HANDBOOK OF CREDIT DERIVATIVES

OTHER TITLES IN THE IRWIN LIBRARY OF INVESTMENT AND FINANCE

HANDBOOK OF CREDIT DERIVATIVES

Edited by
JACK CLARK FRANCIS
JOYCE A. FROST
J. GREGG WHITTAKER

McGraw-Hill

New York   San Francisco   Washington, D.C.   Auckland   Bogotá
Caracas   Lisbon   London   Madrid   Mexico City   Milan
Montreal   New Delhi   San Juan   Singapore
Sydney   Tokyo   Toronto

Library of Congress Cataloging-in-Publication Data

Francis, Jack Clark.
    The handbook of credit derivatives / Jack Clark Francis, Joyce A.
  Frost, J. Gregg Whittaker.
      p. cm.
  Includes bibliographical references (p.).
  ISBN 0–07–022588–5
    1. Credit derivatives. I. Frost, Joyce A. II. Whittaker, J.
Gregg. III. Title.
HG6021.F82   1999
332.63'2—dc21   98–32191
                                                CIP

McGraw-Hill

A Division of The McGraw·Hill Companies

ISBN 0–07–022588–5

*The sponsoring editor for this book was Stephen Isaacs, the editing supervisor was Jacqueline
Brownstein, and the production supervisor was Elizabeth Strange. It was set in Palatino by
ATLIS Graphics & Design, Inc.*

Printed and bound by R.R. Donnelley & Sons Company.

This publication is designed to provide accurate and authoritative information in regard
to the subject matter covered. It is sold with the understanding that neither the author or
the publisher is engaged in rendering legal, accounting, or other professional service. If
legal advice or other expert assistance is required, the services of a competent
professional person should be sought.
    —*From a Declaration of Principles jointly adopted by a Committee of the American Bar
      Association and a Committee of Publishers.*

McGraw-Hill books are available at special quantity discounts to use as premiums and
sales promotions, or for use in corporate training programs. For more information,
please write to the Director of Special Sales, McGraw-Hill, 11 West 19th Street, New
York, NY 10011. Or contact your local bookstore.

          This book is printed on recycled, acid-free paper containing a
          minimum of 50% recycled de-inked fiber.

To Ann, Katie, Zach, and Hannah
                                    —Gregg

To Chris, Sara, and Matthew
                                    —Joyce

To Jim and Steve
                                    —Jack

C O N T E N T S

Chapter 4

Credit Risk Management from a Corporate Perspective   87

Joyce A. Frost, *Head of Marketing, Global Credit Derivatives, Chase
    Securities, Inc.*

PART THREE

DETERMINING EXPOSURE AND PRICING CREDIT DERIVATIVES

Chapter 5

Pricing Credit Derivatives   101

Sanjiv R. Das, Ph.D., *Professor, Harvard Business School*

Appendix

Credit Derivatives Glossary   377

Judah Kaplan, *Associate, Credit Derivatives, Chase Securities, Inc.*
Douglas S. Rolph, Ph.D. Candidate, *Finance Department of the Graduate
     School of Business, University of Washington*

CONTRIBUTORS

Evy Adamidou is a Vice President in the Credit Derivatives Group at Chase Securities, Inc. She is currently a product specialist and marketer for credit derivatives products. Prior to joining Chase she was with Lehman Brothers where she was responsible for trading, structuring, and risk management of credit derivatives products and the Bond Index swap business. She held various positions at Lehman Brothers as a mortgage portfolio strategist and a senior mutual fund specialist. Prior to joining Lehman Brothers she worked as a Mortgage Complex Trades Strategist at Prudential Securities. She holds a Master of Arts and a Ph.D. in Operations Research and Statistics from Princeton University. (CHAP. 2)

Kelly Bryson is a senior Credit Derivatives Marketer for J.P. Morgan Securities Inc. in New York. In addition to structuring and distributing plain vanilla credit derivatives, she was instrumental in structuring BISTRO synthetic securitizations and in the subsequent distribution of BISTRO bonds.

In Ms. Bryson's current role on the Structured Products Syndicate Desk, she is responsible for distributing traditional and synthetic CLOs and CBOs, including BISTRO, with a focus on building the investor base for subordinated credit risk across asset classes.

Ms. Bryson has worked in J.P. Morgan's Structured Products Group since joining the firm in 1995. Prior to joining the credit derivatives desk, Ms. Bryson worked with Yankee issuers in the private placement market. Ms. Bryson is a graduate of Dartmouth College with a B.A. in Asian Studies and Government. (CHAP. 3)

Peter J. Crosbie is a Managing Director of KMV Corporation and is responsible for their Portfolio Management products. He joined KMV in 1995 and has worked in both product development and with clients to implement KMV's technology. Prior to joining KMV, he was Director of Portfolio Management for Barclays Bank in New York. Dr. Crosbie began his career as a consultant to Barclays Bank in 1986 teaching executive development courses in corporate finance and derivatives, and was on the Business faculty of Santa Clara University from 1990 to 1992. Dr. Crosbie is a native of New Zealand and holds a B.Sc. Honours degree in Management Science from Canterbury University and a Ph.D. in Marketing Science and Economics from Purdue University. (CHAP. 7)

Christine M. Cumming has been Senior Vice President responsible for the Bank Analysis and Advisory and Technical Services Functions in the Bank Supervision Group at the Federal Reserve Bank of New York since March 1994.

Ms. Cumming joined the bank's staff in September 1979 as an Economist in the International Research Department, and spent several years leading units in Research which covered the industrial countries and the international financial markets. Later, while in the Bank's International Capital Markets staff, she worked on topics such as the liquidity of banks and securities firms, the international competitiveness of U.S. financial institutions, and the implications of financial innovation.

In January 1992, she was appointed Vice President and assigned to Domestic Bank Examinations in Bank Supervision. A major focus of Ms. Cumming's work in Supervision has involved capital markets issues.

Ms. Cumming holds both a B.S. and a Ph.D. in Economics from the University of Minnesota. (CHAP. 12)

Sanjiv Das joined the finance faculty of the Harvard Business School in 1994. Prior to joining Harvard, Professor Das was a Vice-President at Citibank, N.A. in the Asia-Pacific region.

Professor Das' research looks at the pricing of debt market securities. He has developed models for pricing bonds and options using jump-diffusion processes for interest rates. The research examines the number and types of factors that explain the prices of interest-rate sensitive contingent claims. Das developed numerical methods for the practical implementation of the models, as well. He also built models for pricing of credit risk and credit derivatives, and he has looked at the nature of risk in international portfolios. Professor Das also researches the mutual fund industry, and the performance of portfolio managers. His contributions throughout his research have been both theoretical and empirical in nature. He is also working on computational algorithms for financial problems as well as the behavioral aspects of financial decision-making.

Professor Das has published in the *Review of Financial Studies, The Review of Economics and Statistics, Journal of Financial and Quantitative Analysis, Journal of Derivatives, Review of Derivatives Research, Financial Practice and Education, Journal of Fixed Income, Journal of Financial Engineering, Applied Economics Letters, Journal of Economic Dynamics and Control*, among others, and has made numerous presentations at academic institutions and conferences. The Financial Management Association conferred on him an award for the best Fixed-Income securities paper at the FMA Meetings in St. Louis, 1994, for his work on jump-diffusions in the bond markets. He also won the award for the best thesis in Finance for the year 1994,

awarded by the Financial Management Association. He has worked extensively in several countries in the Asia-Pacific region, namely Australia,
Hong Kong, India, Japan, Malaysia, and Singapore, during his employ-
ment at Citicorp in the derivatives business. Professor Das is also currently
a Faculty Research Fellow of the National Bureau of Economic Research.
He is an Associate Editor of the *Journal of Risk* and the *International Journal
of Theoretical and Applied Finance.*

Professor Das has an undergraduate degree (B.Com) in Accounting
and Economics from the University of Bombay, an MBA (PGDBM) from
the Indian Institute of Management, Ahmedabad, a Master of Philosophy
in Finance from New York University, and a Ph.D. in Finance from New
York University. Professor Das is also a certified cost and works accountant
(AICWA) from the Institute of Cost and Works Accountants of India.
(CHAP. 5)

David Felsenthal is a partner in the New York office of Clifford Chance,
where he works on structured financial products, including derivatives
and repos, and in securities transactions and financial regulation. Mr.
Felsenthal graduated from Princeton University and Harvard Law School.
He is a member of the Banking Committee of the New York City Bar
Association. (CHAP. 11)

Jack Clark Francis received his Bachelors and M.B.A. from Indiana Uni-
versity, served as a Lieutenant in the U.S. Army for two years, and then
earned his Ph.D. from the University of Washington in Seattle. Francis
was on the finance faculty of the University of Pennsylvania's Wharton
School, served as a Federal Reserve Economist for two years; and, is now
Professor of Economics and Finance at Bernard M. Baruch College in New
York City. Dr. Francis authors books published by McGraw-Hill, Prentice-
Hall, and Irwin Publishing Companies. Professor Francis has also had his
research published in numerous academic and business journals. He lives
in Stamford, Connecticut.

Joyce A. Frost is a Vice President of Chase Securities, Inc., where she
heads marketing for Global Credit Derivatives in New York. Ms. Frost
joined Chase in September 1996 from Sumitomo Bank Capital Markets,
where she was responsible for marketing fixed income derivative products
to corporate clients. Previous to joining Sumitomo in February 1991, Ms.
Frost was marketing derivatives to corporate clients at Chase Securities,
Inc. and with The Northern Trust Company in Chicago. Ms. Frost has
been a guest speaker on derivatives throughout the United States, Europe,
and Latin America and has published several articles on the subject of

fixed income and credit derivatives. Ms. Frost holds an MBA with specialization in finance from The University of Chicago and a B.S. in finance from Indiana University. She and her husband Christopher have two children and reside in New York City. (CHAP. 4)

Mark A. Gold is a Vice President at MBIA, a provider of financial guarantees and other financial services. He came to MBIA via Capital Markets Assurance Corporation (CapMAC) which merged with MBIA in February 1998. Participating in the MBIA-AMBAC International joint venture, Mark works particularly where derivative products enter into the transaction or where mathematical modeling issues arise. Mark engineers solutions to client needs involving financial guarantees and capital market access.

From 1993 until joining with CapMAC in the autumn of 1996, Mark held the position of Associate Director in the Derivative Products unit at Standard and Poor's, a credit rating agency. His duties there included the evaluation and analysis of Derivative Product Company risk models including option pricing modules and Monte Carlo simulators, rating criteria development, review and analysis of hedging strategies, review of structured investment vehicles, and quantitative analysis of indexed linked and other structured notes.

Trained as an economist, Mark worked in the industry analysis division of DRI/McGraw Hill from 1990 until moving to S&P. While with DRI, Mark worked on a range of consulting projects involving mathematical modeling and both performed and supervised research on the economic impacts of telecommunications policy. Other responsibilities included industry output forecasting, special industry studies, input-output modeling and model maintenance, productivity research, support for the development of early derivative product company rating criteria, and internal consulting regarding mathematical and statistical modeling. Prior to joining DRI, Mark worked as an independent economic consultant.

Studying under Nobel Laureate Wassily Leontief, Mark obtained his Ph.D. in economics from New York University in 1988. He is the author of numerous articles that have been published in peer review journals and professional texts. (CHAP. 8)

Hardy M. Hodges is a Vice President in Global Credit Derivatives at Chase Securities, Inc., and has been in the group since its inception in early 1995. Among other responsibilities, Mr. Hodges heads up the research effort in credit derivatives and is actively involved in product development, structuring, and pricing. The Credit Derivatives Group at Chase was ranked #1 by *Global Finance* in 1997. Prior to Chase, he was at Goldman Sachs for two years, and on the faculty of Harvard University as a Smithsonian Postdoctoral Fellow. Mr. Hodges holds a Ph.D. from the University of Chicago. He has authored over twenty publications in finance and physics journals. (CHAP. 6)

Judah Kaplan is a Global Markets Officer in the Credit Derivatives Group at Chase Securities, Inc. Mr. Kaplan joined the group in October 1997 in structuring and marketing credit derivative solutions for corporate clients after completing the Associate Training Program at Chase. Prior to joining Chase, Mr. Kaplan was a CPA at the international accounting, tax, and consulting firm of Deloitte & Touche LLP where he audited financial statements of insurance and investment companies. Mr. Kaplan holds a B.S. in Accounting from Yeshiva University and earned an M.B.A. degree with a concentration in Financial Engineering from the Sloan School of Management at the Massachusetts Institute of Technology. (GLOSSARY)

Bruce Kayle is the chair of Milbank's Tax Department and has well-recognized expertise in asset securitization, derivative products, and specialized financing techniques. His practice involves a broad variety of financial products, structured transactions, and U.S. and foreign securities offerings.

Before coming to Milbank, Mr. Kayle served with the U.S. Congress' Joint Committee on Taxation. Mr. Kayle has published articles on tax accounting, derivative products, and tax policy issues. He is on the Executive Committee of the Tax Section of the New York State Bar Association and serves as Co-chair of its Committee on Financial Intermediaries. Mr. Kayle is president of The Tax Club and a member of The Tax Forum. He graduated from the University of Pennsylvania and earned his law degree at Harvard Law School. (CHAP. 10)

John. T. Lawton is a partner in the Audit Business Advisory Services, capital Markets Industry Practice of PricewaterhouseCoopers LLP. He specializes in providing audit, accounting, and business advisory services to financial institutions, particularly money center and international banks, and broker/dealers. He is actively involved in the audit of a large New York based bank and consults on financial risk management issues to both financial institutions and corporate treasury functions. In addition, he consults on difficult matters affecting financial institutions and other enterprises.

Mr. Lawton is a former Practice Fellow of the Financial Accounting Standards Board. During his two-year fellowship, he participated in establishing new accounting standards for financial instruments and helped resolve emerging issues.

Mr. Lawton is a frequent speaker at national and regional conferences on emerging accounting issues.

Mr. Lawton has a masters degree in finance and international business from Columbia Business School and an undergraduate degree in accounting from the University of Notre Dame. He is licensed as a CPA in the States of New York and Connecticut. (CHAP. 9)

M. Sharmini Mahendran is an associate in the International Financial Markets Group at Clifford Chance. Ms. Mahendran is a graduate of Harvard College and Harvard Law School. (CHAP. 11)

Blythe Masters is currently Head of Global Credit Derivatives Marketing, and Co-Head of North American Credit Portfolio at J.P. Morgan Securities Inc., based in New York. She joined J.P. Morgan in 1991 having completed a number of internships in the bank's Interest Rate Swap Group dating back to 1987. She has experience in derivatives marketing and trading (spanning fixed income, commodities, and credit markets), as well as structured finance and securitization.

Ms. Masters has been responsible for credit derivatives marketing and product development for the past four years. Her responsibilities include structuring and distribution of credit derivative products and related credit risk management strategies, both for clients of the bank and internally.

In her portfolio management capacity, Ms. Masters is responsible for the proactive management of capital, balance sheet, liquidity, and credit risks of the bank's retained credit positions arising from lending and derivatives activities.

Ms. Masters is a graduate of Trinity College, Cambridge, with a BA in economics. (CHAP. 3)

David K. A. Mordecai is vice president of financial engineering at AIG Risk Finance, the division of AIG that specializes in Alternative Risk Transfer involving structured transactions that combine insurance and capital market products. Formerly, he was a director at Fitch IBCA, Inc. and the product manager responsible for rating catastrophic risk bonds, synthetic notes, and credit and insurance derivatives. As lead analyst for insurance-linked securities, he developed rating analytics and performed probability and statistical analysis related to event risk and catastrophic risk transactions, as well as new model validation/verification approaches for due diligence of the risk modeling firms. Mr. Mordecai is a recognized authority on credit, weather, and insurance derivatives, and is actively sought as a participant on the international professional and applied conference circuit. He has contributed to several professional texts on credit and catastrophe modeling, structured derivatives, and Alternative Risk Transfer. He is also a participant in the institutional investment management advisory committee of the New York Mercantile Exchange (NYMEX), and a forthcoming research group being formed at the National Bureau of Economic Research (NBER). He received an MBA in finance from the New York University Graduate School of Business (1987), and has over ten years of experience as a capital markets professional. Mr. Mordecai is also currently completing a Ph.D. at the University of Chicago Graduate School of Business. His research focuses on Alternative Risk Transfer, in particular applications of the economics of uncertainty and statistical decision theory to credit arbitrage, intermediation, and the pricing, allocation, and distribution of event risk in the reinsurance and capital markets. (CHAP. 13)

Robert Neal is Associate Professor of Finance in the Kelley School of Business, Indiana University. Mr. Neal holds a Ph.D. in Economics from the University of Chicago. His current research focuses on credit risk and risk management. Prior to joining Indiana University, Mr. Neal was an Economist at the Federal Reserve Bank of Kansas City. He has also worked extensively with the Securities and Exchange Commission on regulatory issues. (CHAP. 1)

Douglas S. Rolph is a Ph.D. candidate in the Finance Department of the Graduate School of Business at the University of Washington in Seattle. Previously, he was an Assistant Economist at the Federal Reserve Bank of Kansas City. At the Federal Reserve, his research has concentrated on derivatives and on models of credit risk. Prior to working at the Federal Reserve, Doug completed his B.A. in Business Administration from the University of Washington. (CHAP. 1)

Daniel C. Staehle is a Capital Markets Examiner in the Treasury and Market Risk Division of the Office of the Comptroller of the Currency (OCC). In that capacity, Mr. Staehle conducts examinations of capital markets activities of large nationally chartered banks and assists the OCC in developing risk management and treasury policy.

Prior to joining the OCC, Mr. Staehle was a Supervising Examiner in the Financial Examinations Department of the Federal Reserve Bank of New York. From November 1997 to January 1999, Mr. Staehle served as the Team Leader of the Federal Reserve System's Asset Securitization Specialty Team. For the prior three years, Mr. Staehle worked in the Bank Analysis Department where his primary responsibilities related to analyzing and assisting in the development of Federal Reserve policy in the areas of capital markets, risk management, and asset securitization, with a special focus on credit derivatives. Prior to joining the Bank, Mr. Staeble spent four years with the Board of Governors of the Federal Reserve System in Washington, D.C. and three years with the Federal Reserve Bank of San Francisco.

Mr. Staehle has a Bachelor of Science degree in accounting from the University of South Carolina in Columbia, South Carolina, and a Master of Management degree in finance and economics from the J.L. Kellogg Graduate School of Management at Northwestern University in Evanston, Illinois. Dan is also a Chartered Financial Analyst (CFA) and a Certified Public Accountant (CPA). (CHAP. 12)

Alden L. Toevs (pronounced Taves) began his professional career as a Professor of Economics at University of Oregon. Then he joined Morgan Stanley and Company in 1983 and became a principal of that firm. In 1990 he joined the First Manhattan Consulting Group (FMCG) and is currently Executive Vice President and heads FMCG's risk management, MIS, and mortgage banking practice areas. In addition, he is an integral part of FMCG Capital Strategies, which focuses on M&A valuation and merger integration.

Alden has published in many of the leading finance and business journals. He has authored or co-authored several books and has lectured at major universities. He has served as keynote speaker for over ten national and international banking conferences.

In 1982 Alden was selected as a Federal Reserve Bank Visiting Scholar. In 1983 he received a similar honorary appointment in the Federal Home Loan Bank System. Other honors include an Institutional Investor All-American Research Team award for Mortgage Research and a Graham and Dodd Scroll from the Financial Analysts Society. He serves or has served on the editorial boards of the *Financial Analysts Journal, Journal of Portfolio Management,* and the *Journal of International Securities Research.*

Mr. Toevs has a Ph.D. with honors from Tulane University. He has also done postdoctoral work at MIT. (CHAP. 14)

J. Gregg Whittaker is a Managing Director and the global head of Credit Derivatives for Chase Securities, Inc. in New York City. He has a Ph.D. in economics from the University of Wisconsin. His dissertation was the first treatise of its kind to integrate options pricing theory with the valuation of financial swaps. Dr. Whittaker began his career as an Economist for the Federal Reserve Bank. He then entered the private sector, managing fixed income and equity derivative groups for The Northern Trust Company and S. G. Warburg & Company, respectively. Whittaker was then recruited by Chemical Bank to build and run its Credit Derivatives operation, a task which he continues after the merger with Chase Manhattan Bank. He also co-edits the *Handbook of Equity Derivatives* among other publications. (CHAP. 2)

A special thanks for help on the production of this book goes to Jacqui Brownstein, Deanna Simonetti, and Faith Bonilla.

ABOUT THE EDITORS

Jack Clark Francis, Ph.D., is a professor of economics and finance at Bernard M. Baruch College in New York City. Among his many published books, Dr. Francis was coeditor with J. Gregg Whittaker and William W. Toy of *The Handbook of Equity Derivatives*. His articles appear regularly in professional journals.

Joyce Frost, MBA, is a vice president in the Credit Derivatives Group of Chase Securities, Inc., where she is a product marketing manager. An adjunct faculty member at Polytechnic University in Brooklyn, New York, Ms. Frost has spoken on derivatives throughout the U.S., Mexico, and Brazil, and her articles appear regularly in *Corporate Finance* magazine.

J. Gregg Whittaker, Ph.D., is a managing director and head of Credit Derivatives for Chase Securities, Inc. Dr. Whittaker previously built and managed the credit derivatives department for Chemical Securities. He coedited *The Handbook of Equity Derivatives* with Jack Clark Francis and William W. Toy.

PART ONE

Introduction

CHAPTER 1

An Introduction to Credit Derivatives

Robert S. Neal*, Ph.D.
Professor, Kelly School of Business, Indiana University

Douglas S. Rolph*, Ph.D.
Ph.D. Candidate, Finance Department of the Graduate School of
    Business, University of Washington

One of the risks of making a bank loan or investing in a debt security is *credit risk*, the risk of borrower default. In response to this potential problem, new financial instruments called credit derivatives have been developed in the past few years. Credit derivatives can help investors and corporations manage the credit risk of their investments by insuring against adverse movements in the credit quality of the borrower. If a borrower defaults, the investor will suffer losses on the investment, but the losses can be offset by gains from the credit derivative. Thus, if used properly, credit derivatives can reduce an investor's overall credit risk.

Estimates from industry sources suggest the credit derivatives market has grown from virtually nothing in 1993 to about $100 billion of transactions in 1997.[1] This growth has been driven by the ability of credit derivatives to provide valuable new methods for managing credit risk.

---

*The authors would like to thank John Crystal at Credit Suisse Financial Products, Russell Ives, Lex Maldutis at Morgan Stanley, Bryant Rother at Yamane Prebon, Dan Steahle at the Federal Reserve Bank of New York, and Gregg Whittaker at Chase Manhattan for helpful conversations, and Stuart Turnbull at Queens University for his additions to the bibliography. An earlier version of this article was published in the Federal Reserve Bank of Kansas City's *Economic Review,* Second Quarter, 1996. The views expressed by the authors do not necessarily reflect the views of the Federal Reserve Bank of Kansas City or the Federal Reserve System.

[1] Dealers Estimates. In addition, the Office of the Comptroller of the Currency's Quarterly Derivative Fact Sheet for the third quarter of 1997 reported that commercial banks held approximately $39 billion in credit derivatives. These holdings were concentrated among seven banks.

As with other customized derivative products, however, credit derivatives expose their users to counterparty, operational, and legal risks. Controlling these risks is likely to be an important factor in the future development of the credit derivatives market.

This chapter provides information on the rationale and use of credit derivatives. The first section describes how to measure credit risk, who it affects, and the traditional strategies used to manage it. The second section shows how credit derivatives can help manage credit risk. The third section examines the risks and regulatory issues associated with credit derivatives. The final section contains a bibliography of current research. A glossary of terms is provided at the end of the book.

CREDIT RISK

Credit risk is important to banks, fixed income investors, and corporations. If a firm defaults, lenders will not receive their promised payments. While there are a variety of methods for managing credit risk, these methods are typically insufficient to reduce credit risk to desired levels. This section defines credit risk, describes how it can be measured, and shows how it affects corporate bond issuers, fixed income investors, and banks. The section also describes the techniques most commonly used to manage credit risk, such as loan underwriting standards, diversification, and asset securitization.

What Is Credit Risk?

Credit risk is the probability that a borrower will default on a commitment to repay financial obligations. Default occurs when the borrower cannot fulfill key obligations, such as making interest payments to bondholders or repaying bank loans. In the event of default, lenders—bondholders or banks—suffer a loss because they will not receive all the payments promised to them.[2]

---

[2]An alternative definition of credit risk relies, not on absolute default rates, but on the variability of actual default rates relative to expected default rates. Suppose a lender expects a 20 percent default rate on a portfolio of high-risk loans and sets the interest rate accordingly. If the subsequent default rate is close to 20 percent, it can be argued that the credit risk of the portfolio is actually low. The lender has earned a high rate of return on the loans and the uncertainty surrounding the rate is low. To keep the presentation simple, the article uses the definition in the text. Use of the alternative definition does not change any of the results in the article.

Credit risk is influenced by both business cycles and firm-specific events. Credit risk typically declines during economic expansions because strong earnings keep overall default rates low. Credit risk increases during economic contractions because earnings deteriorate, making it more difficult to repay loans or make bond payments. Firm-specific credit risk is unrelated to business cycles. This risk arises from events specific to a firm's business activities or its industry, events such as product liability lawsuits. For example, when the health hazards of asbestos became known, liability lawsuits forced Johns-Manville, a leading asbestos producer, into bankruptcy and to default on its bonds.

A broad measure of a firm's credit risk is its credit rating. This measure is useful for categorizing companies according to their credit risk. Rating firms, such as Moody's Investors Services, assign a credit rating to a company based on the firm's anticipated ability to meet scheduled interest and principal payments, its industry, competition, and outlook for the future. Credit ratings range from AAA for firms of the highest credit quality, to CCC for firms likely to default.[3]

A more quantitative measure of credit risk is the credit risk premium. For fixed income securities, the credit risk premium is the difference between the interest rate a firm pays when it borrows and the interest rate on a default-free security, such as a U.S. Treasury bond. For floating rate securities, the premium is typically the difference between the interest rate a firm pays when it borrows and LIBOR, the London Interbank offered rate. The premium is the extra compensation an investor requires for lending to a company that might default. As a firm's credit risk increases, bond investors and commercial banks demand a higher credit risk premium. This increase is necessary to offset the higher expected losses on the bond or loan from the increased probability that the loan will not be repaid.

The characteristics of credit risk premiums are displayed in Figure 1–1. The chart shows the risk premiums for Moody's AAA and BAA industrial bond indices. The data covers January 1984 to August 1997. The top line is the interest rate for all BAA-rated bonds less the interest rate for 10-year Treasury bonds, while the bottom line shows the rate for AAA bonds less the 10-year Treasury rate. There is a strong relation between the credit rating and the credit risk premium—the higher the credit rating, the lower the credit risk premium. As a result, a downgrade

---

[3]From highest to lowest quality, Moody's ratings are AAA, AA, A, BAA, BA, B, and CCC. Categories BAA and above are termed investment-grade bonds, while categories BA and lower are termed non-investment-grade, or junk, bonds.

FIGURE 1-1

Credit Risk Premiums for Bonds

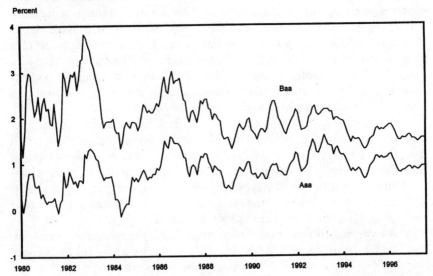

Note: The BAA credit risk premium is the average rate on BAA corporate bonds less the 10-year Treasury bond rate.
The AAA credit risk premium is the average rate on AAA corporate bonds less the 10-year Treasury bond rate.

Source: Moody's Investors Service and Board of Governors of the Federal Reserve System.

in a company's credit rating can significantly increase its borrowing costs. The chart also shows that the cost of borrowing for a company with a constant rating can vary over time. For example, the BAA premium increased from 1.4 percent in August 1981 to 3.0 percent in November 1981.

Who Is Affected by Credit Risk?

Credit risk affects any party making or receiving a loan or a debt payment. Some examples include borrowers, bond investors, and commercial banks.

Borrowers

Borrowers are affected by credit risk because their cost of borrowing depends crucially on their risk of default. A borrower who plans to issue debt in the near future faces the risk that unanticipated events will suddenly increase the costs of borrowing. For example, the recent disclosure of a $1.1 billion trading loss at Daiwa Bank raised fears of the bank's default, which increased its cost of borrowing.[4] Moreover, even without a change in a company's firm-specific credit risk, a downturn in the economy could raise the average credit risk premium and increase the cost of borrowing for all debt issuers.

Bond Investors

Investors in individual bonds are exposed to the risk of a decline in the bond's credit rating. A downgrade in a credit rating will increase the bond's credit risk premium and reduce the value of the bond. Similarly, mutual funds that hold a portfolio of corporate bonds will be affected by fluctuations in the average credit risk premium. Increases in the premium will reduce the price of the bonds and hurt the fund's total return.

Commercial Banks

Banks are exposed to the risk that borrowers will default on their loans. The credit risk faced by banks is relatively high for two reasons. First, banks tend to concentrate their loans geographically or in particular industries, which limits their ability to diversify credit risks across borrowers. Second, credit risk is the predominate risk in loans made to businesses. Most bank loans have adjustable or floating rates, with the interest rate periodically reset to reflect changes in LIBOR. Since the borrowers rate reflects changes in LIBOR, movements in LIBOR pose little risk to banks. The credit risk premium, however, is typically fixed when the loan is made. If the borrowers credit quality decreases, its credit risk premium will rise. Lenders will then suffer because the loan payments are insufficient to compensate for the higher risk.

How Is Credit Risk Managed?

A variety of methods are available to manage credit risk. Traditional methods have focused on loan underwriting standards and diversification. Over the last ten years, an alternative approach to managing credit risk has focused on selling assets with credit risk. Banks can sell individual loans directly using the secondary loan market. Alternatively, they can "securitize," or pool together their assets with similar credit risk and sell

---

[4]Two weeks after the disclosure of the trading loss, Standard and Poors downgraded Daiwa's bonds. The bond market reaction to the disclosure was even swifter. The price of Daiwa's bonds fell immediately, suggesting that investors required a higher credit risk premium to compensate for the additional default risk.

parts of the pool to outside investors. Either approach reduces credit risk because the credit exposure is transferred to the new owner. Unfortunately, these methods are insufficient for managing the credit exposure of many financial firms.

Underwriting Standards and Diversification

The traditional approach to managing credit risk is based on the application of underwriting standards and diversification. For example, take a bank loan officer who is deciding whether to make a loan. After a careful review of the prospective borrower's financial statements, the officer would consider such factors as earnings, profit margins, cash flow, and the amount of outstanding debt. If the prospects for the loan look good, the loan officer then considers the condition of the borrower's industry by examining competitive pressures, product cycles, and future growth prospects. Upon a favorable review, the bank loan officer would manage the credit risk exposure by controlling the terms of the loan. The officer can set limits on the size of the loan, establish a repayment schedule, incorporate covenants, and require additional collateral for higher risk loans. A mutual fund that invests in corporate bonds goes through a similar credit analysis, although it cannot set the terms of the borrowing.

The next step in the traditional approach is to diversify the credit risks across different borrowers. The diversification principle relies on offsetting risks. For example, consider the earnings of two companies, one that sells discounted clothing and another that sells automobiles. During times of economic prosperity, the automobile dealer does well, while the discount retailer does poorly. During times of economic contraction, the discount retailer does well, while the automobile dealer does poorly. Although the individual earnings of the two companies can be quite volatile, the combined earnings would be much less volatile due to the negative relation between their earnings.[5] The same principle holds for a portfolio of bank loans or bonds. The factors that cause industrial companies to default on their loans will differ from the factors that cause farmers to default on their loans. Relative to holding either type of loan separately, combining both types of loans into a portfolio allows the bank to reduce the volatility of its earnings.[6] The earnings from some loans

---

[5]Diversification can also reduce volatility even if the earnings of the firms are positively related. All that is required for diversification to yield benefits is that the earnings of the two firms not be perfectly positively correlated.

[6]Strictly speaking, the gains from diversification are primarily obtained from reducing firm-specific credit risk. Diversification will yield fewer benefits in reducing credit risk associated with business cycles because these fluctuations affect all firms.

will offset the losses from defaulted loans, thereby reducing the likelihood that, on net, the bank will lose money.

While diversification and underwriting standards are necessary first steps for managing credit risk, their ability to reduce credit risk is often limited by a scarcity of diversification opportunities. For example, small commercial banks typically confine their lending to their local area. This lack of geographic diversification means the earnings from their loans will depend heavily on the condition of the local economy. Similarly, the finance divisions of automobile companies face limited diversification opportunities. While a finance division can diversify some credit risk by lending to different dealers, cyclical movements in the economy will affect all dealers, thereby limiting the opportunities for diversification.

Securitization and Loan Sales

In recent years, the development of markets for securitized assets and for loan sales has provided another method for managing credit risk. In the asset securitization approach, bonds or loans with credit risk are pooled together and sold to outside investors. These securities are called asset-back securities because they are collateralized by an underlying pool of loans or bonds. For example, the finance division of an automotive company can combine many of its loans into a single package and sell pieces of the package to institutional investors. From an investor's perspective, purchasing part of the package is attractive because the diversification across many loans reduces the overall credit risk. In addition, to the extent that returns from the package are not closely correlated with the investor's other holdings, diversification allows the investor to reduce the credit risk of his overall portfolio. From the automobile company's perspective, selling the loans eliminates the company's credit exposure to the loans. The substantial growth in the market for nonhousing-related securitized assets is one indication of the success of this approach for managing credit risk. In 1996, $94.1 billion of such securitized assets were issued, up from virtually nothing in 1984.[7]

Banks can use the market for bank loans to manage their credit risk in a similar manner. After making a loan to a company, a bank can sell all or part of the loan to other banks or institutional investors. One common example of a loan sale occurs when a bank provides short-term financing for a corporate takeover. After making the loan, the bank will quickly sell the loan to other investors. This strategy is attractive to banks because

---

[7]Flow of Funds Accounts of the United States, Federal Reserve Statistical Release Z.1, Fourth Quarter, 1996.

they earn a fee from underwriting the loan while the credit risk is assumed by the new investor. Occasionally, banks will lend large amounts in a single takeover, so that controlling the credit risk is extremely important. The use of loan sales by banks to manage their credit risk has increased rapidly in the last few years. In 1996, banks sold $887 billion of loans, up from about $200 billion in 1991.[8]

The markets for securitized assets and loan sales provide valuable tools for managing credit risk. The securitization approach, however, is best suited for loans that have standardized payment schedules and similar credit risk characteristics, such as home mortgages and automobile loans. Loans for commercial and industrial purposes, in contrast, have diverse credit risks. Consequently, a relatively small amount of these loans have been securitized and sold to institutional investors. A more promising way to manage the credit risk of commercial and industrial loans is through credit derivatives.

MANAGING RISK WITH CREDIT DERIVATIVES

Credit derivatives are financial contracts that provide insurance against credit-related losses. These contracts give investors, banks, corporations and debt issuers new techniques for managing credit risk that complement the loan sales and asset securitization methods. This section examines three types of credit derivatives—credit swaps, credit options, and credit-linked notes—and shows how they can help manage credit risk.[9]

Credit Swaps

Credit swaps reduce credit risk through diversification. Credit swaps are appealing to commercial banks whose loan portfolios are concentrated in particular industries or geographic areas. Instead of diversifying credit risk by lending outside its local area or by selling some loans and purchasing others, a bank can swap the payments from some of its loans for payments from a different institution.

Conceptually, the simplest type of credit swap is a loan portfolio swap. Take, for example, two hypothetical banks, San Francisco Technology Bank, which lends mostly to software firms, and Detroit Industrial

---

[8]Loan Pricing Corporation, 1997 Gold Sheets.
[9]Whittaker and Kumar (1996) provide a more detailed discussion on the uses of credit
    derivatives.

Loan Portfolio Swap

Payments from San Francisco
Technology Bank's $50 million loan
portfolio

| San Francisco Technology | → ← | Chicago Risk Management | → ← | Detroit Industrial |

Payments from Detroit
Industrial Bank's $50 million
loan portfolio

Bank, which lends mostly to manufacturers. The swap transaction between the two banks also involves an intermediary, Chicago Risk Management. To execute the transaction, San Francisco Technology Bank sends the interest payments it receives from, say, $50 million of its software loans to Chicago Risk Management. This is shown in Figure 1–2. Simultaneously, Chicago Risk Management receives interest payments on the $50 million loan portfolio from Detroit Industrial Bank. Chicago Risk Management then swaps the interest payments between the two banks. Since there is little common movement in default rates between software firms and manufacturers, both banks are better off. Although difficult to arrange in practice, this type of swap allows each bank to diversify away some of its credit risk. Chicago Risk Management receives a fee for arranging the transaction and assuming the credit risk of both institutions.

The most common credit swap is called a total return swap. In this type of transaction, San Francisco Technology Bank sends its loan payments to Chicago Risk Management, which, in turn, sends the payments to Minneapolis Mutual, a hypothetical insurance company. This is shown in Figure 1–3. In exchange for the loan payments, Minneapolis Mutual sends a floating rate interest payment to Chicago Risk Management, which sends the payment to San Francisco Technology Bank. Based on a $50 million contract amount, Minneapolis Mutual might send Chicago Risk Management a return of LIBOR plus 1 percent. The effect of this swap for San Francisco Technology Bank is to trade the return from its loan portfolio for a return that is 1 percent above LIBOR. While there is still the possibility that the counterparty, Minneapolis Mutual, may default, San Francisco Technology Bank has largely eliminated the credit risk on $50 million of its loan portfolio.

F I G U R E   1–3

Total Return Swap

Payments from San Francisco
Technology Bank's $50 million
loan

Payment equals LIBOR + 1 percent
on a $50 million investment

Relative to loan sales, total return swaps offer two important advantages. First, they allow banks to diversify credit risk while maintaining confidentiality of their client's financial records. In a total return swap transaction, the borrowing firm's records remain with the originating bank. When loans are sold, the firm's records are transferred to the new owner of the loan. Second, the administrative costs of receiving the swap payments can be lower than directly owning the loans. For example, an institution such as an insurance company may be ill suited to monitor loans and ensure that floating rate loans are properly reset for changes in LIBOR. Thus, reducing administrative expenses allows diversification to be achieved at a lower cost.

Credit Options

Credit options are a second type of credit derivative used to hedge the risk of adverse changes in credit quality. A simple way to understand credit options is to use an analogy with car insurance. All car owners pay premiums to purchase car insurance and protect themselves from financial loss. If the car is undamaged, the car owner receives nothing from the insurance company. If the car is wrecked, the insurance company pays the owner enough to replace the car. Thus, for a fee, the insurance policy hedges the value of the car by eliminating the risk of a large financial loss.

Credit options provide a similar hedging function. These options allow investors to protect themselves against adverse moves in the credit quality of financial assets. For example, a bond investor might buy a credit option to hedge the value of a corporate bond. If the bond defaults, the payoff from the option would offset the loss from the bond. If there is no default, the investor would continue to receive the interest payments from the bond but receive nothing from the option.

The key features of credit options are identical to options on stocks. For example, consider a call option on IBM stock. The owner of the call option has the right to buy IBM shares at a previously determined price called a strike price. When the current price of IBM exceeds the strike price, the owner of the call option can earn a profit by purchasing shares of IBM at the strike price and then selling them at the current market price. Similarly, an IBM put option gives the owner of the option the right to sell IBM shares at the strike price. If the market price falls below the strike price, the owner of the option can earn a profit by purchasing IBM shares at the market price and selling the shares at the strike price.

While these examples link the payoff of the option to the price of the underlying stock, options are also available where the payoff is linked to an interest rate. For example, fixed-rate mortgages typically provide a 30-day interest rate lock. Following approval of the loan, the prospective homeowner's mortgage rate is protected against rate increases for 30 days. This interest rate protection is actually a call option on the interest rate because the homeowner implicitly receives a payment if mortgage rates rise following the loan approval. For example, if the rate increases by 0.5 percentage point, the homeowner implicitly pays the increase, but also receives an offsetting payoff from the call option. Thus, the interest rate lock offsets any increases in mortgage rates, ensuring that the homeowner's rates will not rise.

In a similar manner, bond issuers can use credit options to hedge against a rise in the average credit risk premium. As a hypothetical example, suppose Midwest Telephone, a BAA-rated company, is planning to issue $100 million of 1-year bonds in two months. The bonds are to be paid back in one year, and the interest rate Midwest Telephone anticipates paying is 1.5 percentage points above the 1-year Treasury bill rate. If there is an increase in the average credit risk premium for BAA companies before the debt is issued, Midwest's interest payments will also rise. To hedge against this possibility, Midwest could purchase a call option on the credit risk premium.[10] Just as a call option protects a home buyer against a rise in mortgage rates, the call option on the credit risk premium protects Midwest against increases in the premium. If the premium rises above the strike rate specified in the option, Midwest's higher interest payments will be offset by gains from the option.

To illustrate this example, say Midwest Telephone buys a call option on the average BAA credit risk premium. For the $100 million bond, the price of the option is $500,000. The current credit risk premium is 1.5

---

[10]Longstaff and Schwartz (1995) provide a mathematical model for pricing such options.

percent and the call option will pay Midwest if the premium exceeds 1.5 percent in two months. Because the strike rate equals the current risk premium, the option protects Midwest against an increase in the premium. If a downturn in overall economic conditions causes the average premium to rise to 2.5 percent, the one-percentage-point rise in the credit risk premium will cause Midwest's interest payments to increase by $1 million. The higher interest payments, however, will be offset by the payoff from the option (1 percent times $100 million equals $1 million). Since the payment from the call option offsets the increased borrowing costs, purchasing the call option allows Midwest to hedge against increases in the average credit risk premium.[11]

Alternatively, suppose that the credit risk premium falls to 0.5 percent. In this case, the call option has no payoff, but Midwest saves $1 million (1 percent of $100 million) because it can borrow at the lower rate. Thus, purchasing the call option allows Midwest to insure against increases in the credit risk premium while maintaining the benefits of lower borrowing costs if the premium declines. In either case, Midwest would still pay the $500,000 for the option, just as it would pay a premium for any other insurance policy.

Other types of credit options can also be used by bond investors to hedge against a decline in the price of specific bonds. Such a decline might be caused by a downgrade in a company's debt, independent of movements in the average credit risk premium. To hedge this specific risk, the investor can purchase an option that has a large payoff if the credit quality of the bond declines. A decline in quality will trigger a loss on the bond holdings, but this will be offset by the gains from the option. This insurance protects the investor from adverse movements in a firm's credit quality.[12]

To illustrate, suppose an investor owns $10 million of a company's bonds. To insure against an adverse movement in the company's credit quality, the investor might buy a put option on the bonds with a $9 million strike price for $40,000. This option would give the investor the right to sell his bond holdings for $9 million anytime during the next year. Purchasing the option ensures that the investor will get at least $9 million for the

---

[11]In this example, the strike price of the option was set to 1.5 percent, the same as the level of the BAA credit risk premium when the option was purchased. In practice, an issuer could purchase an option with a higher strike price. The advantage of a higher strike price is that the price of the option is lower. The disadvantage is that it offers less protection against an increase in the average credit risk premium.
[12]For a discussion of the methods used to price such options, see the articles by Das (1995) and by Jarrow, Lando, and Turnbull (1997).

bonds. If the market value of the bonds falls to $7 million in one year, the payoff of the option will be $2 million. Alternatively, if the value of the bonds rises to $12 million in a year, the value of the put option will fall to zero. Thus, the put option protects the investor against price declines while still allowing the investor to benefit from price increases.

The most common form of credit option is called a credit default swap. This "swap" is actually a put option on a bond, loan, or portfolio of bonds or loans. The owner of the default swap receives a payoff if more than a prespecified number of the bonds default. For example, suppose an investor's portfolio includes 20 BAA bonds, each of which promises to pay $1,000 in one year. The investor might purchase a credit default swap for $20 that promises to make a payment if three or more of the 20 bonds default. For each bond that defaults, the investor receives the difference between the $1,000 promised payment and the year-end price of the defaulted bond.[13]

The appeal of a credit default swap is that it limits the investor's credit risk. It is designed for investors who are willing to absorb small credit losses but want protection against large losses. In exchange for a relatively small fee, the investor is exposed to the risk that one or two bonds may default but is protected against additional losses.

While investors clearly have an incentive to purchase credit options, it is natural to ask who would agree to sell such options. Industry sources suggest that banks and insurance companies are among the principal providers of credit options. They earn a fee for selling the credit options and can diversify their risks by selling credit options in different industries and in different areas.

Credit-Linked Notes

Credit-linked notes are another type of credit derivative. These notes can be used by borrowers to hedge against credit risk and by investors to increase the yield on their fixed-income investments. A credit-linked note is a combination of a regular bond and a credit derivative. Just as with a regular bond, the credit-linked note promises to make periodic interest

---

[13]The credit default swap is called a swap because of its payment structure. Instead of directly paying the intermediary $20 for the option, the bondholder swaps a payment to the intermediary in exchange for the default protection. The payment is expressed as a fraction of the value of the total promised payments of the bond portfolio. In this case, the payments would be $20/$20,000, or 0.1 percent. The bondholder would swap 0.1 percent of the promised payments to the intermediary in exchange for the default protection.

payments and a payment of the principle when the bond matures. The credit derivative in the note, however, typically allows the issuer to reduce the note's principal if a credit event occurs. Examples of credit events can include a downgrade in the credit rating for an issuer, or a large decline in the price of the issuer's bonds.

A credit card company, for example, may wish to use debt to fund a portfolio of credit card loans. To reduce the credit risk of the loans, the company's debt issue could take the form of a 1-year credit-linked note. This note promises to pay investors $1000 and an 8 percent coupon if a national index of credit delinquency rates is below 5 percent. If the index exceeds 5 percent, however, investors receive $800 and an 8 percent coupon. The credit card company thus has a credit option—the company has the right to lower the principal payment if the overall credit quality of cardholders deteriorates.

A credit card company would issue a credit-linked note because it provides a convenient mechanism to reduce the company's credit exposure. If cardholder defaults are low, then the company can repay the principal in full. If the default rates are high, the company's earnings are reduced, but it only has to pay back part of the principal. By structuring the note in this way, the credit card company is purchasing credit insurance from the investors.

Investors would consider buying such a credit-linked note because they earn a higher rate of return than the credit card company's regular bonds. When the company issues the notes, the price of the notes will be lower than the price of the company's regular bonds. The lower price provides investors with a higher yield and compensates them for the risk that their principal will decline.

CREDIT DERIVATIVES: RISKS AND REGULATORY ISSUES

While credit derivatives provide a valuable tool for managing credit risk, they can also expose the user to new financial risks and regulatory costs. Like other over-the-counter derivative securities, credit derivatives are privately negotiated financial contracts. These contracts expose the user to operational, counterparty, liquidity, and legal risk. In addition, depending on the jurisdiction, there is uncertainty regarding the regulatory status of credit derivatives and the appropriate capital charges for bank loans hedged with credit derivatives. For the most part, these risks are either controllable or relatively small and, therefore, unlikely to restrict the development of the credit derivatives market.

What Are the Risks of Credit Derivatives?

Perhaps the largest risk of using credit derivatives is operational risk. Operational risk is the risk that traders could imprudently use any derivative instrument for speculation instead of hedging. For example, losses from unwarranted derivatives-related trading caused the dissolution of Barings PLC, a British investment bank, and contributed to the default of Orange County, California. While operational risk can be large, it can also be controlled by prudent management and oversight.

A second source of risk is counterparty risk. This is the risk that the counterparty to a transaction will default. If the counterparty defaults, then in most cases the claim would be equivalent to senior, unsecured debt. For example, in the total return swap described earlier, Minneapolis Mutual could default after initiating the swap with San Francisco Technology. If Minneapolis defaults, then San Francisco Technology would have the same claim in bankruptcy as other senior unsecured debt. Because of counterparty default, credit derivatives cannot completely eliminate credit risk.

While counterparty risk is a source of concern, the magnitude of this risk is relatively small. For a firm to suffer a loss from a counterparty default, the counterparty must default and it must owe money on the credit derivative transaction. A proper analysis of counterparty risk requires assessing the joint probability of both these events. The greater the correlation between counterparty default and owing money on the credit derivative transaction, the greater the counterparty risk.

A third source of risk is liquidity risk. Liquidity risk is the uncertainty about being able to sell or offset a previously established position. For firms holding credit derivatives strictly for hedging, liquidity risk is relatively unimportant. For example, consider a bond issuer who uses a credit option to hedge its future costs of borrowing. Because the option will be structured to expire on the borrowing date, the bond issuer will simply hold the option until expiration. In contrast, liquidity risk is typically an important consideration for investors of credit derivatives and for users of credit derivatives who anticipate offsetting their position before the contract matures. Liquidity risk is currently high because there is no active secondary market for participants to hedge their credit exposure or to offset a previously established position. To the extent that the market becomes more active, this risk will decline.

A fourth source of risk for credit derivative users is legal risk. Legal risk is the possibility that a derivative contract may be deemed illegal or unsuitable. The Orange County bankruptcy provides an example of legal risk. For several years, the County successfully invested in risky, fixed-income derivative securities. A sudden and large change in interest rates, however, caused a steep decline in the value of its securities, leaving the County unable to meet margin calls. In the wake of the bankruptcy, the County sued the investment bank that sold them the securities. The County claimed it was illegal for it to hold such securities and, therefore, the derivative securities were unenforceable contracts. The issue is currently being resolved in the courts. If the courts agree with the County, the likelihood will increase that losing parties on other derivative transactions will adopt legal defenses to avoid honoring their derivative contracts. Such a development would strongly restrict growth in the credit derivatives market.

Legal risk also arises from ambiguity regarding the definition of default. Although default terms are specified in the credit derivative contract, the unique nature of the event can make it difficult to precisely define. For example, suppose that Indiana Software provides computer programs that are used by Jakarta General Manufacturing. There is risk in the overseas transaction and Indiana Software purchases default protection for the $10 million account receivable owed by Jakarta General. If the programs sent to Jakarta General do not work properly and payment is refused, then the account receivable could technically be in default. The seller of the credit protection might have to pay Indiana Software unless this scenario was accounted for in the derivative contract. Though the difficulties associated with the documentation of the credit derivative might not preclude two counterparties from entering into an agreement, it can slow the length of time required to complete a trade, and reduce the liquidity of the market. The International Swaps and Derivatives Association (ISDA), has recently developed legal documents that adequately specify when default occurs, thereby reducing legal risk.

Regulatory Issues

Another uncertainty confronting users of credit derivatives is their regulatory status. Should credit derivatives be treated as securities, commodities, swaps, or insurance products? This distinction is important because these contracts are regulated by different agencies and under different terms. Swaps, for example, are under the regulatory jurisdiction of the Commodities Futures Trading Commission. Suppose that a firm enters a credit swap contract. If the regulatory status changes and the contract is subsequently regarded as a "security," it would then be under the jurisdiction of the Securities and Exchange Commission (SEC). Since SEC regulations require additional disclosure, the contract could be considered illegal. A change in regulatory status could therefore potentially invalidate previously established credit derivative transactions.

Another regulatory issue is capital requirements for credit derivatives. Suppose a bank hedges the credit risk of a large loan. Although the hedge reduces the bank's credit exposure, it will not necessarily reduce the bank's capital requirements. If the counterparty to the derivative transaction is also a bank then a reduction in the bank's capital requirement is permitted. According to U.S. regulatory guidance, the hedge reduces the amount of regulatory capital the bank must set aside from 8 percent of the loan (a 100 percent capital charge on 8 percent) down to 1.6 percent of the loan (a 20 percent charge on 8 percent). However, if the counterparty is not a bank, there may not be any reduction in capital requirements.[14] This asymmetry can create a situation where the bank would prefer to have BAA-rated bank counterparty than a AA-rated non-bank counterparty.

As credit derivatives become more available, regulators should re-evaluate the circumstances when credit derivatives reduce a bank's credit exposure. If regulators allow all prudently structured credit hedges to reduce capital requirements, it will encourage the participation of bank and nonbank firms and thereby contribute to the liquidity of the market.

CONCLUSION

Credit risk is an important consideration for banks, bond issuers, and bond investors. The conventional methods of managing credit risk, such as diversification, bank loan sales, and asset securitization, offer only a partial solution to controlling credit risk exposure. In recent years, the growing market for credit derivatives has provided powerful new tools for managing credit risk that can be less costly and more effective than traditional methods. Lenders such as commercial banks and investors such as mutual funds can use credit derivatives to hedge against adverse moves in the credit quality of their investments. Investors can also use credit derivatives to efficiently increase their exposure to different sectors of the credit markets.

Despite its recent growth, the market for credit derivatives is still in its infancy. Many observers believe that the growth in credit derivatives

---

[14]This case would apply if the bank had held the underlying loan for investment. If the bank had held the loan for sale, the penalty might not be as extreme. Chapter 12 contains additional discussion of bank regulatory requirements. See also Federal Reserve System Supervisory Letter 96–17 and Supervisory Letter 97–18 for the regulatory treatment of credit derivatives in the United States.

will parallel the enormously successful interest rate swap market. For this
to occur, however, uncertainties associated with regulatory status, legal
status, and the adequacy of internal control procedures must be resolved.

R E A D I N G   L I S T

This reading list is divided into two sections. The first section lists relevant
regulatory guidance, while the second provides references to academic
research on the pricing of risky debt and credit derivatives.

Regulatory Guidance

Bank of England: "Developing a Supervisory Approach to Credit Derivatives."
    Discussion paper, November 1996.
Bank of France, Commision Bancaire: "Credit Derivatives Issues for Interim Pru-
    dential Treatment." Working paper, June 1997.
Duffee, Gregory, and Chunsheng Zhou: "Credit Derivatives in Banking: Useful
    Tools for Managing Risk?" Working paper, Federal Reserve Board of Gover-
    nors, March 1997.
Federal Deposit Insurance Commision: "Supervisory Guidance for Credit Deriva-
    tives." FIL 62–97.
Federal Reserve System: "Supervisory Guidance for Credit Derivatives." Supervi-
    sory Letter 96–17.
Federal Reserve System: "Application of Market Risk Capital Requirements to
    Credit Derivatives." Supervisory Letter 97–18.
Office of the Comptroller of the Currency: "Credit Derivatives." Advisory Let-
    ter 96–43.
Securities and Futures Authority: "Guidance on Credit Derivatives." Board No-
    tice 414.
Spong, Kenneth: *Banking Regulation: Its Purposes, Implementation, and Effects*, 4th
    ed. Federal Reserve Bank of Kansas City, 1994.

Pricing Defaultable Debt
and Credit Derivatives

Altman, Edward: "Corporate Bond and Commercial Loan Portfolio Analysis."
    Working paper, Financial Institutions Center, Wharton School, University
    of Pennsylvania, 1996.
Altman, Edward: "Defaulted Bonds: Demand, Supply and Performance, 1987–
    1992." *Financial Analysts Journal*, May/June 1993, pp. 55–60.
Altman, Edward: "Measuring Corporate Bond Mortality and Performance." *Jour-
    nal of Finance*, v44, 1989, pp. 909–922.

Amin, K., and Robert Jarrow: "Pricing Options on Risky Assets in a Stochastic Interest Rate Economy." *Mathematical Finance*, v2, 1992, pp. 217–237.

Anderson, Ronald, and Suresh Sundaresan: "Design and Valuation of Debt Contracts." *Review of Financial Studies*, v9, 1996, pp. 37–68.

Asquith, Paul, Robert Gertner, and David Scharfstein: "Anatomy of Financial Distress: An Examination of Junk-Bond Issuers." *Quarterly Journal of Economics*, v109, 1994, pp. 625–657.

Asquith, Paul, David Mullins, and Eric Wolff: "Original Issue High Yield Bonds: Aging Analyses of Defaults, Exchanges, and Calls." *Journal of Finance*, v44, 1989, pp. 923–952.

Barclay, Michael, and Clifford Smith, Jr.: "The Priority Structure of Corporate Liabilities." *Journal of Finance*, v50, 1995, pp. 899–917.

Bensoussan, Alain, Michel Crouhy, and Dan Galai: "Stochastic Equity Volatility Related to the Leverage Effect." *Applied Mathematical Finance*, September 1994, pp. 63–85.

Black, Fischer, and John Cox: "Valuing Corporate Securities: Some Effects of Bond Indenture Provisions." *Journal of Finance*, v31, 1976, pp. 351–367.

Black, Fischer, Edward Derman, and William Toy: "A One Factor Model of Interest Rates and Its Application to Treasury Bond Options." *Financial Analyst Journal*, 46, 1990, pp. 33–39.

Chance, Donald: "Default Risk and the Duration of Zero Coupon Bonds." *Journal of Finance*, v45, 1990, pp. 265–274.

Cooper, I., and A. Mello: "Pricing and Optimal Use of Forward Contracts with Default Risk." Working paper, London Business School, 1990a.

Cooper, I., and A. Mello: "The Default Risk of Swaps." *Journal of Finance*, v45, 1990b, pp. 597–620.

Crosbie, Peter: "Modeling Default Risk." In *Credit Derivatives: Key Issues*. British Bankers Association, 1997.

Cumby, Robert, and Martin Evans: "The Term Structure of Credit Risk: Estimates and Specification Tests." Working paper, Georgetown University, 1997.

Das, Sanjiv, and Rangarajan Sundaram: "A Direct Approach to Arbitrage-Free Pricing of Credit Derivatives." Working paper, Harvard University, 1998.

Das, Sanjiv, and Peter Tufano: "Pricing Credit-Sensitive Debt when Interest Rates, Credit Ratings and Credit Spreads are Stochastic." *The Journal of Financial Engineering*, v5(2), 1996, pp. 161–198.

Das, Sanjiv: "Credit Risk Derivatives." *Journal of Derivatives*, Spring 1995, pp. 7–23.

Das, Satyajit: *Structured Notes and Derivative Embedded Securities.* Euromoney Publications, London, 1996.

Duffee, Gregory: "Estimating the Price of Default Risk." Working paper, Federal Reserve Board of Governors, 1996.

Duffie, Darrell, and Kenneth Singleton: "Modeling Term Structures of Defaultable Bonds." Working paper, Stanford University, 1997.

Duffie, Darrell, and Kenneth Singleton: "An Econometric Model of the Term Structure of Interest Rate Swap Yields." *Journal of Finance*, v52, 1995, pp. 1287–1321.

Eberhart, Allan, William Moore, and Rodney Roenfeldt: "Security Pricing and Deviations from the Absolute Priority Rule in Bankruptcy Proceedings." *Journal of Finance*, v45, 1990, pp. 1457–1489.

Figlewski, Stephen: "The Birth of the AAA Derivatives Subsidiary." *Journal of Derivatives*, Summer 1994, pp. 80–4.

Heath, David, Robert Jarrow, and Andrew Morton: "Bond Pricing and the Term Structure of Interest Rates: A New Methodology for Contingent Claims Valuation." *Econometrica*, v60, 1992, pp. 77–105.

Ho, Thomas, and Sang Bin Lee: "Term Structure Movements and Pricing Interest Rate Contingent Claims." *Journal of Finance*, v41, 1986, pp. 1011–1030.

Hughston, L.P.: "Pricing Models for Credit Derivatives." Lecture notes, Merrill Lynch International, London, U.K., 1997.

Hull, John, and Alan White: "The Impact of Default Risk on Options and Other Derivative Securities." *Journal of Banking and Finance*, v19, 1996, pp. 299–322.

Hull, John, and Alan White: "Pricing Interest Rate Derivative Securities." *Review of Financial Studies*, v3, 1990, pp. 573–592.

Jarrow, Robert, David Lando, and Stuart Turnbull: "A Markov Model of the Term Structure of Credit Spreads." *Review of Financial Studies*, v10, 1997, pp. 481–523.

Jarrow, Robert, and Stuart Turnbull: "When Swaps Are Dropped," *Risk*, May 1997, pp. 70–75.

Jarrow, Robert, and Stuart Turnbull: "Credit Risk." *Handbook of Risk Management and Analysis*. Carol Alexander, editor. Wiley, New York, 1996.

Jarrow, Robert, and Stuart Turnbull: "Drawing the Analogy." *Risk*, v5, 1995a, pp. 63–70.

Jarrow, Robert, and Stuart Turnbull: "The Pricing and Hedging of Options on Financial Securities Subject to Credit Risk." *Journal of Finance*, v50, 1995b, pp. 53–85.

Jarrow, Robert, and Stuart Turnbull: "A Unified Approach for Pricing Contingent Claims on Multiple Term Structures." *Review of Quantitative Finance and Accounting*, 1990.

Johnson, Herb, and Rene Stulz: "The Pricing of Options with Default Risk." *Journal of Finance*, v42, 1987, pp. 267–280.

Kim, Joon, Krishna Ramaswamy, and Suresh Sundaresan: "Does Default Risk in Coupons Affect the Valuation of Corporate Bonds?: A Contingent Claims Model." *Financial Management*, Autumn 1993, pp. 117–131.

Leland, Hayne, and Klaus Toft: "Optimal Capital Structure, Endogenous Bankruptcy, and the Term Structure of Credit Spreads." *Journal of Finance*, v50, 1996, pp. 987–1019.

Longstaff, Francis A., and Eduardo S. Schwartz: "A Simple Approach to Valuing Risky Fixed and Floating Rate Debt." *Journal of Finance*, v50(3), 1995, pp. 789–819.

Longstaff, Francis, and Eduardo Schwartz: "Valuing Credit Derivatives." *Journal of Fixed Income*, June 1995, 6–14.

Madan, Dilip, and Haluk Unal: "Pricing the Risks of Default." *Review of Derivatives Research*, 1995.

Merton, Robert: "A Model of Contract Guarantees for Credit-Sensitive, Opaque Financial Intermediaries." *European Finance Review*, v1. no. 1, 1997.

Merton, Robert: "On the Pricing of Corporate Debt: The Risk Structure of Interest Rates." *Journal of Finance*, v29, 1974, pp. 449–470.

Musiela, Marek, Stuart Turnbull, and Lee Wakeman: "Interest Rate Risk Management." *Review of Futures Markets*, v12, 1993, pp. 221–261.

Nielsen, Lars, Jesus Saa-Requejo, and P. Santa-Clara: "Default Risk and Interest Rate Risk: The Term Structure of Default Spreads." Working paper, INSEAD, France, 1993.

Nielsen, Soren, and Ehud Ronn: "The Valuation of Default Risk in Corporate Bonds and Interest Rate Swaps." Working paper, University of Texas at Austin, 1996.

Pierides, Yiannos: "The Pricing of Credit Risk Derivatives." *Journal of Economic Dynamics and Control*, v5, 1997, pp. 1579–1611.

Ramaswamy, Krishna, and Suresh Sundaresan: "The Valuation of Floating-Rate Instruments." *Journal of Financial Economics*, v17, 1986, pp. 251–272.

Rich, Don: "The Valuation and Behavior of Black-Scholes Options Subject to Intertemporal Default Risk." *Review of Derivatives Research*, v1, 1996, pp. 25–59.

Schonbucher, Philipp: "The Term Structure of Defaultable Bond Prices." Working paper, University of Bonn, 1996.

Schwartz, Alan: "Bankruptcy Workouts and Debt Contracts." *Journal of Law and Economics*, v36, 1993, pp. 595–632.

Shimko, David, N. Tejima, and D. van Deventer: "The Pricing of Risky Debt When Interest Rates are Stochastic." *Journal of Fixed Income*, v3(2), 1993, pp. 58–65.

Skinner, Frank: "A Trinomial Model of Bonds with Default Risk." *Financial Analysts Journal*, 1994, pp. 73–78.

Titman, Sheridan, and Walter Torous: "Valuing Commercial Mortgages: An Empirical Investigation of the Contingent Claims Approach to Pricing Risky Debt." *Journal of Finance*, v44, 1989, pp. 345–373.

Weiss, Lawrence: "Bankruptcy Resolution: Direct Costs and Violations of Priority of Claims." *Journal of Financial Economics*, v27, 1990, pp. 285–314.

Whittaker, Gregg, and Sumita Kumar: "Credit Derivatives: A Primer." In Ravi Dattateya, ed., *The Handbook of Fixed Income Derivatives*. Probus, Chicago, 1996.

Whittaker, Gregg, and Joyce Frost: "An Introduction to Credit Derivatives." *The Journal of Lending and Credit Risk Management*. May 1997, pp. 15–25.

Zhou, Chunsheng: "A Jump-Diffusion Approach to Modeling Credit Risk and Valuing Defaultable Securities." Working paper, Federal Reserve Board of Governors, 1997.

BIBLIOGRAPHY

Das, Sanjiv: "Credit Risk Derivatives." *Journal of Derivatives*, Spring 1995, pp. 7–23.

Jarrow, Robert, David Lando, and Stuart Turnbull: "A Markov Model of the Term Structure of Credit Spreads." *Review of Financial Studies*, Summer 1997, pp. 481–523.

Longstaff, Francis, and Eduardo Schwartz: "Valuing Credit Derivatives." *Journal of Fixed Income*, June 1995, pp. 6–14.

Smithson, Charles, Hal Holappa, and Shaun Rai: "Class Notes: Credit Derivatives (2)." *Risk*, June 1996 pp. 47–48.

Spong, Kenneth: *Banking Regulation: Its Purposes, Implementation, and Effects*, 4th ed. Federal Reserve Bank of Kansas City, 1994.

Whittaker, Gregg, and Sumita Kumar: "Credit Derivatives: A Primer." In Ravi Dattateya, ed., *The Handbook of Fixed Income Derivatives*. Probus, Chicago, 1996.

PART TWO

Investment and Risk Management Applications

CHAPTER 2

Building Efficient Synthetic Positions and Using Credit-Linked Notes

J. Gregg Whittaker, Ph.D.
Managing Director, Chase Securities, Inc.

Evy Adamidou, Ph.D.
Vice President, Chase Securities, Inc.

INTRODUCTION

In the vast and ever changing landscape of financial derivatives, credit derivatives are among the most recent and most rapidly growing innovations. Just as other derivatives allow for management of market factors such as interest rate or currency risks, credit derivatives permit investors to manage credit exposures by separating their view on credit from other market variables. In this chapter, we will explain how investors can efficiently build synthetic positions in a variety of markets by using credit derivatives. We will address what are the advantages of using credit derivatives and who is currently using them, and then we will turn our focus to describing a number of specific products and their applications. Finally, we will consider the possibilities for the future development of this powerful new market.

Credit Derivatives as Synthetic Positions

Credit derivatives are a fairly simple concept. An investor seeking exposure to a specific market or asset class has basically two alternatives: he can either buy the respective instruments in the cash market, or attain the same exposure through a credit derivative structure. Broadly defined, a credit derivative is a financial contract outlining a potential exchange of payments in which at least one leg of the cash flow is linked to the "performance" of a specified underlying credit-sensitive asset or liability. The underlying markets include bank loans, corporate debt, trade receivables, emerging market and municipal debt, as well as the credit exposure generated from other derivatives-linked activities. The performance of

27

such market credits reflects perceived risk and the cost of a potential default.

As in other more traditional derivative markets, swap, note, and option-based products form the foundation for all credit derivative products. For example, a credit option or credit-linked note can be structured to pay the purchaser upon a default or credit downgrade. Moreover, credit derivatives can also take the form of financial swaps where a counterparty exchanges the total return of a certain credit in return for some spread over a specified benchmark, such as LIBOR.

Attractive Features of Credit Derivatives

Credit derivatives provide users with an efficient, tailor-made, on- or off-balance sheet means of synthetically attaining credit risk. Credit derivatives offer tremendous flexibility in terms of tailoring a structure to meet their individual specifications, thereby enabling users to overcome a variety of market and nonmarket impediments in order to achieve their desired investment objectives. By reducing capital requirements and greatly easing the back-office administrative burdens, these derivatives are often a cleaner, lower cost alternative to the underlying cash markets. Moreover, they can provide access to those investors who may be otherwise precluded from the underlying cash markets altogether. Users can also choose the degree of leverage that best suits their particular investment and risk management style.

From an investment standpoint, credit derivatives offer users efficient access to the underlying credit-sensitive markets. Efficiency here is defined as increased flexibility and leverage along with decreased cash, regulatory capital, and back-office requirements. Moreover, the prudent use of credit derivatives can enable users to minimize their tax liabilities, especially in cross border situations. The overall result can be significantly enhanced performance relative to the available cash market alternatives.

Users of Credit Derivatives

The universe of potential users of credit derivatives is as vast as the number of institutions that are exposed to, or that seek exposure to, credit risk. This includes commercial banks, insurance companies, corporations, money managers, mutual funds, hedge funds, and pension funds.

THE BASIC STRUCTURES

The following section provides an overview of the most commonly used credit derivative structures, along with a brief description of some of the specific products. This section is followed by a section that will further expand on these concepts through a series of case studies.

Swaps

A swap is an agreement between two counterparties to exchange disparate cash flows, at least one of which must be tied to the performance of a specified credit-sensitive asset or a portfolio or index of such assets. The other cash flow is usually tied to some floating rate index such as LIBOR, a fixed rate, or linked to some other credit-sensitive asset(s).

While there are a number of different kinds of swaps, we will describe only two:

- Total return swap
- Default swap

Total Return Swap

A total return swap is a swap agreement in which the total return of a bank loan(s) or credit-sensitive security(s) is exchanged for some other cash flow, usually tied to LIBOR or some other loan(s) or credit-sensitive security(s). While no principal amounts are exchanged and no physical change of ownership occurs, the total return swap allows participants to "effectively" go long or short the underlying. As such, a total return swap can be considered a synthetic loan or security.

The maturity of the total return swap need not match that of the underlying, and the swap can typically be terminated at any time. Moreover, at termination, many such structures allow the user to purchase the underlying loan(s) or security(s) at the initial price in lieu of a cash settlement of the swap. However, if the swap is cash settled, the termination payment is typically determined via a dealer poll of the prevailing underlying market value(s).

Default Swap

A default swap is a swap agreement in which a periodic fixed-rate payment, or up front fee, is exchanged for the promise of some specified payment(s) to be made only if a particular, predetermined credit event occurs. The default swap can be structured on a single credit name or a basket of names. A credit event is typically defined as a default or a credit downgrade, where a default could include bankruptcy, insolvency, or failure to make payments within a predetermined amount of time. A lowering of the credit by public rating agencies below a certain prespecified level would constitute a downgrade.

A default swap, then, is comparable to a credit-wrapper. The default payment can be structured in a number of ways. It can be linked to the price movement of a particular security, it can be set at a predetermined recovery rate (binary payoff), or it can be in the form of an actual delivery of the underlying security at a predetermined price. Regardless of the form, a default swap allows for the transference of credit risk from one swap counterparty to the other.

Credit-Linked Notes

Credit-linked notes provide investors with a cost-effective means of monetizing credit views. These notes come in a variety of forms, but the common thread between them is the link between return and the credit-related performance of the underlying. Credit-linked notes are loans or securities, typically issued by an investment grade entity, with coupon, redemption and maturity provisions just like traditional note structures. However, unlike standard notes, the performance of a credit-linked note is a function of the performance of the underlying asset(s), in addition to the performance of the issuer. Therefore, the redemption value of the credit-linked note is directly dependent upon the redemption value of the underlying asset(s).

Credit Options

A credit option is a privately negotiated, over-the-counter option contract between two counterparties which can be customized to meet the specific credit-related hedging or investment objectives of the client. A credit call option gives the purchaser the right, but not the obligation, to buy an underlying credit-sensitive asset, or credit spread, at a predetermined price for a predetermined period of time. A credit put option gives the purchaser the right, but not the obligation, to sell the underlying asset or credit spread at a predetermined price for a prespecified period of time. These basic option structures provide the groundwork for building more exotic credit option structures.

Credit options can be used both as a hedging and an investment vehicle. Purchasing credit options enables investors and hedgers to participate in price or credit spread movement while risking no more than the option premium. Selling credit options can be a valuable source of fee income for those who are looking to enhance portfolio returns. As in other markets, there are a myriad of credit option products, but all fall into one of the following two broad categories:

- Standard credit options
- Exotic credit options

Standard Credit Options

The standard credit option gives the purchaser the right, but not the obligation, to buy (call) or sell (put) an asset or credit spread at a stated price (strike) for a specified period of time (expiry). These structures allow investors to take a view solely on credit-related performance, without any exposure to the absolute level of yields or to any other noncredit market factor. For example, if an investor has the view that a particular credit spread is going to widen in the next year, he can purchase a one year call option on that credit spread. The option will be in-the-money at expiration if the credit spread does indeed widen beyond the strike. If it does not, the investor's loss is limited to the premium paid for the call.

Exotic Credit Options

Exotic credit options are defined as credit options that break at least one of the rules of a standard option with respect to time, price, position, or underlying asset. The most common forms of exotic credit options are the barrier and digital options.

Barrier credit options involve a contingent credit-related mechanism that serves to activate or inactivate the option. In other words, the trigger that turns the option "on" or "off" is a function of the credit quality of the underlying asset(s). Refer again to the example above of an option on a credit spread, but now consider a "down and out" call. The down and out call is structured similarly to the standard call, except that this option ceases to exist if the credit spread narrows below a prespecified knock-out level. Consequently, the premiums for barrier credit options are typically lower than for like standard options. Other forms of barrier credit options include down and ins, up and outs, and up and ins.

Digital (or binary) credit options have payouts at expiration of either zero, if the option expires out-of-the-money, or some preagreed upon fixed amount, if the option expires in-the-money. The fixed payment, unlike a standard option, is independent of how deep in-the-money the option actually is. For example, a digital put option on a bank loan could pay the par amount if the borrower defaulted or nothing if the borrower continued to perform as scheduled, irrespective of the underlying market price.

INVESTMENT APPLICATIONS

The following section takes a closer look at the various credit derivative structures defined in the previous section by developing and working through a number of investment applications.

Synthetic High Yield Debt Trading

Assume an investor seeks to attain $10 million of exposure to an outstanding high yield loan or a loan in syndication. However, this investor has limited access to the cash loan market, limited back-office capabilities, or needs to invest off-balance sheet. The investor can use a total return swap to gain exposure to the loan while keeping it off the balance sheet.

Assume that an investor chooses to leverage a cash investment ten times by holding in reserve, or pledging to Chase, only $1 million against the $10 million underlying exposure. Further, assume that the coupon of the underlying loan is L + 2.5 percent, while the swap payment to Chase Bank is LIBOR + 80 bp. The 170 basis point spread is leveraged ten times to 17 percent with respect to the investors $1 million. Add to this the cash yield on the $1 million of, say, LIBOR, the swap generates current annual income of L + 17 percent.

Capital Structure Arbitrage

Investors can use total return swaps to arbitrage a perceived mispricing between bank loans and subordinated debt of the same issuer. For example, suppose that both assets are priced at par, but the loan yields LIBOR plus 380 basis points while the debt yields LIBOR plus 280 basis points.

F I G U R E   2–1

Total Return Swap to Attain Desired Exposure

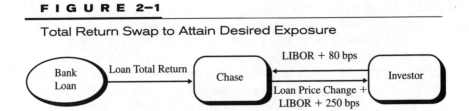

Total Return Swap to Arb Capital Structure Mispricings

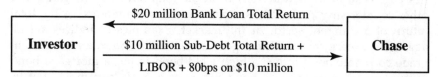

Clearly, in the absence of some overriding technical or other nonmarket factors, a mispricing exists since the senior, secured asset yields more than does the subordinated asset. To efficiently exploit this opportunity, a total return swap can be executed to effectively go long the bank loan and short the subordinated debt at a ratio of, say, two to one.[1]

This swap generates a net spread of 200 basis points [(100bps * $10/$20) + (300bps * $10/$20)] on $20 million. Assuming a $2 million cash investment, this spread is leveraged ten times into a 20 percent return. Add this to the return on the cash itself of, say, LIBOR, and this structure generates a yield of L + 20 percent per annum.

Enhancing Investment Grade Debt Returns

Assume an investor has a positive view about a specific company that is A rated and wishes to book some income by taking the credit risk but without tying up a lot of cash. Let's also assume that she is not willing to take day-to-day price volatility on the name but she is comfortable taking on default risk at 10 times leverage. The investor can enter into a default swap, and post $1 million as collateral. Let's also assume she receives 15 basis points per annum as the premium. The 15 basis point spread is leveraged 10 times to 1.5 percent with respect to her investment. Add to this the cash yield on the $1 million of, say, LIBOR, and the swap generates current income of L + 1.5 percent for an A rated name.

Synthetic Exposure to Various Market Sectors

Investors can efficiently go long or short in the various sectors of the market by using index swaps. An index swap is a simple concept, similar

---

[1]The ratio of two to one, though somewhat arbitrary in this example, seeks to reflect the fact that subordinated bonds tend to be more credit sensitive than their senior secured bank loan counterparts.

to a total return swap; you still have the two counterparties and the periodic exchange of cash flows. However, at least one of the counterparties pays cash flows that are based on the total return of an index. The other counterparty pays LIBOR, another interest rate index, or the total return of a different sector of the market. Examples of indices are an aggregate fixed income index, a government bond index, an investment grade corporate bond index, a high yield bond index, a mortgage bond index, an emerging markets bond index, or a bank loan index. Let us assume that an investor runs an asset allocation fund and wants to have flexibility, depending on his view, to increase or decrease his exposure to the various sectors of the market on a quarterly basis. It may be inefficient for the investor to replicate each sector by structuring a representative portfolio and partially liquidate the portfolio anytime he wishes to decrease his exposure to a specific sector. Alternatively, the investor can use index swaps. For example, whenever he has the view that the bank loan market will outperform the high yield bond market, he can enter into a three month index swap, receive the total return of a bank loan index and pay the total return of a high yield bond index.

Alternatively, let us assume that a fund manager is planning to start a new high yield bond fund, and wishes immediate exposure to the high yield bond market. However, initially he does not have sufficient funds to create a portfolio large enough to be representative of the sector. The portfolio manager can enter into a total return swap and receive the total return of the Chase Securities High Yield Index. In exchange he will pay LIBOR plus 25 basis points on the notional amount of the swap. Through the total return swap the portfolio manager was able to immediately create a long, broadly diversified position to the high yield market. In addition, depending on his credit quality, he can leverage his exposure and at the same time minimize administrative requirements.

Efficient Bank Loan Investment–The Chase Secured Loan Trust Note^{sm}

The Chase Secured Loan Trust (CSLT) Note^{sm} is an investment grade debt security issued by a trust that provides high yields, leveraged upside and limited downside returns linked to a diversified bank loan portfolio. The trust uses the note proceeds to purchase Treasury securities which are then used to collateralize the "effective" purchase of bank loans. From an economic perspective, the note holders are long both the treasuries as well as the underlying bank loans. The collateralization may be as low as 10 percent, allowing investors to achieve an upside leverage of up to 10 to 1, with yields topping 20 percent per annum. However, unlike other leveraged transactions, there are no margin calls with a CSLT^sm, so the investor can lose no more than the initial investment amount.

From an investment perspective, the CSLT^sm is the economic equivalent of purchasing a diversified portfolio of loans on margin but, as mentioned above, without the risk of margin calls. Moreover, due to its innovative structuring, the note itself will carry an investment grade rating even though the underlying portfolio is leveraged and has an average rating that is noninvestment grade.

Bank loans are an underutilized asset class which have historically generated relatively stable, attractive returns. The leveraged (noninvestment grade) bank loan market remains a largely untapped source of high yield paper, with over $300 billion in syndicated leveraged loans outstanding in the United States but only $50 billion held by institutional investors. Between January 1993 and March 1998, the leveraged bank loan annual return was 9.63 percent, compared to 12.02 percent and 22.59 percent for high yield and the S&P 500 respectively. However, because these loans are senior-secured, floating rate assets, they are far less volatile than high yield bonds or equity. Over this same time period, the annual volatility of loans was only 1.49 percent compared to 3.67 percent for high yield and 11.34 percent for the S&P. Consequently, bank loans have provided attractive, highly competitive returns but with a fraction of the volatility that has prevailed in the high yield and equity markets. Credit derivatives, in the form of swaps, notes, or options provide efficient access to this historically strong, underutilized asset class.

Consider an investor (e.g., an insurance company) that is seeking to better utilize its credit analysis capabilities by investing in bank loans. But due to the relatively high capital requirements for noninvestment grade assets coupled with the administrative burdens inherent in the cash loan market, the appeal of this investment strategy is greatly diminished.

The solution to this problem for many is the CSLT Note^sm. A total return swap, while appealing at first blush, may be inappropriate for some investors who can only use swaps and other like derivatives for "risk management" purposes. The note, on the other hand, is allowable for investment purposes because it is a rated, investment grade debt obligation. Moreover, the note can be structured to meet the investor's leverage requirements, or lack thereof, and with relatively simple back-office administrative demands. Consequently, the CSLT Note^sm offers clients an allowable, efficient mechanism for investing in a diversified portfolio of bank loans.

Let's say an investor purchases a $50 million investment grade CSLT Note^sm, issued by a trust. The term of the note is twelve years redeemable by the investor at market prices at the end of the fourth year and annually

F I G U R E   2–3

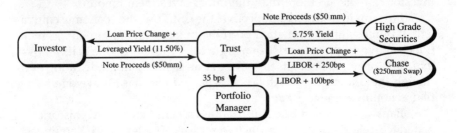

thereafter. The trust uses the note proceeds to purchase T-notes or other high grade securities that are pledged to Chase as collateral for a total return swap. Under the terms of the swap, Chase pays the trust the "total return" on a $250 million loan portfolio, with coupons of LIBOR plus 250 basis points (e.g., in consideration for a payment from the trust of LIBOR plus 100 basis points).

The net swap spread of 150 basis points less the portfolio manager's fee of 35 basis points[2] on $250 million notional is leveraged 5 times to 5.75 percent in respect of the note holder's $50 million investment. Add to this the 5.75 percent T-note yield, and the CSLT Note[sm] generates a yield of 11.50 percent.[3]

Given the historical performance of the leveraged loan market, let us construct a scenario analysis of a typical CSLT Note[sm], with five times leverage, to better understand the potential risks and rewards to the investor over a four-year time horizon.

Consequently, if realized recovery rates and default rates are at historic norms of 87 percent and 5.2 percent respectively, the investment grade rated CSLT Note[sm] total return will be 10.64 percent per annum or LIBOR plus 4.89 percent.

Trading Credit Spreads

Suppose an investor is bullish on, say, Mexican par bonds and seeks to profit from any narrowing of their credit spread relative to U.S. Treasury yields. This can be accomplished by purchasing a "knock-out" (up and

---

[2]Estimate based on current market standards, reflecting a partly fixed and partly performance based fee. The portfolio management agreement is between the investor and the portfolio manager and is independent of Chase.

[3]The coupon can be either fixed or floating, at the investor's discretion.

		Recovery Rate (NPV)	Actual Default Rate			
			2.00%	5.20%[5]	10.00%	16.00%
Initial loan price[4]	99.75%	35.00%	10.10%	8.22%	4.60%	-0.95%
Avg. loan spread	2.50%	55.00%	10.44%	9.17%	7.13%	3.68%
Swap	1.00%	70.00%	10.70%	9.87%	8.57%	6.76%
Curr. port. mgmt fee.	0.20%	87.00%	10.99%	10.64%	10.10%	9.41%
Performance fee over target[6]	20.00%	92.00%	11.07%	10.86%	10.53%	10.12%
Expected annual prepayment	15.00%	100.00%	11.21%	11.21%	11.21%	11.22%
Cash collateral yield	5.75%					
Historical avg. recovery[7]	87.00%					
Historical median recovery[8]	100.00%					

out) put on the credit spread. The premium for this put is moderated by two factors: the knock-out feature and the character of forward credit spreads. First, as discussed previously, the knock-out feature reduces option premiums relative to standard options. Second, the fact that forward credit spreads are typically wider than spot spreads (a function of the positive net carry resulting from buying the underlying emerging market debt and shorting the U.S. Treasury, i.e., the dealers hedge) likewise tends to reduce put premiums.

The investor profits as credit spreads narrow between Mexican par bonds and U.S. Treasury Notes below the strike. If spreads are above the strike but below the barrier, the option has no intrinsic value, but the potential remains that the option could expire in-the-money. However, if spreads ever rise above the barrier (i.e., if the investor is sufficiently incorrect about spreads narrowing) the knock-out put ceases to exist and the investor realizes a loss equal to the premium paid.

Bearish spread strategies can be implemented as well, but are often less efficiently priced than their bullish counterparts because of, again,

---

[4]Assume a diversified portfolio of five-year loans that, if they perform, accrete linearly to par. After four years, the price will be 99.95 percent, given a 25 bps discount to par.
[5]Calculated based upon annual asset weighted average default rates of the five public loan funds from September 1989 to September 1996.
[6]Portfolio management fee assumes 20bps per annum plus performance fee equal to 20 percent of returns in excess of LIBOR + 1.50 percent.
[7]Source: Moody's Investors Service. "Bankrupt Bank Loan Recoveries," June 1998.
[8]Source: Moody's Investors Service. "Bankrupt Bank Loan Recoveries," June 1998.

FIGURE 2-4

Up and Out Put Option

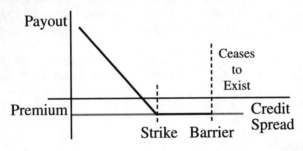

the character of forward credit spreads as well as the potential difficulty and cost of shorting the underlying emerging market debt.

Synthetic Principal Guaranteed Investment

Let us assume that a pension fund wishes to attain exposure to the high yield bond market but has strict guidelines regarding asset principal preservation. An investment in an extendable credit-linked note may be the appropriate solution. The note will have zero or relatively low coupon overtime and, at maturity, would pay principal plus the cumulative total return of a high yield index.

Credit-linked notes ("Notes") can be issued by a credit worthy entity and customized to provide participation in any underlying sector of the market with limited downside risk. There are various ways to create principal guaranteed notes. One simple solution is to invest a portion of the money into Treasury Zeroes of the desired maturity and invest the remaining money into the desired sector through a leveraged total return swap. This type of a principal guaranteed note will provide the principal preservation desired but at the same time will have lower expected returns because only a portion of the money will be invested in the desired sector.

A more efficient alternative, that would allow for all the money to be invested in the desired sector, may be an extendable credit-linked note. An extendable credit-linked note is a note that has a final maturity of 10 years, for example, but has an expected maturity of only 4 years. The payout of the note will be linked to the total return of a specific sector or asset. The note will have zero or relatively low coupon and, at maturity, the payout will be principal plus the total return of the reference asset.

If, at the end of the fourth year, the cumulative total return of the sector is positive, the note will mature. If the cumulative return is negative, the note will extend until the cumulative return becomes positive. If at the end of the tenth year the cumulative total return is still negative, the note will mature at par.

Creating Synthetic Assets with Desired Risk Profiles

A fund manager can use a credit-linked note to synthetically create assets with the desired risk/return profile. For example, assume that the manager wishes to attain exposure to a certain noninvestment grade sector of the market, but is unable to find the desired paper due to a lack of supply. Higher grade paper, which we will assume is more readily available, can be put into a structure to create the desired noninvestment grade exposure with the associated higher yields.

Specifically, assume that the fund manager seeks two-year B-rated credit exposure, but cannot source the paper. However, BB/Ba paper is readily available. A two-year, $10 million, B-rated note yielding LIBOR plus 400 basis points can be structured with four underlying BB/Ba loans, each valued at $10 million and with an average yield of LIBOR plus 275 basis points. The Note is illustrated in Figure 2–5.

The investor is taking on compounded credit risk in that the note effectively defaults if "any" of the underlying loans default. Let's assume that the likelihood of a BB/Ba credit defaulting within two years is about 4 percent. Therefore, the likelihood of any one of four BB/Ba credits defaulting within two years, assuming zero correlation, is about 15 per-

F I G U R E   2–5

Credit-Linked Note to Create Desired Exposure

cent,[9] which is about equal to the likelihood of a B credit defaulting within two years. In other words, the investor has created a B-rated type security yielding LIBOR plus 400 basis points.

From the issuers standpoint, the note provides first loss protection on the underlying loan portfolio. The cost of the protection, the 400 basis point spread on the note over the bank's funding cost of LIBOR, results in a 100 basis point decline in the margin earned on each of the four underlying loans. In the event that any of the loans default, the note is terminated, the bank keeps the $10 million of note proceeds, and the defaulted loan is put to the investor. Consequently, the bank is made whole and the investor bears the risk of the first default. However, any subsequent defaults are the sole responsibility of the bank. The investor can then sell the defaulted underlying loan or hold onto it and go through the workout process.

Synthetic Access to Local Currency and Treasury Markets

Credit-linked notes offer an opportunity for investors to efficiently tap local currency and treasury markets. Let us assume that an investor is bullish about the prospects of the Russian currency over a one year period. He can invest in a coupon bearing, one year, U.S. dollars (USD) denominated note whose principal redemption is linked to a currency factor which is the ratio of the spot value of Russian rubles at note maturity to the spot value of the foreign currency on trade date. As an example, a one year note, issued in May 1998, would pay a coupon of 42 percent.

Currency linked notes are most popular when linked to high yield currencies which provide for relatively high coupons. They can also be packaged to include sovereign credit risk as well. For example, for an investor willing to accept exposure to the Korean currency, a one year note whose principal redemption is linked to the performance of the Korean won would have a USD coupon of 18 percent. But if the investor was also willing to accept sovereign default risk over the note period, the coupon would be 23 percent.

FUTURE MARKET DEVELOPMENT

Credit derivatives are currently growing at an exponential rate and will most certainly become a trillion dollar plus market, given the expanse of

---

[9]Probability of 4 independent BB/Ba credits not defaulting is $0.96^4 = 0.85$. Therefore, probability of first loss note defaulting is 15 percent (100 percent − 85 percent).

the underlying credit markets combined with the compelling investment and risk management applications these products provide. Virtually all aspects of the underlying credit markets as well as the market players themselves point to continued and sustained growth. Corporate bond issuance and bank loan syndications have increased dramatically in recent years.

Moreover, corporate bonds are a large percentage of the holdings of insurance companies, pension funds, and mutual funds. And corporations, regional, commercial, and Ex-Im banks have also become major users of credit derivatives as the market continues to evolve.

Further, we expect that as the market becomes more efficient and further develops, a variety of customized products will emerge as users begin to better understand the possibilities and the varied uses of credit derivatives. Various market indices will develop which will aid market participants in tracking performance. And the growth of the credit derivatives market will see the increased use of loan indices, corporate bond indices, and bond sector indices as investment and hedging benchmarks. Consequently, a liquid, over-the-counter market should develop for options and other derivative products tied to these indices, as well as to the more widely traded underlying bonds and loans themselves.

One of the most dramatic outcomes from the continued development of credit derivatives will be the creation of a market for credit. Currently, the pricing of credit risk is often a subjective undertaking dependent upon an analyst's interpretation of the available financial information. In the not too distant future, however, pricing credit risk will be as simple as pulling up a screen on your PC, with trading opportunities created when your own views differ from those of the market. And efficient credit risk hedging capabilities will be available and affordable to virtually all end-users.

However, one of the impediments to the complete development of credit derivatives is the lack of a credible information infrastructure. Currently, there is only limited historical credit information available for users. Typically, it is the banks and other such credit issuers who have tracked credit performance. But even here, the information is generally fragmented and incomplete. So, for the market to sustain its growth, banks must continue their efforts to enhance and consolidate their analysis, and nonbank users will have to gain access to this information.

CONCLUSION

The credit derivatives market provides clean, efficient access to underlying credit-sensitive markets, thereby providing an effective means by which users can attain their investment and risk management objectives. These derivatives, whether in the form of swap, notes, or options, provide users with a more cost-effective means of reaching their investment goals through reduced cash, capital, and back-office requirements along with increased leverage potential. In addition, they offer the risk manager powerful new hedging tools, capable of isolating credit risk from other market risks.

And because credit derivative structures encompass a variety of markets, there exists a broad array of potential users for whom this market fills a myriad of important investment and risk management needs. The underlying markets include everything from bank loans, corporate and sovereign debt, and municipal bonds to the credit risks inherent in other more traditional derivative markets. Consequently, the list of current and potential users include commercial banks, insurance companies, corporations, money managers, mutual funds, hedge funds, and pension funds.

The credit derivatives market will almost certainly continue to develop quite rapidly for the foreseeable future. However, its long-term prospects hinge on the development of a sound regulatory environment, more readily available historical information, and a better understanding among participants of the advantages and versatility of these products.

CHAPTER 3

Credit Derivatives and Loan Portfolio Management*

Blythe Masters
Managing Director, J. P. Morgan Securities

Kelly Bryson
Credit Derivatives Marketer, J. P. Morgan Securities

INTRODUCTION: CREDIT DERIVATIVES IN THE CONTEXT OF A CHANGING BANKING INDUSTRY

Even in the latter part of the 1990s, we cannot yet argue that most banks actively manage credit risk. Indeed, even in very large banks, credit risk management for the loan portfolio manager is often little more than a strategy of portfolio diversification backed by line limits, with an occasional sale of positions in the secondary market. In recent years, stiff competition among lenders, a tendency by some banks to treat large corporate lending as a loss-leading cost of relationship development, and a benign credit cycle have combined to subject bank loan credit spreads to relentless downward pressure, both on an absolute basis and relative to other asset classes. Despite the benign credit environment, rapidly evolving profitability tools such as risk adjusted return on capital have begun to reveal that corporate loan portfolios are often not generating attractive returns on regulatory or economic capital. Yet at the same time, secondary market illiquidity, relationship constraints, and the luxury of cost rather than mark-to-market accounting have made active bank loan portfolio management either impossible or unattractive. Consequently, the vast majority of banks hold corporate loans from origination until maturity. Market data emphasize this point: in 1997, primary loan syndica-

---

*Opinions expressed in this article are the authors' and do not necessarily reflect those of
    J.P. Morgan or any of its affiliates. The article draws on material previously
    published in J.P. Morgan Securities Inc. *"Credit Derivatives—A Primer,"* March 1998.

43

tion in the U.S. exceeded $1.1 trillion, while secondary loan market volumes were less than $62 billion.[1]

However, five years hence, commentators will look back to the birth of the credit derivative market as a watershed development for bank portfolio management practice. Simply put, credit derivatives are fundamentally changing the way banks price, manage, transact, originate, distribute, and account for credit risk. To put this somewhat radical statement in context, it is necessary to understand that the evolution of credit derivatives is occurring at a critical turning point in bank history and that their development is both being precipitated by—and precipitating change in—the banking industry.

The first dimension of change is that over the past few years, bank loans to large corporations have emerged as an investible asset class. Nonbanks (mutual funds, insurance companies, pension plans) have become significant net investors, with the result that over 40 percent of 1997 syndicated leveraged loans were placed with nonbanks.[2] In parallel, secondary bank loan markets have evolved sufficiently to satisfy the liquidity and mark-to-market requirements of nonbank investors. Investment banks have also entered the lending business to service issuers seeking to tap capital markets across the spectrum from debt to equity. Analytical models for evaluating portfolio credit risk have been made available, and there have been significant improvements in data compilation and dissemination. Finally, the most sophisticated banks have established loan portfolio management groups whose objective is to optimize portfolios by actively buying and selling risk.

The second dimension of change is that bank balance sheets are becoming less and less attractive vehicles for ownership of bank loan assets. Banks are fundamentally disadvantaged relative to other owners of corporate loan assets for at least three simple economic reasons. First, international regulation of minimum capital requirements. In addition to creating a significant compliance cost burden, risk-based capital rules are insensitive to risk and consequently force banks to under leverage high quality assets and encourage them to over leverage low quality assets. Second, the cost of deposit insurance. This is of limited value to high-quality banks whose depositors rely on bank capital over insurance, but it allows low-quality banks to access cheaper funds than would be available in a free market. Third, taxation. Banks pay income tax on loan income, and bank shareholders pay tax on dividend income. Relative to direct investment in loan assets,

---

[1]Source: Loan Pricing Corp. *Gold Sheets*, 1998, volume IV.
[2]Source: Portfolio Management Data.

or investment via a more tax-effective vehicle such as a mutual fund, the impact of "double taxation" clearly disadvantages banks as investment vehicles. In some jurisdictions (e.g., Canada), banks also pay tax on capital.

The inevitable result is that banks are facing rapid disintermediation in the bank loan markets by other financial institutions and capital markets investors. As a result, banks are being forced to reevaluate lending and warehousing activity strategically in order to improve profitability and return on equity in credit businesses. If banks can respond to such change by improving the efficiency with which they deliver loan product to those who are its best longer-run owners while defending key customer relationships and the margins associated with origination and servicing, then disintermediation need not be a threat. In many cases, credit derivatives will form a crucial part of the strategy which allows banks to respond to this imperative. Simply put, this role has evolved because credit derivatives enhance banks' ability to repackage and distribute the credit risk that they are well-positioned to originate, but no longer well-positioned to warehouse. In the same way that securitization made feasible the monoline credit card and mortgage banks, credit derivatives may facilitate the same efficiency of balance sheet usage for corporate lenders.

KEY CHARACTERISTICS OF CREDIT DERIVATIVES

Credit derivatives are bilateral financial contracts that isolate specific aspects of credit risk from an underlying instrument and transfer that risk between two parties. In so doing, credit derivatives separate the ownership and management of credit risk from other qualitative and quantitative aspects of ownership of financial assets. Thus, credit derivatives share one of the key features of historically successful derivative products, which is the potential to achieve efficiency gains through a process of market completion. Efficiency gains arising from disaggregating risk are best illustrated by imagining an auction process in which an auctioneer sells a number of risks, each to the highest bidder, as compared to selling a "job lot" of the same risks to the highest bidder for the entire package. In most cases, the separate auctions will yield a higher aggregate sale price than the job lot. By separating specific aspects of credit risk from other risks, credit derivatives allow even the most illiquid credit exposures to be transferred from portfolios that have but don't want the risk to those that want but don't have that risk, even when the underlying asset itself could not have been transferred in the same way.

In substance, the definition of credit derivatives captures many credit instruments that banks have been using for years, including guarantees, letters of credit, and loan participations. So why attach such significance to this new group of products? Essentially, it is the precision with which credit derivatives can isolate and transfer certain aspects of credit risk, rather than their economic substance, that distinguishes them from more traditional credit instruments. There are several distinct arguments, not all of which are unique to credit derivatives, but which combine to make a strong case for increasing use of credit derivatives by banks.

First, the reference entity, whose credit risk is being transferred, need neither be a party to nor aware of a credit derivative transaction. This confidentiality enables bank treasurers to manage their credit risks discreetly without interfering with important customer relationships. This contrasts with both a loan assignment through the secondary loan market, which requires borrower notification, and a silent participation, which exposes the participating bank to as much credit risk to the selling bank as to the borrower itself.

The absence of the reference entity at the negotiating table also means that the terms (tenor, seniority, size, compensation structure) of the credit derivative transaction can be customized to meet the needs of the buyer and seller of risk, rather than the particular liquidity or term needs of a borrower. Moreover, because credit derivatives isolate credit risk from relationship and other aspects of asset ownership, they introduce discipline to pricing decisions. Credit derivatives provide an objective market pricing benchmark representing the true opportunity cost of a transaction. Increasingly, as liquidity and pricing technology improve, credit derivatives are defining credit spread forward curves and implied volatilities in a way that less liquid credit products never could do. The availability and discipline of visible market pricing enables banks to make pricing and relationship decisions more objectively.

Second, credit derivatives are the first mechanism via which short sales of credit instruments can be executed with any reasonable liquidity and without the risk of a short squeeze. It is more or less impossible to short-sell a bank loan, but the economics of a short position can be achieved synthetically by purchasing credit protection using a credit derivative. This allows the user to reverse the "skewed" profile of credit risk (whereby one earns a small premium for the risk of a large loss) and instead pay a small premium for the possibility of a large gain upon credit deterioration. Consequently, portfolio managers can short specific credits, or a broad index of credits, either to hedge existing exposures or simply to profit from a negative credit view. Similarly, the possibility of short sales opens up a wealth of arbitrage opportunities. Global credit markets today display discrepancies in the pricing of the same credit risk across different asset classes, maturities, rating cohorts, time zones, currencies, and so on. These discrepancies persist because arbitrageurs have traditionally been unable to purchase cheap obligations against shorting expensive ones to extract arbitrage profits. As credit derivative liquidity improves, banks, borrowers, and other credit players will exploit such opportunities, just as the evolution of interest rate derivatives first prompted cross-market interest rate arbitrage activity in the 1980s. The natural consequence of this is, of course, that credit pricing discrepancies will gradually disappear as credit markets become more efficient.

Third, credit derivatives, except when embedded in structured notes, are off-balance sheet instruments. As such, they offer considerable flexibility in terms of leverage. In fact, the user can define the required degree of leverage, if any, in a credit investment. The appeal of off- as opposed to on-balance sheet exposure will differ by institution: the more costly the balance sheet, the greater the appeal of an off-balance sheet alternative. To illustrate, bank loans have not traditionally appealed as an asset class to hedge funds and other nonbank institutional investors for at least two reasons: first, because of the administrative burden of assigning and servicing loans; and second, because of the absence of a repo market. Without the ability to finance investments in bank loans on a secured basis via some form of repo market, the return on capital offered by bank loans has been unattractive to institutions that do not enjoy access to unsecured financing. However, by taking exposure to bank loans using a credit derivative such as a total return swap (described more fully below as well as in a previous chapter), a hedge fund can both synthetically finance the position (receiving under the swap the net proceeds of the loan after financing costs) and avoid the administrative costs of direct ownership of the asset, which are borne by the swap counterparty, which in such trades is generally a bank. Credit derivatives thus allow banks to access new lines of distribution for the credit risk of bank loans and other instruments.

This chapter continues with a brief overview of the two most basic credit derivative structures, then focuses on applications of these tools by risk managers addressing portfolio concentration risk and regulatory capital constraints. The primary theme of this chapter is that credit derivatives are a valuable tool for bank portfolio managers who aim to increase liquidity, take advantage of credit pricing discontinuities, and maximize returns.

CREDIT DERIVATIVE STRUCTURES

Credit Swaps

The credit swap (or "credit default swap") illustrated in Figure 3–1 is a bilateral financial contract in which the protection buyer pays a periodic

Credit Swap

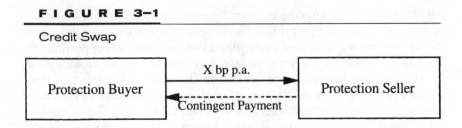

fee in return for a contingent payment by the protection seller following a credit event of a reference entity. The definitions of a credit event and the settlement mechanism used to determine the contingent payment are flexible and negotiated by the counterparties prior to trading. The International Swaps and Derivatives Association, Inc. (ISDA) has produced a standardized letter confirmation for credit swaps transacted under the umbrella of its ISDA Master Agreement. This confirmation allows the parties to specify the terms of the transaction from a number of defined alternatives. The evolution of increasingly standardized terms in the credit derivative market is an important development because it has reduced legal uncertainty that, at least in the early stages, hampered the market's development. This uncertainty originally arose because credit derivatives, unlike many other derivatives, are frequently triggered by an unlikely event, rather than a price or rate move, making the importance of watertight legal documentation for such transactions commensurately greater.

A credit event is usually defined as a bankruptcy, cross acceleration, restructuring, repudiation, or failure to pay; coupled, where measurable, with a significant price deterioration (net of price changes due to interest rate movements) in a specified reference obligation issued or guaranteed by the reference entity. This latter requirement is known as a materiality clause and is designed to ensure that a credit event is not triggered by a technical (i.e., non-credit-related) default such as a disputed or late payment, which is not likely to cause a material price deterioration in the reference entity's obligations. In addition, a credit event generally must be confirmed by publicly available information about the event which is printed in at least two internationally recognized news sources.

The contingent payment is commonly effected by a cash settlement mechanism designed to mirror the loss incurred by creditors of the reference entity following a credit event. This payment is typically calculated as the fall in price of the reference obligation below par, measured in a dealer poll at a specified point in time (or at specified intervals) after the credit event. Since most debt obligations become due and payable in the event of default, plain vanilla senior unsecured loans and bonds will trade at the same dollar price following a default irrespective of maturity or coupon, reflecting the market's estimate of recovery value. Occasionally, the contingent payment is fixed as a predetermined percent of par, which is known as a "binary" settlement.

An alternative settlement mechanism is for the protection buyer to make physical delivery of a specified deliverable obligation in return for a cash payment equal to its face amount. Deliverable obligations may be the reference obligation or one of a broad class of obligations meeting certain specifications, such as any senior unsecured claim against the reference entity. A key distinction between physical delivery and cash settlement is that, following physical delivery, the protection seller has recourse to the reference entity and the opportunity to participate in the workout process as the owner of a defaulted obligation.

Interestingly, credit swaps can be written to provide narrow protection on a specified reference obligation, or they can be written to trigger upon the credit event of any one of a much broader class of obligations of a reference entity. Similarly, while the contingent payment can be determined with reference to a specific instrument, it is also commonly determined by reference to any one of a broad class of qualifying obligations. Thus, while some credit derivatives closely replicate the risks of direct ownership of a specific underlying instrument, others are structured to transfer "macro" exposure to a reference entity. The latter structure provides bank portfolio managers with a unique tool with which to manage the credit risk of an array of different underlying obligations, including bonds, loans, swaps, receivables or letters of credit, of a particular customer.

Counterparty Credit Risk Considerations

In a credit swap the protection buyer has credit exposure to the protection seller, contingent on the performance of the reference entity. If the protection seller defaults, the buyer must find alternative protection and will be exposed to the replacement cost due to changes in credit spreads since the inception of the original swap. If both the protection seller *and* the reference entity default, the buyer is unlikely to recover the full default payment due, although the final recovery rate on the position will benefit from any recovery rate on obligations of both the reference entity and the protection seller.

Counterparty risk consequently affects the pricing of credit derivative transactions. Protection bought from higher-rated counterparties will command a higher premium, and a high correlation between the reference entity and the protection seller will lead to a lower premium. The issue of how to determine and charge for counterparty credit exposure is in large part an empirical one, since it depends on computing the joint

F I G U R E   3–2

Counterparty Credit Charge

$$CCC = (100\% - \text{Recovery Rate}_{CP}) * \sum_{t=t_0}^{t_N} \sum_{R=\text{Def}}^{\text{AAA}} \text{Prob}_{\text{Joint}} \{CP_{\text{In default}} \ RE_{\text{Rating}=R}\} * Op_{\text{Rating}=R}$$

CP = Counterparty

RE = Reference Entity

N = Number of time periods, t

R = Rating of the Reference Entity in time t

Op = Price of an option to replace a risky exposure to RE in state R at time t with a riskless exposure, i.e., when RE has defaulted, value is (100% – Recovery RateRE) i.e., when RE has not defaulted, value is (100% – MTM of Credit Swap, based on credit spreads)

likelihood of arriving in different credit states, which will in turn depend on an estimate of credit quality correlation between the protection seller and reference entity, which cannot be directly observed. As mentioned earlier, significant efforts have been undertaken in the area of default correlation estimation, which also has important applications in credit portfolio risk management.

The equation in Figure 3–2 describes a simple methodology for computing a "counterparty credit charge" (CCC), as the sum of expected losses due to counterparty (CP) default across N different time periods (t) and states of credit quality (R) of the reference entity (RE) from default through to AAA. Given an estimate of credit quality correlation, it is possible to estimate the joint likelihood of the reference entity being in each state, given a counterparty default, from the respective individual likelihoods of arriving in each state of credit quality. Since loss can only occur given a default of the counterparty, we are interested only in the default likelihood of the counterparty. However, since loss can occur due to changes in the mark-to-market (MTM) of the credit swap caused by credit spread fluctuations across different credit states of the reference entity, we are interested in the full matrix of credit quality migration likelihoods of the reference entity.

Typically, the counterparty credit charge is subtracted from the premium paid to the protection seller and accounted for by the protection buyer as a reserve against counterparty credit losses.

Recovery Rate Considerations

Formulating a recovery rate expectation is an integral component of any credit decision, but one that previously could not be isolated from the lending or investment decision. It is possible to structure credit derivatives so that the recovery rate is fixed at inception, introducing the possibility of tailoring transactions to reflect a recovery rate view.

For example, a bank would take exposure to a credit at the senior unsecured level at a spread of 40 basis points (bp). Another bank with existing exposure would sell this credit at the same spread. However, the first considers the likely recovery rate for the credit to be 50 percent, while the second considers it to be 70 percent.

The two banks may enter into a credit swap in which the contingent payment is fixed at 50 percent rather than at the floating recovery rate of senior unsecured debt, as usually determined by dealer poll of a reference obligation after default. The second bank, the protection buyer, might be prepared to pay up to 40 × 50/30 bp or 67 bp for the fixed recovery contract, since it offers more protection than the floating recovery contract given the bank's recovery rate expectation of 70 percent (50/30 is the ratio of expected losses upon default in the fixed versus the floating recovery transaction). Conversely, the first bank is happy to receive any premium over 40 bp for the 50 percent fixed recovery transaction since in its view this is equivalent to the floating recovery transaction. A transaction completed at, say, 55 bp would leave both banks satisfied given their divergent recovery rate views.

Total Rate of Return Swaps

A total return swap (or "total rate of return swap" or "TR swap") is also a bilateral financial contract designed to transfer credit risk between parties, but a TR swap is distinct from a credit swap in that it exchanges the *total* economic performance of a specified asset for a fixed cash flow. That is, payments between the parties to a TR swap are based upon changes in the market valuation of a specific credit instrument, irrespective of whether a credit event has occurred.

As illustrated in Figure 3–3, one counterparty (the "TR payer") pays to the other (the "TR receiver") the total return of a specified asset, the

F I G U R E 3–3

Total Return Swap

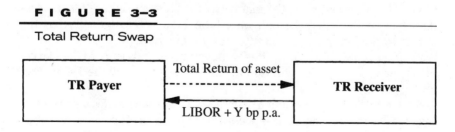

reference obligation. "Total return" comprises the sum of interest, fees, and any change-in-value payments with respect to the reference obligation. The change-in-value payment is equal to any appreciation (positive) or depreciation (negative) in the market value of the reference obligation, as usually determined on the basis of a poll of reference dealers. As an alternative to cash settlement of the change-in-value payment, TR swaps can allow for physical delivery of the reference obligation at maturity by the TR payer in return for a payment of the reference obligation's initial value by the TR receiver. The maturity of the TR swap is not required to match that of the reference obligation, and in practice rarely does. In return, the TR receiver typically makes a regular floating payment of LIBOR plus a spread (Y bp p.a. in Figure 3–3).

The key distinction between a credit swap and a TR swap is that the former results in a contingent or floating payment only following a credit event, while the latter results in payments reflecting changes in the market valuation of a specified asset in the normal course of business.

Transferring Credit Risk via Total Return Swaps

Upon entering into a TR swap on an asset residing in its portfolio, the TR payer has confidentially removed all economic exposure to the underlying asset without the need for a cash sale. Typically, the TR payer retains the servicing and voting rights to the underlying asset, although occasionally certain rights may be passed to the TR receiver. The TR receiver has exposure to the underlying asset without the cash outlay which would be required to purchase it. The economics of a TR swap resemble a synthetic secured financing of a purchase of the reference obligation provided by the TR payer to the TR receiver.

Since the maturity of a TR swap does not have to match the maturity of the underlying asset, the TR receiver in a swap with a maturity of less than that of the underlying asset may benefit from the positive carry associated with being able to roll forward a short-term synthetic financing of a longer-term investment. The TR payer may benefit from being able to purchase protection for a limited period without having to liquidate the asset permanently. At the maturity of a TR swap whose term is less than that of the reference obligation, the TR payer essentially has the option to reinvest in that asset (by continuing to own it) or to sell it at the market price. At this time, the TR payer has no exposure to the market price since a lower price will lead to a higher payment by the TR receiver under the TR swap.

In addition to providing a "synthetic repo" market, TR swaps effectively make the loan asset class accessible to investors for whom administrative complexity or lending group restrictions imposed by borrowers have traditionally presented barriers to entry. Recently, banks have made use of TR swaps to provide insurance companies and levered fund managers with access to the bank loan markets in this way.

Exploiting a Funding Advantage or Avoiding a Disadvantage

For a bank that owns a credit-risky asset, the return for assuming that credit risk is only the net spread earned after deducting that bank's cost of funding the asset on its balance sheet. Thus, it makes little sense for an A-rated bank funding at LIBOR flat to lend money to a AAA-rated entity that borrows at LIBID: after funding costs, the A-rated bank takes a loss but still takes on risk. Consequently, banks with high funding levels often extend risky loans to generate spread income. However, since there is no upfront principal outlay required for most protection sellers when assuming credit swap positions, these trades provide an opportunity to take on credit exposure in off-balance sheet positions that do not need to be funded. Credit swaps are therefore fast becoming an important source of investment opportunity and portfolio diversification for certain banks and other investors who would otherwise continue to accumulate concentrations of lower-quality assets due to their own high funding costs.

Conversely, banks with low funding costs can benefit by funding assets on the balance sheet and purchasing default protection on those assets, perhaps for less than the net spread which such a bank would earn over its funding costs. Hence, a low-cost bank may offset the risk of the underlying credit but still retain a net positive income stream by renting its balance sheet to a higher-cost institution. Of course, the counterparty credit risk to the protection seller must be covered by this residual income. However, the combined credit quality of the underlying asset and the credit protection, even from a lower-quality counterparty, may often be very high since two defaults (by both the protection seller and the reference entity) must occur before losses are incurred, and such losses would be mitigated by the recovery rate on claims against both entities.

Other Credit Derivatives

Dynamic Credit Swaps

A recent credit derivative innovation is the dynamic credit swap (or "credit intermediation swap"), which is a credit swap with the notional

F I G U R E   3–4

Coverage of Dynamic Credit Swaps

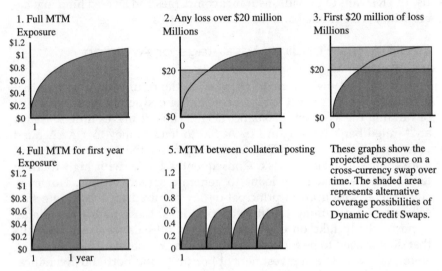

1. Full MTM
Exposure

2. Any loss over $20 million
Millions

3. First $20 million of loss
Millions

4. Full MTM for first year
Exposure

5. MTM between collateral posting

These graphs show the projected exposure on a cross-currency swap over time. The shaded area represents alternative coverage possibilities of Dynamic Credit Swaps.

amount linked to the mark-to-market of a reference swap or a portfolio of swaps. In this case, the notional amount applied to computing the contingent payment is equal to the mark-to-market value, if positive, of the reference swap at the time of the credit event (see Figure 3–4, Chart 1). The protection buyer pays a fixed fee, either upfront or period-ically, which, once set, does not vary with the size of the protection provided. The protection buyer will only incur default losses if the swap counterparty *and* the protection seller fail. This dual credit effect means that the credit quality of the protection buyer's position is com-pounded to a level better than the quality of either of its individual counterparties. The status of this credit combination should normally be relatively impervious to market moves in the underlying swap, since, assuming an uncorrelated counterparty, the probability of a joint default is small.

A dynamic credit swap may be employed to hedge exposure be-tween margin calls on collateral posting (Figure 3–4, Chart 5). Another structure might cover any loss beyond a preagreed amount (Figure 3–4, Chart 2) or up to a maximum amount (Figure 3–4, Chart 3). The protection horizon does not need to match the term of the swap; if the buyer is primarily concerned with short-term default risk, it may be cheaper to hedge for a shorter period and roll over the dynamic credit swap (Figure 3–4, Chart 4).

A dynamic credit swap avoids the need to allocate resources to a regular mark-to-market settlement or collateral agreements. Furthermore, it provides an alternative to unwinding a risky position, which might be difficult for relationship reasons or due to underlying market illiquidity.

Additional Innovations

Like most derivatives, credit derivatives have already evolved into a multitude of structural variations. Hybrid credit derivatives are triggered by credit events *plus* an additional requirement of a material movement in equity prices, commodity prices, interest rates, and so on. Basket credit swaps are triggered by a credit event not just of a single reference entity, but of, say, the *first credit in a basket* or *the first 10 percent of a portfolio.* Credit spread forwards allow two parties to take opposing views on the level of a specified credit spread at a specified point in the future—a payment is made (in either direction) by one of the parties to the other depending on the amount by which the spread is wider or narrower than a specified strike at maturity. Similarly, credit spread options are options on forward credit spreads in which one party pays an upfront premium in return for a payment linked to the amount by which a spread is wider than the strike (a credit spread cap or call) or narrower than the strike (a credit spread put or floor) at a specified point in time. Credit options are put or call options on the price of floating rate bonds, loans, or asset swaps, rather than options on credit spreads. Alternatively, fixed rate bond options are a hybrid of credit and interest rate derivatives in which both risks change hands.

The common denominator among all credit derivatives is their ability to transfer some form of credit risk between counterparties in isolation of both other risks and the underlying source of credit risk. This chapter focuses on this key feature and the applications of credit derivatives that arise naturally from it. In what follows, we concentrate primarily on credit swaps since these represent the most plain vanilla structure, although in many cases alternative structures could be employed to achieve substantially similar results.

The next section considers the use of credit derivatives in credit portfolio management, particularly in the context of recent innovations in credit portfolio risk modeling.

A PORTFOLIO APPROACH TO CREDIT RISK MANAGEMENT

Credit Has Become a Risk Management Challenge

Capital market bond issuance increased from $1.2 trillion in 1996 to $1.5 trillion in 1997.[3] Syndicated loans have also enjoyed an origination boom, increasing from $888 billion to $1.11 trillion over the same period. However, only a small fraction of outstanding volumes trades in the secondary bond market while secondary loan trading, although rapidly improving, is even thinner. Even in the United States, where secondary loan markets are most liquid, the difference between volumes transacted in the primary versus the secondary loan markets is remarkable: secondary transaction volumes are less than 6 percent of new origination. Elsewhere, such statistics are even more skewed. Clearly, banks and institutional investors in competitive lending markets are retaining more credit risk.

Moreover, an increasingly varied array of institutions is intermediating and extending credit. Corporations, insurance companies, and their reinsurers are taking on increasing credit exposures through commercial contracts, trade receivables, insurance, derivative trades, and complex financial instruments. Many of these credit risks are troublesome to manage because they do not derive from standardized or marketable credit instruments and in many cases involve uncertain and market-sensitive counterparty exposures that are more challenging to manage than traditional instruments. Credit derivatives have for the first time made the active management of such exposures a possibility.

Meanwhile, by mid-1997, credit spreads across the spectrum had become compressed on both an absolute and relative basis versus historical comparisons. In late 1997, currency devaluations had highly correlated effects on credit quality across the east Asian region and knock-on effects on credit spreads in the United States and around the globe. Spreads have widened further in the first half of 1998 as the flight to quality has continued. In such an environment, institutions are increasingly vulnerable not only to a potential turn in the credit cycle leading to default-related losses, but also to mark-to-market losses caused by a reversion in credit spreads toward historical levels. At the same time, many banks

---

[3]Source: IFR Omnibase. Includes Eurobonds, International, and excludes domestic governments and U.S. and European domestics.

are experiencing constraints on regulatory and/or economic capital, and following recent high-profile risk management mishaps, there has been intensified focus on risk monitoring and controls. Common sense dictates that, if institutions are demanding better performance in terms of return on economic capital, management must have a solid grasp of all forms of risks being taken.

Consequently, as credit exposures have multiplied and become more complex, the need for more sophisticated risk measurement and management techniques for credit risk has also increased. Of course, more active credit risk management could be achieved by more rigorous enforcement of traditional credit processes such as stringent underwriting standards, limit enforcement, and counterparty monitoring. Increasingly, however, bank risk managers are also seeking to quantify overall credit risk within benchmark value-at-risk statements that treat exposure to both market and credit risks consistently. Moreover, having identified credit risks, risk managers are becoming increasingly inclined to take actions to manage them.

In response to increased focus on credit risk management by banks and other financial institutions, the past few years have seen the evolution of sophisticated techniques for the measurement and evaluation of credit transactions in the context of specific portfolios. The first of these to be made readily available was J.P. Morgan's CreditMetrics®,[4] a portfolio model for evaluating credit value-at-risk across an array of different instruments in a mark-to-market framework. The relationship between credit derivatives and such models is an important one: by combining better credit risk trading tools with more sophisticated methodologies for evaluating credit risk, credit derivatives are making more active credit portfolio management a possibility.

The Need for a Portfolio Approach
to Credit Risk Management

A portfolio approach to credit risk analysis has two aspects. First, exposures to each obligor are restated on an equivalent basis to produce integrated statements of credit risk across the entire institution, irrespective

---

[4]CreditMetrics® is a registered trademark of J.P. Morgan & Co. Incorporated. It is written with the symbol® on its first occurrence in this article and as CreditMetrics thereafter. The CreditMetrics® methodology, datasets, and Credit Manager software application are exclusively managed by the RiskMetrics Group, LLC.

of the underlying asset class. This is particularly useful when combined with a risk management strategy that makes use of credit derivatives to transfer credit risk independently of the underlying instruments in a portfolio. Thus, both the methodology used to assess risk and the tools used to take action to manage risk are uninhibited by asset class barriers. Second, correlations of credit quality across obligors are taken into account. Consequently, portfolio effects—the benefits of diversification and costs of concentrations—can be properly quantified.

Until recently, portfolio managers had very little to say in quantified terms about the concentration risk in their credit portfolios, since it is only in the context of a portfolio model that concentration risk can be evaluated on anything other than an intuitive level. Concentration risk arises from an acceleration in the expected loss of a portfolio due to increased exposure to one credit, or groups of highly correlated credits, perhaps in a particular industry or location. The problem can be mitigated only through diversification or transactions such as credit derivatives that hedge the specific risk of the concentrated exposure. On the whole, financial systems have historically proven to be very robust in the face of isolated credit failures. By contrast, correlated credit deterioration has been the cause of many occurrences of financial distress (consider agricultural loans in the U.S. Midwest, oil loans in Texas, the Latin American debt crisis, the recent Asian debt crises, and so on). A portfolio approach to credit risk analysis allows portfolio managers to quantify and stress-test concentration risk along many different dimensions such as industry, rating category, country, or type of instrument. Traditionally, credit limits have been the primary defense against unacceptable concentrations of credit risk. Fixed exposure limits may be intuitive, but are somewhat arbitrary in that they do not recognize the relationship between risk and return. A more quantitative approach would make credit lines a function of marginal portfolio volatility (i.e., an *output* of the portfolio management model rather than an *input* to it).

Another key reason to take a portfolio view of credit risk is to more rationally and accurately evaluate and prioritize credit extension decisions and risk-mitigating actions. For example, rightly or wrongly, in mid-1997, financial markets indicated a widespread perception of diminished risk due to credit, as illustrated by the historically tight level of credit spreads. In this environment, the bank lending marketplace became increasingly competitive. As a result, good customer relationships have often become synonymous with heavily concentrated exposures as corporate borrowers command smaller bank groups and larger commitments from relationship banks. Yet banks are often caught in a paradoxical trap of their own making whereby those customers with whom they have developed the most valued relationships are precisely the customers to whom they have the least capacity to take incremental risk. Bank portfolio managers have begun to harbor suspicions that they may be vulnerable to a turn for the worse in global credit cycles and that current levels of spread income may not justify the concentration of risks being accumulated. Such concerns cannot easily be evaluated or systematically reflected in pricing and credit extension decisions in the absence of a portfolio model. In a portfolio context, the decision to take on ever higher exposure to an obligor will meet with ever higher risk—risk that grows geometrically with the concentration on that obligor. If a relationship demands the extension of credit to a customer to whom the portfolio is overexposed, a portfolio model allows the portfolio manager to quantify (in units of under-compensated risk) exactly the extent of envisaged investment in relationship development. As a result, the risk-return tradeoff of concentrated lending activity can be better managed. Conversely, the portfolio manager can rationally take increased exposure to under-concentrated names. Indeed, such names may be *individually* risky yet offer a relatively small marginal contribution to overall *portfolio* risk due to diversification benefits. In this context, the ability of credit derivatives to assume and shed risk on a purely economic basis has become increasingly valuable.

Thus, by capturing portfolio effects, recognizing that risk accelerates with declining credit quality, and treating credit risk consistently, regardless of asset class, a portfolio credit risk model can provide the foundation for rational risk-based capital allocation and rational pricing of both cash credit instruments and credit derivatives. Such a model is equally appropriate for economic and regulatory capital purposes, but, as we shall see, differs fundamentally from the capital measures currently mandated for bank regulation by the Bank for International Settlements (BIS).

The Challenges of Measuring Portfolio Credit Risk

Modeling portfolio credit risk is neither analytically nor practically easy, presenting at least two significant challenges. The first problem relates to the remote probability of large losses in credit portfolios, combined with the limited potential for upside capital appreciation. As illustrated in Figure 3–5, this produces skewed return distributions with long, fat tails that differ significantly from the more normally distributed returns typically addressed by market value-at-risk models. Because of this feature, to understand the risks of credit portfolios completely requires that the nature of these tails be explored, a computationally onerous exercise.

Comparison of Distribution of Market Returns and Credit Returns

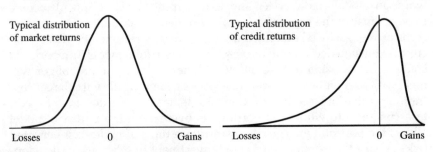

The second problem is empirical. Unlike market portfolios where the data necessary to compute correlations are readily available, correlations in credit portfolios cannot easily be directly observed. Consequently, credit quality correlations must either be derived indirectly from other sources, such as equity prices, or tabulated from historical data at a relatively high level of aggregation (e.g., treating all A-rated obligors identically).

Expected versus Unexpected Losses

The *expected* loss calculation is, in one sense, the most straightforward aspect of portfolio theory. That is, the ability to estimate credit quality and the expected size of losses given changes in credit quality allows the risk manager to price, and reserve for, expected loss. Summing across all credit states, probability of loss multiplied by expected size of loss equals expected loss. If there were no further uncertainty relating to possible credit losses, computing expected loss would be the extent of the risk management problem: predictable credit losses year after year would be no more than a budgeted expense. *Risk*, however, entails not just an estimated possibility of loss but also the *uncertainty* of loss, namely the chance that the estimate of expected loss may be incorrect. Unexpected loss measures the potential for error in the estimate of expected loss. Typically, this has been estimated as a function of portfolio volatility. For example, if unexpected loss is deemed to be that level of loss which is, say, 95 percent likely not to be exceeded, then in a normal distribution this level would be 1.65 standard deviations from the portfolio mean.

While it is difficult to estimate *expected* credit portfolio values, it is harder still to predict *unexpected* loss, or *uncertainties* around these values. This is because the distribution of credit-related losses is heavily skewed, with the result that meaningful probabilities of loss can occur many standard deviations distant from the expected level. Because of this, modeling the full distribution of portfolio values requires a great deal of information beyond simple summary statistics such as the mean and standard deviation (volatility). Without a full specification of the portfolio value distribution, it is not possible to compute the percentile levels necessary to describe risk in credit portfolios. By considering every possible combination of credit states across every obligor in the portfolio, the full distribution of a credit portfolio can be constructed mechanistically, but this is computationally complex for portfolios of more than a few obligors. One approach, adopted in CreditMetrics, is to estimate the portfolio distribution by a process of simulation that reduces the computational burden by sampling outcomes randomly across all possibilities. Once the portfolio distribution has been approximated in this way, it is possible to compute percentile levels and summary statistics that describe the shape of the distribution.

The Significance of Diversification

At first glance, it would seem that two loans held to maturity will have a default correlation much lower than their corresponding equity price correlation (due to the low likelihood that two extremely remote events will occur simultaneously). For the layperson, a natural conclusion to draw might be that the benefits of diversification in a credit portfolio are not significant precisely because default correlations are so low. But this is not a correct conclusion. The implication of very low default correlations is that the systematic risk in a credit portfolio is small relative to the nonsystematic or individual contribution to risk of each asset. Nonsystematic risk is hedgeable or diversifiable risk. The greater the component of nonsystematic risk, the greater the benefits of diversification, and vice versa. The problem can be viewed another way. Indices provide great hedges of risk in equity portfolios because most equity portfolios are sufficiently diversified to resemble the market. However, because a portfolio of debt of those same names is unlikely to be sufficiently diversified to resemble the market, this same type of index hedge will not work in debt portfolios. The portfolio management consequences of a full characterization of credit risks are thus not insignificant: it takes many more names to fully diversify a credit portfolio than an equity portfolio, but when those diversification benefits are achieved, they are considerable. An inadequately diversified portfolio, on the other hand, can result in significantly lower return on risk ratios than would seem intuitively obvious. Absent cash market alternatives, the case for proactive management of credit risk using derivatives is compelling.

The Importance of Liquidity and Active Risk Management

Credit exposure has sometimes been modeled as analogous to a portfolio of short, deep out-of-the-money put options on firm assets, an insight first suggested by Robert Merton.[5] The analogy is intuitively sound given the expected yet limited upside and remote but large downside profile of credit risk. This short option analogy allows us to draw some insights on the consequences of illiquidity in credit portfolios. In equity portfolios, it has been argued, independence of daily returns allows time to diversify risk. If credit portfolios are similar to a portfolio of out-of-the money puts, however, it can be argued that as the market declines (credit quality deteriorates) the "delta" equivalent of that portfolio increases and the portfolio becomes more leveraged (riskier). Consequently, any persistent serial correlation in credit returns, as suggested by the historical tendency of one downgrade to be followed by another, can cause poor performance to increase volatility and create accelerating portfolio riskiness. An ability to rebalance the portfolio in response to credit deterioration is the only effective way to materially offset this effect. The consequences of illiquidity and absence of active risk management in credit portfolios are therefore more severe than in market risk portfolios.

Applying a quantitative approach to portfolio concentration risk does not, of course, necessitate the use of credit derivatives as a portfolio management tool. However, where existing positions are illiquid for whatever reason, credit derivatives offer a new solution for reducing exposure, or at least quantifying the tradeoff of *not* reducing exposure.

The illiquidity of credit positions can be caused by any number of factors, both internal and external to an organization. Internally, in the case of bank loans and derivative transactions, relationship concerns often lock portfolio managers into credit exposure arising from key client transactions. Corporate borrowers prefer to deal with smaller lending groups and typically place restrictions on transferability and on which entities can have access to that group. Credit derivatives allow users to reduce credit exposure without physically removing assets from their balance sheet. Loan sales, or the assignment, or unwinding of derivative contracts typically require the notification and/or consent of the customer. By contrast, a credit derivative is a confidential transaction that the customer need neither be party to nor aware of, thereby separating relationship management from risk management decisions.

---

[5]"On the Pricing of Corporate Debt: The Risk Structure of Interest Rates," *The Journal of Finance*, Vol. 29, 1974.

Similarly, the tax or accounting position of an institution can create significant disincentives to the sale of an otherwise relatively liquid position, as in the case of a bank that owns a loan in its hold-to-maturity account at a low tax base. Purchasing default protection via a credit swap can hedge the credit exposure of such a position without triggering a sale for either tax or accounting purposes. Recently, credit swaps have been employed in such situations to avoid unintended adverse tax or accounting consequences of otherwise sound risk management decisions.

Illiquidity generally results from factors external to the bank in question. The secondary market for most loans is not deep and, in the case of certain forms of trade receivables or insurance contracts, may not exist at all. Some types of credit exposure, including the regional and industrial concentration risk to key customers faced by many banks (meaning not only the default risk, but also the risk of customer replacement cost), are simply not transferable at all. In such cases, credit swaps can provide a hedge of exposure that would not otherwise be achievable through the sale of an underlying asset. Simply put, credit swaps deepen the secondary market for credit risk far beyond that of the secondary market of the underlying credit instrument.

Analyzing Credit Risk on a Portfolio Basis: Methodology

Applying modern portfolio theory to credit risk measurement continues to evolve rapidly and has had little standardization to date. As the first readily available portfolio model for evaluating credit value-at-risk, the following discussion focuses on CreditMetrics methodology, recognizing that it is not necessarily the only approach to the problem. The purpose here is to illustrate how such analysis may be integrated with a portfolio risk management strategy incorporating the use of credit derivatives in a fashion that allows the user to identify, prioritize, and ultimately evaluate or "price" the opportunities presented by credit derivatives.

CreditMetrics employs a three-step process to compute individual and portfolio credit value-at-risk. First, it computes the exposure profile of each obligor in a portfolio. Where the portfolio incorporates instruments such as derivatives whose credit exposure is a dynamic function of underlying market moves and the passage of time, this requires some preprocessing to estimate the exposure profile of each instrument. Second, it computes the volatility of each instrument caused by credit events (including upgrades, downgrades, and defaults). Likelihoods derived from a transition matrix are attributed to each possible credit event. Each event results in an estimated change in value (derived from credit spread data and, in default, recovery rates). Finally, taking into account correlations between each of these events, the model combines the volatility of the individual instruments to give an aggregate portfolio volatility. Recently, there have been significant developments in the field of default and migration correlation estimation. As a result, some of the difficulties encountered in direct estimation of historical correlations due to the small historical sample set have been avoided by inferring such information from equity price correlations.[6]

Because it is a measure of symmetrical dispersion about the expected portfolio value, portfolio volatility is not an accurate measure of risk in a skewed distribution. The standard deviation measure cannot, for example, capture the fact that the maximum upside might be only one standard deviation above the average, while meaningful occurrences of loss can be many standard deviations below the average. Consequently, CreditMetrics includes a simulation engine that estimates the entire distribution of a credit portfolio and computes percentile levels. These percentile levels reflect the likelihood that the portfolio value will fall below a specified level (e.g., that the likelihood of its falling below the first percentile level is 1 percent).

In the next section, we go on to discuss practical applications of a portfolio approach to credit risk measurement, many of which identify opportunities for specific credit derivative transactions.

Practical Applications of a Portfolio Approach to Credit Risk Management

Prioritizing Risk-Reducing Transactions

Decisions to buy, sell, or hold an exposure should be made in context of an existing portfolio. The relevant calculation is then not the stand-alone

---

[6]The assumptions and mathematics required to estimate default correlations from equity price correlations are complex and beyond the scope of this chapter. The interested reader is referred to the "CreditMetrics—Technical Document," J.P. Morgan, 1997 and "On the Pricing of Corporate Debt: The Risk Structure of Interest Rates," *Journal of Finance*, Vol. 29, 1974. Conceptually, if liabilities are assumed fixed and default is defined as occurring instantaneously when asset values fall below liabilities, then the volatility of asset levels as inferred from equity price behavior should directly predict the chance of default by any firm. By extension, these asset volatilities will also drive the joint default probability between any pair of firms. A positive correlation between asset returns (as implied by equity prices) would, therefore, in turn imply some expected positive correlation in credit quality migration.

risk of that exposure but the *marginal* increase to the portfolio risk that would be created by adding that exposure to it. Marginal risk refers to the difference between the total portfolio risk before and after the marginal transaction. If the new transaction adds to an already over-concentrated portion of the portfolio, then the marginal risk is likely to be high. If the new transaction is diversifying (or in the extreme is actually hedging a position), then the marginal risk may be quite small or even negative. The importance of calculating the marginal risk is that it captures the specific characteristics of a particular portfolio. It would not be unusual for a given credit to be considered risky in one bank's portfolio but of considerably lower risk in another bank's portfolio. Mechanically, a marginal risk statistic can be calculated using either standard deviations or percentile levels. The point is the same: to show the change in total portfolio risk upon the addition of a new transaction.

Thus, marginal credit value-at-risk analysis may be used to direct and prioritize risk-mitigating actions, and as such it is a useful tool for identifying opportunities for the use of credit derivatives to restructure a portfolio's composition. To illustrate, Figure 3–6 shows marginal risk versus size of exposures within a typical credit portfolio.

F I G U R E 3–6

Marginal Risk versus Exposure Size

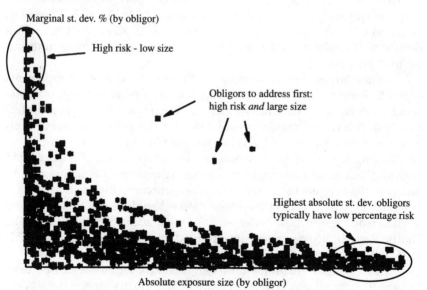

When considering risk-mitigating actions, it is useful to prioritize transactions which have the greatest impact on the absolute amount of portfolio risk (which appear in the upper right corner of Figure 3–6) since this prioritizes exposures that are both a relatively high contribution to portfolio risk on a percentage basis and a large dollar amount of exposure. In practice, such outliers may be the result of "fallen angels," whose now excessive exposures were appropriate when originated, or simply relationship-driven concentrations. Where a relationship is a driving concern, purchasing protection via a credit derivative is often preferable to an outright sale of the asset.

Portfolio analysis highlights where an asset may contribute differently to the risk of distinct portfolios and yet yield the same returns in either case. Consequently, it is easy to imagine a situation in which two managers identify two credit risks of the same maturity, yield, and credit quality, but—because of the composition of the two portfolios—the risk of both portfolios is reduced by the swap. This is often accomplished most easily using credit derivatives and, moreover, without a loss in return (i.e., the financial equivalent of a free lunch). The importance of identifying the contribution of each asset to portfolio risk is obvious. The risk of credit assets is largely due to concentrations particular to the portfolio. Thus, opportunities may exist to restructure the portfolio to reduce risk with no change in profitability.

The following case shows measures of portfolio value-at-risk due to credit taken from a hypothetical 20-obligor portfolio of assets with various maturities, ratings, and exposure amounts. In Figure 3–7, the plots of marginal portfolio risk against exposure size identify "asset 15" a B-rated, $3.26 million bond as the highest marginal and absolute contributor to overall risk.

As the largest risk contributor to the portfolio, asset 15 represents only 4.8 percent of the portfolio value, but 23.79 percent of the portfolio standard deviation. The solution? Selling asset 15 or buying credit protection against it would reduce portfolio risk by 23.8 percent. However, this leaves a reinvestment problem, so we should compute the impact of substituting this asset for another; for this purpose, we choose a bond with identical stand-alone statistics and with the same return. Importantly, however, the new asset is assumed to have a *zero* correlation with the rest of the portfolio. The effect of this substitution is to reduce portfolio standard deviation by 7 percent. Since the portfolio yield is unaffected, the portfolio Sharpe Ratio (ratio of excess return to risk) improves accordingly, by 7.5, or $(1/0.93-1)$ percent.

This example illustrates how marginal risk measures can be used to suggest transactions which generate better returns for the risks being

Marginal Risk against Exposure Size

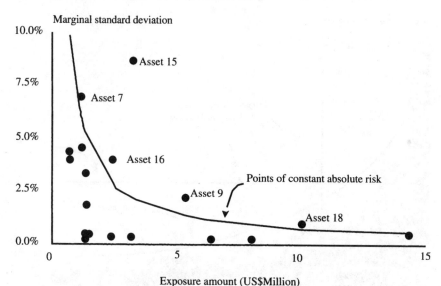

Exposure amount (US$Million)

taken or take less risk for the returns being generated. However, many sources of credit risk are not associated with liquid or readily transferable instruments. Consequently, when over-concentrated or under-compensated risks are identified within a portfolio, such as that presented by asset 15, the portfolio manager is often constrained from simply being able to sell that exposure or replace it with another. Similarly, when seeking to diversify away concentration risks, such as when seeking a substitute for asset 15, the portfolio manager is frequently constrained by limited availability of diversifying assets. Clearly, credit derivatives provide the portfolio manager with an important new means to shed existing illiquid exposures and to source new ones which diversify the portfolio.

Setting Risk-Based Credit Limits

Traditionally, credit risk limits have been based on intuitive but arbitrary exposure amounts, which is unsatisfactory because resulting decisions are not properly risk-driven. Consequently, the next step beyond using risk statistics for prioritizing transactions is to use them for limit-setting. Just as it is best to address exposures with the highest level of absolute risk first, it makes sense to set credit limits according to the absolute contribution to portfolio risk. This would correspond to a limit resembling

FIGURE 3-8

Risk-Based Limit Setting

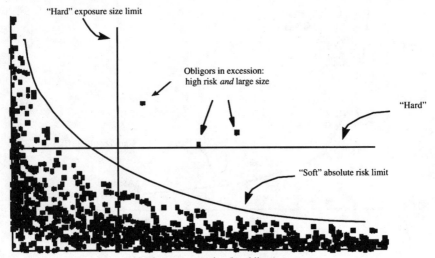

Marginal st. dev. % (by obligor)

Absolute exposure size (by obligor)

the curve defined by the boundary of non-outlying scatter points in Figure 3-7, as illustrated in Figure 3-8 above. Such a limit would prevent the addition to the portfolio of any exposure that increased portfolio risk by more than a given amount, rather than the more traditional approach of limiting absolute exposure size (a vertical line) or individual riskiness (a horizontal line).

Figure 3-9 demonstrates how marginal risk statistics can be used to make credit allocation decisions sensitive to the trade-off between risk and return. The left-hand illustration reflects how marginal contribution to portfolio risk increases geometrically with exposure size of an individual obligor, which is noticeable for weaker credits. Consequently, as illustrated in the right-hand graph, proportionately more return is required with each increment of exposure to an individual obligor to maintain a constant balance between risk and return. The marginal risk of the obligor is shown by the curve labeled "Risk-based minimum required return." This represents the set of points at which return-on-risk is constant—the curvature of this line reflects the fact that as exposure size and, hence, portfolio risk increases, proportionately greater return is required to maintain a constant risk-return trade-off. The horizontal straight line represents the

FIGURE 3-9

Exposure Targets Based on Risk-Return Tradeoff

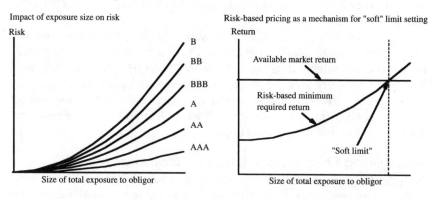

available market return for the obligor, as reflected, perhaps, in the premium available for a credit swap on that name. Areas to the right of the intersection between the two lines represent situations in which the portfolio manager might rationally decrease exposure, because doing so would more than proportionately reduce risk relative to the loss in return. Areas to the left of the intersection represent situations in which the portfolio manager might increase exposure because doing so would more than proportionately increase return relative to the increase in risk. The vertical line marking the point of intersection is thus the "soft" risk-based target for exposure to the obligor given available market pricing, the portfolio targeted risk-return balance, and the relationship between the obligor and the existing portfolio. The appeal of a limit that is an output of a model that is sensitive to both risk and return is unmistakable.

Determining Risk-Based Capital Allocations

To assess the risk a firm takes by holding a credit portfolio requires an understanding of the risk of that portfolio with regard to what this implies about the stability of the organization. Essentially, in this framework, risk is measured in terms of its threat to shareholder capital: if a firm's liabilities are constant, then it is taking risk by holding assets that are volatile. Such risk-taking capacity is not unlimited and must be allocated as a scarce resource. For example, if a manager found that there was a 10 percent chance of a decline in portfolio value occurring in the next year that would be severe enough to cause organization-wide insolvency, then he or she would likely seek to decrease the risk of the asset portfolio. For a portfolio with a more reasonable level of risk, the manager cannot add new exposures indiscriminately, since eventually the portfolio risk will surpass the "comfort level." Thus, each additional exposure utilizes a scarce resource, which is commonly thought of as risk-taking capacity or "economic capital."

As a result, a percentile level seems to be an appropriate indicator of economic capital. Using, for example, the first percentile level, economic capital could be defined as the level of losses on the portfolio that, with 99 percent certainty, will not be exceeded in the next year. Such a measure would be sensitive to obligor credit quality, would reflect the risk of portfolio concentrations, and would allow uniform treatment of risk, irrespective of the underlying instrument.

Measuring Regulatory Capital Allocations

If credit derivatives are to change the way in which institutions measure and manage credit risk, it is necessary to assume that banks in particular will not continue to face the disincentives to portfolio risk management currently caused by regulatory capital requirements.

Accordingly, the risk-based approach to economic capital allocation described above contrasts starkly with the so-called risk-based capital framework currently mandated for bank regulation under the Bank for International Settlements (BIS) accord. Under the current BIS rules, the required capital reserve for a portfolio of credit positions residing in the banking book (as the vast majority do) is a simple summation of the capital for the portfolio's individual transactions. In turn, each transaction's capital requirement depends on a broad categorization of the obligor (rather than credit quality), on the transaction's exposure type (e.g., drawn loans versus undrawn commitments), and, for off-balance sheet exposures, on whether the transaction's maturity is more or less than one year. Moreover, as described more fully below, there are very limited opportunities for banks to offset capital requirements where exposures have been hedged using credit derivatives because the current guidelines require virtually complete offset of risks with a lower risk-weighted counterparty (irrespective of credit quality) in order to recognize any capital relief. The weaknesses of this structure, such as its one-size-fits-all risk weight for all corporate loans and its inability to distinguish between diversified and undiversified portfolios, are increasingly apparent to regulators and market participants. Particular concern has been paid to the uneconomic incentives created by the regulatory regime and the inability of regulatory capital adequacy ratios to accurately portray actual bank risk levels.

Were regulatory capital ratios used only as originally intended, namely as supervisory tools measuring minimum prudent capitalization levels in the context of a more thorough regulatory review of a bank's risks, the issue of regulatory capital calculations would be immaterial. Banks would report the required ratios but continue to manage their businesses so as to optimize *economic* capital utilization. However, perhaps because regulatory capital ratios are one of the few standardized public risk measures for banks, they are closely monitored by a number of observers including the public rating agencies and stock analysts as an indicator of a financial institution's stability and credit quality. Consequently, the management of regulatory capital ratios has become as much of an imperative as the management of economic capital for those banks that are focused on maximizing shareholder value.

Continually increasing use of credit derivatives by both dealer and end-user banks has highlighted the need to reform the bank regulatory capital framework and over the next few years will likely contribute to bringing such reform to the front of the regulatory agenda. The point is a simple one: if discrepancies continue to exist between economic and regulatory measures of risk, then banks, once equipped with tools such as credit derivatives, will be either forced to avoid entering into economic transactions because of their adverse effect on regulatory capital or incented to enter into uneconomic transactions because of their beneficial effect on regulatory capital.

By contrast, the appeal of the internal models approach described above is illustrated by the analogy of a parent dividing a pie between two squabbling children. As the knife moves to and fro over the pie, each child protests at the size of its share. To resolve the problem, the parent gives the knife to one child, but tells them both that once the division is made, the other may choose which piece to eat. The analogy illustrates the point that, by enforcing a system that is inherently unbiased, the regulator is able to supervise without interfering with the efficient allocation of resources.

In response to these concerns, both banks and bank regulators are looking for insights in credit risk models such as CreditMetrics that generate expected losses and a probability distribution of unexpected losses and would close the gap between economic and regulatory capital measures, thereby encouraging proactive credit risk management and promoting the further growth of credit derivatives.

REGULATORY TREATMENT OF CREDIT DERIVATIVES

Over the past year, North American and European bank regulators have responded to banks' rapidly increasing use of credit derivatives by publishing supervisory guidance including guidelines on appropriate regulatory capital treatment. These include papers from the following:

- Federal Reserve Board (SR 1996–17, August 12, 1996, and SR 1997–18, June 13, 1997)

- Office of the Comptroller of the Currency (OCC Bulletin 96–43, August 12, 1996)

- Federal Deposit Insurance Corporation (FIL–62–96, August 15, 1996)

- Bank of England ("Discussion Paper: Developing a Supervisory Approach to Credit Derivatives," November 1996; and "Credit Derivatives: Amended Interim Capital Adequacy Treatment," June 5, 1997)

- Financial Services Authority ("Regulatory Treatment of Credit Derivatives," FSA/PN/48/98, July 22, 1998)

- Securities and Futures Authority (Board Notice 414: "Guidance on Credit Derivatives," April 17, 1997)

- Commission Bancaire ("Credit Derivatives: Issues for Discussion on Interim Prudential Treatment," June 1997; and "Traitement Prudentiel des Instruments Dérivés de Crédit," April 18, 1998)

- OSFI (Policy for Credit Derivatives. Statement # 1997–04, October 31, 1997)

This guidance encourages many users by reducing uncertainty surrounding the potential legal and regulatory treatment of such new products.[7] Moreover, the regulatory guidelines broadly agree that credit derivatives are a viable tool to manage credit risk and approve their use to reduce credit exposure. In certain circumstances, recognizing the economic

---

[7]In this regard, a paper by the Financial Law Panel ("Credit Derivatives: The Regulatory Treatment, A Guidance Notice," May 1997) and an opinion commissioned by ISDA from Robin Potts, Q.C., of Allen and Overy ("Credit Derivatives: Opinion," June 24, 1997), also reduce uncertainty by making a strong case that under U.K. law, credit derivatives that are not entered into by way of "insurance business," are not contracts of insurance, and are not void under waging or gaming laws. A recently issued letter by the State of New York Insurance Department on June 25, 1998, which states that derivative instruments "do not constitute insurance . . . unless . . . payment to the purchaser is dependent upon that party suffering a loss" provides strong support for the conclusion that credit derivatives are not insurance contracts under New York law.

effect of buying credit protection, the guidelines also allow for some required regulatory capital relief.

However, credit derivatives, in combining certain features of traditional credit products that are subject to one capital regime (the "banking book"), with those of traded instruments that are subject to a quite different capital regime (the "trading book"), and those of derivative contracts that are subject to yet a third capital regime ("counterparty risk capital"), present a significant challenge to any one-size-fits-all solution to regulatory capital treatment. Indeed, some of the regulators' suggested solutions have served to highlight the shortcomings of all three approaches.

Nonetheless, some of the regulatory papers cited above are helpful in providing a broad discussion of the issues rather than a narrow prescriptive approach. Moreover, the emergence of credit derivatives in conjunction with more sophisticated internal credit risk models has stimulated debate that may ultimately lead to reform of the regulatory treatment of credit risk as a whole. The following discussion provides a very broad summary of the regulatory capital treatment of simple banking book transactions in some jurisdictions. Banks should consult with their own advisors as to the appropriate regulatory capital treatment of specific transactions in their own jurisdiction.

Credit derivatives, as off-balance sheet transactions, need to be translated to an on-balance sheet equivalent for regulatory capital purposes. When a bank sells protection in a TR swap or credit swap, the guidelines require that the bank's position be treated as if it had written a standby letter of credit or guarantee (collectively known as "direct credit substitutes"). These are translated to on-balance sheet equivalents with a conversion factor equal to 100 percent of the notional amount of the contract. Risk-weighting then proceeds according to the weighting of the reference entity (0 percent for an OECD sovereign, 20 percent for an OECD bank, and 100 percent for corporations).

If a bank buys protection via a TR swap or credit swap to hedge an underlying asset, the bank can, in certain circumstances, achieve the same capital relief as if it had purchased a guarantee from its counterparty. Although different regulators apply different standards and some are more specific than others, broadly speaking, the transaction will have to achieve a significant degree of risk transference to achieve capital relief (e.g., by exactly matching the maturity and seniority of the underlying asset). Provided there is no material mismatch between the underlying asset and the protection purchased, this would result in a reduction in the risk-weighting of the underlying asset to a level equal to that of the protection seller, if lower than that of the reference entity (e.g., from 100 percent to 20 percent for corporate default protection purchased from an

OECD bank). Under current regulations, as with guarantees, no such relief would be available for a bank buying protection from a 100 percent risk-weighted entity (including all corporations and most nonbank financial institutions), even if this entity were AAA-rated. Similarly, where the degree of risk transference is considered inadequate due to a mismatch in maturity, seniority, or the credit event definition, the arrangement may not be considered an effective guarantee, and *no* capital relief, rather than partial capital relief, will be allowed.

This treatment clearly creates a significant disincentive for banks that are protection buyers seeking to simultaneously manage economic risk and regulatory capital. Despite the fact that hedged positions represent a very small residual risk (since the hedging bank can only lose if its counterparty *and* the underlying reference entity default), the bank would be required to hold capital against at least 20 percent, and possibly 100 percent (if selling risk to a nonbank), of the notional contract sizes. Banking book capital treatment clearly presents even more severe problems for dealer banks accumulating large portfolios of mostly hedged positions as a function of their intermediation business. This problem may be somewhat alleviated for dealers and larger, more sophisticated banks that maintain a trading book.

Assets in trading accounts are subject to BIS-mandated market risk capital rules. Under these rules, capital is required to be held for counterparty risk, general market risk (usually zero for a credit derivative that does not embody market risk), and specific risk. As with all derivatives, the amount of counterparty risk capital required to be held will depend on a conversion factor that is equal to the current exposure to the counterparty on the contract, if positive, plus an add-on that is determined by reference to maturity and underlying risk type. Although no factors have yet been developed for credit derivatives specifically, the conservative approach adopted by the Federal Reserve requires the use of equity swap factors for investment grade exposures and commodity add-ons for others. Applying the logic that the use of equity add-ons should be a conservative treatment for debt positions since debt is senior to equity in the capital structure of the firm, other regulators, including the Bank of England, have required equity add-ons to be used for all credit derivatives. Risk-weighting proceeds according to the weighting of the swap counterparty (0 percent for OECD sovereigns, 20 percent for OECD banks, 50 percent for corporations).

As with general market risk, banks may elect either to adopt the standardized approach to specific risk or to use their own internal models. Table 3–1 illustrates standardized specific risk factors that vary by the category of the underlying instrument and by maturity. These differ most

T A B L E 3–1

Specific risk factors for trading book assets
(standardized approach)

Category	Remaining Maturity	Weighting Factor	Old "Conversion Factor" Equivalence
Government	N/A	0.00	0.00
Qualifying	6 months or less	0.25	3.125%
	Over 6 to 24 months	1.00	12.500%
	Over 24 months	1.60	20.000%
Other	N/A	8.00	100%

Source: J.P. Morgan Securities Inc.

notably from the older banking book risk-weightings in the case of "qualifying" debt positions. Qualifying positions include OECD bank debt and OECD corporate debt if investment grade or of equivalent quality and issued by a corporation with instruments listed on a recognized stock exchange. For qualifying debt positions, the risk factors equate to weightings of 3.125 percent for positions with tenor of six months or less, 12.5 percent for positions with tenor between six and 24 months, and 20 percent for positions with tenor of over 24 months. Non-qualifying debt carries a factor equivalent to 100 percent, and OECD government debt has a factor of 0 percent. This is most significant in that the market risk capital rules link capital charges to maturity and credit quality and consequently treat open exposures to investment grade corporations significantly more favorably than exposures held in the banking book.

The Federal Reserve guidelines for the treatment of credit derivatives in the trading book under the standardized approach (SR 97–18) envisage some netting of specific risks in long and short positions, but only in the case of "matched" positions, defined as those with identical maturities, reference assets, and structures. The requirement for identical structures means that a loan or bond may only be hedged with a total return swap of identical maturity referencing that specific asset, but not with a credit swap, even one with identical maturity and referencing that specific asset. In addition, total return swaps and credit swaps may only be offset by identical transactions but not by each other. Offsetting positions that do not meet the necessary requirements to be considered matched do not achieve any capital relief but require capital to be held against the specific risk of either the long or the short position, whichever is greater. Given the additional requirement to hold capital against counterparty risk, this treatment can result in *increased* capital requirements.

In summary, current guidelines suggest that banks can, in certain circumstances, use credit derivatives to hedge risks to free up regulatory capital, although not yet in a manner remotely consistent with the true reduction in economic risk. It is hoped that the development of more sophisticated internal models for credit risk measurement may stimulate a more flexible approach to regulatory capital that involves less restricted use of internal models.

BALANCE SHEET MANAGEMENT: TRADITIONAL AND SYNTHETIC SECURITIZATIONS USING CREDIT DERIVATIVES

In the last year, credit derivatives have entered the mainstream of global structured finance as tools in a number of large, high profile securitizations of assets that cannot as easily be managed using more traditional techniques. By combining credit derivatives with traditional securitization tools in collateralized loan obligations (CLOs), structures can be tailored to meet specific balance sheet management goals with much greater efficiency. Specifically, credit derivatives have assisted banks in reducing economic and/or regulatory capital, preserving a low funding-cost advantage, and maintaining borrower and market confidentiality.

Collateralized Loan Obligations

Consider a portfolio of bank loans to corporations. Traditional securitization techniques for such a portfolio would involve the creation of a CLO, in which the originating bank would assign or participate its loans to a special purpose vehicle (SPV), which in turn would issue two or more classes of securities in the capital markets. Typically, the originating bank would retain much of the economic risk to the pool of loans by purchasing the most junior (equity) tranche of the SPV securities. The extent to which the transaction would achieve regulatory capital relief for the bank would depend upon the size of the retained first loss position. According to the low level recourse rules governing securitizations in the United States, a retained first loss piece of 8 percent or greater would result in no capital relief, but smaller retained first loss positions would result in required capital equal to the lesser of 8 percent and the size of the recourse position.

While a CLO can achieve a number of goals including regulatory capital relief, financing of a loan portfolio, and off-balance sheet treatment of the portfolio for Generally Accepted Accounting Principles (GAAP) purposes, it has some inefficiencies. For example, for a bank that enjoys low-cost unsecured financing, the cost of funding usually achieved by such transactions is unattractive, since even the most senior, typically triple A rated, securities are sold at the LIBOR "plus" spreads which prevail in the asset-backed securities market. Thus, in seeking to manage regulatory capital, the bank is effectively forced to accept an inefficient financing cost. Moreover, transferring the legal ownership of assets to the SPV via assignment requires borrower notification and consent, introducing the risk of adverse relationship consequences. The alternative of participating loans to the vehicle will normally cause the vehicle's overall rating to be capped at that of the originating bank with adverse consequences for the overall cost of funding. Structures that avoid this particular problem can be structurally and legally complex and require extensive rating agency involvement. Finally, CLOs cannot be readily applied to loans that are committed but undrawn, such as revolving credit lines, or backstop liquidity facilities.

Synthetic Securitizations

As alternatives to traditional CLOs, transactions are being developed that make use of credit derivatives to transfer the economic risk but not the legal ownership of the underlying assets. Credit derivatives can be used to achieve the same or similar regulatory capital benefits of a traditional securitization by transferring credit risk synthetically. However, as privately negotiated confidential transactions, credit derivatives allow the originating bank to avoid the legal and structural risks of assignments or participations and maintain both market and customer confidentiality.

Thus, credit derivatives are stimulating the rapidly growing asset-backed securitization market by stripping out and repackaging credit exposures from the vast pool of risks that do not naturally lend themselves to securitization, either because the risks are unfunded (off-balance sheet), because they are not intrinsically transferable, or because their sale would be complicated by relationship concerns. In so doing, by enhancing liquidity and bringing new forms of credit risk to the capital markets, credit derivatives achieve the financial equivalent of a free lunch whereby both buyers and sellers of risk benefit from the associated efficiency gains. We introduce both credit-linked notes (CLN) and credit-swap structures on the following pages.

Credit-Linked Notes

In several recent securitizations, the credit risk of loans on the originating bank's balance sheet has been transferred to the securitization SPV via the sale of credit-linked notes rather than the assignment or participation of the loans themselves. CLNs are funded assets that offer synthetic credit exposure to a reference entity or a portfolio of entities in a structure designed to resemble a synthetic corporate bond or loan. The simplest form of CLN is a bank deposit issued by the originating bank whose principal redemption is linked to a credit event of a reference credit. Alternatively, CLNs may be issued by an SPV that holds collateral securities (government securities or repurchase agreements on government securities) which are financed through the issuance of those notes. The SPV enters into a credit swap with the originating bank in which it sells default protection in return for a premium that subsidizes the coupon to compensate the investor for the reference entity default risk. In each case, the investor receives a coupon and par redemption, provided there has been no credit event of the reference entity.

The value of a CLN as opposed to a traditional sale or participation of assets is that (a) the structure is confidential with respect to the bank's customers and (b) the CLN or credit swap terms generally allow the bank the flexibility to use the contract as a hedge for any senior obligation of the reference entity (including loans, bonds, derivatives, receivables, and so on).

Broad Index Secured Trust Offering ("BISTRO")

Since late 1997, the market has seen several innovative structures which have exploited the unfunded, off-balance sheet nature of credit derivatives (as opposed to funded CLNs) to allow a bank to purchase the credit protection necessary to mimic the regulatory capital treatment of a traditional securitization while preserving its competitive funding advantage. Such structures have the advantage of being equally applicable to the exposure of both drawn and undrawn loans.

This type of structure is exemplified by a transaction known as BISTRO, a J.P. Morgan proprietary product which has been applied to approximately $40 billion of bank credit risk since first introduced in December 1997. In this structure, an originating bank buys protection on a specified portfolio of corporate credit exposures via a portfolio credit swap from J.P. Morgan. Morgan, in turn, purchases protection on the same portfolio from an SPV. The credit protection may be subject to a "threshold" (in Figure 3–10, equal to 1.50 percent) relating to the aggregate level of losses experienced on the reference portfolio. Since this threshold represents economic risk retained by the originating bank, it is analogous to the credit enhancement or equity stake that a bank would provide in a traditional securitization using a CLO.

F I G U R E 3–10

BISTRO Structure

Credit swap on $10 bn portfolio | Credit swap on first $700 mm of losses

Originating Bank
— Fee →
Contingent payment on losses exceeding 1.5% of portfolio ←

Intermediary Bank
— Fee →
Contingent payment on losses exceeding 1.5% of portfolio ←

BISTRO SPV
$700 mm US Tsy Notes

Under market risk capital rules, the intermediary bank can model the capital requirement of its residual risk position based upon VaR calculations

$700 mm ↑↓ Senior & Subordinated Notes

Capital markets investors

The BISTRO SPV is collateralized with government securities or repurchase agreements on government securities which it funds via the issuance of notes which are credit-tranched and sold into the capital markets. In a critical departure from the traditional securitization model, the BISTRO SPV has substantially less collateral than the notional amount of the reference portfolio. Typically, the BISTRO collateral will amount to only 5 to 15 percent of the portfolio notional. Thus, only the first 5 to 15 percent of losses (after the threshold, if any) in a particular portfolio are funded by the vehicle, leaving the most senior risk position unfunded. The transactions are structured so that, assuming the portfolio has a reasonable amount of diversification and investment grade-average credit quality, the risk of loss exceeding the amount of BISTRO securities sold is, at most, remote, or in rating agency vernacular, better than "triple A."

To achieve regulatory capital relief, it is necessary for the originating bank to make use of a third party bank (J.P. Morgan in this example) to intermediate between the BISTRO SPV and itself because of the large notional mismatch between the underlying portfolio and the hedge afforded by the SPV. Provided that the third party bank is able to apply internal models to its residual risk position in a trading book, this risk will not consume a disproportionate amount of regulatory capital for the intermediating bank. The fact that such a structure allows sophisticated banks to be efficient distributors of third party risk but not their own risk is another ironic consequence of the current risk-based capital rules.

Credit derivative structures such as BISTRO significantly reduce the legal, systems, personnel, and client relationship costs associated with a traditional securitization. They reduce the amount of time needed to execute a transaction of significant size. They can achieve efficient leverage in leaving the senior most risks in diversified portfolios unfunded and distributing substantial volumes of credit risk in many small capital markets transactions. In addition, while a CLO can efficiently hedge only funded credit risk, a credit derivative transaction can hedge a much broader universe of credit exposures including unfunded commitments, letters of credit, derivatives, revolvers, settlement lines, mortgage insurance lines, and trade receivables. The wider universe of credits available via a credit derivative structure means a larger, more diverse, portfolio can be executed with clear benefits in terms of cost, regulatory capital, and economic risk. Furthermore, in a BISTRO, the originating bank avoids any linkage of the transaction to its own name, thereby avoiding reputation risk with respect to the market and individual borrowers. This arms-length nature of the BISTRO is a benefit when rating agencies assess credit implications for the bank.

CONCLUSION

The market for credit derivatives has grown exponentially since the beginning of the 1990s. Transaction volumes have increased from the occasional tens of millions of dollars to regular weekly volumes measured in hundreds of millions, if not billions, of dollars. Banks remain among the most active users of credit derivatives, but the list of market participants is rapidly expanding to include a broad range of broker-dealers, institutional investors, money managers, hedge funds, insurers, reinsurers, and corporations. Growth in market participation and market volume is likely to continue at its current rapid pace, based on the unequivocal contribution credit derivatives are making to efficient risk management, rational credit pricing, and ultimately systemic liquidity. Credit derivatives can offer both the buyer and seller of risk considerable advantages over traditional alternatives and represent an important innovation for global financial markets, both as an asset class and a risk management tool, with the potential to revolutionize the way that credit risk is originated, distributed, measured, and managed.

Portfolio Credit Risk Modeling and Credit Derivatives

It is no coincidence that the use of credit derivatives has emerged simultaneously with the development of increasingly sophisticated credit portfolio models. The launch of J.P. Morgan's CreditMetrics® in April 1997 with the support of a large group of cosponsors provided the first readily available benchmark model for evaluating credit value-at-risk in a full portfolio context. This technology allows portfolio managers to quantify concentration risk arising from large exposure to one credit or to groups of highly correlated credits in a particular industry or location. Traditionally, arbitrary credit line limits have been the primary defense against concentrations of credit risk. By contrast, the CreditMetrics approach makes credit allocation decisions sensitive to risk and return (that is, an output of the portfolio management model rather than an input to it). The approach allows portfolio managers to identify those credits contributing most significantly to portfolio risk and evaluate options for replacing them with other, less correlated and, hence, less risky, exposures.

These innovations in the application of modern portfolio theory to credit portfolios have revealed powerful arguments for more active credit risk management. For example, loans have a lower default correlation than their corresponding equity correlation due to the low likelihood that two remote events will occur simultaneously. The implication of low default correlations is that the systematic risk in a credit portfolio is small relative to the nonsystematic or individual contribution to risk of each asset. The greater the component of nonsystematic risk in a portfolio, the greater the benefits of diversification, and vice versa. To view the problem another way, indices provide good hedges of risk in equity portfolios, but not in debt portfolios: it takes many more names to fully diversify a credit portfolio than an equity portfolio, but when those diversification benefits are achieved, they are considerable. An inadequately diversified portfolio, on the other hand, can result in significantly lower return on risk ratios than would seem intuitively obvious. The conclusion? Given the opportunity, portfolio managers should actively seek to hedge concentrated risks and diversify with new ones.

The development of better models for credit risk *measurement* and better tools for credit risk *management* are mutually reinforcing: traditionally, without the tools to transfer credit risk, it was not possible to properly respond to the recommendations of a portfolio model. Conversely, without a portfolio model, the contribution of credit derivatives to portfolio risk-return performance has been difficult to evaluate. However, as such technology becomes more widespread, as the necessary data become more accessible, and as credit derivative liquidity improves, the combined effect on the way in which banks and others evaluate and manage credit risks will be profound. Banks will adopt a more proactive approach to trading and managing credit exposures, with a corresponding decline in the typical holding period for loans. It will become more common to observe banks taking exposure to borrowers with whom they have no meaningful relationships and shedding exposure to customers with whom they do have relationships to facilitate further business. Such transactions will occur on both a one-off and portfolio basis. In a sense, the use of large bilateral portfolio swaps is simply a less radical and more effective solution than a bank merger to the problem of a poorly diversified customer base. Banks will increasingly have the ability to choose whether to act as passive hold-to-maturity investors or as proactive, return-on-capital driven originators, traders, servicers, repackagers, and distributors of loan product. Ironically, this process will resemble the distribution techniques employed by those institutions that have been disintermediating banks in the capital markets for years. It also seems inevitable that the occurrence of more frequent secondary trading and the availability of more objective credit pricing will prompt a movement toward the marking-to-market of loan portfolios.

Implications of Credit Derivatives

While it is true that banks have been the foremost users of credit derivatives to date, it would be misleading to suggest that banks will be the only institutions to benefit from them. Credit derivatives are bringing about greater efficiency of pricing and greater liquidity of all credit risks. This will benefit a broad range of financial institutions, institutional investors, and also corporations in their capacity both as borrowers and as takers of trade credit and receivable exposures. Just as the rapidly growing asset backed securitization market is bringing investors new sources of credit assets, the credit derivative market will strip out and repackage credit exposures from the vastly greater pool of risks which do not naturally lend themselves to securitization, either because the risks are unfunded (off-balance sheet), because they are not intrinsically transferable, or because their sale would be complicated by relationship concerns. By enhancing liquidity, credit derivatives achieve the financial equivalent of a "free lunch" whereby both buyers and sellers of risk benefit from the associated gains.

It is not surprising, then, to learn that credit derivatives are a group of products that, while innovative, are coming of age. When they first emerged in the early 1990s, credit derivatives were used primarily by derivatives dealers seeking to generate incremental credit capacity for derivatives counterparties with full credit lines. Since then, they have evolved into a tool used routinely by commercial and investment banks and other institutional investors in the course of credit risk management, distribution, structuring, and trading, with liquidity beginning to rival,

FIGURE 3–11

Size of U.S. Credit Derivatives Market

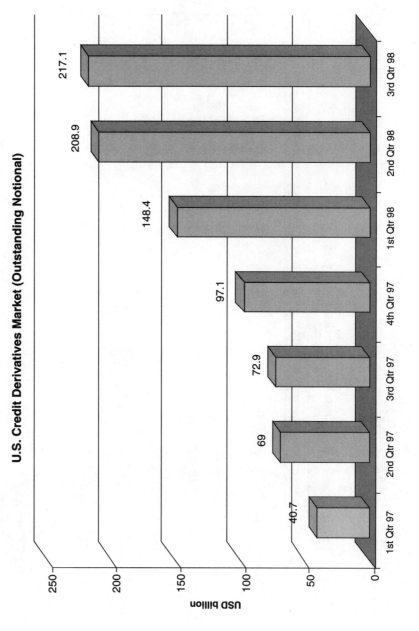

U.S. Credit Derivatives Market (Outstanding Notional)

FIGURE 3-12

Top Ten Credit Derivatives Participants

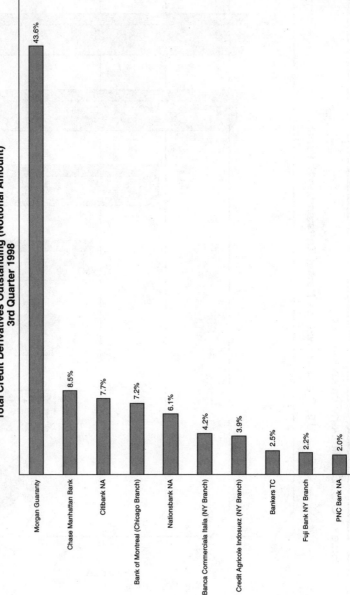

**Top 10 Institutions
Total Credit Derivatives Outstanding (Notional Amount)
3rd Quarter 1998**

Morgan Guaranty — 43.6%
Chase Manhattan Bank — 8.5%
Citibank NA — 7.7%
Bank of Montreal (Chicago Branch) — 7.2%
Nationsbank NA — 6.1%
Banca Commerciale Italia (NY Branch) — 4.2%
Credit Agricole Indosuez (NY Branch) — 3.9%
Bankers TC — 2.5%
Fuji Bank NY Branch — 2.2%
PNC Bank NA — 2.0%

Percent of Market

or even exceed, that of the secondary loan trading market in the United States and the asset swap market in Europe. Most recently, corporate risk managers have begun to explore the use of the product as a mechanism for hedging their own costs of borrowing, as well as managing credit exposures to key customers.

There is evidence to suggest that credit derivative activity has picked up significantly in recent months. For example, data recently released by U.S. regulators,[8] illustrated in Figures 3–11 and 3–12, show rapid growth in the credit derivatives market among U.S.-based commercial banking institutions. The reported outstanding notional amount of credit derivatives jumped by over $50 billion in the first quarter of 1998, from $97 billion at the end of 1997 to $148 billion. This represents growth of 53 percent in the quarter, compared to average growth of 36 percent over the previous three quarters. The statistics are compiled from quarterly call reports filed only by FDIC-insured U.S. domestic commercial banks and U.S. branches of foreign commercial banks. Consequently, the data understates the size of the global market significantly. Excluded are all non-commercial banking institutions (e.g., investment banks, securities houses, insurance and reinsurance companies, corporations, funds and money managers) and all activity of non-U.S. commercial banks outside their U.S. branches. This omission could amount to 50 percent of global activity, suggesting that total outstanding notional volumes approached $300 billion at the end of the first quarter of 1998.

This evidence is corroborated by a recent BBA (British Bankers' Association) 1997–98 survey[9] which reveals credit derivatives to be the fastest-growing OTC derivatives market and projects global credit derivatives volumes will reach $740 billion by the year 2000.

While these numbers are tiny relative to the size of the global credit markets and other derivatives markets (both measured in the trillions of dollars), credit derivatives today remind many of the nascent interest rate and equity swap markets of the 1980s—a product whose potential for growth derives from both enormous need and an enormous underlying marketplace.

---

[8]Source: Federal Reserve and OCC quarterly call report filings through March 30, 1998.
[9]Source: BBA Survey June 17, 1998.

CHAPTER 4

Credit Risk Management from a Corporate Perspective

Joyce A. Frost
Head of Marketing, Global Credit Derivatives, Chase Securities, Inc.

Corporations face a myriad of operational and financial risks. The operational risks of a company are managed from the executive office down to the individual operating units while financial risks are typically overseen by the chief financial officer and managed through the treasurer's office. To date the active management of financial risk by corporations has focused mostly on interest rate, currency, and commodity price risk. Credit risk, on the other hand, has typically been more actively managed in situations where a creditor to the company is already experiencing credit problems, evidenced by a slowdown or nonpayment of trade receivables. With the introduction of credit derivatives, corporations are beginning to be more proactive in identifying credit risk and managing it, similar to what was experienced in the early to mid-1980s with the inception of interest rate derivatives. This chapter will begin by identifying different sources of credit risk to the corporation and how they are commonly managed and will explore potential solutions using credit derivatives. The chapter will conclude by introducing credit derivatives to liability management.

IDENTIFYING AND MANAGING CREDIT RISK

Unlike other financial risks faced by a corporation, such as interest rate, currency or commodity risk, credit risk in many cases is not so readily observable or quantifiable. Direct sources of credit risk are the easiest to identify and quantify. Direct sources of credit risk originate in investment portfolios, commercial contracts (e.g., short-term trade receivables), or other contracts, usually longer term (e.g., customer financing commitments, leases, long-term fixed price commodity, or take or pay contracts). The most common direct source of credit risk is through standard trade receivables. Depending on the size of the receivables relative to its capital or the general credit quality of its receivables, a company may take a more active role in managing the credit risk. When a particular credit starts to become problematic, a company traditionally has had several options to manage the risk. It can reduce business to the customer which is not particularly appealing if the credit in question is one of the firm's best customers, or do nothing, maintaining the status quo. Although the latter is a cross-your-fingers approach, it is a route often taken. Other traditional ways of managing the risk is: through factoring, which tends to be relatively expensive; securitization, although the company typically retains a first loss position in the portfolio so it does little to reduce the risk; or accounts receivable insurance. Credit derivatives can be an efficient and effective solution and will be discussed in greater detail later in the chapter.

Direct sources of credit risk are also inherent in the short-term and long-term investment portfolio. Most short-term investment portfolios are highly liquid and limited to high quality securities, such as treasuries, commercial paper or bank deposits. Although easily identifiable the exposure is of little concern because of its high quality, short term nature. Debt instruments in longer term, held to maturity investment portfolios (e.g., bonds, notes, or long-term bank deposits) are potentially of greater concern. These longer term investments originate from a variety of sources. They could be part of a traditional investment portfolio for companies with excess cash which is commonly seen in technology or other cash rich companies. These investments, typically public bonds, tend to be actively managed either inside or outside by a professional money manager. The management of the credit risk associated with these bonds is usually done by selling out of a specific position given the liquidity of the bond market. However, there may be reasons why a corporation may want to retain the position on its books (e.g., recognition of capital gains and losses), but reduce or eliminate the inherent credit exposure. The reduction of credit risk can efficiently be done through credit derivatives.

Other longer-term investments could originate as a result of structured transactions, such as Japanese leverage leases, where a corporation must purchase a long-term yen bank deposit to defease its own credit risk to a group of investors. Because of the lack of liquidity in the cash markets for these long-term structured deposits, the corporation has little flexibility to sell its position if the quality of the issuing bank has deteriorated. Credit derivatives again may be an excellent tool to help the corporate reduce or eliminate the credit risk.

Corporations may also be exposed to longer term, third party credit exposure as a result of acquisition or trade finance. For example, it is not uncommon for a company who is selling a subsidiary to partially finance the purchase by taking back a note from the acquirer. The same holds true for trade finance when a manufacturer is selling large equipment to a third party and must provide financing as part of the deal. These bilateral agreements are typically illiquid and difficult to sell but are sometimes purchased by a bank, or other financial institution, at a discount. Explicit or implicit guarantees of third party debt are an obvious source of credit risk and can be a result of supporting a strategically important supplier, or customer, who is in need of financing. These exposures are more difficult to manage since the corporation can not readily step out of the contract effectively "selling" off its exposure. Credit derivatives can be applicable to all these situations either by reducing the credit exposure associated with the note trade receivable, or guarantee, or reducing the balance sheet impact of ownership.

The sources of risk attained from the above examples are all fairly easy to identify and quantify. However, there are "hidden" sources of credit risk that are not so easily identifiable, predictable, or quantifiable. Two examples come to mind and both stem from customer concentrations. The first is the impact of a "disruption" at a customer business (e.g., a strike), and the second is the impact of a major downturn, or bankruptcy, of a major customer. In the case of the latter, not only would the corporation suffer as a result of losses on its trade receivables, but future revenue could also be lost if the customer files Chapter 7 or 11.

Another major source of credit risk to corporations is country risk. This exposure is pervasive since most corporations "think globally" and many look to the emerging markets either as a big source of new revenue or as strategically important for operations given relatively cheap labor pools. Country risk is inherent in many cross-border transactions but tends to be more problematic in longer term investments through project financings, joint ventures, and direct subsidiaries. Country risk is typically identified by three major events, inconvertibility, expropriation, or political violence. Companies mitigate this risk in a variety of ways such as protection offered through traditional letters of credit issued by banks, programs through the Export Development and Multilateral Agencies, and insurance companies. Companies can now also look at credit derivatives as a potentially viable alternative.

CREDIT DERIVATIVES AS A HEDGING TOOL

The Steps to Hedge Credit Exposure

As highlighted above, credit derivatives may be an effective tool for a corporation to hedge its credit risk.

As a short summary, a credit derivative is a financial contract with a payout typically linked to loan or bond values, credit events, credit spreads, or credit ratings of single names, baskets, or indices.

There are predominantly three forms of credit derivatives which are used by corporates to hedge credit risk: credit swaps (often referred to as default swaps), receivable puts, and total return swaps. Depending on the circumstances, any one of the three structures may be an effective hedge of credit risk.

In the credit swap, one counterparty, the protection buyer, makes periodic payments to the other counterparty, the protection seller, in return for a contingent payment if a predefined credit event[1] occurs in the reference credit. The contingent payment can be based on cash settlement, typically par minus recovery value of the reference asset, or physical delivery of the reference asset, in exchange for a cash payment equal to the initial notional amount.

In a *receivable put*, the purchaser of the put pays an upfront premium and has the right to put a specific trade receivable(s) to the seller at a predetermined price upon a payment default of the receivable. The receivable put is typically not documented under an ISDA[2] agreement and is often used for post-petition trade receivables, or in cases where a credit swap is not feasible.

A total return swap is a contract between two parties whereby one party, the total return payor, pays the total rate of return (fees, coupons, and price appreciation) on a specific reference asset to the other party, the total return receiver, in exchange for receiving LIBOR plus or minus a spread and any price depreciation on the reference asset.

The first step in hedging credit risk is obviously to identify and quantify the credit exposure that is causing concern. For example, $20 million of trade receivables to XYZ Incorporated, the reference entity. The next step is to determine the best credit derivative structure to hedge the particular risk. This decision will largely depend on the characteristic of

---

[1]Credit events are typically defined as payment default, cross default or cross-acceleration, and bankruptcy.
[2]International Swap and Derivative Association.

the hedged item. For most credit exposures, the credit swap is the desired hedging instrument since the buyer of protection has known fixed payments (i.e., the premium) while the seller of protection will make a contingent payment upon credit event which is the "event" from which the corporation is seeking protection. Credit swaps are commonly used to hedge risk from trade receivables, notes, or third party guarantees. Since total return swaps require two way payment flows in respect to price appreciation and depreciation of the reference asset, it may not be the structure of choice for certain hedged items. For example, if the reference credit improves over the life of the swap and as a result the price on the reference asset appreciates, the company would have to make a payment equal to the price appreciation to its swap counterparty. If there is no commensurate appreciation that can be realized on the hedged item, there would be a negative cash flow effect in respect to the swap. This mismatch is somewhat mitigated if using bank loans as the reference asset since bank loans tend not to trade significantly above par for any length of time.

The third step is to identify an appropriate reference asset that will be used to hedge the exposure and the settlement method upon credit event. Ideally, the reference asset should be the hedged item with physical delivery upon credit event. In many circumstances, though, it will need to be a publicly traded or a broadly distributed debt instrument, such as a bond or loan issued by the reference entity. In this case since the hedged item is not the reference asset, cash settlement would be necessary upon credit event since the company would not be able to deliver the specific reference asset.

There is a growing trend in credit swaps, however, whereby the reference asset can be a class of assets, such as any senior unsecured obligation. Obligations can be defined as any form of indebtedness, or financial commitment including trade receivables, guarantees, letters of credit, or derivative transactions. In this case, physical delivery is often the settlement method upon credit event and the protection buyer can deliver the hedged item to the protection seller even though it was not specifically identified in the swap documents.

An important factor in determining the appropriate reference asset is its ranking in bankruptcy. Ideally, the reference asset should rank pari passu with the credit risk exposure being hedged to eliminate or reduce basis risk. Basis risk is the risk that gains or losses on the hedged item and are not equally offset by gains or losses on the hedge. Basis risk can arise in two circumstances. First, there may be basis risk associated with timing. For example, if a default or loss is experienced on the hedged item but a credit event has not been triggered on the credit swap, or vice versa, the corporate may not be protected. A way to mitigate this risk is

T A B L E   4–1

	B or L[1]	Trade Receivables Recovery (%)	Secured Debt Recovery (%)	Unsecured Debt Recovery (%)
Best	B	45.7%	60.3%	13.6%
Federated	B	73.9%	100.0%	41.6%
Hills	B	71.0%	105.0%	43.6%
Macy's	B	37.5%	118.0%	35.8%
Woodies	L	54.0%	100.0%	47.0%
Zales	B	18.6%	100.0%	24.6%
Average Recovery		50.1%	95.2%	34.4%

to include cross default or cross acceleration as a credit event in the credit derivative and ensure that the payment and default thresholds in respect to payment default and cross default are appropriate. Second, basis risk arises if the market value of the reference asset at the time of credit event differs from that of the hedged item. This form of basis risk is only relevant when using total return swaps or credit swaps with cash settlements upon credit event. The risk is that the payment under the hedge does not cover losses experienced on the hedged item. Physical delivery of the hedged item (e.g., the receivables), eliminates this basis risk, however, physical settlement of the credit derivative may not always be feasible.

The recovery value of liabilities in the capital structure of bankrupt retailers highlights the potential basis risk between hedging one class of liabilities with another.

As shown in Table 4–1, the average recovery value for trade receivables was 50.1 percent compared to 95.2 percent on secured debt and 34.4 percent on unsecured debt.

To mitigate basis risk associated with cash settlement where a specific credit exposure is hedged with a different reference asset, it is important that the corporation determine the appropriate notional amount of the swap, which, if necessary, is the next step in structuring a credit derivative. This step may be the most challenging since the determination will be based on expected recovery rates of the hedged item versus that of the reference asset.

Using the retailer example in Table 4–1, it would appear that hedging trade receivables with unsecured debt would be the most appropriate if physical delivery of the receivable through a credit swap, or receivable put, were not available. Comparing the values of unsecured debt to that of receivables, a dollar-for-dollar hedge would have more than covered losses on the receivables in almost all circumstances, except for Zales. A more precise hedge, had we known the actual recovery of Zales, would have been to buy $10.8 million of protection for every $10 million of exposure to Zales receivables. However, in practice this hedging ratio approach is not widely used since the actual outcome is quite unpredictable; therefore, most companies will hedge their receivable dollar-for-dollar.

The notional amount of protection can be determined as follows where:

$$N = \frac{1 - RVh}{1 - RVr} * E$$

RVh = Expected Recovery Value hedged item

RVr = Expected Recovery Value of reference asset

E = Dollar amount of Exposure to hedge

Using the Zales example to illustrate the cash flows, a credit default swap referencing secured debt may have been structured as shown in Figure 4–1. This example assumes that the highest price in the market for $10.79 million of secured debt equaled the actual recovery value experienced in bankruptcy and MS Manufacturing was perfectly hedged.

If the hedged item is the same as the reference asset there obviously is no basis risk so a dollar-for-dollar hedge would be appropriate. If the hedged item is in the same liability class as the reference asset, such as senior unsecured debt, a dollar-for-dollar hedge would most likely still be appropriate. However, there could still be differences in the market

F I G U R E 4–1

The notional amount was determined as follows:

$$\$10,795,756 = \frac{1 - .186}{1 - .246} * \$10mm$$

Assume Credit Event occurs and swap terminates.
Recovery Value of Unsecured Debt = .246%
Initial Price = 1.00%
Cash Settlement of Swap = [1% − .246%] * $10,795,000 = $8,139,430
Cash Settlement of MS receivables = $10,000,000 * .186% = 1,860,000

value of the hedged item and that of the reference asset upon a cash settlement These differences could reflect the expected liquidity of the reference asset versus the hedged item or how substantial the supporting documentation. If the hedged item is in a different liability class, the determination of the appropriate notional amount may be more difficult.

When hedging country risk associated with longer term credit exposures, determining the appropriate reference asset may present some challenges. To eliminate the basis risk, the reference asset would ideally be that of the specific exposure for example, however, this is not always feasible and the reference entity may not have other liquid debt instruments to reference. Therefore, referencing one of the sovereign bonds of that country may be most practical. Let's take an example of a company with significant operations in Mexico through a joint venture. The company is cognizant of the political risk associated with its investment, and if it could, it would prefer to isolate its exposure to the commercial risks of the venture and not the unpredictable country risks. To help mitigate the risk, the corporate enters into a three year total return swap referencing one of the Mexican Sovereign bonds whereby the corporate synthetically shorts Mexico by paying the total return on the bonds and receiving LIBOR $\pm$ spread. If the credit quality of Mexico decreases, so does the price of the bonds and the corporate has a gain in its swap contract. This gain may help to offset any unrealized losses on the value of its investments. Presumably if there is political unrest in Mexico the value of the joint venture has declined since the political risk has increased. Conversely, if Mexico improves and bond spreads tighten there would be a loss on the swap contract that may be offset by an unrealized gain on the value of the joint venture. However, even though there may be a fairly strong correlation between the sovereign Mexican bonds and the value of the joint venture there is basis risk in that the dollar-for-dollar gains or losses in the value of the subsidiary may not be offset by gains or losses on the total return swap. The cost of this hedge would be the negative carry associated with the synthetic short position. If the coupon on bonds was LIBOR + 4.00 percent, the corporate would pay LIBOR + 4.00 percent on the swap and receive say, LIBOR − .25 percent from the swap dealer. In this case the cost would increase by 3.75 percent per annum on the notional amount plus or minus periodic depreciation or appreciation.

The other solution to mitigate the country risk associated with the joint venture would be to purchase protection through a credit swap for three years. In the credit swap, the corporate would also pay 3.75 percent per annum and would receive a cash settlement from the swap counterparty if there were a credit event for Mexico. By the maturity of the swap, if there were no credit event over the three years, there would be no payment to the corporate even though Mexico's credit could have significantly deteriorated during the three years. If Mexico became a better credit over the three year period, there would be no final payment by either party unlike the total return swap where the corporate is responsible for paying the price appreciation on the reference bonds. Both structures hedge the corporate at the extreme, when there is a credit event. The cash settlement upon credit event under both structures would also be identical if the reference assets were the same for both. The decision to hedge with either a total return swap or a credit swap will reflect the corporate hedging objectives including scope, maturity, cash flow, and relative price.

The last step is to choose the appropriate dealer in which to hedge the exposure. Practically, up to this point, most corporations would have been working closely with a bank to help appropriately structure the transaction. However, there are several things to keep in mind prior to execution. Depending on the underlying reference asset and the time to maturity, there could be significant counterparty credit exposure. In essence the corporation is transferring the risk of the reference entity to that of the swap counterparty. However, the corporate is only at risk of loss on its hedge if the underlying reference entity defaults and at the same time so does the swap counterparty. Theoretically, this exposure can be as large as the notional amount of the swap.

Therefore, the corporate should be cognizant of the correlation between the reference asset and the swap counterparty. The higher the correlation of the two entities, the weaker the actual protection since it is more likely that both entities will default at the same time than if they were not correlated. This is a real risk that was recently proven out during the Asia crisis when several Korean corporations defaulted on bonds which were used as reference assets in credit swaps. A few Korean banks sold protection on these reference assets and were unable to meet its obligations under credit swaps upon credit event of these corporates. The entities which bought protection were left with similar losses it would have had were the exposures not hedged. In the United States and most other G7 countries the correlation risk is minimal but should still be considered under certain circumstances. There are ways to mitigate this risk, if necessary, by requiring collateral on the swap or purchasing the protection vis-à-vis a credit linked note (i.e., a liability issued by the corporate that is linked to a credit event of the reference entity).

Figure 4–2 illustrates and summarizes the steps to hedge credit exposure.

F I G U R E 4–2

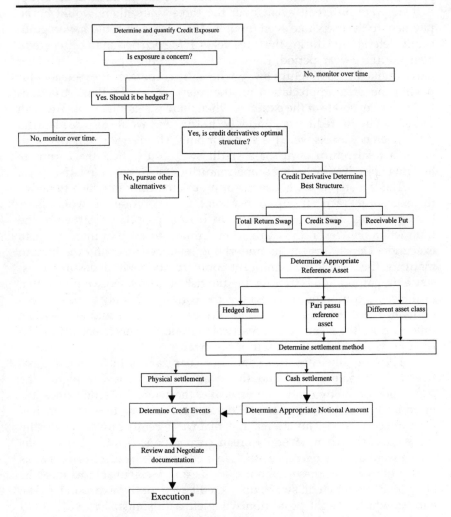

LIABILITY MANAGEMENT

In the previous section, we looked at using credit derivatives to manage credit exposure. In this section, we examine the use of credit derivatives to manage liabilities primarily through the use of swaps. Some corporates, particularly those with high yield debt outstanding, will tender or re-purchase their debt in the open market for a variety of reasons. The tender process is usually considered expensive as a result of the upfront fees

F I G U R E   4–3

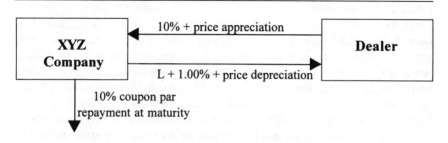

payable to a securities firm to tender the bonds and the increased price usually demanded by investors to make it a successful tender. With a total return swap, a company can synthetically "repurchase" its bonds in the market by receiving the total return on it's targeted bonds and paying LIBOR plus a spread to the swap counterparty. By receiving the total return, the company has effectively hedged the market value of its debt. It locked in the current price of its bonds since it will receive any appreciation on the bonds from the counterparty and will pay any price depreciation. Effective, the total return swap has hedged against any price appreciation associated with its bonds. Presumably the dealer has purchased the bonds in the market, most likely over a period of time, at prices that are more favorable than if a public tender had been announced by the company, however, there is no requirement that the dealer actually purchase the bond as its hedge.

Figure 4–3 illustrates the cash flows.

In this example, two things have happened. First XYZ eliminated its price risk in respect to a tender offer. If the price of its bonds appreciate from say 102 to 104 percent, the dealer pays XYZ 2 percent at maturity of the swap. If the price of the bond declines to say par, XYZ is responsible for the 2 percent depreciation. Second, XYZ has effectively converted its financing costs to floating since it will be receiving the 10 percent cash flow on the swap which will offset its bond coupon and will be paying LIBOR + 1.00 percent. Note that the LIBOR + 1.00 percent payment is based on the initial price of the bonds, 102 percent, times the notional amount of the swap, say $100 million. Assuming current six month LIBOR is at 5.75 percent, the payment on the swap by XYZ over the first six months is $3,490,312. XYZ is receiving $5 million resulting in net positive carry of $1,509,687. XYZ, however, is still responsible for price depreciation and as the swap gets closer to maturity the market price of the bonds will migrate to 100 percent. Assuming no credit event the final payment by XYZ would be $2 million.

Credit derivatives can also be used to hedge credit spread risk of a future bond issuance (e.g., if a corporate is planning to issue a ten year bond six months from now). Practically speaking, although possible, it is very difficult to hedge an issuers specific credit spread for large issue amounts. However, an issuer can use an index swap as a proxy. In this structure, the issuer pays the total return (an effective short) on an index that is highly correlated to its own credit spreads. For example, a B/BB issuer may look to use a high yield index, such as the CSI High Yield Index, to hedge against widening spreads. Conversely, a high grade issuer could structure a swap using a high grade index, such as a sub-component of the Lehman Aggregate or Merrill Lynch indices to hedge its spread risk. In return, the issuer receives either (1) LIBOR ± spread if it also wishes to hedge against interest rate movement since most indices have long durations, or (2) a fixed rate, if it does not wish to hedge against treasury movements.

Using the index total return swap tied to LIBOR, the issuer would hedge the general levels of issuing costs (interest rates and spreads) six months from the trade date. If interest rates and/or credit spreads increased, the issuer would receive a payment under the swap which would help offset costs on its own bond issue. Conversely, if rates and/or credit spreads decline, the issuer would make a payment under the swap which would be offset by lower borrowing costs. However, because the issuer is using an index swap to hedge its own issue costs, there is basis risk in the transaction.

CONCLUSION

Certainly, as the market continues to develop and as more corporations become familiar with credit derivatives, the potential applications may reach far beyond the ones identified in this chapter. The hope is that credit derivatives will drive more active credit risk management within a corporation just as interest rate and currency swaps propelled the active management of interest rate and currency risk. Accounting, regulatory and other outside factors will also affect, either positively or negatively, the growth of this important market, but the potential is enormous.

PART THREE

Determining Exposure and Pricing Credit Derivatives

CHAPTER 5

Pricing Credit Derivatives*

Sanjiv R. Das, Ph.D.
Professor, Harvard Business School

ABSTRACT

This chapter summarizes some leading models for the pricing of credit derivatives. The models are presented in a simplified fashion, with examples, so as to make the details of the engineering more accessible to a broader audience. The role of interest rate risk, default risk, and recovery risk are all given play in these models. While several modeling methods have now been proposed, this chapter deals with those that (a) are implementable using observables, and (b) easily provide risk-neutral pricing in a manner free from arbitrage.

INTRODUCTION

Since 1992, when credit derivatives were first proposed at an annual meeting of the ISDA, the market and interest in this product has grown rapidly. The products are now well set to be mainstream securities, are well traded, and have global markets.

---

*This chapter has been prepared specifically for this book. The contents of this chapter have been immensely influenced by discussion with several people, both academics and practitioners, and the perspectives in the chapter emanate from an opinionated perusal of the burgeoning literature on the subject. Many thanks to Peter Tufano, who rekindled my interest in this subject, and made it all the more fun.

Essentially, risk on a defaultable bond may be broken into three separate components:

1. **Interest rate risk:** this is standard, any bond, defaultable or not, must possess interest rate risk. There are several models dealing with interest rates, most notably the Heath-Jarrow-Morton (1992) model, which provides a universal framework for interest rate risk modeling and risk management.

2. **The risk of default:** this risk pertains to the pure possibility of the bond entering default, irrespective of the magnitude of loss from default. *Default* risk is what rating agencies have usually been concerned with. S&P and Moodys ratings usually refer to the likelihood of default. To quote S&P:

   "Likelihood of default is indicated by an issuer's senior debt rating . . . Subordinated debt usually is rated lower than senior debt to better reflect the relative position of the obligation in bankruptcy. Unsecured debt, where significant secured debt exists, is treated similarly to subordinated debt."

   Therefore, one simple way to track default risk is through credit ratings, which provide a good proxy, since rich information on this aspect is readily available.

3. **The risk of insufficient recovery in the event of default:** this may be called *recovery* risk. This risk is quite different from that of default risk; it pertains to the market value for residual assets of a firm in default.

Clearly, the last two risks outlined above together determine credit spreads on a bond. It is important to segregate them since credit derivatives may be written on either or both risks—hence, from a modeling viewpoint, it is essential not to treat them as one composite entity. Moreover, the sources of empirical information in the modeling process will be quite disparate. Ratings and other industry-level information are quite effective in providing market participants with a good idea of default likelihood, whereas a more accurate assessment of the individual firm's recovery risk is necessary in understanding why spreads tend to be different for firms within the same rating category and industry.

In this article, we shall examine a range of models which deal with the pricing of credit-sensitive securities. Starting with simple models, we will eventually progress on to sophisticated models which embed all three of the above mentioned sources of risk. The structure of the article is as follows. First, we take a look at the most popular credit derivatives merely to set the stage for the models. Then we will examine the first of many models, restricting attention to modeling approaches which directly model the credit spread. In the next section, we look at the components of the credit spread in greater detail, and then, move onto an explicit model, the Jarrow-Lando-Turnbull (1997) approach. Then we deal with the Das-Tufano (1996) extension of the Jarrow-Lando-Turnbull model, and the Duffie-Singleton (1995) framework. The last section concludes, and also raises some conceptual issues on relative pricing and its relationship to pricing to provide a rate of return on capital. We also discuss in brief the application of the methods in this chapter to credit portfolios.

The definition of the three most common credit derivatives will provide a good idea of why the basic risk classification is useful.

STANDARD CREDIT DERIVATIVE CONTRACTS

While credit derivatives are usually tailor-made given the solely OTC nature of the market, they tend to be classified into three types of transactions.

1. *Default swaps:* In the default swap, one party receives a fixed stream of payments in return for which he pays nothing unless the underlying bond defaults. This is basically an insurance contract protecting the holder of the underlying from the consequences of default. One way in which the default swap is implemented is that when default occurs, the underlying is delivered to the party providing the insurance against a par value payment. It's clear that the event of default is necessary to make the default swap pay off for the party making the steady constant stream of payments. Reductions in value of the underlying unaccompanied by default do not compensate the fixed rate payer in the swap in any way. Values of default swaps are not affected directly by changes in the riskless rate of interest or by changes in credit spreads (though there is an indirect effect). Only the probability of default matters. To the extent that the probability of default is correlated with interest rates and spreads, those variables matter too, but not directly.

2. *Total return swaps:* In a total return swap, one party makes a fixed set of payments in return for a variable stream of payments indexed to the total return (coupon plus capital appreciation) of the bond. Here, unlike in the case of a default swap, reductions in value, even without the occurrence of default make for changes in payments streams. A total return swap is affected directly by changes in spreads and default probabilities.

3. *Credit spread options:* Credit spread options are options written on the terminal value of credit spreads over some horizon. For example, an option may be written such that it pays off when the spread after a year exceeds a threshold value. These are directly option-like in nature, unlike the preceding two contracts. Since spreads are affected by both, default and variations in spreads prior to default, it has similar risk elements as does the total return swap.

There are several other contracts which are credit risk related and the 3-way risk classification may be employed to provide an interesting view of these securities.

Hence, in order to effectively run a portfolio of credit spread options, we need a model that:

- Accommodates a wide range of products, some of which are listed in Table 5–1, and

- Encompasses all the risk categories possible, so as to enable the investor to avail of any possible credit structure that may be desired, and offer the dealer a working solution to be able to offer new products at ease.

It is important to note here that credit risk is not well traded, and is also complex, resulting in several modeling difficulties. A quick listing of these issues are:

- Credit derivatives are still non-standard products.

- There is poor historical information on credit risks, and changing economic conditions makes past data unreliable.

T A B L E 5–1

Security	Interest Risk	Default Risk	Recovery Risk
Corporate debt	Y	Y	Y
FRN	N	Y	Y
Credit sensitive note	Y	Y	N
Auction rate notes	N	N	N
Spread adjusted notes	Y	Y	Y
Default swaps	N	Y	N
Total return swaps	N	Y	Y
Credit spread options	N	Y	Y

- Prices evidence slow adjustment to rating changes, and ratings do not always adjust concurrently with real credit quality changes.
- Illiquid underlying securities permeate the market, making replication of derivatives somewhat difficult.
- There are few useful indices for credit related instruments.
- A large number of deals are in the emerging markets arena where information is poor and the statistical properties of asset prices are underresearched.

TECHNICAL APPROACHES TO PRICING CREDIT DERIVATIVES

To be suitable for practitioners, pricing models must use easily observable data, and price securities off a lattice scheme, consistent with the absence of arbitrage. Here we will look at an entire range of models, where the calibration of the model is done using a simple bootstrapping method, proceeding maturity by maturity in developing the model, as is usual in term structure models of the Heath-Jarrow-Morton (1992) class. The models will incorporate interest rate risk, default risk and recovery risk.

Before proceeding to a full-blown model, it is instructive to consider simpler approaches to modeling credit sensitive securities. One such approach consists of directly modeling the credit spread.

Spread Models

Spread models do not break down the spread into default risk and recovery risk components. It is easier to directly model the spread itself. This approach is ideal in modeling credit spread options. The approach consists of designating the model for the spread by choosing an appropriate stochastic process. Derivatives pricing models are characterized first and foremost by the assumptions made about which stochastic process drives the underlying risks that are being traded. It is analogous to defining the road conditions when designing special purpose cars. While the tools used primarily by rocket-scientists in finance are continuous-time tools, this chapter will exposit models primarily in simpler discrete numeric terms. Hence, apart from a few differential equations to begin the exposition, the calculations in this chapter will be simple arithmetic computations. Readers unfamiliar with stochastic differential calculus may skip these equations, and proceed on to the numerical exposition without loss of conceptual content.

For example, the square-root diffusion provides one possible candidate for a physical process. The following stochastic differential equation may well be a likely candidate for modeling credit spreads:

$$ds = k(\theta - s)dt + \sigma\sqrt{s}dz \qquad (5.1)$$

where s is the spread, k is the rate of mean reversion, θ is the long run mean of the spread, and σ is the volatility coefficient. The Wiener increment is dz. In the simplest case, the model assumes that interest rates are constant, which is a reasonable assumption to make when the spread option has short maturity. Moreover, the volatility of the riskless rate of interest is low in comparison to that of the spread making such an assumption tenable for the moment. To represent this stochastic process in a more simple fashion, we discretize it

$$s(t) = s(0) + k[\theta - s(0)]t \pm \sigma\sqrt{s(0) \times t} \qquad (5.2)$$

which simply means that next period's spread $s(t)$ given this period's spread $s(0)$ will be given by the equation above, resulting in two possible values, an "up" value and a "down" value depending on the sign of the shock term $\sigma\sqrt{s(0) \times t}$. The spread also changes by an amount $k[\theta - s(0)]t$ which is positive when the spread is below its average level θ and negative when the spread is above its average. This term accounts for "mean reversion" in the spread, for which there is plenty of empirical evidence. Hence, the process above for the spread, while fairly simple, is a reasonably good modeling device.

In order to price options on spreads, all that is needed is the range of outcomes of the spread at the option maturity T, and the probabilities assigned to these outcomes. This is dependent on the specific choice of the spread model. For example, in the discrete version above, there are two outcomes each period, and the probabilities are equal (i.e., 0.5).

The probability function $f(s_T)$ may also be more complex, in its continuous form. But, once it is known options on the spread may be easily priced. The spread option-pricing equation below would emerge:

$$Option = e^{-RT} \int_0^\infty \max(0, s_T - K)f(s_T)ds_T$$

where R is an appropriate discount rate, and K is the threshold spread or exercise price. This is simply the present value of expected payoffs on the spread option. However, the choice of discount rate is one matter that needs resolving. The second matter to be resolved is how the stochastic process above needs to be risk-adjusted to make the solution for options prices free of arbitrage. Hence, the equation above cannot be directly applied without the resolution of these conceptual questions.

For the uninitiated, a digression here on *risk-neutral pricing* is in order. Twenty-five years ago, the development of the Black-Scholes option pricing equation highlighted the fact that in order to price derivatives, it was necessary to discount the expected cash flows on an option, provided the expected cash flows at maturity of the option were computed using "risk-neutral" processes. These processes are different from observed, statistical processes. They are pseudoprocesses that make the existing prices of securities equal to the discounted, expected future values of the security. The process above in equation 5.2 is the statistical process. This would need to be modified to make it risk-neutral. The simple way to do this is to add a term to it, and then solve for this term such that the expected discounted values of securities under the new process were equal to its current price. We shall see several examples of this as we proceed through the pricing models in this chapter.

In order to illustrate the technicalities involved, a two-period lattice implementation is sufficient, especially since it avoids the need for technical and often complex stochastic calculus based expositions.

A One-Factor Spread Model

Assume a two-period model with each period equal to one year. The current observed term structure of interest rates from the government bond market (the riskless zero coupon rate curve) is made of up of two rates: 8 percent (for one year) and 9 percent (over two years). Therefore,

$$r = \begin{bmatrix} 0.08 \\ 0.09 \end{bmatrix}$$

The notation adopted for the spot rate curve above is a vector. Each element contains the value of the interest rate for a specified period in the model. Likewise, assume that the credit spread curve for two periods is given by

$$s = \begin{bmatrix} 0.010 \\ 0.015 \end{bmatrix}$$

Hence, the risky zero coupon curve is simply the sum of these two curves, i.e.,

$$r + s = \begin{bmatrix} 0.090 \\ 0.105 \end{bmatrix}$$

Therefore, the price of a risky zero coupon bond of maturity two years (face value $100) is

$$81.8984 = \frac{100}{(1 + 0.105)^2}$$

The riskless forward rate between 1 and 2 years is

$$f_{12} = \frac{1.09^2}{1.08} - 1 = 0.1001.$$

Now, make the following assumptions about our model based on equation 5.1 above.

$$k = 0.2$$
$$\theta = 0.02$$
$$\sigma = 0.03$$

A simple (though certainly not the most ideal) discrete binomial representation of the model is:

$$s(t) = s(0) + k[\theta - s(0)] \pm \sigma\sqrt{s(0)},$$

since the unit of time is 1 year (i.e., $t = 1$). Therefore, the one period credit spread after a year would take one of two values (with equal probability) based on the equation above, where $s(0) = 0.010$. In order to undertake pricing without violation of arbitrage, under a risk-neutral regime, it is necessary to risk-adjust the stochastic process above by modifying its drift term. Hence, our model can be extended to include an adjustment term γ:

$$s(t) = s(0) + k[\theta - s(0)] + \gamma \pm \sigma\sqrt{s(0)}.$$

Plug in the assumed parameter values, and then, using this difference equation, the spread at the end of period 1 in the model will be equal to either of the following two values:

$$s(1) = \begin{cases} \gamma + 0.015 \\ \gamma + 0.009 \end{cases}$$

Therefore, at the end of one period, the price of a two period zero coupon risky bond [denoted B(t)] will have one of the following two values:

$$B(1) = \begin{cases} \dfrac{100}{1 + f_{12} + \gamma + 0.015} \\[2mm] \dfrac{100}{1 + f_{12} + \gamma + 0.009} \end{cases}$$

and accordingly, the price of the bond at time 0 will then have a price determined by discounting these two values back at the risky rate assuming equal probabilities for each:

$$B(0) = \frac{1}{2}\left[\frac{100}{1 + 0.1001 + \gamma + 0.015} + \frac{100}{1 + 0.1001 + \gamma + 0.009} \right]$$
$$\times \frac{1}{1 + 0.08 + 0.01}$$
$$= 81.8984$$

Since we already know that this price must equal 81.8984, we have a single equation in the unknown parameter γ, which we solve to obtain the risk adjustment term. The value is computed to be:

$$\gamma + 0.0081$$

Plugging this back we find that the spread after one period is equal to one of the following two values:

$$s(1) = \begin{cases} 0.0231 \\ 0.0171 \end{cases}$$

This simple analysis has provided the risk adjustment required to make the risk-neutral process for spreads consistent with the absence of arbitrage.

Spread options are easily priced on this lattice. For example, a one period call option on the spread struck at an exercise price of $K = 0.02$ would pay off when the spread was equal to 0.0231 and would expire worthless when the spread was 0.0171. The price of this simple spread option would be

$$\text{Spread } (K = 0.02) \text{ option} = \frac{1}{1.08} \times N \times (0.0231 - 0.0200) \times 0.5$$

where N is the face value of the contract, $(0.0231 - 0.0200)$ is the final intrinsic value per dollar, and $\frac{1}{1.08}$ is the discount factor to present value the option, which ends up in the money with probability 0.5.

Since the model above prices risky and riskless bonds exactly so as to be consistent with the term structures we started with, it is arbitrage-free. Readers familiar with interest rate models will find this approach identical to that originally developed by the Ho-Lee (1986) and Black-Derman-Toy (1990) models. It is quite straightforward to:

1. Extend these models to more periods, and
2. To incorporate an additional factor.

A Two-Factor Model

We can also make the interest rate stochastic and correlated with the credit spread, using a simple extension of the one-factor model. Assume in addition to the stochastic process [equation (5.1)] for the spread, we also have a square root process for the interest rate, which mimics the Cox-Ingersoll-Ross (1985) model. We simplify the interest rate process using the same discretization model as before:

$$r(t) = r(0) + \alpha[\beta - r(0)] \pm \eta\sqrt{r(0)}.$$

We assume that changes in the spread and riskless rate are correlated with parameter ρ. As before, the rate of mean reversion is α, the long run mean of the riskless rate is β, and the volatility coefficient is η. Assume the following parameters for this process:

$$\alpha = 0.3$$
$$\beta = 0.10$$
$$\eta = 0.01$$
$$\rho = 0.3$$

In order to establish the lattice for pricing credit sensitive debt, we need two steps. First, we build the lattice for riskless debt, and then, using this lattice as a base, we shall build the risky debt lattice on top of the riskless one.

Of course, reading from the term structure, $r(0) = 0.08$. Since the riskless rate of interest is stochastic, in order to undertake risk-neutral pricing, we need to make a risk-adjustment to the drift of the process, using an additional parameter.

$$r(t) = r(0) + \alpha[\beta - r(0)] + \delta \pm \eta\sqrt{r(0)}.$$

With the given parameter values, the one period rate of interest will take one of the following two values after one period:

$$r(1) = \begin{cases} \delta + 0.0888 \\ \delta + 0.0832 \end{cases}$$

Therefore, the price of a two-period riskless bond [denoted P(t)] after one period will be

$$P(1) = \begin{cases} \dfrac{100}{1 + \delta + 0.0888} \\[2ex] \dfrac{100}{1 + \delta + 0.0832} \end{cases}$$

And as before, the price of the riskless bond at time 0 will be

$$B(0) = \frac{1}{2}\left[\frac{100}{1 + \delta + 0.0888} + \frac{100}{1 + \delta + 0.0832}\right]\frac{1}{1.08} = \frac{1}{1.09^2}$$

Solving this equation gives us a value of δ = .0141 which is the rough value of the term premium for the second period in the model. Substituting this value back into the model gives the evolution of the riskless rate over time, under the risk-neutral probability measure:

$$r(1) = \begin{cases} 0.1029 \\ 0.0973 \end{cases}$$

Having derived the risk-neutral process for the riskless interest rate, we can complete the exercise by deriving the model for the entire tree comprising changes in riskless interest rates and spreads. Since, we are in a two-factor world, and we represent each factor with a binomial process, at each node on our pricing lattice we will now extend out four branches. This is because for two stochastic processes, the combination of two binomial processes may be established as a four-way branching process.

We can visualize the four states of the world in the future (at the end of the first period) as combinations of up and down moves by the riskless interest rate and the spread. Assume that in states 1 and 2 the riskless interest rate is up, and in states 3 and 4 it is down. Also assume that in states 1 and 3 the spread is up and in states 2 and 4 it is down. Therefore, the state-space for the riskless rate of interest will be

$$r(1) = \begin{bmatrix} 0.1029 \\ 0.1029 \\ 0.0973 \\ 0.0973 \end{bmatrix}$$

Likewise, the state space for the credit spread will be:

$$s(1) = \begin{bmatrix} \gamma + 0.015 \\ \gamma + 0.009 \\ \gamma + 0.015 \\ \gamma + 0.009 \end{bmatrix}$$

Since we have yet to work out the risk adjustment (γ) for the spread curve, the state space in spreads is incomplete and expressed as a function of γ.

It is also necessary to determine the probabilities so as to ensure that the correlation between r and s is achieved. Notice that the two risk-neutral processes for r and s could be written in discrete-time as

$$r(t) = r(t - \Delta) + \alpha[\beta - r(t - \Delta)]\Delta + \delta + \eta\sqrt{r(t - \Delta)} \times w\sqrt{\Delta}$$
$$s(t) = s(t - \Delta) + k[\theta - s(t - \Delta)]\Delta + \gamma + \sigma\sqrt{s(t - \Delta)} \times z\sqrt{\Delta}$$
$$corr(z, w) = \rho$$

where Δ is the discrete time interval on the lattice and (w, z) are shocks to (r, s). With this structure, the state-space for the random shocks (w, z) to the two processes may be discretized as:

$$w = \begin{bmatrix} +1 \\ +1 \\ -1 \\ -1 \end{bmatrix}, z = \begin{bmatrix} +1 \\ -1 \\ +1 \\ -1 \end{bmatrix}$$

The following probability structure achieves the desired correlation between w and z:

$$q = \begin{bmatrix} \dfrac{1 + \rho}{4} \\[2mm] \dfrac{1 - \rho}{4} \\[2mm] \dfrac{1 - \rho}{4} \\[2mm] \dfrac{1 + \rho}{4} \end{bmatrix}$$

where it is important to note that q is a *risk-neutral* probability vector.
Note that this scheme always ensures probabilities between zero and one,
and also that the correlation lies in the range $[-1, 1]$. With an assumed
value of correlation, $\rho = 0.3$, the resultant probabilities are:

$$q = \begin{bmatrix} 0.325 \\ 0.175 \\ 0.175 \\ 0.325 \end{bmatrix}$$

At this point, we have solved for all desired values except the risk
adjustment for credit spreads (i.e., parameter γ). To do so, we compute
the prices of the two period bond at the end of the first period. Since
there are four states, we will have four distinct prices.

$$B(1) = \begin{bmatrix} \dfrac{100}{1 + 0.1029 + \gamma + 0.015} \\[3mm] \dfrac{100}{1 + 0.1029 + \gamma + 0.009} \\[3mm] \dfrac{100}{1 + 0.0973 + \gamma + 0.015} \\[3mm] \dfrac{100}{1 + 0.0973 + \gamma + 0.009} \end{bmatrix}$$

Using identical logic to that earlier, we can solve for the risk adjustment γ using the no-arbitrage equation below:

$$\frac{1}{1.105^2} = \frac{1}{1.09} \times q'B(1)$$

$$= \frac{1}{1.09} \times [0.325 \quad 0.175 \quad 0.175 \quad 0.325] \begin{bmatrix} \dfrac{100}{1 + 0.1029 + \gamma + 0.015} \\[2mm] \dfrac{100}{1 + 0.1029 + \gamma + 0.009} \\[2mm] \dfrac{100}{1 + 0.0973 + \gamma + 0.015} \\[2mm] \dfrac{100}{1 + 0.0973 + \gamma + 0.009} \end{bmatrix}$$

where q and B are vector forms of the probabilities and bond prices respectively. The solution from this model is once again $\gamma = 0.0081$. This implies that the state space for the spread is

$$s(1) = \begin{bmatrix} 0.0231 \\ 0.0171 \\ 0.0231 \\ 0.0171 \end{bmatrix}$$

This lattice is also extendable in the same way to many periods. However, there is no assurance that it will recombine, and, hence, the computing load may be quite severe. However, with the current levels of available computing power, this is usually not a serious problem. There are several ways to manage the lattice to ensure some modicum of recombination, but this is beyond the scope of this chapter.

The extension of the one-factor model to two factors brings several advantages. First, it accounts for correlation between interest rates and spreads. This correlation is often the driving factor behind some of the derivative structures we see in the marketplace. Second, it is useful when credit swaps are being priced where the swap involves a payment of LIBOR versus a fixed rate plus spread. These swaps are sensitive to the stochastic processes of both the riskless rate and credit spread. Pricing of credit swaps would not be complete with a one-factor model.

DETAILED MODELING OF THE SPREAD

So far, we have examined one and two factor models of the spread. These models considered the aggregate spread, and did not decompose it into its default and recovery components. Doing so is essential if we are to price more intricate forms of credit derivatives. For instance, the one factor model enables the pricing of spread options but not credit default swaps, and total return swaps. When we extend the model to two factors, we are able to price some forms of credit swaps, but not default swaps, because the model does not characterize the event of default in any way. Hence, it is critical to model default itself so as to make the components of the spread separately tradeable. Often, buyers of credit derivatives are seeking default protection, and do not mind tolerable levels of overall spread risk. This is analogous to the protection offered by municipal bond insurance.

Decomposing the credit spread requires modeling choices of the processes governing:

1. Default, and

2. Recovery rates in the event of default.

First, we need to establish the notation for this. Let the rate at which default occurs be denoted λ. This "hazard" rate may be a constant or a function of time to maturity of the bond, the level of the current interest rate, or some other factors in the economy. The recovery rate is denoted ϕ, and represents the cents per dollar of the face value of the bond that are recovered when default occurs. Clearly, $\phi \in [0,1)$. For a more detailed and in-depth discussion of hazard-rate models the reader is referred to the work of Madan and Unal (1994, 1998).

There is a well known simple relationship between these parameters and spreads. If the one period riskless rate of interest is r, then the risk-neutral value of a credit risky bond maturing in a single period from now must be equal to the discounted value of expected cash flows in the future. Thus, the pricing equation will be

$$B = \frac{\lambda \phi + (1 - \lambda)}{1 + r}$$

Since we have simply taken the expected value, we have clearly ignored risk aversion (i.e., assumed that the investor is risk-neutral) which means that the parameters λ and ϕ have been set to their risk-neutral values. We shall see why this is important later in the chapter.

It is also true that we can price the risky bond off the spread curve directly. This means that

$$B = \frac{1}{1 + r + s}$$

Therefore, equating the two equations for B, we develop a relationship between the spread and the determinants of the spread. Solving for s, we obtain:

$$s = \frac{\lambda(1 - \phi)(1 + r)}{1 - \lambda(1 - \phi)}$$

It is quite clear that:

1. The spread increases as the hazard rate (λ) rises.
2. The spread declines when the recovery rate (ϕ) improves.

An observation that follows quite simply from this model is that the spread is a function of the term $\lambda(1 - \phi)$ which makes separate identification of the hazard rate and the recovery rate impossible. One way to separate the two rates is to use debt of different seniority from the same firm, since presumably the debt would have the same hazard rate but different recovery rates (see Duffie and Singleton [1995] for a discussion of this issue).

In this article, we shall examine three recent models that have attempted a detailed modeling of default risk.[1] The model by Jarrow, Lando, and Turnbull (1997) models in great detail the event of default and does not focus extensively on recovery rate risk. The model by Das and Tufano (1996) focuses on the modeling of the recovery process as well, along with the attendant no-arbitrage conditions. The model of Duffie and Singleton (1995, 1996) exploits the relationship between spreads and its components in modeling the term structure of swap yields. To make inroads into the concepts behind these models, we first examine the Jarrow-Lando-Turnbull model (which we shall denote as the JLT model).

THE JARROW-LANDO-TURNBULL (JLT) MODEL

This model focuses on modeling default and credit migration in preference to modeling recovery rates. Hence, in this model changes in spreads will be a function of changes in credit rating and the event of default.

The elegant feature of this model is its focus on the changes in bond rating through the use of rating migration matrices. The major rating agencies regularly publish plenty of information on rating changes. In particular, the rating transition matrix is directly available for use in the

---

[1]Several models apart from these have also dealt with this issue, and are equally relevant. However, for parsimony in exposition, we focus here on a limited set.

JLT model. The transition matrix is a simple square matrix depicting the probability in one period of migrating from any one given credit rating to another (including the default class of securities). As an example, consider the following matrix.

$$d = \begin{array}{c} I \\ J \\ D \end{array} \begin{bmatrix} 0.90 & 0.05 & 0.05 \\ 0.10 & 0.80 & 0.10 \\ 0 & 0 & 1.00 \end{bmatrix}$$

It has three states, I, J, and D, standing for "investment grade (I)," "junk grade (J)," and "default (D)." Reading across the rows, we get the probabilities of going from one state to another in one period. For example, the first row provides the probabilities of the rating level changing from I to any of the three possible states. It may remain in state I with a probability of 0.90, change to rating level J with a probability of 0.05, and finally, it may go into default with a probability of 0.05.

The last row is a special row in the sense that it embodies the assumption that once the default state is reached, the system will remain in default for sure (i.e., state D is an absorbing state). The rating transition matrix depicted here is a simplified version of the true matrix, which usually comprises many different rating levels, ranging from AAA to default (D).

In order to set up the model, we also need information on riskless interest rates, and the spreads for each of the rating levels, I and J. As before, we shall assume a two period model, and the riskless zero coupon rates are

$$r = \begin{bmatrix} 0.08 \\ 0.09 \end{bmatrix}$$

The spreads for each rating level are as follows:

$$s_I = \begin{bmatrix} 0.01 \\ 0.015 \end{bmatrix}, s_J = \begin{bmatrix} 0.02 \\ 0.03 \end{bmatrix}$$

The JLT model requires the assumption that there is no correlation between rating migration and interest rates. For simplification of the exposition here, we shall also assume that the riskless rates are nonstochastic, which, given the prior assumption of no correlation, should not affect the pricing of credit risky instruments in any significant way.

The prices of risky debt of maturity one and two periods are computed using the information above:

$$B_I(1) = \frac{1}{1.09}$$

$$B_I(2) = \frac{1}{1.105^2}$$

$$B_J(1) = \frac{1}{1.10}$$

$$B_J(2) = \frac{1}{1.12^2}$$

In the event of default, the JLT model assumes a recovery rate, denoted ϕ. However, it also makes the assumption that the recovery amount is received at the maturity of the bond, not at the time of default. This assumption is a simplification which makes the mathematics of the model highly tractable. It is not a modeling feature which cannot be dispensed with, as the basic strength of the model (i.e., rating migration, would be preserved nevertheless). For our example, we assume that

$$\phi = 0.40$$

At maturity, the bond will be in one of the three states (I, J, or D). If it is in the first two states, the payoff on a zero coupon bond will be 1. If it ends up in default, the payoff is ϕ. The payoff or cash-flow vector for all possible three states is therefore written as

$$C = \begin{bmatrix} 1 \\ 1 \\ \phi \end{bmatrix}$$

In states I and J the bond is not in default and returns a dollar. In state D it defaults and is worth ϕ. In order to get the risk-neutral values of the bonds, which must equal the prices above, we need to get expected cash flows at maturity and discount them back to the present using *risk-neutral* default probabilities. What we have so far in transition matrix d are the *statistical* probabilities. What is necessary is to convert the statistical probabilities into risk-neutral probabilities using a risk adjustment. Therefore, in the JLT model, the off-diagonal probabilities in d will be multiplied by an adjustment, denoted π. As an example, assume a one-period bond is currently in state I. At maturity, the three states have probabilities given by vector

$$d_I = \begin{bmatrix} 0.90 \\ 0.05 \\ 0.05 \end{bmatrix}$$

We transform d_I into the risk-neutral vector q_I with an adjustment π_I as follows:

$$q_I = \begin{bmatrix} 1 - 0.10\pi_I \\ 0.05\pi_I \\ 0.05\pi_I \end{bmatrix}$$

so that the last two elements of d_I have been multiplied by π_I, and the first element is simply the plug required to make the probabilities add up to 1. In order to solve for the risk-adjustment, we find the value of π_I which makes the expected value of discounted cash flows equal to the traded price of the bond:

$$B_I(1) = \frac{1}{1+r} C' q_I$$

$$\frac{1}{1.09} = \frac{1}{1.08} \begin{bmatrix} 1 & 1 & 0.4 \end{bmatrix} \begin{bmatrix} 1 - 0.10\pi_I \\ 0.05\pi_I \\ 0.05\pi_I \end{bmatrix}$$

The solution is

$$\pi_I(1) = 0.30581$$

A similar computation may be undertaken for one-period junk debt, so as to get the required risk adjustment.

$$B_J(1) = \frac{1}{1+r} C' q_J$$

$$\frac{1}{1.10} = \frac{1}{1.08} \begin{bmatrix} 1 & 1 & 0.4 \end{bmatrix} \begin{bmatrix} 0.10\pi_J \\ 1 - 0.20\pi_J \\ 0.10\pi_J \end{bmatrix}$$

which results in

$$\pi_J(1) = 0.30303$$

In general if we define the cumulative probability of default over n periods from any state $i = \{I, J\}$ as $q_{di}(n)$, then the risk adjustment for the nth period for a bond initially in state i, will be written as follows:

$$\pi_i(n) = \left[1 - \left(\frac{1 + r(n)}{1 + r(n) + s(n)}\right)^n\right]\frac{1}{(1 - \phi)q_{di}(n)}$$

For example, to recheck

$$\pi_J(1) = \left[1 - \left(\frac{1 + 0.08}{1 + 0.08 + 0.02}\right)^1\right]\frac{1}{(1 - 0.4) \times 0.1} = 0.30303$$

Therefore, we now obtain the risk-neutral transition matrix for one period from these calculations. In general, we shall denote this matrix as $Q(n)$.

$$Q(1) = \begin{array}{c} I \\ J \\ D \end{array}\begin{bmatrix} 0.9694 & 0.0153 & 0.0153 \\ 0.0303 & 0.9394 & 0.0303 \\ 0 & 0 & 1.00 \end{bmatrix}$$

Moving on, similar logic can be applied to obtain the two-period risk-neutral transition matrix. First, recognize that the two-period statistical transition matrix is easily derived from the one-period matrix d. This follows from a simple property of these transition matrices where squaring the one period matrix delivers the two period *cumulative* default probability transition matrix, assuming that the periods are identical in terms of default risk. Likewise the three period matrix would be simply the one period matrix taken to the power three.

$$d(2) = d^2$$

$$= \begin{bmatrix} 0.90 & 0.05 & 0.05 \\ 0.10 & 0.80 & 0.10 \\ 0 & 0 & 1.00 \end{bmatrix}\begin{bmatrix} 0.90 & 0.05 & 0.05 \\ 0.10 & 0.80 & 0.10 \\ 0 & 0 & 1.00 \end{bmatrix}$$

$$= \begin{bmatrix} 0.815 & 0.085 & 0.100 \\ 0.170 & 0.645 & 0.185 \\ 0 & 0 & 1 \end{bmatrix}$$

Therefore,

$$q_i(2) = \begin{bmatrix} 1 - 0.185\pi_i(2) \\ 0.085\pi_i(2) \\ 0.100\pi_i(2) \end{bmatrix}$$

and

$$q_j(2) = \begin{bmatrix} 0.170\pi_j(2) \\ 1 - 0.355\pi_j(2) \\ 0.185\pi_j(2) \end{bmatrix}$$

Using our equation, we can solve for the risk adjustments:

$$\pi_i(2) = \left[1 - \left(\frac{1 + 0.09}{1 + 0.09 + 0.015} \right)^2 \right] \frac{1}{(1 - 0.4) \times 0.1} = 0.449417$$

$$\pi_j(2) = \left[1 - \left(\frac{1 + 0.09}{1 + 0.09 + 0.03} \right)^2 \right] \frac{1}{(1 - 0.4) \times 0.185} = 0.476162$$

which we plug back to adjust the statistical matrix $d(2)$ to give the two period risk-neutral transition matrix $Q(2)$:

$$Q(2) = \begin{bmatrix} 0.9169 & 0.0382 & 0.0449 \\ 0.0809 & 0.8310 & 0.0881 \\ 0 & 0 & 1 \end{bmatrix}$$

This completes the implementation of the JLT model in its simplest form. Armed with the risk-neutral rating transition matrices, computed off observable term structures, the pricing of several credit risk derivatives becomes possible. For example, in order to price a default swap we need to multiply the cumulative probability of default by the loss on default, and discount it at the interest rate for two periods. All this information is provided from the risk-neutral analysis above.

The following are the advantages of the JLT model:

1. The model explicitly accounts for default risk.

2. It also models default not as a sudden occurrence, but correctly, as a process of migration from better credit quality to default. By modeling a spectrum of credit ratings, the approach also allows credit derivatives indexed to ratings to be

easily valued. A direct example of such a derivative is a credit-sensitive note, where the issuer pays a coupon indexed to the current rating of the bond.

3. The model also allows the pricing of default swaps, since the event of default is explicitly modeled. So far, we have seen that pure spread models do not admit the pricing of credit default swaps.

The simple version of the model has some drawbacks:

1. Even when interest rates are stochastic, the model requires the assumption that riskless rates are uncorrelated with default, thereby making credit spreads uncorrelated with interest rates, which usually contradicts stylized phenomena.

2. The Markov transition matrix is obtained from historical data, which may not reflect accurately future credit scenarios—however, this is not a critical problem, and adjustments may be made to this matrix to reflect the trader's view or forecasts without amending the technical structure of the model in any way.

3. Assuming that recovered cash flows on default are received at maturity is necessary to make the model tractable, but violates practice. However, here too, the model may be modified to account for reality with little damage to its essential structure.

4. The model implies that all securities with the same credit rating have the same spread. The model is intended to be an explanation of average spreads for a rating class rather than to explain spreads for individual bonds.

Overall, this is an excellent structure on which more sophistication may be placed so as to make the model reflect most features of credit risky instruments, and thereby make for a rich framework in which to price credit derivatives. Extensions to the JLT model have been undertaken in the Das-Tufano (DT) (1996) model, where making the recovery rate stochastic surmounts the drawbacks of the JLT model. Another approach is to make the probability of default correlated with the riskless interest rate. These models, which make the hazard (default) rate uncertain are those of Jarrow and Turnbull (1995), Lando (1994), and Duffie-Singleton (1995).

THE DAS-TUFANO (DT) MODEL

This model is an extension of JLT, and uses credit ratings to characterize the probability of default. In the JLT model, on default, there is a *constant* recovery rate. Therefore, the JLT model is characterized by a variability in spreads which is driven purely by changes in credit ratings. The DT model makes the recovery rate in the event of default stochastic as well, and provides a two-factor decomposition of credit spreads. The effect of this innovation is:

1. It allows more variability in the spreads on risky debt. The additional source of variability is key in reaching acceptable levels of spread volatility.

2. Spreads are now a function of factors other than pure quality levels. In the pure JLT model credit spreads change only when credit ratings change, whereas in the debt markets credit spreads change even when ratings have not changed.

3. Recovery rates are correlated with the term structure of interest rates. This results in a model where credit spreads are correlated with interest rates.

4. By choosing different recovery rate processes for firms within the same credit rating class, variability of spreads may be made firm specific, rather than rating class specific.

5. Making recovery rates stochastic enables the pricing of a wide range of spread-based exotic debt and option contracts. The model provides a means to price resetting debt when the yardstick for the reset may be the riskless interest rate, the firm's credit rating, or its spread over Treasuries. It also enables the valuation of risky debt when the counterparties have different credit risks (e.g., in the pricing of risky coupon swaps).

The model's explicit link to observable credit ratings and credit spreads is critical. Not only does it make the implementation of the model feasible, but also it permits us to value standard bonds, and credit-contingent instruments.

In general, models for pricing risky debt can be expressed simply using the following equation:

$$B(r, t, .) = P(r, t) - L(.)Q(.)P(r, t) \qquad (5.3)$$

where r is the riskless interest rate, t is maturity, $B(.)$ is the price of zero coupon risky debt, $P(.)$ is the price of riskless debt of the same maturity, $Q(.)$ is the pseudoprobability of default and $L(.) = 1 - \phi(.)$, the loss rate, is equal to one minus the amount of the bond's value recovered in the event of default. And $\phi(.)$, as before, is the recovery rate on default, which is now assumed to be stochastic.

This conceptual specification was first examined and modeled in detail by Longstaff and Schwartz (1995). Once again, notice that the spread is a function of the composite $L(.)Q(.)$ (i.e., recovery rate and probability of default), and neither is separately identifiable. Hence, this corresponds to a similar point made in the Duffie-Singleton (1995) framework. By making any of the two components $L(.)$ or $Q(.)$ correlated with r, it is possible to make credit spreads correlated with the riskless rate. The DT model assumes the recovery rate $\phi(.)$ to be stochastic and correlated with r thereby getting the required correlation. It is usually more tractable to do it this way than to make $Q(.)$ correlated with r (to see the alternative approach refer to Lando [1994]).

Model

The pricing model has two parts: (1) the term structure model, and (2) the default model. Any model may be used for the term structure (e.g., Heath-Jarrow-Morton [1992], Hull-White [1990], Black-Derman-Toy [1990], etc.)

The probabilities of moving from one credit rating to another are specified by a transition probability matrix, which is easily estimated (the JLT model). The approach involves an amalgam of existing models, as well as an extension to stochastic default recovery rates, as in Jarrow and Turnbull (1995), which may be correlated with the term structure of interest rates.

Modeling proceeds as follows: First, obtain the risk-neutral set up for the evolution of the term structure of interest rates; Second, ascertain the risk-neutral probabilities of the default process. The combination of the two provides a stochastic framework for the arbitrage-free pricing of risky debt. Notice that this is exactly in the spirit of the spread models presented earlier in this chapter.

Implementation

We illustrate the model with a simple two-period example. Assume similar initial term structure variables as in the section on the JLT model. The model has two periods of unit length of time each. The riskless rates and spreads are:

$$r = \begin{bmatrix} 0.08 \\ 0.09 \end{bmatrix}, s_l = \begin{bmatrix} 0.010 \\ 0.015 \end{bmatrix}, s_J = \begin{bmatrix} 0.02 \\ 0.03 \end{bmatrix}$$

Assume a binomial lattice with equal probabilities on each branch. And as before, the interest rate process is a discrete square-root model.

$$r(t) = r(0) + \alpha[\beta - r(0)] + \delta \pm \eta\sqrt{r(0)}$$

where we set $\alpha = 0.3$, $\beta = 0.10$, and $\eta = 0.1$. Then δ is the risk adjustment which works out to be 0.0141. As worked out before, the two risk-neutral spot interest rates in the next period will be

$$r(1) = \begin{cases} 0.1029 \\ 0.0973 \end{cases}$$

This completes the set up of the riskless interest rate model. With this setting, we can price riskless debt out to a maturity of two periods.

We now develop a stochastic process for recovery rates as required in the DT model. Any process can be chosen for recovery rates as long as they remain with the range [0,1]. The recovery rates will be chosen so as to be correlated with riskless rates, and, hence, we can achieve the correlation of credit spreads with the term structure. At time 0, we assume that the recovery rates are as follows:

$$\phi_I(0) = 0.59$$
$$\phi_J(0) = 0.41$$

With this initial choice, we can then choose a stochastic process for recovery rates so as to obtain rates in future periods. A simple process may be chosen such as $\phi_i(t) = \phi_i(0) \pm \sigma_i$, where σ_i is some appropriately chosen parameter. Here, we simply pick values for the evolution of the spread over time as a binomial process. Since we have two stochastic variables now, both binomial, we shall represent the joint evolution of the lattice as a tree with a four-way branching scheme. Also, assume that the recovery rates are negatively correlated with riskless interest rates and that this correlation is $\rho = 0.5$. Then, at the end of one period, four possible states arise, and the values of the model variables in these four states are as follows:

$$r(1) = \begin{bmatrix} 0.1029 \\ 0.1029 \\ 0.0973 \\ 0.0973 \end{bmatrix}$$

$$\phi_I(1) = \begin{bmatrix} 0.62 \\ 0.58 \\ 0.62 \\ 0.58 \end{bmatrix}$$

$$\phi_j(1) = \begin{bmatrix} 0.45 \\ 0.35 \\ 0.45 \\ 0.35 \end{bmatrix}$$

$$prob = \begin{bmatrix} 0.125 \\ 0.375 \\ 0.375 \\ 0.125 \end{bmatrix}$$

The exact details of the way in which the state space is generated is not critical to the theory of the model. The example above is just one scheme that may be implemented. It has negative correlation between riskless rates and the spreads. This is easily seen from the fact that when riskless rates and interest rates move (from time 0) in the same direction, lower probabilities are assigned than when they move in opposite directions.

As we shall see, it is quite useful to compute *state prices* (denoted by variable w) off the riskless interest rate tree in order to speed up calculations in the model.[2] At time zero the state price is simply unity, i.e.,

$$w(0) = 1$$

At each of the four states in the next period, the state price vector is given by the product of the probability of the branch times the previous state price divided by the riskless rate at the initial node of the branch:

$$w(t + 1) = prob \times w(t) \times \frac{1}{1 + r(t)}$$

---

[2]State prices are the current value of a security that pays off a dollar in a single specific state in the future, and zero in all other states. For example, if there are two possible states ("up" and "down") at the same time in the future, then the state price of the "up" state would be the value of a dollar received in that state times the risk-neutral probability of that state, discounted to the present, using a riskless discount rate. State prices are useful since they allow us to compute the price of any security by multiplying the payoffs of the security by state prices in each state, and then add these values up.

Imposing these calculations, we get the state prices at time 1 to be:

$$w(1) = \begin{bmatrix} 0.115741 \\ 0.347222 \\ 0.347222 \\ 0.115741 \end{bmatrix}$$

We shall also assume the same rating transition matrix as before

$$d = \begin{matrix} I \\ J \\ D \end{matrix} \begin{bmatrix} 0.90 & 0.05 & 0.05 \\ 0.10 & 0.80 & 0.10 \\ 0 & 0 & 1.00 \end{bmatrix}$$

and now, the problem is to compute the risk-neutral transition matrix so that various credit sensitive derivatives may be priced. We start with the one period risky bond of rating class I. At the end of a period, it may default, with risk-neutral *first passage probability* $q_i^0(t)$ in which case it will return an amount $\phi_i(1)$. The first-passage probabilities are written with superscript zero, so as to distinguish them from cumulative probabilities, written as $[q_i(t)]$. We call these "first-passage" probabilities as they are the probability of defaulting in any period t, assuming no previous default. Since there are four states of the world at time 1, in each state the expected cash flow is

$$C_i(1) = q_i^0(1)\phi_i(1) + (1 - q_i^0(1))1$$

This is the "expected" cash flow, (i.e., the recovery rate multiplied by the probability of default plus one times the probability of no default). The present value of this expected cash flow for a bond of rating class I is

$$w(1)'C_I(1) = [0.115741 \quad 0.34722 \quad 0.347222 \quad 0.115741] \quad (5.4)$$

$$\begin{bmatrix} 0.62q_I^0(1) + 1 - q_I^0(1) \\ 0.58q_I^0(1) + 1 - q_I^0(1) \\ 0.62q_I^0(1) + 1 - q_I^0(1) \\ 0.58q_I^0(1) + 1 - q_I^0(1) \end{bmatrix} \quad (5.5)$$

In equilibrium, this must equal the price of the one year risky bond, which is

$$\frac{1}{1.09} = w(1)'C_I(1)$$

Solving this equation provides the value of the risk-neutral first passage default probability,

$$q_I^0(1) = 0.0229$$

A similar calculation undertaken for rating class J gives the probability

$$q_J^0(1) = 0.0303$$

Working back from these probabilities gives the risk adjustment to the statistical probability of default

$$\pi_I(1) = \frac{q_I^0(1)}{d_I(1)} = \frac{0.0229}{0.05} = 0.4580$$

$$\pi_J(1) = \frac{q_J^0(1)}{d_J(1)} = \frac{0.0303}{0.10} = 0.3030$$

This allows the adjustment to matrix d to provide the entire risk-neutral rating change matrix for one period, the calculations being exactly those of the JLT model:

$$Q(1) = \begin{bmatrix} 0.9542 & 0.0229 & 0.0229 \\ 0.0303 & 0.9394 & 0.0303 \\ 0 & 0 & 1.00 \end{bmatrix}$$

In this implementation, the procedure may be actually simplified quite drastically by noticing that the equation (5.4) can be written as

$$\frac{w(0)}{1 + r(0)}[\overline{\phi}q_i^0(1) + 1 - q_i^0(1)] = \frac{1}{1 + r(0) + s_i(0)}$$

where $\overline{\phi}$ represents the average recovery rate over the entire time period one. Then, the calculations become the solutions to the following equations:

$$\frac{1}{1 + 0.08}[0.6q_I^0(1) + 1 - q_I^0(1)] = \frac{1}{1.09}$$

$$\frac{1}{1 + 0.08}[0.04q_J^0(1) + 1 - q_J^0(1)] = \frac{1}{1.10}$$

giving the solution values above. This is possible since recovery rates enter the payoffs to the bond in a linear fashion.

Using the same logic, the values for the second period are developed. At the end of period one, there are four end nodes. Each of these branches out to four nodes each, providing a total of 16 end nodes after two periods. The procedure to be imposed here is to obtain the expected cash flows in each end node (accounting for default and recovery), and then discount these cash flows back. Also, since we are valuing a two-period bond, default is possible at the end of the first period as well, and a possible cash flow may arise in any of the four nodes after one period. This must also be probabilistically weighted and discounted back.

If recovery rates enter the cash flows in a linear way (i.e., they are linear in default probabilities, or are not functions of default probabilities), then the simplification suggested above allows the calculation of the lattice without investigating the 16 end nodes in detail. All we really need is the average recovery rate over the time period two, emanating from the appropriate state at the end of period one. Since there are four states at the end of period one, there are four average values of recovery corresponding to each of these states. Assume, for illustrative purposes, the following state space for average recovery rates:

$$\overline{\phi_I}(1) = \begin{bmatrix} 0.63 \\ 0.59 \\ 0.63 \\ 0.59 \end{bmatrix}, \ \overline{\phi_J}(1) = \begin{bmatrix} 0.46 \\ 0.34 \\ 0.46 \\ 0.34 \end{bmatrix}$$

The value of the two period risky zero coupon bond is the present value of cash flows at time one and time two. At time one a cash flow is generated only if default occurs. The present value of this cash flow for both classes of bonds is as follows:

$$PV[\text{Cash flow}] = \text{prob(default)} \times \text{average recovery} \times \frac{1}{1+r}$$

$$PVC_I(1) = 0.0229 \times 0.6 \times \frac{1}{1.08}$$

$$PVC_J(1) = 0.0303 \times 0.4 \times \frac{1}{1.08}$$

The expected cash flows in the second period comprise the probability weighted cash flows at the 16 nodes at the end of period two. Since recovery rates are linear, the present value of these cash flows is

$$PVC_i(2) = \sum_{k=1}^{4} \left(\frac{w_k(1)}{1 + r_k(1)} [\overline{\phi}_k q_i^0(2) + 1 - q_i^0(2)] \right)$$

where k simply indexes the four states, and as before $\overline{\phi}$ is the average recovery rate proceeding from the each of the four states. Hence, plugging in the actual parameter values provides the following cash flows for each rating class at maturity:

$$PVC_i(2) = \frac{0.115741}{1.1029} [0.63 q_i^0(2) + 1 - q_i^0(2)]$$

$$+ \frac{0.347222}{1.1029} [0.59 q_i^0(2) + 1 - q_i^0(2)]$$

$$+ \frac{0.347222}{1.0973} [0.63 q_i^0(2) + 1 - q_i^0(2)]$$

$$+ \frac{0.115741}{1.0973} [0.59 q_i^0(2) + 1 - q_i^0(2)]$$

$$PVC_j(2) = \frac{0.115741}{1.1029} [0.46 q_j^0(2) + 1 - q_j^0(2)]$$

$$+ \frac{0.347222}{1.1029} [0.34 q_j^0(2) + 1 - q_j^0(2)]$$

$$+ \frac{0.347222}{1.0973} [0.46 q_j^0(2) + 1 - q_j^0(2)]$$

$$+ \frac{0.115741}{1.0973} [0.34 q_j^0(2) + 1 - q_j^0(2)]$$

The following two equations then provide the solutions for $\{q_i^0(2), q_j^0(2)\}$.

$$PVC_i(1) + PVC_i(2) = \frac{1}{1.105^2}$$

$$PVC_j(1) + PVC_j(2) = \frac{1}{1.12^2}$$

Solving we obtain

$$q_i^0(2) = 0.107905$$
$$q_j^0(2) = 0.110326$$

These probabilities are "first passage" probabilities (i.e., the probability of defaulting in the second period, conditional on no prior default). In order to develop the matrix $Q(2)$ for the two-period cumulative ratings transitions, we convert the risk-neutral first-passage default probabilities above into cumulative ones.

$$q_i(2) = q_i(1) + [1 - q_i(1)]q_i^0(2)$$
$$= q_i^0(1) + [1 - q_i^0(1)]q_i^0(2)$$

since for the first period, first-passage and cumulative probabilities are the same. The resultant values we need are

$$q_i(2) = 0.0229 + [1 - 0.0229](0.107905) = 0.128334$$
$$q_j(2) = 0.0303 + [1 - 0.0303](0.110326) = 0.137283$$

Therefore the risk adjustments for the second period are:

$$\pi_i(2) = \frac{0.128334}{0.100} = 1.28334$$

$$\pi_j(2) = \frac{0.137283}{0.185} = 0.74207$$

These adjustments may be applied to the statistical matrix d^2

$$d^2 = \begin{bmatrix} 0.815 & 0.085 & 0.100 \\ 0.170 & 0.645 & 0.185 \\ 0 & 0 & 1.000 \end{bmatrix}$$

to get the risk-neutral cumulative transition matrix

$$Q(2) = \begin{bmatrix} 0.7626 & 0.1091 & 0.1283 \\ 0.1262 & 0.7365 & 0.1373 \\ 0 & 0 & 1.00 \end{bmatrix}$$

Hence, after these calculations we have several items of computed data, which allows the pricing of almost any kind of credit derivative. The data that is available now are:

- Risk-neutral ratings transition matrices for both periods [i.e., $Q(1)$, $Q(2)$]. These, of course, contain the cumulative probabilities of default [$q_i(t)$]. The required risk adjustments [$\pi_i(t)$] to the statistical transition matrix (d) are also achieved as a by-product.

- A bivariate lattice of riskless interest rates (r) and recovery rates (ϕ) satisfying no-arbitrage conditions, and providing for correlation between recovery rates and interest rates.

- State prices (w) which help speed up calculations on the lattice.
- First-passage probabilities of default for each rating class: $[q_i^0(t)]$, $i = I, J$.

Using this information, the following derivative products are priced by generating the necessary cash flows at each node on the lattice and discounting the cash flows back by multiplication by the state prices to obtain present values:

1. Plain-vanilla risky debt for any rating class: Using first passage probabilities, generate the desired cash flows, and then multiply the cash flows at each node by the corresponding state prices gives the security value.

2. Rating-sensitive debt: bonds may be floated where the issuer agrees to reset the coupon depending on the credit rating of the bond. At inception, an agreed upon coupon menu is offered and as the rating changes, the coupon may move up or down. The DT model is ideally suited to price such debt since the rating transition matrix provides risk-neutral information on rating changes which can be directly used to generate cash flows at each node on the tree.

3. Spread-adjusted notes: The coupon may also be indexed to the spread at each node. This is achieved by computing the forward spread at each node on the lattice. Since the price of risky debt is known at each node, and so is the riskless rate, it is quite simple to compute the credit spread at each node as well. Then pricing spread-adjusted debt becomes feasible.

4. Spread options: Given the computed spread at each node, it's easy to price spread options since cash flows may be generated at each node by comparing the spread at the node with the strike rate.

5. Total return swaps: Since the price of any underlying risky bond is computable at each node on the tree, the total return on the bond may also be easily calculated. This enables the pricing of total return swaps. For example, a total return swap on an I-rated instrument versus LIBOR is easily priced because the return and LIBOR (riskless rate) information is already available on the tree.

6. Credit default swaps: The probabilities and loss from default may be computed at every node. Using the state prices at each node, the product of loss, probabilities, and state prices

provides the value of the default swap. Care must be taken to use the first-passage probabilities.

7. Floating rate debt: FRNs are instruments with credit risk but very little interest rate risk. The credit risk component is easily valued off the tree.

8. Swaps by counterparties of differing credit standing: Since the model derives the risk-neutral transition matrix for each rating class, cash flows for swaps where the two counterparties differ in credit rating are easily priced. At each node on the lattice, the probabilities of being in default for various counterparties is available, as well as the information required to ascertain whether the swap is in or out of the money. Applying the swap cash flows to the probabilities gives the credit risk adjusted cash flows which can then be multiplied by state prices to give the required swap value.

Therefore, we have seen that the JLT model may be extended to a larger framework in which almost all models of pricing risky debt may be subsumed.

THE DUFFIE-SINGLETON ANALYSIS

In a recent paper Duffie and Singleton (1995) show how the pricing of risky debt may be analyzed in the same way as riskless debt, where the discount rate comprises the riskless rate plus an adjustment made up of a function of the hazard rate and recovery rate. Maintaining the same notation as before, and assuming that we are operating under the risk-neutral measure, we can argue that, in a very small interval of time Δ, the value of a risky bond is equal to

$$B = e^{-r\Delta}[(1 - \lambda\Delta) + (\lambda\Delta)\phi]$$
$$\simeq (1 - r\Delta)[(1 - \lambda\Delta) + (\lambda\Delta)\phi]$$

Here λ is the annualized hazard rate, and r is also annualized. Expanding this expression and then eliminating terms in Δ^2 (which in continuous time would be zero), we arrive at

$$B \simeq 1 - \Delta[r + \lambda(1- \phi)]$$
$$\simeq e^{-\Delta[r+\lambda(1-\phi)]}$$
$$= e^{-R\Delta}$$

where R may be thought of as the "risky" rate of interest. Using this model, the risky rate of interest may be written as the sum of the riskless rate, and a spread term equal to the product of the hazard rate (λ) and the proportionate loss on default ($1 - \phi$).

$$R = r + \lambda(1 - \phi)$$
$$= r + s$$

This analysis also reinforces the fact that the spread is not easy to decompose into default and recovery risk components, unless additional information is brought into the model. Note here that the spread is once again a composite of the two risks, and each elements is not separately identifiable.

The Duffie-Singleton (1995) model is completely general, and R comprises three elements of risk (i.e., the riskless rate, hazard rate, and recovery rate), all of which may be treated as stochastic and correlated with each other in the most general version of their formulation. These models may be implemented on lattices which, with all three stochastic processes, makes for a difficult implementation in order to match the existing prices of riskless and risky debt exactly. In lattice implementations, a branching process needs to be chosen to provide for a default event branch. However, this model may be thought of as a very general framework in which to price risky debt derivatives.

We can exemplify this model with a brief example. Let $\lambda = 0.1$ (i.e., a 10 percent chance of default in a year). Also, assume that the recovery rate is $\phi = 0.5$. We let today's one-year riskless rate of interest be 9 percent, and after a year assume that this changes to either 11 percent or 7 percent with equal probability. The price of a two-period riskless zero-coupon bond will be

$$100 \times 0.5 \times [e^{-0.11} + e^{-0.07}] \times e^{-0.09} = 83.54$$

Under the model the risky discount rates are simply the riskless rate plus spread, i.e.,

$$R = r + 0.1(1 - 0.5) = r + 0.05$$

Therefore, to price risky bonds we use a current rate of 14 percent (0.09 + 0.05), and the rates after one year will be 16 percent (0.11 + 0.05) and 12 percent (0.07 + 0.05). The price of the bond will be

$$100 \times 0.5 \times [e^{-0.16} + e^{-0.12}] \times e^{-0.14} = 75.59$$

This can be confirmed by working with the risky cash flows on the bond. At the end of two years, the expected cash flow is

$$100 \times e^{-0.1} + 50 \times (1 - e^{-0.1}) = 95.24$$

where $(1 - e^{-0.1})$ is the probability of default. Discounting this back at the two possible values of the riskless rate gives

$$95.24e^{-0.07} = 88.80$$

and

$$95.24e^{-0.11} = 85.32$$

Taking 95 percent of these values and discounting back gives

$$[88.80 + 85.32] \times 0.9524 \times e^{-0.09} = 75.78$$

which is roughly equal to that from the direct calculation (rounding occurs since the recovery rate has not been handled in continuous time). The Duffie-Singleton model thus allows users of regular term structure models for government bonds to directly apply them to risky debt, by replacing the riskless rates with risky rates from the formula above. These models are now known as "reduced-form" models of risky debt pricing.

CONCLUSIONS AND OTHER IMPORTANT ISSUES FOR CREDIT RISK MODELS

This chapter focused almost entirely on pricing models. We surveyed a range of approaches to modeling credit derivatives, and examined simple versions of some major extant models. One strand of the literature was given short shrift here: those of the Merton (1974) type, where the value of the firm is modeled instead of the prices of risky and riskless securities, which are functions of the value of the firm. Papers of this class are theoretically appealing [see Longstaff and Schwartz (1995), Bhattacharya and Mason (1981), Black and Cox (1976), Shimko, Tejima, and Van Deventer (1993), Nielsen, Saa-Requejo, and Santa-Clara (1993), Das (1995)], yet pose enormous implementation problems, especially when dealing with risky bonds of firms with complicated capital structures. Moreover, to examine that entire stream of work would have led to an enormous diversion from the simple models pursued here. There is no doubt that the Merton approach is enormously important too, and the modeler of credit derivatives is well-advised to take a careful look at these models in addition to those in this chapter, before making an engineering decision on pricing approach.

While this chapter aims to focus primarily on the pricing of credit derivatives, there are several other issues that bear addressing in conjunction with pricing. In this section, I shall focus on only two of these issues, since they pertain directly to pricing models. These are (a) portfolio credit risk and (b) pricing to obtain a rate of return on capital.

The pricing models we have discussed so far, envisage a framework for the no-arbitrage pricing of derivatives with credit risk. Quite clearly, since these models fit the existing term structure of interest rates and credit spreads, the lattices that are developed may be used to price several differently structured products. Moreover, for each security that is priced, the initial conditions (parameters) may be perturbed and numerical derivatives calculated, so that "hedge" ratios with respect to all the underlying sources of risk may be obtained, and then, these hedge ratios may be used to put in place the required hedges. Thus, it is clear that the pricing technology directly supports portfolio risk management. It is in no way any different from the technology already in place for equity, foreign exchange, commodity, and interest rate derivatives.

Recently, simulation methods have also been developed to undertake credit portfolio management, the essence of these methods being that a wide variety of default scenarios may be generated, and complete and satisfactory stress testing of credit portfolios can also be undertaken. In addition, the simulation approach allows for a large number of sources of risk, and can be combined with other risk management methods. For example, it allows the comingling of price and credit risk into one risk management system. Simulation is a very powerful approach towards credit risk management. It is also directly extensible, and can support large portfolios adequately. The choice of a pricing technology versus risk management by simulation is one every institution dealing in credit derivatives must face. If the pricing technology has been developed, it clearly makes sense to use it for risk management, thereby ensuring consistency of the front end dealing process with the ex-post management of positions. This also ensures that the risk measures are also consistent with no-arbitrage, since the model accounts for this issue. With simulation off the statistical matrices, risk measures do not in any way conform to risk-neutral (i.e., no-arbitrage pricing).

Using pricing technology, such as that developed in this chapter, is often described as "relative pricing." The models here used observed values of riskless rates and spreads, developed a lattice, and then enabled pricing off the lattice which ensured (a) that no arbitrage was admitted, and (b) that all securities were priced correctly relative to each other. This leads to the second major issue of this section (i.e., an often adopted approach by most financial institutions): when not availing of a relative pricing model. This is the method of pricing a security to ensure a risk-adjusted rate of return on capital. If the same derivative were priced by two financial houses with differing balance sheets, quite clearly, the same security would have two different prices. In fact, differential valuations will make it hard to create a market, since when there is little agreement on price, how can one expect to see price formation. On the other hand, when pricing using relative pricing technology, the simple fact that consistency across security prices is achieved makes for better establishment of markets.

One must not fail to recognize however, that even relative pricing fails when the inputs used by participants differs, because they have differential information. However, relative pricing markets evidence a convergence of information that does not come with pricing for a rate of return. The mechanism of relative pricing offers boundless hope that prices, models, and information will all converge to the optimal welfare maximizing one. We can only wait and see whether this optimism on pricing technology leads to the rapid growth of this new market in credit derivatives.

B I B L I O G R A P H Y

Bhattacharya, S., and S.P. Mason: "Risky Debt, Jump Processes, and Safety Covenants," *Journal of Financial Economics*, v9(3), 1981, pp. 281–307.

Black, F., and J.C. Cox: "Valuing Corporate Securities: Some Effects of Bond Indenture Provisions," *Journal of Finance*, v31(2), 1976, pp. 351–367.

Black, F., E. Derman, and W. Toy: "A One-Factor Model of Interest Rates and Its Application to Treasury Bond Options," *Financial Analysts Journal*, v46, 1990, pp. 33–39.

Cox, J., J. Ingersoll, and S. Ross: "A Theory of the Term Structure of Interest Rates," *Econometrica*, v53, 1986, pp. 385–407.

Das, Sanjiv: "Credit Risk Derivatives," *Journal of Derivatives*, v2(3), 1995, pp. 7–23.

Das, Sanjiv, and Stephen Lynagh: "An Overview of Credit Derivatives," Harvard Business School Case No. 9–297–086, 1997.

Das, Sanjiv, and Peter Tufano: "Pricing Credit Sensitive Debt when Interest Rates, Credit Ratings and Credit Spreads Are Stochastic," *Journal of Financial Engineering*, v5, 1996, pp. 161–198.

Duffie, D., and K. Singleton: "An Econometric Model of the Term Structure of Interest Rate Swap Yields," *Journal of Finance*, v52, 1997, pp. 1287–1323.

Duffie, D., and K. Singleton: "Modelling Term Structures of Defaultable Bonds," Working paper, Stanford University, 1997, forthcoming *Review of Financial Studies*.

Harrison, J.M., and D.M. Kreps: "Martingales and Arbitrage in Multiperiod Security Markets," *Journal of Economic Theory*, v20, 1982, pp. 381–408.

Heath, D., R. Jarrow, and A. Morton: "Bond Pricing and the Term Structure of Interest Rates: A New Methodology for Contingent Claims Valuation," *Econometrica*, v60, 1992, pp. 77–106.

Ho, T., and S. Lee: "Term Structure Movements and Pricing Interest Rate Contingent Claims," *Journal of Finance*, v41, 1986, pp. 1011–1029.

Hull, J, and A. White "Pricing Interest Rate Derivative Securities" *Review of Financial Studies*, 1990, v3(4), pp. 573–592.

Jarrow, R., D. Lando, and S. Turnbull: "A Markov Model for the Term Structure of Credit Spreads," *Review of Financial Studies*, v10, 1997, pp. 481–523.

Jarrow, R., and S. Turnbull: "Pricing Options on Financial Securities Subject to Default Risk," *Journal of Finance*, v50, 1995, pp. 53–86.

Lando, D.: "On Cox Processes and Credit Risky Bonds," *Review of Derivatives Research*, 1998, v2(3), pp. 99–120.

Longstaff, F., and E. Schwartz: "A Simple Approach to Valuing Risky Fixed and Floating Rate Debt," *Journal of Finance*, v50(3), 1995, pp. 789–819.

Madan, D., and H. Unal: "Pricing the Risks of Default," Working paper, University of Maryland, *Review of Derivatives Research*, 1998, v2, pp. 121–160.

Madan, D., and H. Unal: "A Two Factor Hazard Rate Model for Pricing Risky Debt in a Complex Capital Structure," Working paper, University of Maryland, 1998.

Merton, R.C.: "On the Pricing of Corporate Debt: The Risk Structure of Interest Rates," *Journal of Finance*, v29, 1974, pp. 449–470.

Nielsen, T.N., J. Saa-Requejo, and P. Santa-Clara: "Default Risk and Interest Rate Risk: The Term Structure of Default Spreads," Working Paper, INSEAD, 1993.

Shimko, D., N. Tejima, and D.R. Van Deventer: "The Pricing of Risky Debt when Interest Rates are Stochastic," *Journal of Fixed Income*, September 1993, pp. 58–65.

Credit Derivatives Pricing Dictionary

Hardy M. Hodges, Ph.D.
Vice President, Global Credit Derivatives, Chase Securities, Inc.

The pricing of credit derivative products is still largely in a developmental phase. This is evidenced by the increasing number of academic papers on this topic over the last few years, and the number of differing pricing methodologies. In this guide to pricing credit derivatives, only the most simplistic and practical pricing approaches are presented.

Since the pricing of many credit derivative products are linked to those of other products, the format of this guide is dictionary-style, which enables products or pricing concepts to be easily cross-referenced. Terms that are defined elsewhere in the pricing dictionary are capitalized. The modular approach presented here allows a substantially condensed exposition of credit derivatives pricing.

An important general observation is that there are a number of credit derivative products that have pricing models and can be priced, but they cannot be hedged efficiently via available instruments that trade in the credit marketplace. Examples of such products include Credit Spread Options, Credit Rating Options, and Digital Default Swaps. This situation is fairly unique compared to other types of derivatives (e.g., equity or currency), where hedging is typically achieved by dynamically trading the underlying asset(s). The pricing of such credit derivatives is then based upon the statistical likelihood of a payout, risk tolerance, and a selected pricing model. Since there is dependency upon the pricing model chosen, the pricing is subject to model risk. At some point, when the credit derivative markets develop further and dynamic hedging becomes feasible, pricing will be directly linked to hedging and model risk should be less of a concern.

ASSET SWAP PRICING

A par asset swap combines the sale of an asset, typically a fixed-rate bond, to a party at a price of par without accrued interest, and an interest rate swap whereby the coupons on the asset are swapped for an index (typically LIBOR) plus a spread. The asset swap spread reflects the pricing of the asset swap. Economically, an asset swap allows parties who fund on a floating-rate basis (typically LIBOR) to receive, on a net basis, the asset swap spread. The spread, to a large degree, reflects the credit risk of the underlying asset and is therefore an important benchmark for the pricing of other credit derivative products.

A good estimate of the pricing of a par asset swap is obtained as follows:

Asset Swap Spread = Asset Yield over Treasuries − Interest Rate Swap Spread,

where the asset yield is on a yield-to-maturity basis, and the interest rate swap spread reflects the cost of converting fixed-rate treasuries into floating-rate LIBOR over the life of the asset.

CREDIT RATING OPTIONS

A Credit Rating Option is a financial instrument with a payout contingent upon a rating event (e.g., a rating downgrade or upgrade). At present, this type of product is one of the most difficult credit derivatives to hedge. Since the pricing cannot be linked to a direct hedge, there is significant model risk associated with the pricing of credit rating options. For credit rating options, the relevant Pricing Models are clear: they must be of the class that incorporates transitions between various ratings. Pricing Models such as Das and Tufano create a risk neutral transition probability matrix between different rating categories which can be directly used to price a host of Credit Rating Option products.

CREDIT SPREAD

This terminology has been used in several different ways. One meaning is the spread, based upon subtracting the yield-to-maturity of a risky asset (usually fixed-rate) versus a comparable maturity riskless U.S. Treasury bond. This spread is a measure of the credit risk of an asset, as the asset pricing is compared directly to riskless Treasuries. This is a popular measure of credit risk in the primary and secondary bond markets. A second interpretation has been a spread of the risky asset to that of a comparable maturity swap rate (i.e., the asset swap spread). This latter meaning is very relevant to credit derivatives, as it reflects the residual credit risk after interest rate risk is stripped out of an asset via an interest rate swap—the spread over LIBOR is a tradeable, practical, measure of credit risk. Since the credit spread is a positive quantity, analogous to stock price, the simplest model for its behavior is described by a Wiener process (also known as Brownian motion):

$$\frac{d(credit\ spread)}{credit\ spread} = \mu dt + \sigma dz$$

where μ is the drift in credit spread, σ is the credit spread volatility, and dz is a random variable characterized by zero mean and variance dt in a small time interval dt. The above model implies a lognormal distribution for the credit spread.

It is worth noting that over long periods of time credit spreads have historically exhibited *mean reversion*. That is, there is a tendency for credit spreads to remain within a band of spreads and also to revert back towards average spreads from unusually large or small spreads. Recent work on this effect can be found in Longstaff and Schwartz. The lognormal model may be safely applied over time horizons significantly smaller than the time scale for mean reversion to occur.

CREDIT SPREAD LOCK

Suppose a corporation plans to issue fixed-rate debt (maturing at time T) at a future time t, and is concerned about credit spreads substantially widening from the Forward Credit Spread c_{fwd}. The issuer can hedge against issuing into the market at an uncertain credit spread c_{mkt} by locking-in the Forward Credit Spread. In theory, the required economics could be accomplished by a combination of two Default Swap positions: (1) a short credit-risk position with maturity T and (2) a long credit-risk position maturing at time t. In practice, long and short bond positions may be more cost-effective means of creating the forward position, although this can create basis risk since it is unlikely that there exist bonds in the marketplace maturing exactly at times t and T (e.g., a mix of several bonds may be required to construct a position with the same duration as the new issue).

CREDIT SPREAD OPTIONS

Credit Spread Options are financial instruments with a payoff linked to an underlying Credit Spread or credit-sensitive asset price. Typically the options are structured to knock-out (i.e., expire worthless) upon a default, so that the economics of the instruments separate spread risk and default risk. The standard call and put spread options have the following payouts:

$$Call = Duration\ Factor \times Max(0,\ Spread\ Strike - Credit\ Spread)$$
$$Put = Duration\ Factor \times Max(0,\ Credit\ Spread - Spread\ Strike)$$

where the *Duration Factor* is used to translate spreads into price terms. Underlying assets that fit into the above option payoff framework include asset swaps and fixed-rate bonds.

Alternatively, the economics of spread options is also reflected in the prices of credit-sensitive assets, such as floating rate bank loans or floating rate notes. In these cases, the spread options can be cast in price, rather than spread, terms:

$$Call = Max(0,\ P - X)$$
$$Put = Max(0,\ X - P)$$

where X is the strike price and P is the price of the underlying credit-sensitive asset. Note that the spread or the price representations of the spread options presented above are effectively the same, linked through the standard price-duration-spread relationship.

To illustrate the essential features of credit spread option pricing, a very simple European-style model is presented within the price, rather than credit spread, framework presented above. The payout of the option at maturity T is contingent upon a default event not occurring (to obtain default protection as well, an off-par Default Swap with an $X - P$ payout can be purchased). Option pricing can then be obtained from Black's model for bond options, with an adjustment for the knock-out feature in the event of a default:

$$Call = Survival(T) \times e^{-rT}[FN(d_+) - XN(d_-)]$$
$$Put = Survival(T) \times e^{-rT}[XN(-d_-) - FN(-d_+)]$$

where F is the forward value of the underlying asset, given by

$$F = e^{rT} \times (P(0) - I)$$

$P(0)$ is the initial asset price, I is the present-value of all estimated cash flows generated from the asset over the life of the option, r is the risk-free rate, $Survival(T)$ is the Survival Probability that a default has not occurred up to time T, N is the cumulative normal distribution, and

$$d_{\pm} = [\ln(F/X) \pm \sigma^2 T/2]/\sigma\sqrt{T}$$

where σ is the volatility of the forward asset price.

Example

Consider a one year option to put a new seven year senior secured bank loan, issued at a price of 99.5 percent, at a strike price $X = 98$ percent. Suppose that $r = 6.0$ percent, the coupon on the loan is LIBOR + 300 bps and is paid quarterly, the one year Credit Spread is 200 bps, and that the volatility σ is estimated to be 3.0 percent p.a.

First, we calculate the Survival Probability. Using the 29 percent Loss in the Event of Default for the senior secured loans, Risk-Neutral Pricing yields the following:

$$p_{def} = 6.90\% \ (= 200 \text{ bps p.a.} \times 1 \text{ Yr}/29\%)$$
$$\Rightarrow Survival(T) = 1 - 6.90\% = 93.1\%,$$

where, for simplicity, the Survival Probability is calculated without subdividing the one year period. The present value of the quarterly loan cash flows (assumed to be 9.0 percent p.a.) over the life of the option is estimated to be $I = 8.7$ percent. Hence, the forward value is given by $F = 96.4$ percent. Substituting these results into the above formulae, it follows that the cost of the option is:

$$Put = 186 \text{ bps}$$

DEFAULT CORRELATIONS

The pair-wise default correlation ξ_{12} of two assets (labeled 1 and 2) is defined through the following relation:

$$\xi_{12} = \frac{E([d_1 - E(d_1)] \times [d_2 - E(d_2)])}{\sigma(d_1)\sigma(d_2)} = \frac{p_{12} - p_1 p_2}{\sigma(d_1)\sigma(d_2)}$$

where d_i is a discrete random variable ($0 \Rightarrow$ no default, $1 \Rightarrow$ default) characterizing the event of default for asset i, p_{12} is the joint probability that both assets will default, p_i is the default probability of asset i, and $\sigma^2(d_i) = p_i(1 - p_i)$ is the variance of the event of default of asset i about the expected likelihood of default (see Default Distribution for details).

The above formula has intuitive limiting cases. If both assets behave identically the same, then $d_1 = d_2$ and it follows that $\xi_{12} = 1$ (perfect correlation). If the assets behave completely opposite one another, then $d_1 = -d_2$ and it follows that $\xi_{12} = -1$ (perfect inverse correlation). If the assets behave independently, then $\xi_{12} = 0$ (no correlation).

Correlations are not only relevant for baskets of assets, but also for default and total return swaps on a single asset. The swaps can be viewed as an asset whose performance is guaranteed by a counterparty. The pricing of the credit swap, in general, will depend upon the correlation ξ_{12} between the asset (labeled by 1) and the guarantor (labeled by 2). It is worth noting that ξ_{12} is constrained from the observation that the joint probability of default, reflecting the likelihood of default on the guaranteed asset, must be: (a) greater than or equal to zero, and (b) less than or equal to the probability of default associated with the asset or guarantor that has the better credit quality (i.e., lowest default probability). Mathematically,

$$-\frac{p_1 p_2}{\sigma(d_1)\sigma(d_2)} \le \xi_{12} \le \frac{\min(p_1, p_2) - p_1 p_2}{\sigma(d_1)\sigma(d_2)}$$

For further discussion of the upper correlation bound, see Lucas (1995). One available source of Default Correlations, based upon an underlying model for the default process, is Kealhofer, McQuown, & Vasicek Corporation (KMV).

DEFAULT DISTRIBUTION

There are only two possible credit outcomes from a risky asset: (1) a default event occurs, or (2) a default event does not occur. Either outcome is randomly determined. The Binomial (also known as Bernoulli) distribution is appropriate for discrete random variables which can have only two different attributes or values. Let d be defined as the random variable that characterizes the event of default:

$$d = \begin{cases} 1 \text{ if default} & , \quad \text{probability } p \\ 0 \text{ if no default} & , \quad \text{probability } 1 - p \end{cases}$$

and p be defined as the likelihood that a default will occur. Then, moments of the distribution of d are calculated as follows:

$$E(d) = p \times 1 + (1 - p) \times 0 = p \qquad \text{(mean)}$$
$$\sigma^2(d) = p \times (1 - p)^2 + (1 - p) \times p^2 = p(1 - p) \qquad \text{(variance)}$$

DEFAULT PUT OPTION

Similar to a par Default Swap, but with an upfront *Premium* paid by the option buyer in exchange for the right to put a defaulted asset in exchange for par. Alternatively, for a cash settled option, the option seller pays par less the market price of the asset following a default. The *Premium* is not simply the present-value of the periodic Default Swap Pricing—

consideration must be given for the likelihood that each periodic payment is actually made. This is done as follows:

$$Premium = \sum_{t=1}^{M} D(t) \times Survival(t) \times Default\ Swap\ Pricing(t), \text{ where}$$

M is the number of periodic payments that would take place in a Default Swap over the maturity of the Default Put Option, $D(t)$ is the discount factor applicable to time t, $Survival(t)$ is the Survival Probability that a default has not occurred at t and that a default swap premium payment is made, and *Default Swap Pricing(t)* is the swap pricing in terms of dollar cash flow over each payment interval.

DEFAULT SWAP

In a par default swap, periodic payments representing the default swap pricing are made to a counterparty (the "guarantor") in return for a payment of par less the market price of a reference asset contingent upon an event of default. To a good approximation, if there are bonds of the same issuer as the reference asset that bracket the maturity of the default swap, the pricing is obtained from the maturity-interpolated asset swap pricing levels. That is,

Par Default Swap Pricing ≅ *maturity-interpolated Asset Swap Pricing*

Alternatively, the asset swap pricing of a different company, that is comparable to that of the issuer of the reference asset, may be used for pricing purposes.

Differences between the pricing that clears the market and the above estimate of the *Default Swap Pricing* can arise for a variety of reasons: (1) hedging costs, (2) liquidity of the default swap, (3) supply/demand factors, (4) the credit quality of the guarantor, and (5) potential default correlations between the guarantor and the reference asset.

In an off-par default swap, periodic payments are made to a counterparty in return for a payment of a contractually stated price X (different than par, possibly related to the initial market value of the asset) less the market price of a reference asset contingent upon a default. The pricing of an off-par default swap is related to that of a par Default Swap and a Digital Default Swap as follows:

Off − Par Default Swap Pricing

= Par Default Swap Pricing ± Digital Default Swap,

where the *Digital Default Swap* has a fixed payout of $|100$ percent $− X|$

contingent upon a default, and the + or − sign in the above relation corresponds to the cases $X > 100$ percent and $X < 100$ percent, respectively, indicating a long or short position in the default risk.

As an example, an off-par default swap with a 95 percent less recovery value payout on $10mm notional of risk can be synthesized (and priced) via a $10mm par default swap with an offsetting (short credit risk) Digital Default Swap that has a $500,000 (= 5 percent × $10 mm) payout.

DIGITAL DEFAULT SWAP

In a Digital Default Swap, payments (represented by *Dollar Pricing*, on a p.a. basis) are made to a counterparty in return for a fixed *Dollar Payout* contingent upon an event of default of a reference asset. This type of swap is easily valued under the simplifying assumption that the Loss In the Event of Default (*LIED*) of the reference asset is well approximated. Given the *Credit Spread* for the maturity of an ordinary *par-recovery* Default Swap with the same maturity as the Digital Default Swap, it follows that the digital pricing is merely a pro-rata portion of ordinary Default Swap Pricing:

$$Dollar\ Pricing = Dollar\ Payout \times \left[\frac{Credit\ Spread}{Loss\ in\ the\ Event\ of\ Default}\right]$$

Note that the last bracketed term also represents the risk-neutral default rate, so that the pricing represents the expected (probability-weighted) digital default swap payout.

EXPECTED LOSS/GAIN

The present-valued expected loss $E(Loss)$ associated with a credit instrument can be calculated as follows:

$$E(Loss) = \sum_{t=1}^{M} D(t) \times p(t-1,t) \times Survival(t-1) \times LIED(t), \text{ where}$$

M is the number of periods ($= T/\tau$) that the maturity time T has been sub-divided into time intervals τ for the purpose of modeling the time behavior of defaults within time T, t is a discrete time index $0,1,\ldots,M$ that corresponds to an actual time $t \times \tau$ within the interval $[0,T]$, $p(t-1,t)$ is the probability that the underlying asset will default between $t-1$ and t, $Survival(t)$ is the cumulative Survival Probability of there not being a default over all prior periods in the interval [0,t], $D(t)$ is the discount factor, and $LIED(t)$ is the Loss In the Event of a Default.

The present-valued expected gain $E(Gain)$ associated with a credit derivative instrument, net of any riskless cash flows associated with a potential upfront cash investment, is calculated as follows:

$$E(Gain) = \sum_{t=1}^{M} D(t) \times Survival(t) \times Credit\ Spread \times \tau$$

where the same notation as in the $E(Loss)$ calculation is used, *Credit Spread* is expressed as an annualized spread, and τ is the time period over which periodic cash flows occur (again, time is measured in discrete units of τ). The *Survival(t)* weighting factor accounts for the possibility that the spread cash flow will actually be received, based upon the likelihood that there is not a default in the time interval [t − 1,t], contingent upon there not being a default over the cumulative prior periods [0,t − 1].

FIRST-TO-DEFAULT NOTES

In the note form of the first-to-default basket product, a cash investment equal to the face value of one of N equally-weighted credits is made, which is used to provide default protection on the first asset to default during the life of the note. The cash is typically invested in high-grade securities. The notes have a stated coupon, and principal will be returned if no defaults occur. If any underlying asset defaults, the note defaults and terminates early, no interest is paid, and settlement may be (a) physical, whereby the investor's principal in an amount equivalent to the face value of the defaulted asset is forfeited in exchange for physical delivery of the defaulted asset, or (b) cash, whereby the investor forfeits principal in the amount of par value (or, in an alternate structure, initial market value) less the market value of the defaulted asset to the note issuer.

A methodology for pricing the first-to-default basket product begins with a calculation of the risk associated with the product (i.e., the Expected Loss). Assuming Risk-Neutral Pricing, the pricing of the note is extracted by equating the Expected Gain on the note, net of the risk-free rate earned on the cash investment, to the Expected Loss. An alternative approach is to translate the $E(Loss)$ into a rating. As an example, Moody's rating scale is based upon expected loss, although it is calculated based upon stressed assumptions of default rate, default timing, and Loss In the Event of Default—see Backman and O'Connor Moody's Report (1995) for further details. The market rate associated with the rating, for the maturity of the product T, is then easily estimated—which is a good benchmark for the pricing of the first-to-default basket. Deviations from this benchmark pricing may arise from several sources: (1) liquidity or "highly structured transaction" premia, (2) supply or demand imbalances in the market, and (3) potential costs associated with issuing the product, such as capital or hedging costs.

The key calculation for either of the above approaches is the Expected Loss. The equation provided for the $E(Loss)$ may be used with the proviso that all of the underlying assets are of the same seniority (i.e., they all have the same recovery rate R). A simple and general formula for the marginal note default probability $p(t - 1,t)$ in the interval $[t-1,t]$, a key component to the $E(Loss)$ calculation, is available for the case that the Default Correlations between the N underlying assets are zero:

$$p(t - 1,t) = \left[1 - \prod_{j=1}^{N} (1 - p_j(t - 1,t)) \right]$$

where $p_j(t - 1,t)$ is the default probability of the jth asset out of the N assets in the basket, in the time interval $[t - 1,t]$. This is the probability that one or more assets default over the interval $[t - 1,t]$, thereby triggering a default on the note.

Example: Three Assets, and Correlations

Suppose three bonds are the reference assets in a First-to-Default Note maturing in one year, with the underlyer pricing and correlation information in Table 6–1.

Default Correlations are potentially important for pricing purposes, as this example shall illustrate. In the example, for simplicity, non-zero default correlations ρ exist only between Bonds No. 1 and No. 2. In general,

T A B L E   6–1

Bond No.	Bond Mat.	Asset Swap Pricing (bps)	1 Year Default Risk Pricing* (bps)	Seniority	Correlation Coefficients
1	8 yrs	400	350	sub	$\xi_{12} = \rho, \xi_{13} = 0$
2	5 yrs	375	350	sub	$\xi_{21} = \rho, \xi_{23} = 0$
3	2 yrs	325	300	sub	$\xi_{31} = 0, \xi_{32} = 0$

*One year default risk pricing differs from Asset Swap Pricing due to differences in the maturity of the credit risk, potential demand premia for synthetic 1 year risk, etc.

inclusion of correlations is cumbersome as it requires specification of all the pair-wise, triplet-wise, etc., correlations of the underlying assets.

Using the Risk-Neutral Pricing approach, calibration of the default probabilities to market prices is achieved based upon a recovery rate assumption and the pricing of one year default risk (corresponding to the note maturity). For simplicity and illustrative purposes, given the short maturity of the note, we do not subdivide the time period or apply a discount factor. Using an average Loss In the Event of Default of 66 percent for subordinated debt, the following risk-neutral default rates are obtained:

Bond No.:	1	2	3
1 Yr Default Rate:	5.30%	5.30%	4.55%
	(=350bps/66%)	(=350bps/66%)	(=300bps/66%)

For the case that all correlations are zero (i.e., $\rho = 0$), the simple formula for the probability of a note default can be used:

$p = 14.40\% = 1 - (1 - 0.0530) \times (1 - 0.0530) \times (1 - 0.0455)$
in which case:
$E(Loss) = 14.40\% \times 66\% = 950$ bps.

Assuming the cash is invested at LIBOR, the estimated investor pricing is L + 950 bps, which is the bulk of the total available one-year risk spread (1000 bps) from the underlying assets. The issuer retains the residual 50 bps as compensation for exposure to the residual default risk.

To account for a nonzero correlation ρ, the probability that at least one bond defaults is calculated from the more general relation:

$$p = p_1 + p_2 + p_3 - p_{12} - p_{13} - p_{23} + p_{123}$$

where p_{12} is the joint probability that Bond No. 1 and No. 2 will default, $p_{13} = p_1 p_3$ and $p_{23} = p_2 p_3$ since Bond No. 3 is uncorrelated with Bond No. 1 and 2, and p_{123} is the joint probability that all three of the bonds will default. The latter is simplified to $p_{123} = p_{12} p_3$ since Bond No. 3 is uncorrelated with Bond No. 1 and 2. Hence, there is only one additional piece of information required to specify this problem, the joint probability of default p_{12}, which can be calculated in terms of the correlation coefficient $\xi_{12} = \rho$ (see Default Correlations).

The pricing to the investor, expressed as a spread over LIBOR and as a function of the correlation ρ, is shown in Table 6–2. As illustrated in Table 6–2, correlations between the underlying reference assets in a first-to-default basket can have a significant impact on pricing. With increasing

T A B L E 6–2

Pricing as a Function of Correlation between Bonds 1 and 2								
Correlation ρ:	0.00	0.05	0.10	0.15	0.20	0.25	0.50	0.75	1.00
Pricing (bps):	950	935	919	903	887	871	792	713	634

correlations, the net risk to the issuer (underlying assets + first-to-default protection) increases, more spread is retained by the issuer for compensation of the additional risk, and a smaller payout results to the investor.

FORWARD CREDIT SPREAD

An important concept for credit derivatives is how the market is pricing future credit spreads, which can be obtained from forward credit spread curves. The curves are obtained via the same methodology as forward interest rate curves. Table 6–3 is provided for the calculation of one year credit spreads of XYZ Corp., a BB industrial company, 1 to 4 years hence.

Forward LIBOR rates can be obtained directly from the Eurodollar futures markets.

FORWARD DEFAULT PROBABILITY

Using the Risk-Neutral Pricing technique, the Forward Default Probability can be backed-out by dividing the Forward Credit Spread (multiplied by the term of the spread) by an assumed Loss In the Event of Default for

T A B L E 6–3

Time Yrs	Forward Time N (Yrs)	XYZ Corp. Zero Yield	XYZ Corp 1 Yr Forward	LIBOR Rate 1 Yr Forward	1 Yr Credit Spread N Yrs Forward (bps)
1	0	6.65	6.65	5.98	67 (Spot)
2	1	6.75	6.86	6.14	72
3	2	6.92	7.27	6.25	101
4	3	7.09	7.58	6.34	125
5	4	7.30	8.18	6.42	176

the asset. Empirically, it is observed that actual historical marginal default rates increase (decrease) with time for investment (non-investment) grade assets.

KMV

KMV is a firm that provides several products which can be used to facilitate the pricing of credit derivatives, and to optimize the risk/return characteristics of credit portfolios. Their software provides outputs of expected default rates and Default Correlations for specific companies. The Pricing Models driving these outputs is based upon Merton's model, which requires financial statement data for each company KMV tracks. Their model is calibrated through the use of historical equity prices, and a historical database of payment defaults since 1977.

LOSS IN THE EVENT OF DEFAULT (LIED)

Relative to the face par value of an asset, the loss in the event of a default is given by the following:

$$LIED(t) = (100\% - R), \text{ where}$$

R is the recovery rate of the defaulted asset. The recovery rate can be interpreted as the ultimate post-bankruptcy recovery level present-valued to the date of default. Alternatively, market prices of the asset following a default serve as a reasonable proxy for the recovery level. Moody's has studied historical (1989–1996) recovery levels based upon traded prices approximately thirty days following a default, summarized in Table 6–4.

Refer to Carty and Lieberman Moody's Report (1997) for further details. The level of the recovery is sensitive to the claim status of the debt instrument within the capital structure of the obligor. In addition,

T A B L E   6–4

Asset Seniority	Recovery R	LIED	Std Dev
Senior Secured Bank Loans	71	29	21
Senior Secured Bonds	63	37	26
Senior Unsecured Bonds	48	52	26
Subordinated Bonds	34	66	23

the recovery distributions are fairly broad, as indicated by the large standard deviations.

PRICING MODELS

There are two general classes of credit derivative pricing models. The first, and oldest, class of models originated with Merton's work in 1974. This class is characterized by a modeling of the behavior of a firm's asset value, which provides the likelihood of a firm default as a model output, and credit derivative pricing sometimes in the form of a compound option. Difficulties arise since a firm's asset value, and the parameters modeling the behavior of asset value, are not directly observable in the marketplace. The second class of models separates the default process from the behavior of asset value, with default rates being inferred from traded credit instruments. This class of models, with the elimination of the unobservable asset value process, is more practical and more commonly used to price credit derivatives. Both classes of models are discussed in more detail below.

Merton modeled the asset value V of a firm as a lognormal process, which requires specification of the expected asset return and asset volatility. In a simple model with one zero coupon bond of face value F and maturity T in the firm's capital structure: $Equity\ Payout = Max(V(T) - F, 0)$. Similarly, the firm's debt can be expressed in terms of a put option on the firm's assets: $Debt\ Payout = F - Max(F - V(T), 0)$. If $V < F$ at maturity, the firm is in default. Credit derivatives such as options on debt are essentially options on options, or compound options. [See, e.g., Das (1995).] The main problem with Merton's model is in specifying the unobservable asset value stochastic process, and the complete capital structure for the firm. Several improvements to Merton's model were made recently by Longstaff and Schwartz: (1) a boundary level is introduced such that if the asset value ever falls below the level, the firm is in default; (2) a recovery level in the event of default can be specified, an attractive alternative to specifying the claim structure on the firm's assets; and (3) interest rates are allowed to be stochastic.

The second class of models can be found in the following academic literature: Jarrow and Turnbull (1995), Jarrow, Lando, and Turnbull (1997), Das and Tufano (1996) (DT), and Duffie and Singleton (1996). There are several essential features of these models: (1) the assumption of a complete and arbitrage-free credit market (i.e., risk-neutrality), (2) the default process is modeled as a binomial tree with branches corresponding to a default or no default, (3) default can occur randomly over time, (4) the recovery rate must be specified (DT incorporate stochastic recovery levels), and (5) credit derivatives linked to credit ratings can be accommodated in the models via rating agency information on the migration probabilities between different rating categories. The last item is important for pricing credit derivatives such as Credit Rating Options. In the risk-neutral framework, the observed historical transition matrix between different ratings must be transformed into a risk-neutral transition matrix. These models are quite general, fairly easy to implement, and can be used to price most credit derivative products. Unfortunately, some of the assumptions underpinning these models are currently questionable. For example, (a) negligible trading costs/bid-ask spread between long and short positions, (b) good liquidity, and (c) underlying assets are perfectly divisible. The last point is particularly relevant for the loan asset class, where the minimum lot size is typically $5mm.

RISK-NEUTRAL PRICING

The assumption of risk-neutrality greatly facilitates the pricing of credit derivatives. The assumption can be expressed as follows:

$$E(Gain) = E(Loss)$$

where all variables and terminology are defined under Expected Loss/Gain. Since $E(Gain)$, by definition, is net of any risk-free cash flows associated with a potential upfront cash investment, the above expression is equivalent to the condition that the expected profit be equal to that obtained in a riskless investment. Alternatively, if no cash is put upfront, risk-neutrality states that the investor should not have an expected profit. The above formula can be used to obtain risk-neutral probabilities given spread pricing, or the credit spread can be obtained given the probabilities:

$$Credit\ Spread = \frac{\sum_{t=1}^{M} D(t) \times p(t - 1,t) \times Survival(t - 1) \times LIED(t)/\tau}{\sum_{t=1}^{M} D(t) \times Survival(t)}$$

Assuming a constant marginal default rate $p(t - 1,t)$, with a cumulative default rate $p_{def} = p(t - 1,t)\ xM$, and a time-independent $LIED$, it follows that in the continuous limit where M tends to infinity, the Credit Spread is given by:

$$Credit\ Spread = p_{def} \times LIED/T = p_{def} \times (100\% - R)/T$$

where $T = M\tau$ is the maturity of the risk.

SURVIVAL PROBABILITY

The Survival Probability is the probability that a default has not occurred up to a given point in time t. Divide a time period T into M equal periods with $M + 1$ time points labeled by index i (1 represents the end of the first period). The default probability $p(i - 1, i)$ corresponds to the likelihood of default in the time interval $[i - 1, i]$, and $1 - p(i - 1, i)$ corresponds to the likelihood of no default (i.e., survival). The survival probability up to the time $i = t$ is then given by the product of the survival probabilities in all prior intervals:

$$Survival(t) = \prod_{i=0}^{t} (1 - p(i - 1, i))$$

where $p(-1, 0) = 0$; this boundary condition ensures that the the survival probability at the onset $(t = 0)$ is 100 percent.

TOTAL RETURN SWAP

A Total Return Swap (TRS) can be viewed as a funding trade, whereby one party funds an underlying asset and passes the full economics of the asset to a counterparty in exchange for a floating rate index (usually LIBOR) plus a *spread*. The level of the *spread* can depend upon a multitude of factors: (a) the credit quality of the TRS counterparty; (b) the amount of collateral, if any, posted for the TRS; (c) funding costs relative to the floating rate index/credit quality of the TRS provider; (d) capital costs of the TRS; (e) required profit margins; (f) operational costs; (g) the specifics of margin agreements, if any; and (h) the credit quality or risk of the underlying asset.

From the risk perspective of the TRS provider, there are two important cases to be considered: (1) the TRS receiver defaults and the underlying asset has declined in value, and (2) the underlying asset defaults and then the TRS receiver defaults before payment is made of the decline in value of the asset to the TRS provider. The first risk is sensitive to the default probability of the TRS receiver, and the volatility of the underlying asset. The second risk relates to the joint probability of default of both the underlying asset and the TRS receiver, and the recovery level of the underlying asset.

One important limit worth noting is the case that the maturity of the underlying asset matches the tenor of the TRS. In this case, since the terminal underlying asset price is known with certainty (par) if a default does not occur, the economics is equivalent to that of an Off-Par Default

Swap with a payout based upon the initial asset price less the market price of the asset following an event of default.

B I B L I O G R A P H Y

Backman A., and G. O'Connor: "Rating Cash Flow Transactions Backed by Corporate Debt, 1995 Update," *Moody's Investors Service Report*, April 1995.

Black, F.: "The Pricing of Commodity Contracts," *Journal of Financial Economics*, vol. 3, 1976, pp. 167–179.

Carty L., and D. Lieberman: "Historical Default Rates of Corporate Bond Issuers, 1920–1996," *Moody's Investors Service Report*, January 1997.

Das, S.: "Credit Risk Derivatives," *The Journal of Derivatives*, Spring 1995, pp. 7–23.

Das, S., and T. Tufano: "Pricing Credit Sensitive Debt when Interest Rates, Credit Ratings and Credit Spreads are Stochastic," *Journal of Financial Engineering*, vol. 5, 1996, pp. 161–198.

Duffie, D., and K. Singleton: "An Econometric Model of the Term Structure of Interest Rate Swap Yields," *Journal of Finance*, vol. 52, 1997, pp. 1287–1321.

Jarrow, R., and S. Turnbull: "Pricing Options on Financial Securities Subject to Default Risk," *Journal of Finance*, vol. 50, pp. 53–86.

Jarrow, R., D. Lando, and S. Turnbull: "A Markov Model for the Term Structure of Credit Spreads," *Review of Financial Studies*, vol. 10, 1997, pp. 481–523.

Longstaff, F.A., and E.S. Schwartz: "Valuing Credit Derivatives," *The Journal of Fixed Income*, vol. 5, pp. 6–12.

Longstaff, F.A., and E.S. Schwartz: "A Simple Approach to Valuing Risky Fixed and Floating Rate Debt," *Journal of Finance*, vol. 50, 1995, pp. 789–819.

Lucas, D.J.: "Default Correlation and Credit Analysis," *The Journal of Fixed Income*, June 1995, pp. 32–41.

Merton, R.C.: "On the Pricing of Corporate Debt: The Risk Structure of Interest Rates," *Journal of Finance*, vol. 29, 1974, pp. 449–470.

CHAPTER 7

Using Equity Price Information to Measure Default Risk*

Peter J. Crosbie, Ph.D.
Managing Director, KMV Corporation

OVERVIEW

Default risk is the uncertainty surrounding a firm's ability to service its debts and obligations. Prior to default, there is no way to discriminate unambiguously between firms that will default and those that won't. At best we can only make probabilistic assessments of the likelihood of default. As a result, firms generally pay a spread over the default-free rate of interest that is proportional to their default probability to compensate lenders for this uncertainty.

Default is a deceptively rare event. The typical firm has a default probability of around 2 percent in any year. However, there is considerable variation in default probabilities across firms. For example, the odds of a firm with a AAA rating defaulting are only about 2 in 10,000 per annum. A single A-rated firm has odds of around 10 in 10,000 per annum, five times higher than a AAA. At the bottom of the rating scale, a CCC-rated firm's odds of defaulting are 4 in 100 (4 percent), 200 times the odds of a AAA-rated firm.

The loss suffered by a lender or counterparty in the event of default is usually significant and is determined largely by the details of the particular

---

contract or obligation. For example, typical loss rates in the event of default for senior secured bonds, subordinated bonds and zero coupon bonds are 49 percent, 68 percent, and 81 percent, respectively.

Cross default clauses in debt contracts usually ensure that the default probabilities for each of the classes of debt for a firm are the same. That is, the default probability of the firm determines the default probability for all of the firm's debt or counterparty obligations. However, the loss in the event of default for each of the classes of obligations can vary widely depending on their nature (e.g., security, collateral, seniority, etc.).

Although, in general, a poor investment strategy, it is possible to be rewarded for taking on large concentrations of risk in equities because these concentrations at times produce large returns. However, overwhelming evidence of the ineffectiveness of this *stock-picking* strategy has been available since the early 1970s and, as a result, the majority of equity investments are managed in diversified portfolios. Unlike equities, debt has no upside potential and, thus, the case for managing default risk in well-diversified portfolios is even more compelling. The limited upside potential of debt spreads means that there are no possible circumstances under which an investor or counterparty can be rewarded for taking on concentrations of default risk. Like other rare events with high costs, default risk can only be effectively managed in a portfolio.

In addition to knowing the default probability and loss given default, the portfolio management of default risk requires the measurement of default correlations. Correlations measure the degree to which the default risks of the various borrowers and counterparties in the portfolio are related. The elements of credit risk can therefore be grouped as follows:

Stand-alone Risk

- *Default probability.* The probability that the counterparty or borrower will fail to service its obligations.
- *Loss given default.* The extent of the loss incurred in the event the borrower or counterparty defaults.
- *Migration risk.* The probability and value impact of changes in default probability.

Portfolio Risk

- *Default correlations.* The degree to which the default risks of the borrowers and counterparties in the portfolio are related.

- *Exposure.* The size, or proportion, of the portfolio exposed to the default risk of each counterparty and borrower.

While each of these items is critical to the management of credit portfolios, none are more important or more difficult to determine, than the default probability. The remainder of this chapter will focus on the determination of default probability using information from a firm's financial statements and the market price of its equity.

MEASURING DEFAULT PROBABILITY: THE PROBLEM

There are three main elements that determine the default probability of a firm:

- **Value of Assets:** the *market value* of the firm's assets. This is a measure of the present value of the future free cash flows produced by the firm's assets discounted back at the appropriate discount rate. This measures the firm's prospects and incorporates relevant information about the firm's industry and the economy.

- **Asset Risk:** the *uncertainty* or *risk* of the asset value. This is a measure of the firm's business and industry risk. The value of the firm's assets is an estimate and is thus uncertain. As a result, the value of the firm's assets should always be understood in the context of the firm's business or asset risk.

- **Leverage:** the extent of the firm's contractual liabilities. Whereas, the relevant measure of the firm's assets is always their market value, the book value of liabilities relative to the market value of assets is the pertinent measure of the firm's leverage, since that is the amount the firm must repay.

For example, Figure 7–1 illustrates the evolution of the asset value and book liabilities of Venture Stores, a Midwestern retailer which defaulted in January 1998.

The default risk of the firm increases as the value of the assets approaches the book value of the liabilities, until finally the firm defaults when the market value of the assets is insufficient to repay the liabilities.

In our study of defaults, we have found that in general firms do not default when their asset value reaches the book value of their total liabilities. While some firms certainly default at this point, many continue to trade and service their debts. The long-term nature of some of their liabilities

FIGURE 7–1

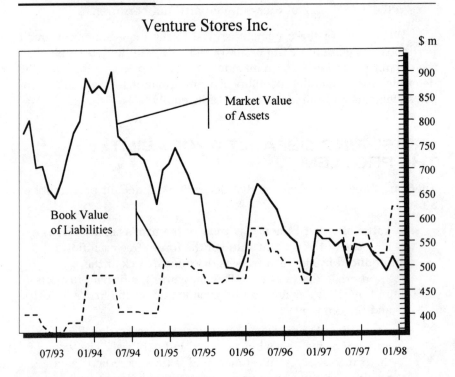

Venture Stores Inc.

$ m

Market Value
of Assets

Book Value
of Liabilities

900
850
800
750
700
650
600
550
500
450
400

07/93   01/94   07/94   01/95   07/95   01/96   07/96   01/97   07/97   01/98

provides these firms with some breathing space. We have found that the *default point*, the asset value at which the firm will default, generally lies somewhere between total liabilities and current, or short-term, liabilities.

The relevant net worth of the firm is therefore the market value of the firm's assets minus the firm's default point:

$$
\begin{bmatrix} Market\ Value \\ Assets \end{bmatrix} - \begin{bmatrix} Default \\ Point \end{bmatrix}
$$

A firm will default when its market net worth reaches zero.

Like the firm's asset value, the market measure of net worth must be considered in the context of the firm's business risk. For example, firms in the food and beverage industries can afford higher levels of leverage (lower market net worth) than high technology businesses because their businesses, and consequently their asset values, are more stable and less uncertain.

For example, Figure 7–2 shows the evolution of asset values and default points for Compaq Computer and Anheuser-Busch. Figure 7–3

F I G U R E 7-2

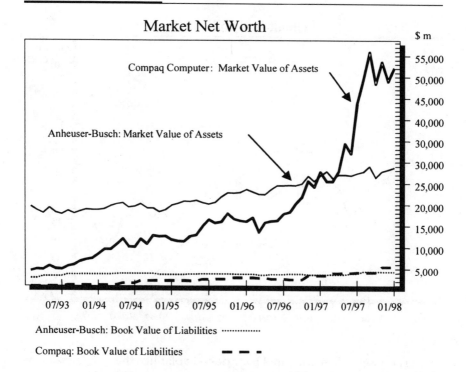

Market Net Worth

$ m

Compaq Computer: Market Value of Assets

Anheuser-Busch: Market Value of Assets

55,000
50,000
45,000
40,000
30,000
30,000
25,000
20,000
15,000
10,000
5,000

07/93   01/94   07/94   01/95   07/95   01/96   07/96   01/97   07/97   01/98

Anheuser-Busch: Book Value of Liabilities ·············

Compaq: Book Value of Liabilities   ▬ ▬ ▬

shows the corresponding evolution of the annual default probabilities. The default probabilities shown in this figure are the one year default rates, the probability that the firm will default in the ensuing year, and are displayed on a logarithmic scale.

The effect of the relative business risks of the two firms is clear from a comparison of the two figures. For instance, as of January 1998, the relative market values, default points, asset risks, and resulting default probabilities for Compaq and Anheuser-Busch were:

	Anheuser-Busch	**Compaq Computer**
Market Value of Assets	28.7	52.1
Default Point	5.4	4.3
Market Net Worth ($b)	23.3	47.8
Asset Volatility	14%	33%
Default Probability (per annum)	.02%	.16%

FIGURE 7–3

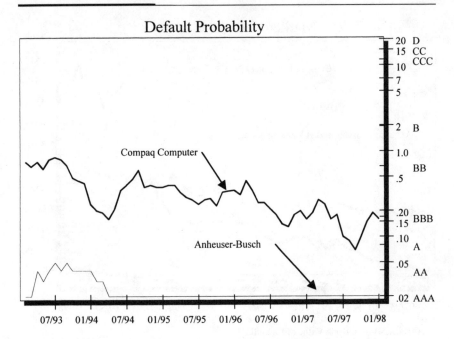

Default Probability

The asset risk is measured by the asset volatility, the standard deviation of the annual percentage change in the asset value. For example, Anheuser-Busch's business risk is 14 percent, which means that a one standard deviation move in their asset value will add (or remove) $4 billion from its asset value of $28.7 billion. In contrast, a one standard deviation move in the asset value of Compaq Computer will add or remove $17.2 billion from its asset value of $52.1 billion. The difference in their default probabilities is thus driven by the difference in the risks of their businesses, not their respective asset values or leverages.

As you would expect, asset volatility is related to the size and nature of the firm's business. For example, Figure 7–4 shows the asset volatility for several industries and asset sizes.

Asset volatility is related to, but different from, equity volatility. A firm's leverage has the effect of magnifying its underlying asset volatility. As a result, industries with low asset volatility (e.g., banking) tend to take on larger amounts of leverage while industries with high asset volatility (e.g., computer software) tend to take on less. As a consequence of these compensatory differences in leverage, equity volatility is far less differentiated by industry and asset size than is asset volatility.

F I G U R E   7–4

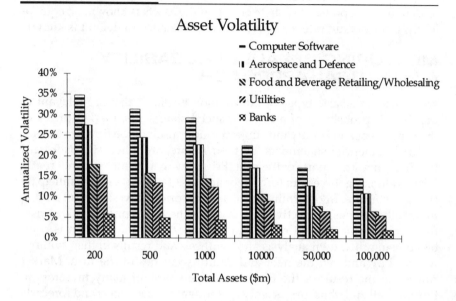

Asset Volatility

- Computer Software
- Aerospace and Defence
- Food and Beverage Retailing/Wholesaling
- Utilities
- Banks

Asset value, business risk, and leverage can be combined into a single measure of default risk which compares the market net worth to the size of a one standard deviation move in the asset value. We refer to this ratio as the *distance-to-default* and it is calculated as:

$$\begin{bmatrix} Distance \\ Default \end{bmatrix} = \frac{\begin{bmatrix} Market\ Value \\ Assets \end{bmatrix} - \begin{bmatrix} Default \\ Point \end{bmatrix}}{\begin{bmatrix} Market\ Value \\ Assets \end{bmatrix}\begin{bmatrix} Asset \\ Volatility \end{bmatrix}}$$

For example, in January 1998 Anheuser-Busch was approximately 5.8 standard deviations away from default while, in contrast, Compaq Computer was only 2.8 standard deviations away from default. That is, it would take a 5.8 standard deviation move in the asset value of Anheuser-Busch before it will default while only a 2.8 standard deviation move is required in Compaq's asset value to result in its default.

The distance-to-default measure combines three key credit issues: the value of the firm's assets, its business and industry risk, and its leverage. Moreover, the distance-to-default also incorporates, via the asset value and volatility, the effects of industry, geography, and firm size.

The default probability can be computed directly from the distance-to-default if the probability distribution of the assets is known, or, equivalently, if the default rate for a given level of distance-to-default is known.

MEASURING DEFAULT PROBABILITY: A PRACTICAL APPROACH

There are three basic types of information available that are relevant to the default probability of a firm: financial statements, market prices of the firm's debt and equity, and subjective appraisals of the firm's prospects and risk. Financial statements, by their nature, are inherently backward looking. They are reports of the past. Prices, by their nature, are inherently forward looking. Investors form debt and equity prices as they anticipate the firm's future. In determining the market prices, investors use, among many other things, subjective appraisals of the firm's prospects and risk, financial statements, and other market prices. This information is combined using their own analysis and synthesis and results in their willingness to buy and sell the debt and equity securities of the firm. Market prices are the result of the combined willingness of many investors to buy and sell and, thus, prices embody the synthesized views and forecasts of many investors.

The most effective default measurement, therefore, derives from models that utilize both market prices and financial statements. There is no assertion here that markets are perfectly efficient in this synthesis. We assert only that, in general, it is difficult to do a better job than they are doing. That is, in general, it is very difficult to consistently beat the market. Consequently, where available, we want to utilize market prices in the determination of default risk because prices add considerably to the predictive power of the estimates.

KMV Corporation has developed a model of default probability, Credit Monitor™, that uses equity prices and financial statements. Credit Monitor (CM) calculates the Expected Default Frequency™ (EDF™) which is the probability of default during the forthcoming year, or years (CM calculates EDFs for years 1 through 5). Default is defined as the nonpayment of any scheduled payment, interest, or principal. The remainder of this section describes the procedure used by CM to determine a public firm's probability of default.

There are essentially three steps in the determination of the default probability of a firm:

1. **Estimate asset value and volatility:** In this step the asset value and asset volatility of the firm is estimated from the market value and volatility of equity and the book value of liabilities.

2. **Calculate the distance-to-default:** The distance-to-default (DD) is calculated from the asset value and asset volatility (estimated in the first step) and the book value of liabilities.
3. **Calculate the default probability:** The default probability is determined directly from the distance-to-default and the default rate for given levels of distance-to-default.

Estimate Asset Value and Volatility

If the market price of equity is available, the market value and volatility of assets can be determined directly using an options pricing based approach which recognizes equity as a call option on the underlying assets of the firm. For example, consider a simplified case where there is only one class of debt and one class of equity. See Figure 7–5.

The limited liability feature of equity means that the equity holders have the right, but not the obligation, to pay off the debt holders and take over the remaining assets of the firm. That is, the holders of the other liabilities of the firm essentially own the firm until those liabilities are paid off in full by the equity holders. Thus, in the simplest case, equity is the same as a call option on the firm's assets with a strike price equal to the book value of the firm's liabilities.

CM uses this option nature of equity to derive the underlying asset value and asset volatility implied by the market value, volatility of equity, and the book value of liabilities. This process is similar in spirit to the procedure used by option traders in the determination of the implied volatility of an option from the observed option price.

F I G U R E   7–5

Assets	Liabilities
100	80
	20

FIGURE 7-6

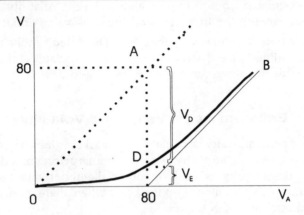

For example, assume that the firm is actually a type of levered mutual fund or unit trust. The assets of the firm are equity securities and, thus, can be valued at any time by observing their market prices. Further, assume that our little firm is to be wound up after five years and that we can ignore the time value of money (discounting adds little to our understanding of the relationships and serves only to complicate the picture). That is, in five years time, the assets will be sold and the proceeds divided between the debt and equity holders.

Initially, assume that we are interested in determining the market value of the equity from the market value of the assets. This is the reverse of the problem we face in practice but provides a simpler perspective to initially understand the basic option relationships. See Figure 7–6.

To be specific, assume that we initially invest $20 in the firm and borrow a further $80 from a bank. The proceeds, $100, are invested in equities. At the end of five years what is the value of equity? For example, if the market value of the assets at the end of year five is $60 then the value of equity will be zero. If the value of the assets is $110, then the value of the equity will be $30, and so on. Thus, in Figure 7–6, the lines from $0 to $80 and from $80 to point B represent the market value of the equity as a function of the asset value at the end of year five.

Assume now that we are interested in valuing our equity prior to the final winding up of the firm. For example, assume that three years have passed since the firm was started and that there are two years remaining before we wind the firm up. Further, we have marked the equities to market and their value is determined to be $80. What is the value of the equity? Not zero. It is actually something greater than zero because it is the value of the assets two years hence that really matters and there is still a chance that the asset value will be greater than $80 in two years time. In Figure 7–6, the value of the equity with two years to go is represented by the curve joining $0 and point B.

The higher the volatility of the assets the greater is the chance of high asset values after two years. For example, if we were dissatisfied with our fund's performance after three years because it has lost $20 in value, dropping from $100 to $80, we may be tempted to invest in higher-potential, higher-risk, equities. If we do, what is the effect on the equity value? It increases. The more volatile assets have higher probabilities of high values, and consequently, higher payouts for the equity. Of course, there are accompanying higher probabilities of lower asset values, because volatility works both ways, but with limited liability this does not affect the equity value. At the end of the five years, it makes no difference to the equity if the final asset value is $79 or $9; its payout is the same, 0.

Where did the increase in the equity's value come from? It did not come from an increase in the asset value. We simply sold our original portfolio for $80 and purchased a new portfolio of higher-risk equities for $80. There was no value created there. The value of course came from the bank holding our firm's debt. In Figure 7–6, the value of the firm can be divided between the debt and equity holders along the line joining the points $80 and A, where the line 0 to A plots the asset value against itself. Thus, the only way the value of equity can increase while the asset value remains constant is to take the value from the market value of the debt. This should make sense. When we reinvested the firm's assets in higher-risk equities, we increased the default risk of the debt and consequently reduced its market value.

The value of debt and equity are thus intimately entwined. They are both really derivative securities on the underlying assets of the firm. We can exploit the option nature of equity to relate the market value of equity and the book value of debt to determine the implied market value of the underlying assets. That is, we solve the reverse of the problem described in our simple example. We observe the market value of the equity and solve backwards for the market value of assets (see Figure 7–7).

In practice, we need to take account of the more complex capital structures and situations that exist in real life. For example we need to consider the various terms and nature of debt (e.g., long- and short-term debt, and convertible instruments), the perpetuity nature of equity, the time value of money, and, of course, we also have to solve for the volatility

F I G U R E 7–7

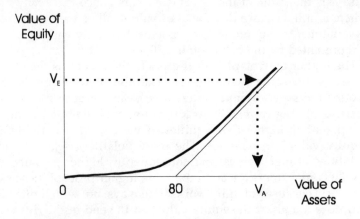

of the assets at the same time. Thus, in practice, we solve the following two relationships simultaneously:

$$\begin{bmatrix} Equity \\ Value \end{bmatrix} = OptionFunction \left(\begin{bmatrix} Asset \\ Value \end{bmatrix}, \begin{bmatrix} Asset \\ Volatility \end{bmatrix}, \begin{bmatrix} Capital \\ Structure \end{bmatrix}, \begin{bmatrix} Interest \\ Rate \end{bmatrix} \right)$$

$$\begin{bmatrix} Equity \\ Volatility \end{bmatrix} = Volatility\ Function \left(\begin{bmatrix} Asset \\ Value \end{bmatrix}, \begin{bmatrix} Asset \\ Volatility \end{bmatrix}, \begin{bmatrix} Capital \\ Structure \end{bmatrix}, \begin{bmatrix} Interest \\ Rate \end{bmatrix} \right)$$

Asset value and volatility are the only unknown quantities in these relationships and, thus, the two equations can be *solved* to determine the values implied by the current equity value, volatility, and capital structure.

Calculate the Distance-to-Default

There are six variables that determine the default probability of a firm over some horizon, from now until time H (see Figure 7–8).

1. The current asset value.
2. The distribution of the asset value at time H.
3. The volatility of the future assets value at time H.
4. The level of the default point, the book value of the liabilities.

F I G U R E 7–8

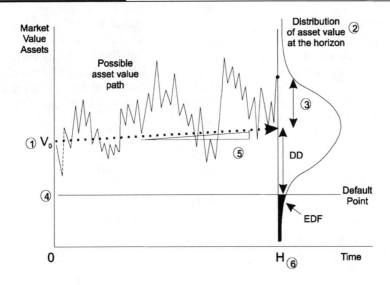

5. The expected rate of growth in the asset value over the horizon.

6. The length of the horizon, H.

The first four variables, asset value, future asset distribution, asset volatility, and the level of the default point, are the really critical variables. The expected growth in the asset value has little default discriminating power and the analyst defines the length of the horizon.

If the value of the assets falls below the default point, then the firm defaults. Therefore, the probability of default is the probability that the asset value will fall below the default point. This is the shaded area (EDF) below the default point in Figure 7–8.

Figure 7–8 also illustrates the causative relationship and trade-off among the variables. This causative specification provides the analyst with a powerful and reliable framework in which they can ask what-if questions regarding the model's various inputs and examine the effects of any proposed capital restructuring. For example, the analyst can examine the effect of a large decrease in the stock price or the effects of an acquisition or merger.

If the future distribution of asset values were known, the default probability (Expected Default Frequency, or EDF) would simply be the likelihood that the final asset value was below the default point (the shaded area in Figure 7–8). However, in practice, the distribution of the asset values is difficult to measure. Moreover, the usual assumptions of normal or lognormal distributions cannot be used. For default measurement, the likelihood of large adverse changes in value are critical to the accurate determination of the default probability. Consequently, CM measures the distance-to-default as the number of standard deviations the asset value is away from default and uses empirical data to determine the corresponding default probability. As discussed in a previous section, the distance-to-default is calculated as:

$$\begin{bmatrix} Distance \\ Default \end{bmatrix} = \frac{\begin{bmatrix} Market\ Value \\ Assets \end{bmatrix} - \begin{bmatrix} Default \\ Point \end{bmatrix}}{\begin{bmatrix} Market\ Value \\ Assets \end{bmatrix}\begin{bmatrix} Asset \\ Volatility \end{bmatrix}}$$

and is marked as DD in Figure 7–8.

Calculate the Default Probability

We obtain the relationship between distance-to-default and default probability from data on historical default and bankruptcy frequencies. Our database includes over 100,000 company-years of data and over 2000 incidents of default or bankruptcy. From this data, a lookup or frequency table can be generated which relates the likelihood of default to various levels of distance-to-default.

For example, assume that we are interested in determining the default probability over the next year for a firm that is seven standard deviations away from default. To determine this EDF, we query the default history for the proportion of the firms, seven standard deviations away from default that defaulted over the next year. The answer is about five basis points (bp), 0.05 percent, or an equivalent rating of AA.

We have tested the relationship between distance-to-default and default frequency for industry, size, time, and other effects and have found that the relationship is constant across all of these variables. This is not to say that there are no differences in default rates across industry, time, and size but only that it appears that these differences are captured by the distance-to-default measure. Our studies of international default rates are continuing but the preliminary results of studies by KMV Corporation and some of its clients indicate that the relationship is also invariant across countries and regions.

T A B L E 7–1

Variable	Value	Notes
Market value of equity	$22,572 bn*	(Share Price) × (Shares Outstanding).
Book liabilities	$49,056 bn	Balance sheet.
Market value of assets	$71,994 bn	Option-pricing model.
Asset volatility	10%	Option-pricing model.
Default point	$36,993 bn	Liabilities payable within one year.
Distance-to-default	4.8	Ratio: $\dfrac{72-37}{72 \times 10\%}$ (In this example we ignore the growth in the asset value between now and the end of the year.)
EDF (one year)	21 bp	Empirical mapping between distance-to-default and default frequency.

*billion

Putting It All Together

In summary, there are three steps required to calculate an EDF: (1) estimate the current market value and volatility of the firm's assets; (2) determine how far the firm is from default, its distance-to-default; and (3) scale the distance-to-default to a probability. For example, consider Chrysler Motors, which, at the end of January 1998, had a one-year EDF of 21 bp, close to the median EDF of firms with a BBB rating. Table 7–1 illustrates the relevant values and calculations for the EDF.

A CLOSER LOOK AT CALCULATING EDFs

Merton's general derivative pricing model was the genesis for understanding the link between the market value of the firm's assets and the market value of its equity. It is possible to use the Black-Scholes (BS) option-pricing model, as a special case of Merton's model, to illustrate some of the technical details of estimating EDFs. The BS model is too restrictive to use in practice, but is widely understood and provides a useful framework to review the issues involved. This section works an example of the calculation of an EDF using the BS option-pricing model. This section also discusses some of the important issues that arise in practice and, where necessary, highlights the limitations of the BS model in this context.

Equity has the residual claim on the assets after all other obligations have been met. It also has limited liability. A call option on the underlying assets has the same properties. The holder of a call option on the assets has a claim on the assets after meeting the strike price of the option. In this case the strike of the call option is equal to the book value of the firm's liabilities. If the value of the assets is insufficient to meet the liabilities of the firm then the shareholders, holders of the call option, will not exercise their option and will leave the firm to its creditors.

We exploit the option nature of equity to derive the market value and volatility of the firm's underlying assets implied by the equity's market value. In particular, we solve backwards from the option price and option price volatility for the implied asset value and asset volatility.

To introduce the notation, recall that the BS model posits that the market value of the firm's underlying assets follows the following stochastic process:

$$dV_A = \mu V_A dt + \sigma_A V_A dz \tag{7.1}$$

where

V_A, dV_A = the firm's asset value and change in asset value,
μ, σ_A = the firm's asset value drift rate and volatility, and
dz = a Wiener process.

The BS model allows only two types of liabilities, a single class of debt and a single class of equity. If X is the book value of the debt which is due at time T, then the market value of equity and the market value of assets are related by the following expression:

$$V_E = V_A N(d1) + e^{-rT} X N(d2) \tag{7.2}$$

where

V_E = the market value of the firm's equity,

$$d1 = \frac{\ln(V_A/X) + \left(r + \frac{\sigma_A^2}{2}\right)T}{\sigma\sqrt{T}}$$

$d2 = d1 - \sigma_A\sqrt{T}$, and
r = the risk free interest rate

It is straightforward to show that equity and asset volatility are related by the following expression:

$$\sigma_E = \frac{V_A}{V_E}\Delta\sigma_A \tag{7.3}$$

where

σ_E = the volatility of the firm's equity, and
Δ = the hedge ratio, $N(d1)$, from (7.2).

Consider the example of a firm with a market capitalization of $3 billion, an equity volatility of 40 percent per annum and total liabilities of $10 billion. The asset value and volatility implied by the equity value, equity volatility, and liabilities are calculated by solving the call price and volatility equations, (7.2) and (7.3), simultaneously. In this case[1] the implied market value of the firm's assets is $12.511 billion, and the implied asset volatility is 9.6 percent.

In practice it is important to use a more general option-pricing relationship that allows for a more detailed specification of the liabilities and that models equity as perpetuity. CM currently incorporates five classes of liabilities, short-term, long-term, convertible, and preferred and common equity.

The model linking equity and asset volatility given by equation (7.3) holds only instantaneously. In practice the market leverage moves around far too much for equation (7.3) to provide reasonable results. Worse yet, the model biases the probabilities in precisely the wrong direction. For example, if the market leverage is decreasing quickly then equation (7.3) will tend to overestimate the asset volatility and, thus, the default probability will be overstated as the firm's credit risk improves. Conversely, if the market leverage is increasing rapidly then equation (7.3) will underestimate the asset volatility and, thus, the default probability will be understated as the firm's credit risk deteriorates. The net result is that default probabilities calculated in this manner provide little discriminatory power.

Instead of using the instantaneous relationship given by equation (7.3), CM uses a more complex iterative procedure to solve for the asset volatility. The procedure uses an initial guess of the volatility to determine the asset value and to *de-lever* the equity returns. The volatility of the resulting asset returns is used as the input to the next iteration of the procedure that in turn determines a new set of asset values and, hence, a new series of asset returns. The procedure continues in this manner until it converges. This usually takes no more than a handful of iterations if a reasonable starting point is used. In addition, the asset volatility derived above is combined in a Bayesian manner with country, industry,

---

[1] All liabilities are assumed to be due in one year, $T = 1$, and the interest rate r is assumed to be 5 percent.

and size averages to produce a more predictive estimate of the firm's asset volatility.

The probability of default is the probability that the market value of the firm's assets will be less than the book value of the firm's liabilities by the time the debt matures. That is:

$$p_t = \Pr[V_A^t \le X_t \,|\, V_A^0 = V_A] = \Pr[\ln V_A^t \le \ln X_t | V_A^0 = V_A] \qquad (7.4)$$

where

   p_t = the probability of default by time t,
   V_A^t = the market value of the firm's assets at time t, and
   X_t = the book value of the firm's liabilities due at time t.

The change in the value of the firm's assets is described by equation (7.1) and, thus, the value at time t, V_A^t, given that the value at time 0 is V_A, is:

$$\ln V_A^t = \ln V_A + \left(\mu - \frac{\sigma_A^2}{2}\right)t + \sigma_A\sqrt{t}\epsilon \qquad (7.5)$$

where

   μ = the expected return on the firm's asset, and

   ϵ = the random component of the firm's return.

The relationship given by equation (7.5) describes the evolution in the asset value path that is shown in Figure 7–8. Combining equations (7.4) and (7.5), we can write the probability of default as:

$$p_t = \Pr\left[\ln V_A + \left(\mu - \frac{\sigma_A^2}{2}\right)t + \sigma_A\sqrt{t}\epsilon \le X_t\right] \qquad (7.6)$$

and after rearranging:

$$p_t = \Pr\left[-\frac{\ln\frac{V_A}{X_t} + \left(\mu - \frac{\sigma_A^2}{2}\right)t}{\sigma_A\sqrt{t}} \le \epsilon\right] \qquad (7.7)$$

The BS model assumes that the random component of the firm's asset returns is normally distributed, $\epsilon \sim N(0,1)$ and as a result we can define the default probability in terms of the cumulative normal distribution:

$$p_t = N\left[-\frac{\ln\frac{V_A}{X_t} + \left(\mu - \frac{\sigma_A^2}{2}\right)t}{\sigma_A\sqrt{t}} \right] \qquad (7.8)$$

Recall that the distance-to-default is simply the number of standard deviations that the firm is away from default, and thus in the BS world is given by:

$$DD = \frac{\ln\frac{V_A}{X_t} + \left(\mu - \frac{\sigma_A^2}{2}\right)t}{\sigma_A\sqrt{t}} \qquad (7.9)$$

Continuing with our example, assume that the expected return on the assets, μ, is equal to 7 percent and that we are interested in calculating the one-year default probability. The distance-to-default, DD, in this case[2] is 2.8, and the corresponding default probability from equation (7.8) is 25 bp.

In practice, we need to adjust the distance-to-default to include not only the increases in the asset value given by the rate $\left(\mu - \frac{\sigma_A^2}{2}\right)$ but also any cash outflows to service debt, dividends and so on. In addition, the normal distribution is a very poor choice to define the probability of default. There are several reasons for this but the most important is the fact that the default point is in reality also a random variable. That is, we have assumed that the default point is described by the firm's liabilities and amortization schedule. Of course, we know that this is not true. In particular, firms will often adjust their liabilities as they near default. It is common to observe the liabilities of commercial and industrial firms increase as they near default while the liabilities of financial institutions often decrease as they approach default. The difference is usually just a reflection of the liquidity in the firm's assets, and thus their ability to adjust their leverage as they encounter difficulties.

---

[2]The distance-to-default is calculated by equation (7.9),

$$DD = \frac{\ln\frac{12.5116}{10} + \left(0.05 - \frac{0.0092}{2}\right)}{0.0961}.$$

Unfortunately ex ante we are unable to specify the behavior of the liabilities, and thus the uncertainty in the adjustments in the liabilities must be captured elsewhere. We include this uncertainty in the mapping of distance-to-default to EDF. The resulting empirical distribution of default rates has much wider tails than the normal distribution. For example, a distance-to-default of four, four standard deviations, maps to a default rate of around 45 bp. The equivalent probability from the normal distribution is essentially zero.

CALCULATING LONG-TERM EDFs

The extension of the model to longer terms is straightforward. The default point, asset volatility, and expected asset value are calculated as before except they take into account the longer horizon, see Figure 7–9. For example, suppose we are interested in calculating the EDF for a three-year horizon. Over the three years, we can expect that the default point will increase as a result of the amortization of long-term debt. This is a conservative assumption that all long-term debt is refinanced short-term. We could just as easily model the asset value decreasing as the debt is paid down but in practice debt is usually refinanced. In any case it really doesn't matter, whether the assets go down by the amount of the amortiza-

FIGURE 7–9

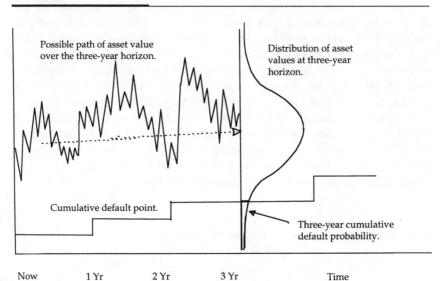

Possible path of asset value over the three-year horizon.

Distribution of asset values at three-year horizon.

Cumulative default point.

Three-year cumulative default probability.

Now   1 Yr   2 Yr   3 Yr   Time

tion or the default point increases by the same amount, the net effect on the default point is the same.

In addition to the default point changing, as we extend the horizon the future expected asset value is increasing as is our uncertainty regarding its actual future value. The expected asset value increases at the expected growth rate and the total asset volatility increases proportionally with the square root of time.[3]

The distance-to-default is therefore calculated using the relevant three-year asset value, asset volatility, and default point. The scaling of the default probability again uses the empirical default distribution mapping three-year distance-to-defaults with the cumulative default probability to three years. That is, the mapping answers the question, what proportion of firms with this three-year distance-to-default actually default within three years. The answer to this question is the three-year cumulative default probability. EDFs are annual default probabilities and the three-year EDF is calculated as the equivalent average annual default probability.[4] For example, suppose the three-year cumulative probability is 250 bp then the three-year EDF is 84 bp.

SOME FREQUENTLY ASKED QUESTIONS ABOUT EDFs

How does the model deal with off-balance-sheet liabilities?

This is a critical question for many firms, particularly financial institutions where these liabilities can obviously be quite significant. Fortunately, the model is surprisingly robust to the precise level of the liabilities.

For example, consider the firm used previously in our BS example. Assume that in addition to the $10 billion in liabilities the firm has a further $5 billion in off-balance-sheet commitments. That is, the true default point is actually $15 billion not $10 billion. The *actual* EDF of the firm can therefore be calculated using the BS model as follows. The firm's market capitalization remains $3 billion, and its equity volatility is still 40 percent

---

[3] The asset variance is additive and, therefore, increases linearly with time. The asset volatility is the square root of the variance and, therefore, increases with the square root of time.

[4] The EDF is calculated from the cumulative default probability using survival rates. For example, the three-year cumulative probability of default and the three-year EDF are related by the following expression: $1 - CEDF_3 = (1 - EDF_3)^3$. The probability of not defaulting within three years, $1 - CEDF_3$, and the average annual probability of not defaulting, $1 - EDF_3$.

per annum. The implied asset value and volatility, with liabilities of $15 billion, are calculated again by solving the call price and volatility equations, (7.2) and (7.3), simultaneously. In this case[5] the implied market value of the firm's assets is $17.267 billion, and the implied asset volatility is 6.9 percent. The asset value is about $5 billion higher and the asset volatility is lower reflecting the higher leverage of the firm. (Recall the equity volatility was kept the same but we increased the leverage, as a result the implied asset volatility must be lower.)

The corresponding distance-to-default is 2.7 and the implied EDF is 34 bp. Compare this with the 2.8 distance-to-default and 25 bp EDF calculated using only the on-balance sheet liabilities of $10 billion. This is a difference in about one minor rating grade, BBB− to BB+, for an increase in liabilities of 50 percent.

Obviously, if you have more complete or up-to-date information on the firm's liability structure it should be used in the model. Credit Monitor includes an add-on product called EDF Calculator™ (EDFCalc™) that enables the user to enter a more complete, or more recent, statement of the firm's liabilities.

Does the model incorporate the possibility of large changes in the market value of the firm?

Yes. In addition to incorporating the uncertainty in the liability structure of the firm, the empirical distance-to-default to EDF captures the possibility of large jumps, up or down, in the firm's market value. The empirical distribution includes data from several serious market downturns including the crash of October 1987.

Can the model be used to simulate market downturns or crashes?

The EDF already includes the effects of market downturns and crashes weighted by their appropriate probabilities. However, it is quite straightforward to ask questions such as, in the event of a 30 percent drop in the market what will be the effect on a firm's, or a portfolio of firms', EDFs? The effect of a market downturn on the equity value of any particular firm can be estimated using the firm's equity beta.

$$\Delta V_E = \beta_E \Delta V_m \qquad (7.10)$$

---

[5]All liabilities are assumed to be due in one year, $T = 1$, and the interest rate r is assumed to be 5 percent.

Should EDFs be averaged or smoothed to remove their variation over time?

No. It is certainly true that the EDF of a firm can vary over time but these variations are reflecting changes in credit quality as perceived by the equity market. Therefore, any smoothing or averaging is simply masking the signals from the market.

The volatility in EDF over time can pose problems for some bank's credit processes where the EDF directly determines the grade. However, this issue is usually simply overcome by determining actions by range of EDF. That is, action triggers are attached to grades that are defined in terms of EDF ranges. As a result, small, economically insignificant, movements within a grade do not trigger any action and movements between grades trigger an appropriate review.

A related question is whether or not there is any trend information in EDFs. There is not. EDFs are driven by market prices and, thus, are directly analogous to prices. If there isn't any trend information in the equity price there isn't any in the EDF.

What is the confidence interval around an EDF?

Confidence intervals are commonly used in statistics to account for sampling error. That is, because a survey, or other measure, covers the entire population of the statistic of interest, the average for example, can only be known within certain limits and the limits are generally referred to as the confidence interval. There is not an analogous concept for an EDF. With the exception of parts of the volatility estimation, EDFs are calculated from the option-pricing based causal model linking debt and equity. There really is no sampling measure.

In addition, the concept of a confidence interval around a probability really leads you to some quite philosophical issues.[6] Probabilities already encode a measure of uncertainty. Low EDFs mean that we are quite *confident* that the firm will not default. Conversely, high EDFs imply we are less *confident* that the firm will not default. For example, what is the expected default frequency when there is a 50 percent chance the default probability is 30 bp and a 50 percent chance the default probability is 20 bp? The answer is of course 25 b, the average of the confidence interval.

In practice, it is better to understand the sensitivity of the EDF to changes in the underlying variables, leverage, volatility, and asset value. The EDF calculator is the most common tool for analysts to do this type of analysis.

---

[6]There are some Bayesian decision models that can incorporate uncertainty in probabilities, but these models are complicated and not in common use.

Why isn't information from the bond or credit derivatives market included?

There is a whole class of models, usually called reduced-form models, that relate credit spreads and default probabilities. Our experience implementing these approaches has not been successful to date. There is nothing wrong with the models per se, indeed in theory they hold the promise of some advantages over the causal model described in this chapter. However, the data required to calibrate and implement reduced-form models is not yet widely available. In most cases credit risk simply is not as actively and cleanly traded as equities at the moment. This situation will undoubtedly change as the credit derivative and other markets grow, but to date we have not found credit spread information to be of sufficient quality to support the estimation of individual level default probabilities.

To date, the most successful use of credit spread data that we are aware of has been in the cross-sectional[7] estimation of credit spread curves. These curves describe the typical market spread for a given level of credit quality.

Are the default probabilities applicable across countries and industries?

The distance-to-default measure incorporates many of the idiosyncrasies of different countries and industries. For example, the business risk, as measured by the asset volatility, varies for a given industry across countries. Volatilities tend to be the lowest in Europe and the highest in the United States, with Asian countries usually in between. With exception of the difficulty posed by differing accounting standards, the default point can be measured appropriately for each firm regardless of its country of incorporation. The different economic prospects for countries are obviously captured by the individual equity and asset valuations. As a result, we believe that the distance-to-default captures most of the relevant inter-country differences in default risk. However, the question does remain whether differences in bankruptcy codes, culture, and so on may result in different default rates for a given distance-to-default. That is, is the distance-to-default to EDF mapping constant across countries?

The empirical default distribution that is used to map distance-to-default and EDF is built from publicly listed defaults in the United States. As a result its translation to other countries should be questioned. However, we believe that the default probabilities resulting from this U.S.

---

[7]Cross-sectional in this context means combining data from many different firms and issues. This is in contrast to the problem tackled in this chapter—the estimation of the default probability for each individual firm.

based mapping are good measures of economic default risk. That is, it is possible as a result of political or other intervention that a firm will be saved from default in say Europe when in the United States it might have been left to fail. However, these interventions are not free and are costly to someone, often the taxpayer, or in the case of Asia, more commonly the shareholders of related firms. It seems unwise to us to measure default risk incorporating a reliance on the uneconomic behavior of another group. The uneconomic behavior may well continue but it certainly seems unwise to institutionalize it in a measure of default risk. We do believe it is possible to reliably model uneconomic behavior and, thus, we aim to provide a hard economic measure of default and allow the analyst to factor in their own measure of implied government or other support.

Philosophy aside, our experience with EDFs internationally has been very good. Over half the users of EDFs operate outside of the United States. During the recent credit problems in Asia the model performed extremely well, see Figure 7–10. The model has also been tested anecdotally in most European countries. We continue to collect default data internationally and expect to be able to release a comprehensive study of Credit Monitor's performance as this data accumulates.

Does the EDF contain any measure of country (translation) risk?

We believe there is some measure of country risk impounded in EDFs but exactly how much we don't know. The calculations for EDFs are done in the local currency and, therefore, the country risk measure comes from the discount in the local equity price as a result of international investors concerns regarding the convertibility of the currency. Obviously

F I G U R E   7–10

Daito Kogyo, a Japanese construction company, defaulted in July 1997. Bangkok Metropolitan Bank (Thailand) was taken over in January 1998.

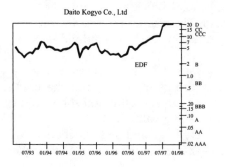

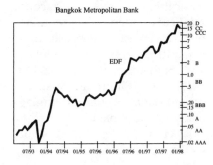

it is impossible to separate this influence from all the others and, as a result, we do not know how much country risk, if any, is present in the EDF. The amount is likely to vary by country as a function of the accessibility of their equity market and on the interest of international investors.

How well does the EDF work on thinly traded or closely held firms?

Surprisingly well. This question often arises in connection with efficient markets and the culture of Anglo-Saxon markets. While the results of the international default studies will have to speak for themselves we already actually know quite a lot about the performance of the model in thinly traded markets.

Our experience with these firms is drawn from the bottom end of the U.S. equity market where the companies are smaller and less actively traded than most of the firms on international exchanges. Our coverage of the United States is almost total and the bottom 2000 or so companies have market caps of less than U.S. $20 million, (almost 1000 have a market capitalization of less than U.S. $7 million). Most of these companies are not even listed on an exchange and are traded instead over the counter. Obviously trading in these companies is going to be thin and many are likely to be very closely held.

This is also a group of firms that default a lot and, thus, we have a large body of evidence on the model's performance on these firms. It is very good. It appears that it doesn't seem to take many economically motivated investors to move the equity price to reflect the risk of the firm.

Does the model assume that the equity market is efficient?

No. In fact it is important to realize that the equity is not always going to be right. Nor does it necessarily always reflect all the information regarding a company. In fact with hindsight the market is often wrong and, of course, it frequently changes its mind. However, we also know that it is difficult to consistently beat the market, over 90 percent of managed funds were unable to outperform the market in 1997. That is, it is difficult to pick stocks consistently, and difficult to know when the market is under- or overvaluing a firm. The market reflects a summary of many investors forecasts, and it is unusual if any one individual's, or committee's, forecast is better.

Sometimes the market is simply caught by surprise as in Figure 7–11. Burns Philip, an Australian food company (spices and the like), caught the market and rating agencies by surprise although some credit analysts undoubtedly worried that it was overvalued.

Fraud is often the cause of extremely large and sudden changes in credit quality. For example, in Figure 7–12 it is not hard to spot when the

F I G U R E   7–11

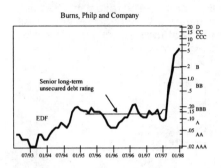

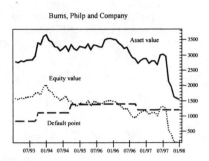

announcement regarding the improprieties in the reporting of Mercury Finance's assets was made.

However, most of the time the market will be well aware of problems, or opportunities, and this information will be fairly reflected in the EDF, see Figure 7–13.

How well does the model work on financial institutions?

The credit risk of financial institutions is notoriously difficult to assess. Financial institutions are typically very opaque and, thus, judging the quality of their assets and determining the extent of their liabilities is almost always very difficult. In addition, the liquidity of their assets means that their true size is sometimes difficult to judge. The window dressing of balance sheets at reporting dates is common place.

The equity market is well aware of these issues and no doubt does better than most at sorting them out. In addition, we are fortunate that

F I G U R E   7–12

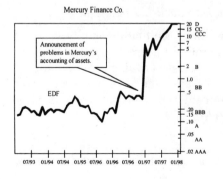

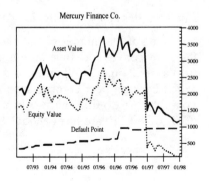

F I G U R E 7–13

Toshoku, a Japanese food trading company, failed in December 1997. The equity value of Safeway, a U.S. food retailer, has increased by $12.5 billion over the last four years while its liabilities have increased by only $1.5 billion.

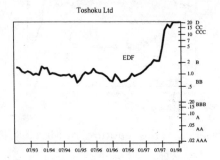

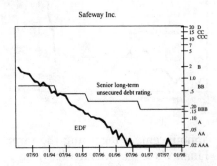

EDFs are relatively robust to the understatement of a firm's liabilities (see our earlier discussion on this issue). However, it is undoubtedly true that many financial institutions stretch this property of the model to its limits. In addition to these challenges, most financial institutions are tightly regulated and, thus, the appropriate definition of default may not be the point when their asset value falls below their liabilities. Unfortunately, there are very few financial institution defaults and, thus, testing and calibrating the model on just financial institutions is difficult.

Overall, despite these challenges we believe that the model performs very well on financial institutions, certainly better than any alternative approach that we know of. The lack of actual defaults means it is difficult for us to determine if the level of the EDF is as precise as it is for commercial and industrial firms, but the anecdotal evidence is clear; the model provides timely and reliable early warning of financial difficulty (see Figure 7–14).

How does this apply to firms that do not have publicly traded equity?

One of the themes of this chapter has been that the equity value of the firm conveys a considerable amount of information regarding the firm's credit quality. When this information is not available, we are forced to fall back on peer comparisons to determine the asset value and asset volatility. We do this analysis in a companion product to Credit Monitor (CM) called Private Firm Model™ (PFM).[8]

---

[8]The PFM is discussed more fully in other publications available from KMV Corporation.

F I G U R E   7–14

Yamaichi Securities defaulted during November 1997 and Siam City Bank (Thailand) was taken over by regulators in February 1998. First Central Financial Corp., a U.S. property and casualty insurance company, filed for Chapter 11 protection on March 5, 1998. First Bangkok City Bank, Thailand, was taken over February 1998.

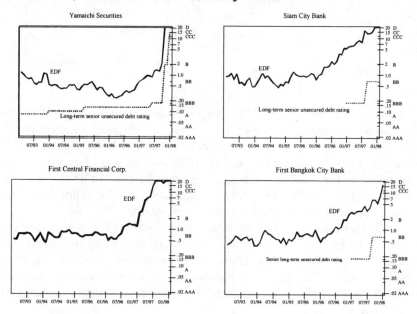

PFM uses the same framework as CM except the asset value and asset volatility are estimated using financial statement data and industry and country comparables. The estimation of the asset volatility is relatively straightforward. As we have seen, asset volatility can be explained quite well by size, industry, and country. Estimating the asset value is much more challenging. PFM uses a broad set of comparables and essentially determines an appropriate EBITDA[9] multiple. That is, given the set of comparables, what is a reasonable multiple to apply to the private firm's EBITDA to determine its asset value.

In spite of the obvious challenges that the absence of market data poses, overall the PFM does rather well. For example, in Figure 7–15 we

---

[9]We use EBITDA, earnings before interest, taxes, depreciation, and amortization, as a proxy for the firm's free cash flow.

F I G U R E 7-15

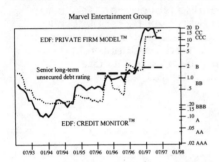
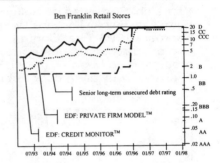

plot the EDFs from CM and PFM along with senior unsecured debt rating for two public firms. Marvel Entertainment, a U.S. publishing company that defaulted in December 1996 and Ben Franklin Retail Stores, a U.S. retail company, that defaulted in July 1997. As you would expect, at any one point in time, the correspondence between the public and private EDFs is far from perfect. However, longitudinally the correspondence can be quite remarkable as it is in both of these cases.

PFM's performance on truly private companies has been tested extensively in the United States and efforts are underway to extend this testing to Europe and Asia. There are some sectors in which the PFM does not do well at all. Most notably, it cannot be used on financial institutions. The operating cash flow for these firms is a very poor indicator of asset value.

The public market comparables tie the PFM's EDFs into the credit cycle. That is, because the EBITDA multiples adjust to reflect the current market conditions and outlook, the EDFs from the PFM change over time even if the financial statements of the firm remain stable. This is obviously a key property of the model, and within the limitations of financial statement data keeps the EDFs as forward looking as possible.

TESTING THE DEFAULT MEASURE'S PERFORMANCE

Determining the performance of a default measure is both a theoretical and an empirical problem. For example, what exactly do we mean by performance or predictive power? In practice, we can only hope to estimate probabilities of default. That is, we will not be able to definitively classify firms into *will default* and *will not default* categories. As a result, in assessing the performance of a model, we face the task of assessing its ability to discriminate between different levels of default risk.

For example, consider the policy of never lending to firms below 2 percent EDF, around a B rating. The benefit of this policy is that we avoid lending to firms that have a relatively high probability of default and, thus, avoid lending to a lot of firms that do eventually default. The cost of this policy is that we do not lend to any firms below a B rating and many of these firms, about 98 percent, do not default. Thus, one measure of a model's performance is the trade-off between the defaulting firms we avoid lending to and the proportion of firms we exclude. This trade-off is commonly called the power curve of a model.

For example, in Figure 7–16 we plot the power curves for EDF and the senior unsecured debt rating from a major bond rating agency. The cutoff points for the population are plotted along the horizontal axis and the proportion of defaults excluded at each cutoff point is plotted on the

F I G U R E   7–16

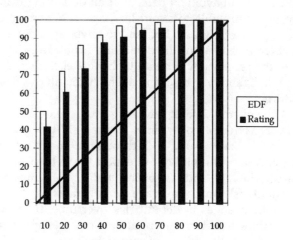

Default Predictive Power
EDF and Bond Ratings
Rated Universe

Percent of
Defaults
Excluded

Percent of
Population Excluded

FIGURE 7–17

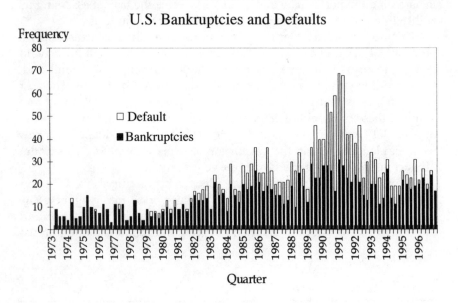

U.S. Bankruptcies and Defaults

vertical axis. If we rank all firms by their EDFs and impose a cutoff at the bottom 10 percent, then we avoid lending to 50 percent of the defaulting firms. That is, by not lending to the bottom 10 percent as ranked by EDF we can avoid 50 percent of all defaulting firms. At a cutoff of 30 percent we are able to avoid lending to 85 percent of defaulting firms and, of course, if we do not lend to anybody, a cutoff of 100 percent, we avoid lending to all of the defaulting firms. Thus, for a given cutoff, the larger the proportion of defaults that are excluded, the more powerful is the model's ability to discriminate high default risk firms from low default risk firms.

The overall default rate, and, thus, the default probability of firms, varies considerably over time. Figure 7–17 plots the default history for the United States from 1973 through 1997. The chart shows that as a general rule of thumb we can expect the default rate to double or triple between the high and low of the credit cycle. Thus, an effective measure of default risk cannot average default rates over time; instead, it must reflect the changes in default risk over time. Because EDF incorporates asset values based on information from the equity market, it naturally reflects the credit cycle in a forward-looking manner. For example, Figure 7–18 shows the median EDF for U.S. BBB rated firms from February 1993 through January 1997, and Figure 7–19 shows the EDF quartiles for financial institutions in Korea and Thailand over the same period.

F I G U R E 7–18

Median EDF BBB Rated U.S. Corporates

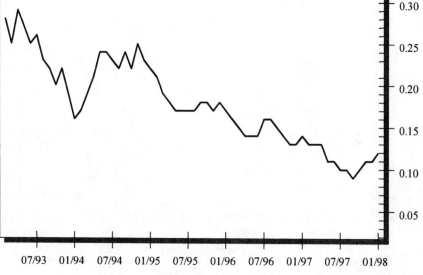

At the individual firm level, the model's ability to reflect the current credit risk of a firm can be assessed by observing the change in the EDF of a firm as it approaches default. Figure 7–20 plots the medians and quartiles of the EDF for five years prior to the dates of default for rated companies. Default dates are aligned to the right such that the time moving

F I G U R E 7–19

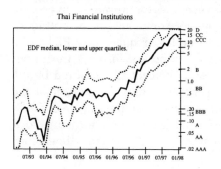

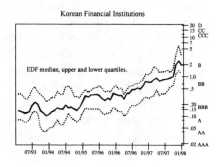

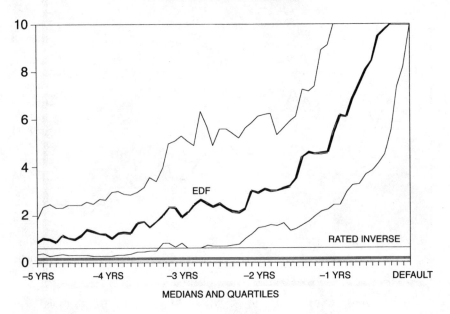

EDF PRIOR TO DEFAULT
RATED COMPANIES ONLY

MEDIANS AND QUARTILES

to the left indicates years prior to default. EDF is plotted along the vertical axis. The level of EDFs is sloping upward, towards increasing levels of default risk, as the date of default draws closer. Moreover, the slope increases as the date of default approaches.

Five years prior to default, the median EDF of defaulting companies is approximately 1 percent, around BB. One year prior to default the median has increased to over 6 percent. During the time of this sample, the median EDF for all rated companies, both default and non-default, was around 0.16 percent. (The median and percentiles for the rated universe are the straight lines running parallel to the horizontal axis at the bottom of the chart.) Two years prior to default, the lower quartile of EDFs (the riskiest 25 percent) of the defaulting firms breaks through the upper quartile of the rated universe (the safest 25 percent as measured by the rating agency). Thus, two full years prior to default 75 percent of the defaulting firms had EDFs in the bottom quartile of the universe.

There is no single measure of performance for default measures such as an EDF. Performance must be measured along several dimensions including discrimination power, ability to adjust to the credit cycle and the ability to quickly reflect any deterioration in credit quality. The EDF generated from the equity market and financial statement information of a firm does all of these things well. The dynamics of EDF come mostly from the dynamics of the equity value. It is simply very hard to hold the equity price of a firm up as it heads towards default. The ability to discriminate between high and low default risks comes from the distance-to-default ratio. This key ratio compares the firm's net worth to its volatility and, thus, embodies all of the key elements of default risk. Moreover, because the net worth is based on values from the equity market, it is both a timely and superior estimate of the firm's value.

SUMMARY AND DISCUSSION

A three-step process is used to calculate EDFs:

1. Estimate the market value and volatility of the firm's assets;
2. Calculate the distance-to-default, the number of standard deviations the firm is away from default; and
3. Scale the distance-to-default to an expected default frequency (EDF) using an empirical default distribution.

Because EDFs are based on market prices they are forward looking and reflect the current position in the credit cycle. They are a timely and reliable measure of credit quality. As a final example of the forward-looking strength of EDF, Figure 7–21 shows Venture Stores, which defaulted in January 1998. (Venture Stores was presented in our first example, Figure 7–1.) The first sign of a serious deterioration in the credit quality is in October 1994 when the EDF jumps from 2 percent to 5 percent (B to B-). The EDF climbed as high as 11 percent in February 1996, recovering a little as they secured additional financing before finally reaching 20 percent (D) in February 1997, eleven months prior to default.

EDFs are an effective tool in any institution's credit process. Accurate and timely information from the equity market provides a continuous credit monitoring process that is difficult and expensive to duplicate using traditional credit analysis. Annual reviews and other traditional credit processes cannot maintain the same degree of vigilance that EDFs calculated on a monthly or a daily basis can provide. Continuous monitoring is the only effective early warning protection against deteriorating credit quality. EDFs are also often used to help the focus of the efforts

FIGURE 7–21

Venture Stores Inc.

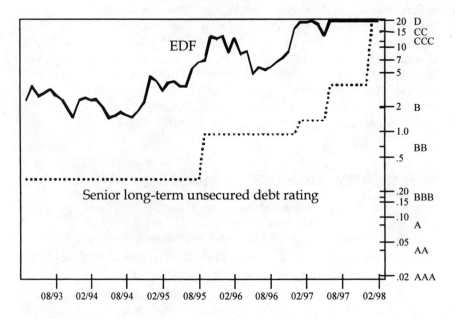

of traditional credit processes. They provide a cost-effective method to screen credits quickly and to focus credit analysis where it can add the most value. Further, because EDFs are real probabilities, they are the key data items in many institutions' provisioning, valuation, and performance measurement calculations.

CHAPTER 8

Challenges in the General Valuation of Credit Derivatives

Mark A. Gold, Ph.D.
Vice President, MBIA Insurance Corporation

Derivatives, especially in the form of futures on agricultural commodities, have been an applied financial technology for many decades. The last fifteen years, however, have witnessed an explosive growth in derivatives both through the development of new instruments and through the extensive adoption of these forms as essential elements in the day-to-day activities of large financial institutions and corporations. In a financial environment characterized by interest rate and foreign exchange variability, interest rate and currency derivatives in particular have become key components of risk management. Facilitating the application of such contracts has been a wide recognition and acceptance of associated valuation methods.

In recent years, new derivative instruments have been created which link cash flows to credit (or credit sensitive) events. These contracts such as default and total return swaps and credit-linked notes are included under a generic umbrella name: credit derivatives. Like, their interest rate and currency cousins, credit derivatives involve contingent cash flows determined by outcomes in underlying reference indices or instruments.

It is the point of this chapter, however, that there are fundamental differences between interest rate and currency derivatives, on the one hand, and credit derivatives, on the other. In the case of the former, capital markets establish conditions in which competition, in the form of arbitrage opportunities in markets of the underlying, compels a valuation that permits formulaic representation. In the case of credit derivatives, such market arbitrage opportunities are not generally available due to the general lack of futures or forward markets in credit risky instruments. While payouts on credit derivatives are "derived" by reference to external indices or instruments, it cannot be said that the price of such contracts is strictly determined by the market for the underlying. Pricing of such contracts must instead emerge as an outcome of supply and demand for credit insurance products; a market that is guided but not fully determined by conditions in the markets of the underlying. Moreover, the development of supply and demand functions in this market is one that necessarily is subjective and involves challenges in subjective determination. Further complicating the issue of pricing is the fact that regulatory views of credit enhancement differ from authority to authority and may condition balance sheet relief on the form rather than the substance of the provided credit support.

VALUATION OF INTEREST RATE AND CURRENCY DERIVATIVES

Why is it possible to value a fixed-floating interest rate swap when the value of the floating rate in the future is unknown? There are two parallel reasons. The first reason is given by the fact that a LIBOR floating rate bond, evaluated at the interbank level of credit quality, is a par instrument at reset, and that the cash flows of a fixed-floating swap can be replicated (at the interbank level of credit quality) by the issuance of a floating rate (fixed rate) bond, and the purchase of a fixed rate (floating rate) bond. Since such bonds may be valued on reset dates (the floating at par, the fixed according to discounted cash flows), a swap must have the same value as the self financed and replicating composite bond portfolio; if it doesn't, an arbitrage opportunity will exist in the capital markets of the underlying. The parallel reason is that, in liquid currencies with developed forward markets, a floating rate obligation may be hedged to the forward curve. Again, if the swap does not have a value very close to that given by the forward curve projection of floating payments against the payments of a fixed rate bond, an arbitrage opportunity will exist in capital markets within boundaries established by methodologies for forward curve determination and futures market frictions. In both cases, arbitrage opportunities will impose a valuation on the derivative. It is not difficult to prove that the resulting two swap valuation formulas, the par bond approach and the forward curve method, generate equivalent swap valuations.

As long as the prerequisite term curves and spot markets exist, arbitrage also permits valuation of foreign exchange futures, forwards, and swaps. This is so since today one can exchange at spot and invest in some credit risk free asset denominated in the second currency. Alternatively, one may invest in a credit risk free asset in the first currency until the targeted forward date and then exchange. The two investment strategies have the same initial condition, a given value in one currency, and must have the same terminal outcome. If not, one strategy will be preferred over the other. The underlying instruments, risk free bonds and the spot exchange rate thus serve to determine the forward exchange rate. Here, as in the case of interest rate derivatives, arbitrage opportunities in capital markets serve to impose a valuation on a derivative contract.

With respect to the valuation of options, it was the vital contribution of Fischer Black and Myron Scholes that, for an array of assets, specific positions in underlying assets could replicate the payout of a European option. To obtain the value of the option derivative, one proceeded to project the value of the replicating portfolio. While such projections involve important assumptions, including, in particular, an assumption concerning underlying price volatility, if the assumptions are largely correct, once again, arbitrage in capital markets will serve to enforce a valuation on the derivative.

PROBLEMS IN THE ENFORCEMENT OF CREDIT DERIVATIVE VALUATIONS

It would seem plausible that the value of a credit derivative on a credit risky bond would be related to the credit spread. Let us examine how that might be enforced.

The credit spread may be understood as the difference in yield between a credit risky asset and a credit risk free asset denominated in the same currency; it may be taken to represent the premium investors require to cover the contingent event of default loss, making them comfortable that the expected return on the portfolio of credit risky assets would be no less than a portfolio of credit risk free assets. As a practical matter, such spreads may fluctuate for reasons that have nothing to do with the immediate perspective of relative long term prospects for credit loss but rather are outcomes e.g., of fluctuating liquidity for credit risk free instruments of particular tenor or coupon. Let us here, however, abstract from such issues.

If I want to be "long" credit risk, that is fairly easy; I buy a credit risky bond. Again, this might not be quite so simple if I am seeking a particular credit, tenor, or coupon. Abstracting from such particularities, however, obtaining exposure to credit risk is not a hard thing to do.

Suppose I want to be long the credit spread. In currencies with liquid forward markets in highly rated sovereigns, this also is not difficult. In the case of the U.S. dollar, I buy a credit risky asset and "short" an appropriate strip of Treasury futures. To the extent that the general level of interest rates rises, my capital loss on the bond I own will be offset by the gain in the short Treasury futures. My exposure exists only to the relative movement of prices between the credit risky bond and the

Treasuries that underlie my short strip. Once the position is established, a widening of credit spreads reduces its value while a reduction in credit spreads raises its value.

Suppose, however, I want to take the opposite position with respect to the credit spread. Clearly, I must go long the Treasury strip and short the credit risky bond. Such a position would establish financial protection against the deterioration of credit quality of the entity issuing the credit risky debt instrument. Unfortunately, capital markets in general do not present a ready mechanism to sell short or sell forward credit risky bonds. The general inability to sell forward credit risky debt instruments in capital markets means that there is no strong enforcement mechanism for imposing capital market conditions directly upon the market for financial insurance products, generally, and upon the market for credit derivatives, in particular.

It should be noted in passing that while it is often possible to short equity positions, the use of such positions to hedge the credit risk of senior unsecured debt involves substantial basis risk. To the extent that an issuer has senior debt outstanding, the loss exposure of an equity holder in an insolvency may be materially larger than that of the senior bond holder since the bond holder will have a prior claim on assets relative to the equity holder.

Consequently, one cannot establish general valuation formulas for credit derivatives based on capital market conditions since there is no direct competitive mechanism for enforcing such results. While credit spreads must shape the supply and demand functions of individual market agents for credit insurance, such conditions do not impose a value on respective credit insurance products. Unlike interest rate and currency derivatives, where both payout and pricing are essentially determined in underlying markets, only the payout of credit derivatives is determined in the market of the underlying. Their price is established in a separate market for credit derivatives, a submarket of the broader market for credit insurance products.

To discuss the determination of credit derivative valuation, one must therefore consider the factors shaping the demand and supply functions of the individual agents participating in credit derivative markets. As will be made clear below, such a discussion bears substantial challenges.

PROBLEMS IN THE APPLICATION OF OPTION THEORY TO CREDIT DERIVATIVE VALUATION

While capital markets do not permit a general mechanism for selling credit risky debt forward, casual observers have suggested the application of options as a method of establishing a synthetic short position. Suppose in the over-the-counter market one purchased a put on a credit risky bond. When combined with a long Treasury strip, the put would establish credit protection since a credit-event induced drop in the value of the bond could be recovered in the contingent payout of the put. Wouldn't option valuation methods pioneered by Merton, Black, and Scholes provide a mechanism for the valuation of the option?

A review of the particular features of the Black-Scholes option valuation methodology will make clear that the answer, unfortunately, is "no."

The strategy of Black and Scholes was to establish a position in the underlying that would mimic the payout of a European option at expiry for every price outcome. Valuation of the option would then follow from the stochastic time-path in the movement of the underlying. So long as this stochastic evolutionary process could be defined in a way that permitted an analytical solution, the option could be valued. On the assumption that the underlying was credit risk free, a log normal stochastic process could be applied for a wide class of assets with the rate of return of a credit risk free asset as the trend return (or, if you like, since we are concerned with bonds, an alternative Wiener evolutionary process with a no-intertemporal-arbitrage drift could be applied). Here was a valuation methodology for the "risk-neutral" world.

Clearly, such a strategy cannot be applied in the case of credit risky assets. First, as stated above, a position in the underlying to reproduce the payout conditions of the derivative cannot be established because of a general inability to short credit risky debt instruments. Suppose, for argument's sake, however, that one could; even then, the Black-Scholes approach would break down since we would have to establish a stochastic evolutionary process for the underlying. Such a process, given the characteristics of bond values in default, will not be easy to characterize, and almost certainly will not be log normal. Moreover, we are left with the problem of defining the appropriate trend return for the process; the yield of a short-term highly rated sovereign would hardly be appropriate.

***

In the absence of a capital markets enforcement mechanism, prices for credit derivatives emerge out of markets for credit insurance products. This requires market agents to determine subjective valuations of credit derivatives as suppliers or consumers of such products. To the extent that products were standardized and pricing was transparent, such a market might replicate the effects of arbitrage opportunities in the underlying. Unfortunately, products tend to be customized, pricing is not always transparent, and the subjective conditions of the agents will vary to such a large extent that sellers may easily apply segmented price schemes.

Indeed, the determination of a subjective valuation for a credit derivative is one that will vary from valuing agent to valuing agent not only due to differences in portfolio conditions but also due to differences of objectives and analytical approaches.

The development by market agents of independent views concerning the value of credit derivatives conditioned on the subjective portfolio situation and evaluation of default risks is one that poses a range of challenges. Should valuation of credit derivatives be studied based upon credit events other than default (e.g., credit rating downgrade), or should credit derivative valuation be based strictly upon the probability of default loss? How should one characterize the value time path of a credit risky underlying instrument? How does a portfolio manager make judgements concerning the risk that assets in the portfolio will default in tandem? These questions will be considered in detail below. It will ultimately be clear that market participants with different portfolios will evaluate a given credit derivative differently and that even in the case where the portfolio is the same, different managers need not draw the same conclusions concerning pricing, supply, or demand given their respective subjective views on the questions above.

MODELING THE CREDIT EVOLUTIONARY PROCESS

The expectations of agents concerning the credit loss exposure of their portfolios must be constructed based on some views on the likelihood of credit devolution and default. Before examining what those expectations might be, let us first consider to what extent the analysis of credit devolution is necessary.

If one is maintaining a large portfolio of credit risky assets, the projection of credit devolution may be of interest in order to adjust reserves against the change in likelihood of portfolio loss. Beyond such a risk control concern, the portfolio may be exposed to credit derivatives the payout of which is conditioned not on default but on some intermediate, credit devolution condition. Derivatives subject to credit related barriers would be an example of contracts the payout of which may be contingent on a credit event other than default; a total return swap could also establish payouts due to credit devolution as well as default. Where the portfolio is exposed to contingent payments in the event of credit devolution, the modeling of the credit evolutionary path becomes important.

If, however, the portfolio of credit exposures is not large and does not contain contracts the payout of which is credit devolution sensitive, the intermediate stages a credit might take between its current state and default are not of any particular interest. The probability of default is the essential concern.

Whether or not one includes the analysis of credit devolution in the projection of contingent losses, some judgements will be necessary regarding the application of default histories. Over what classes of assets should one try to develop inferences? Should one be concerned only with the history of corporate debt or should one include default histories involving other debt categories (e.g., municipal or structured debt)? Clearly the outstanding tenor of a security is relevant in the analysis of contingent credit risk exposure; is there also, however, some relevance to be associated with the amount of time that has elapsed since the date of issuance? To the extent that an estimate of the probability of default over the outstanding tenor of a security has been established, what are probabilities over subintervals? Should one apportion the probability evenly over time or establish some other path? Of course, the questions here concerning default probabilities may be applied to the analysis of credit ratings transitions through nondefault states over time. Depending on one's answers to these questions, an evolutionary approach to rating transition and default, such as a first order Markov process, may, or may not, be appropriate.

CREDIT INTERRELATIONSHIPS AMONG PORTFOLIO ASSETS

The subjective valuation of a given credit derivative will also be conditioned by specific portfolio conditions since default exposures of separate credits are not necessarily independent and, indeed, are likely to bear some interconnection. Establishing the extent of such interrelationships is by no means clear-cut. If one is evaluating the contingent credit risk embedded in a portfolio using an analysis of credit devolution, it may be possible to establish credit downgrade correlations between different asset segments based on historical observations, though the stability of such relationships will be questionable. If, on the other hand, one is analyzing contingent credit loss exposure in terms of default events only, the concept of correlation will not be applicable; one will need to apply, instead, the concept of conditional probability. While formally, conditional probability will allow an agent to weight contingent default losses among assets in an interrelated fashion, the practical application of the concept is much more difficult than the application of rating downgrade correlations. There are far fewer defaults than downgrades so data sets will be nowhere near as rich. Moreover, the actual evaluation of the data will be difficult. How does one judge whether observed events were interrelated? Are they interrelated because of the combination of commonality of class and time proximity? What criteria does one apply to establish proximity of time and commonality of class? Finally, whatever judgements are made concerning historical observation, are the relationships stable enough to project them forward? If not, what approaches are reasonable to establish a credit reserve "tax" against joint credit event interrelationships that may be extant in a particular portfolio at a particular time?

***

The challenges to the valuation of credit derivatives expressed here are by no means exclusive to this class of contracts but extend as well to the much broader class of credit insurance instruments. While formulaic valuation may, therefore, be problematic for this class of products, the spectrum of credit support vehicles serves to establish competition in the market for financial insurance that provides the potential for boundaries around pricing. It is worth noting that the different products, while close substitutes for each other, are by no means perfect substitutes. Moreover, the different regulatory regimes of the providers and the differing regulatory credit given to instruments offering the same payout properties can establish irrationalities in pricing and demand. Finally, a market for insurance products will establish competitive prices near costs as long as there is a high degree of market transparency. However, there is not a centralized marketplace for credit insurance products, nor are there centralized price-posting centers. Impeding the development of such information gathering centers is the customized character of many credit enhancement products. Unfortunately, limits on transparency contribute to a range of practices such as concessionary pricing, which, in turn, further add to the lack of clarity concerning real prices and costs.

To better understand the market for external credit support products, let us review five kinds of alternatives: (1) third party guarantees, (2) stand-by letters of credit, (3) surety bonds issued by regulated financial guarantors, (4) credit derivatives, and (5) recourse arrangements. These forms of credit risk mitigation extend beyond such bilateral arrangements as netting agreements, recouponing, and mark-to-market and collateral posting agreements.

FORMS OF THIRD PARTY CREDIT ENHANCEMENT

Generally, there are two basic types of third party guarantees, guarantees of collection and guarantees of payment. In the case of the former, an obligor obtains enhancement of its performance of specified obligations (the specification of which may be highly particular or quite general) in the form of a promise (made for value) by the guaranteeing third party to pay to a creditor sums on the referenced obligations which the creditor was unable to collect from the obligor after exhausting its legal remedies, up to any contracted limit. Collection guarantees obviously provide credit support—but not timely support. In the case of payment guarantees, the obligor obtains (for value) from the guaranteeing third party a promise to pay to creditors sums due on referenced obligations upon demand when due. Collection of recovery against the obligor is pursued later by the guarantor.

Standby letters of credit (LOCs) are essentially obligor contracted payment guarantees issued by banks, stipulating specific beneficiaries and covered performance obligations. Collection against the obligor in the event of a draw under an LOC is made by the issuing bank under terms of a reimbursement agreement contracted by the obligor in conjunction with the LOC.

A surety bond is essentially (and sometimes formally) a contracted payment guarantee issued (for value) by a regulated financial guarantor, a financial institution the business of which is to write financial insurance policies under conditions established and monitored by the regulating authority. Typically it is obligor contracted, though not always.

Credit derivatives are contracts under which, in exchange for a premium or schedule of fixed payments, a third party promises to make certain specified payments to a counterparty upon a specified credit linked (or credit sensitive) event involving a referenced obligor. The obligor need not, and often is not, a party to the transaction except as a reference under the payment terms. Typically, it is a creditor or contingent creditor that contracts a credit derivative to obtain relief against contingent losses due to credit events affecting obligors to which it is exposed.

Recourse arrangements are those in which a financial institution (or, in some instances, a nonfinancial business) retains certain credit exposures in connection with a transaction, such as a securitization. The retention may be for reasons of promoting the transaction (e.g., in the sale of the asset-backed notes), or it may be as an investment.

These different forms of third party credit enhancement are often close substitutes—but they are seldom perfect substitutes. They may differ as to the character of the contracting parties and they often are affected differently by regulation. These differences tend to impose segmentations into the market for credit enhancement services that may serve to reduce efficiency.

REGULATORY INCONSISTENCIES IN THE TREATMENT OF DIFFERENT FORMS OF CREDIT INSURANCE

As an object lesson in the differences in regulatory treatment between the different forms of third party credit support, consider U.S. bank regulatory capital rules for capital charges arising due to bank exposures to securitizations.

Under rules prevailing for many years, bank recourse exposures with respect to assets transferred in a securitization were capital-charged as a risk weighting with reference to the total amount of assets sold into the securitization and not conditioned on the size of the recourse, except as modified by the low-level recourse rule. This rule limits the maximum risk based capital requirement to the maximum contractual exposure of the bank. If, however, a bank retained recourse not through a contractual arrangement of risk retention in conjunction with the asset sale but via an off-balance sheet direct credit substitution in the form of a standby letter of credit, the charge would be based on the size of the enhancement and not the size of the pool being enhanced. The anomaly in the rules permitted banks to reduce capital requirements merely by changing the form of the support provided to a securitization.

To correct this loophole, various regulatory authorities prepared a joint release on new proposed rules that strove to establish charges according to the substance of exposure and not the form. The new rules establish general uniformity, informed by credit ratings issued by nationally recognized statistical ratings organizations, for capital charges related to bank support of bank exposures to securitizations. Some inconsistencies remain, however, where external support for a bank on its retained securitization exposure is provided by a nonbank guarantee or a Surety Bond. Such inconsistencies, while present under U.S. rules, are not necessarily present in rules governing financial institutions domiciled outside the United States and regulated under other authorities.

Of course, differences in regulatory capital treatment accorded the various forms of credit support are not confined to the area of securitization. Generally, differences will exist in conjunction with differences in the formal and informal regulating authority governing the issuer of the support. These differences have a tremendous impact upon pricing since the critical component of the cost of credit support is the cost of capital allocated against the associated exposure.

CONCESSIONARY PRICING

Occasionally, financial institutions will offer concessionary pricing of credit enhancement products either as an inducement to engage the institution as part of a broader transaction, or as part of a broad client relationship touching upon many different areas of business. Such arrangements distort the market for credit insurance products by reducing the transparency of real costs and prices. The victims of the resulting lack of transparency may include the conceding firm itself if such concessions are not the result of carefully reasoned and calculated shadow prices for services and associated incomes.

CREDIT ARBITRAGE

Regulatory inconsistencies and impediments to transparency contribute to conditions in which pricing inefficiencies may persist. In addition to these impediments are scale issues. To the extent that credit spreads reflect market views concerning the particular credit quality of respective issuers, implicitly they do so with respect to a portfolio of a certain size and diversification. To the extent that exposures may be contracted only on a relatively lumpy basis, a portfolio scale is required (along with skill in portfolio construction and management) before the credit spread offers a meaningful return on a risk-adjusted basis.

Ironically, the capital markets which fail to provide an enforcement mechanism for the valuation of derivatives on individual risky credits provide the foundation, via credit-linked notes and securitization, for the arbitrage of scale, regulatory, and opaque pricing inefficiencies. While the activities in the market, both in terms of the everyday marketing of credit insurance products and the steady growth in the securitization of credit-risky assets create mechanisms by which competition may work to assert a consistent price set, the persistence of arbitrage action indicates that practical barriers continue to impede the emergence of clear valuations for credit derivatives and other credit enhancement products.

CONCLUSION

Securitization of credit exposure raises interesting issues at the periphery of the subject of credit derivative valuation.

Many of the obstacles to the general valuation of credit support products rest in the specificities associated with them. Such specificities are not associated with interest rate or currency products transacted at the interbank level of credit. In part, LIBOR may be hedged efficiently because it is general. Exposure to XYZ Corp. can only be hedged by a specific offsetting credit support transaction. This is particularly of importance with respect to the function of intermediation.

Until recently, the market for the underwriting of credit exposure was largely a buy and hold proposition. The allure of credit derivatives rested in part in the prospect for a liquid secondary market that would fundamentally transform the nature of credit support products. Credit derivatives, as such, however, permit only a limited transcendence beyond the specificity of credit exposure. True, through credit derivatives, exposure many be delinked from origination and formal instrument ownership—but this delinkage has long been available through a range of credit support products.

Over the last year, however, new products have emerged combining credit derivatives and securitization techniques. In these products, huge pools of credit exposure, in some cases accumulated through the intemediation activities of credit derivative desks, are established as references for credit-linked notes which pay principal less reference losses and interest representing, in part, an insurance premium, to classes of noteholders at various levels of subordination. By pooling a very large number of exposures, in many cases diversified across geographic and/or industry categories, note issuers offer to investors (the functional insurers) a more generic type of credit risk that is far more amenable to objective acturarial calculation. In such condition are the seeds of general hedge instruments and, perhaps, a potential foundation for new market boundaries to credit support product pricing.

PART FOUR

Accounting, Tax, Legal, and Regulatory Environment

CHAPTER 9

Accounting for Credit Derivatives

John T. Lawton
Partner, PricewaterhouseCoopers LLP

INTRODUCTION

There are a variety of concepts that seemingly conflict in the various manners by which we account for different types of financial assets and liabilities. Sometimes in accounting one looks to a group of assets or liabilities to determine the amount that should be reported in the financial statements. For example, entities often times evaluate the losses inherent in a portfolio of loans or other receivables when evaluating the appropriate amount to report in a reserve for credit losses. Other times, one must focus solely on a single transaction or asset for financial reporting purposes, even though there may be relationships between that asset and other assets or liabilities reported in the financial statements. For example, the fair value reported for an available for sale security must be the amount at which a single security could be traded, regardless of how large or how liquid the entity's overall position is in that security. In still other circumstances, we account for parts of a transaction, asset or liability separately, such as when a detachable warrant is accounted for separately from the debt to which it is attached. Other conflicts that exist in accounting involve the timing of when a transaction or event is recognized in the financial statements, while still others involve different ways of measuring assets and liabilities in the financial statements (e.g., amortized cost, market value, lower of cost or market, etc.).

The financial innovations of the last twenty-five years have in many instances highlighted these areas of conflict, and often it has been difficult to determine the appropriate concept or principle to apply to a particular financial instrument or transaction. This has been particularly true in the area of credit derivatives and, in my experience, many transactions that are similar have been accounted for in alternative ways as a result of the ambiguity in accounting guidance. Until recently, there has been no authoritative accounting literature that addresses how to account for these instruments. Accountants have had to rely on analogies to other types of transactions and instruments, together with an understanding of a transaction's purpose and intent, to determine a reasonable and fair approach to presenting the results of credit derivative transactions in the financial statements.

Accounting standard setters around the globe are struggling to address the spate of new financial products and the rapid development of the capital markets. In the United States, the Financial Accounting Standards Board (FASB) issued Statement of Financial Accounting Standards No. 133, "Accounting for Derivative Instruments and Hedging Activities," (SFAS 133) in June 1998, becoming the first comprehensive standard for accounting for derivative instruments, including most credit derivatives, to be issued. That statement becomes effective for most entities in the year 2000. Other standard setters have proposals in various stages of development, and it is virtually certain that a steady flow of additional accounting guidance will be issued in the foreseeable future with implications on the accounting for credit derivative transactions. Consultation with a locally qualified accountant is recommended when considering how to account for a specific transaction. This chapter will focus on the accounting standards applicable in the United States, but the general concepts have applicability in most instances in other countries.

There are a variety of credit derivative types, but much of the accounting discussion to date has focused on three general categories of credit derivatives, total return swaps, credit spread options, and credit default products. Credit derivative contracts may combine an endless number of terms and conditions resulting in products with different payment events, amounts, and underlying assets. Nevertheless, for accounting purposes these contracts generally can be categorized into these three groups.

TOTAL RETURN SWAPS

In general, a total return swap buyer exchanges the economic performance of a reference asset for a more stable return. In a typical contract, the buyer owes to the seller all the contractual amounts that would be received during the period if the reference asset were held plus any appreciation of the reference asset based on observed prices. The seller owes to the buyer an amount equal to a fixed or floating annual percentage rate of the notional value of the reference asset (usually tied to the seller's short-term borrowing costs) plus any depreciation in the observed value of the reference asset. Only the net amounts owed under the contract are exchanged. The observed price differential component may be determined and/or paid periodically, or at contract maturity. During the life of a total return swap, the buyer effectively shifts the credit and market risk of holding the reference asset to the seller. Nevertheless, neither the buyer nor the seller is required to hold the underlying reference asset in a total return swap.

In the absence of authoritative accounting literature addressing total return swaps, accountants have sought to apply accounting treatments that follow the economic substance of the transactions. In doing so, all of the specific contract terms must be evaluated so that all payment flows and contingencies are analyzed. Total return swaps are highly customized instruments and terms vary from transaction to transaction. In addition, the intent of the party in entering the transaction and the relationship of the swap to other assets and liabilities of the entity must be considered.

As the name implies, total return swaps transfer a variety of risk elements that would be incumbent to holding the underlying reference asset. Interest rate and foreign currency risks may be transferred, as well as the more pervasive credit risk. Total return swaps are similar to interest rate swaps and other derivatives in the manner in which they transfer risks and returns separately from the funding and holding of underlying assets. Consequently, accountants have generally analogized to the accounting treatment for interest rate swaps and other derivative contracts when accounting for total return swaps. Total return swaps are particularly analogous to equity swaps, because of the mechanisms for exchange of the market appreciation, or depreciation, of the underlying assets. The new accounting guidance in SFAS 133 confirms this treatment. Virtually all total return swaps would be considered derivatives under the new definition established in this standard.

In recent years, the focus in accounting for derivatives has been increasingly placed on the individual contract, with market value considered to be the most appropriate measurement. Consequently, mark-to-market accounting has generally been applied to individual total return swap transactions from inception of the contract, with the total return swap reported at its fair value and changes in value reported in income in the period of change.

Accountants also consider the relationship of a total return swap to other assets and liabilities in determining the overall accounting treatment of a transaction. Some entities hold the related reference asset as an asset or liability and enter into total return swaps to manage risk. Given the inconsistencies in accounting methods, the underlying asset or liability may be accounted for differently than the total return swap. For example, a loan underlying a total return swap may be reported at amortized cost, with any potential credit loss considered in an overall allowance for credit losses in a loan portfolio. As a result, earnings and the balance sheet may reflect amounts differing from fair value in a given reporting period. Gains and losses on the market value of the swaps may not offset the accrual of net interest income and provision for loan losses related to the loan, despite the overall neutral market risk position in the loan. To mitigate the effects of these types of situations, accountants look to the application of hedge accounting.

Unfortunately, it has been difficult for an entity to meet the requirements for hedge accounting when using total return swaps. This is primarily due to the requirement that the item to be hedged exposes the entity to accounting risk of loss for the price risk. Referenced assets that management intends to hold to maturity, such as an originated loan, will theoretically mature at par, except in the case of default. Economic gains and losses associated with interest rate and other risks are not recognized. Since losses related to price movements would not be recognized and offset price movements on the total return swap during the contract period, hedge accounting criteria would not be met. Total return swaps that mature concurrently with the underlying asset may overcome this obstacle.

Historically, the accounting treatment for a total return swap transaction that does qualify as an accounting hedge has been to conform the accounting for the total return swap to the accounting for the underlying asset, rather than apply mark-to-market accounting. Generally, period interest exchanges resulting from the swap would be recorded as an adjustment of interest income arising from the designated loans or securities being hedged. Payments attributed to any actual or expected change in value are treated in the same way as the offsetting change in the value of the designated loans or securities. For U.S. reporting purposes, SFAS 133 has dramatically changed this accounting by requiring a change to the accounting for the underlying reference asset when a fair value hedge of an asset or liability is being made.

Under SFAS 133, a derivative contract, including a total return swap, can be used to hedge the exposure to changes in fair value of a recognized asset or liability, or of a firm commitment attributable to a particular risk. The hedge must be part of a formally documented strategy that details how the effectiveness of the hedge will be measured. In addition, throughout the life of the hedge, there must be an expectation of achieving offsetting changes in fair value attributable to the risk being hedged. That risk may be the entire change in fair value of the hedged item, or for financial instruments, interest rate risk, credit risk, or foreign exchange risk. The hedged item must present an exposure to changes in fair value that could effect reported earnings, but not be measured at fair value with changes in value reported directly in earnings.

If the qualifications for a fair value hedge are met, the change in the fair value of the hedging derivative is still reported as an asset or liability on the balance sheet with changes in its value reported in earnings. The change in the fair value of the designated asset or liability attributable to the hedged risk adjusts the basis of the hedged asset or liability with the corresponding amount also reported in earnings. For hedges of an available-for-sale security, the change in fair value of the available-for-sale security attributable to the hedged risk is recorded in earnings as opposed to in the separate component of equity. Under SFAS 133, any ineffectiveness, or imperfection in the hedge impacts earnings. Under previous hedge accounting rules, if the hedging relationship qualified for hedge accounting, hedge ineffectiveness was generally not immediately recognized in earnings.

A total return swap may also qualify as a cash flow hedge. A cash flow hedge is a hedge of the exposure to variability in the cash flows of a recognized asset or liability or of a forecasted transaction that is attributable to a particular risk. An example of a cash flow hedge would be the use of a total return swap to ensure the total amount of cash to be paid for a tender offer on an outstanding debt issue of an entity. Like a fair value hedge, the hedge must be documented at inception, specify the hedged item, the nature of the risk being hedged, and describe how effectiveness will be assessed. Forecasted transactions must be probable and their terms identified with a fair degree of specificity.

Under SFAS 133, a total return swap used in a cash flow hedge would still be reported in the balance sheet at its fair value. However, only the portion of the change in market value that is not effective in offsetting the cash flows being hedged would be reported directly in earnings. The effective portion of the change in value would be reported in other comprehensive income, which is reported separately under new accounting guidance and in essence bypasses net income and goes directly to the equity section of the balance sheet. When the cash flows being hedged are reported in earnings, the accumulated balance in other comprehensive income would then also be recognized in earnings. In effect, accumulated other comprehensive income acts as a holding pen for the changes in market value in the total return swap until the effects of the cash flows being hedged are reported in earnings. Needless to say, the accounting for this type of hedge is cumbersome, and detailed tracking of balances in accumulated other comprehensive income is necessary to ensure that the adverse effects of the differing timing, or method, of recognizing the hedged item and the total return swap are correctly mitigated.

The many variants of total return swaps are generally addressed by SFAS 133. Transaction structurers will be challenged to determine how best to fit the variety of existing and new products into the hedging concepts of the new accounting guidance. Because of the strong undercurrent of market value accounting in the new rules and the shift to recognizing the ineffective portion of a hedge currently, there will be increased volatility in earnings as a result. Unbundling products into separate contracts may provide one means by which this volatility may be minimized.

CREDIT SPREAD OPTIONS

Not all credit derivative products provide for the unconditional exchange of payments as in a total return swap. Many products provide the buyer an option to effect an exchange or receive payment when specific conditions are met. One type of credit derivative with this feature is a credit spread option. Credit spread options are generally used to lock in a credit spread above some interest rate index for a specific period of time. For example, a corporation planning to issue three-year floating-rate debt instruments in three months may desire to ensure that the spread above LIBOR will not exceed the spread at which it could currently issue debt. It could buy a credit spread option from a derivative dealer to provide protection from increasing credit spreads. Under the terms of the agreement, the corporation could require the dealer to pay the difference between the current spread above LIBOR and the spread available at the time of issuance if the credit spread widens during the three month option term. In exchange, the corporation would pay the dealer a premium.

Accountants have accounted for credit derivative options by analogy to other types of financial options. Existing practice for those options generally calls for mark-to-market accounting unless specific hedge criteria are met. A seller of these products would not qualify for hedge accounting treatment and would report the contract at market value with changes in value reported in earnings. When a buyer of these contracts meets criteria for hedge accounting, the buyer has historically split the value of the option in two pieces. The intrinsic value of the option (the value attributable to the amount that an option is in-the-money) has been accounted for as an adjustment of the hedged item. In the example, cited above, this would mean synthetically reducing the interest rate over the five-year period that interest is paid on the underlying debt. The time value of the option (i.e., the remaining value of the option after deducting the intrinsic value) has been amortized over an appropriate period.

Again SFAS 133 has changed this reporting model going forward under U.S. accounting principles. Credit spread options and similar option contracts are considered derivatives for accounting purposes. Consequently, the options will always be reported at market value like all other derivatives. For those options that qualify as a hedge, the same guidance described above for total return swaps would be applicable to credit spread options. For the corporation in the example above, it seems quite likely that the credit spread option could qualify as a cash flow hedge of the interest payments on the anticipated debt issuance. If the debt issuance is probable, the corporation could report the changes in the credit spread option's fair value that would be effective in offsetting the effects of increases in credit spreads in other comprehensive income until the related interest expense is recognized. The portion of value change attributable to time decay of the option and other factors would continue to be reported in income in the current period. If the option is in the money at maturity and is exercised, the accumulated balance in accumulated other comprehensive income would be recognized in income as a reduction of interest expense in the periods where the related interest expense is accrued.

Despite the economic differences between total return swaps and credit spread options, the accounting is essentially the same under SFAS 133. This is the result of the FASB's attempt to create more uniform accounting for derivative instruments. However, not all credit derivatives are derivatives as defined by SFAS 133.

CREDIT DEFAULT PRODUCTS

Credit default products are contracts that are designed to provide protection against credit loss on an underlying reference asset as a result of a specific event, usually default by the reference asset issuer. The writer or seller of the product receives a premium in exchange for making a payment to the buyer should the specified event occur. The conditional payment may be a fixed amount or an amount determined at the time of the credit event, such as the difference between the market value and face value of the reference asset. The premium received may also be received at contract inception, or it may be received over time in fixed or variable payments. As with total return swaps, the permutations of what could be done are seemingly endless.

Contracts with these characteristics have attributes that are analogous to several different types of products, each with different prescribed accounting practices. Consequently, there has been diversity in the way credit default products have been treated for financial reporting purposes. Many credit default contracts have been analogized to products such as standby letters of credit and financial guarantees. Others have been analogized to derivatives, while still others have been analogized to insurance contracts.

The Financial Accounting Standards Board recognized this diversity in practice when developing the new accounting rules for derivatives. Consequently, they established guidance for determining which contracts should be considered derivatives and which should be analogized to other types of products such as financial guarantees. Contracts may be considered financial guarantees only if one of the parties to the contract will receive payment as reimbursement for actual losses incurred because the underlying debtor fails to make payment when due. It requires this type of insurable event to be considered a guarantee. Contracts for payment based on a change in an underlying, such as a change in a debt rating, will be considered derivatives.

This guidance will cause many contracts that have previously been treated by analogy to standby letters of credit and other credit products to be considered derivatives from the date of adoption of SFAS 133. That means contracts which were accounted for by amortizing premiums through date of maturity on a systematic basis and reporting loss accruals when losses become probable will suddenly be accounted for at market value.

One characteristic of this new guidance is that form, as well as substance, will play a critical role in determining which contracts may be considered to be a financial guarantee. The FASB staff has indicated that in order for a contract to be considered a financial guarantee, and not a derivative, the contract provisions must require that the buyer have exposure to loss as a precondition for payment. The exposure to loss can arise from holding the reference asset or from other contractual provisions. The buyer's holding of an underlying asset is therefore not a sufficient condition for a contract to be considered a guarantee. Buyers and sellers of credit default products can thus choose the accounting model for a given transaction by inserting or omitting contract language that links the payments under the contract to the loss exposure being hedged.

Credit default products that are within the scope of SFAS 133 will be accounted for just the same as total return swaps and other derivatives. Consequently, they will be mark-to-market each period and reported on the balance sheet at fair value. The corresponding change in fair value for each period will be reported in earnings or in other comprehensive income, depending upon whether the product is part of an effective cash flow hedge. If the credit product is part of a fair value hedge, the basis of the hedged item may be adjusted for changes in fair value attributable to changes in credit risk, thus offsetting changes in the fair value of the credit derivative product reported in current period earnings.

For those credit default products that are outside the scope of SFAS 133 and thus analogized to financial guarantees, the accounting would differ somewhat for the buyer and seller of the transaction. The seller would accrue into income the premium received over the life of the contract. Each period the seller would evaluate the likelihood that a payment would have to be made under the contract. If payment is probable, then a loss would be reported in earnings equal to the discounted or undiscounted amount of loss expected, with a liability established. Until the loss became probable, there would not be any separate accounting for the potential payments to be made under the contract. This accounting treatment is consistent with the general principles for accounting for contingencies described in Statement of Financial Accounting Standards No. 5.

Like sellers, buyers would account for the payment of the premium over the life of the transaction. In essence, the amount paid in advance or over time is like an insurance premium, which for fixed amounts is recognized on a straight-line basis. If the buyer's payments are variable, they are recognized evenly within the periods for which payment is due. Since the buyer has the related underlying exposure, it would evaluate its overall exposure to loss from its combined position. The buyer would consider the probability of loss in a broader context, grouping the protection afforded by the credit default product with the loss exposures it may have in its loan portfolio or elsewhere. Losses inherent in the overall portfolio would then be reported when they are probable.

Some credit default products may have features that would distinguish them from the general types described above. In those cases, other accounting analogies may be appropriate. For example, contracts that include other aspects that parallel insurance contracts as defined in the accounting literature might better be accounted for using an insurance model. Despite the new accounting rules in the United States, there is still not a complete roadmap for all the innovative credit derivative products that are yet to be developed.

SECURITIES WITH EMBEDDED CREDIT PRODUCTS

Aspects of credit protection and risk transferal are inherent in the credit markets, and it is not new that bonds include elements to protect the investors or to shift interest rate or other risks to the bond investors. However, in recent years there has been innovation in how those features can be combined in a security. For example, some bonds have been issued under which repayment is contingent upon another party meeting its obligation on a reference security. These bonds have combined credit derivative features with the usual elements of debt to create attractive returns and to target specific investors.

The accounting for securities in general varies depending on the type of entity, the purpose of the investment, the ability and intent to hold the investment to maturity and other factors. In the United States, accounting rules may require securities to be mark-to-market value with the changes in value reported in earnings or other comprehensive income. Other times, securities may be reported at historical or amortized cost. With this existing diversity, it is no surprise that securities with embedded credit derivatives have been accounted for in a myriad of ways.

Generally, securities with unusual features have been accounted for based on the predominant characteristics of the overall contract. If overall, the usual credit features such as fixed principal with set maturity dates predominate over the unusual features, accountants have looked to the security model to account for the transaction, with modifications to adapt to the special attributes caused by the embedded derivative. For example, a bond issue that pays contingent interest based on the performance of a referenced asset would be accounted for as debt, with interest accrued based on the amount that would be payable assuming the conditions existing at the balance sheet date (sometimes called marked-to-index accounting).

Under the new accounting standard, SFAS 133, the rules have dramatically changed for these types of securities. The new derivative guidance has embraced the concept of bifurcation (i.e., splitting the transaction or contract into its components and accounting for the components separately). Thus, when the criteria specified are met, a separate derivative contract would be inferred and reported separately at the estimated market value of a freestanding derivative with similar features. The remaining debt portion of the contract or transaction would be accounted for in a manner that is similar to a contract or transaction that does not have the embedded derivative features. Thus, an issuer would report outstanding debt as a liability at historical cost, with implied terms for interest accrual and disclosure. Similarly, the buyer of these securities would follow general guidance for reporting investment securities, using terms implied in the bifurcation to record interest income and to estimate fair value.

The criteria used to determine if an embedded derivative should be separated from its host contract are threefold:

1. the economic characteristics and risks of the embedded derivative are not clearly and closely related to the economic characteristics and risks of the host,

2. the combined contract is not reported at fair value with changes in value reported directly in earnings, and

3. the embedded instrument would be a derivative contract under the provisions of SFAS 133.

The concept of clearly and closely related is judgmental, and requires careful consideration. Specific examples are cited in SFAS 133 to help apply the above criteria. Generally, many of the specialized products introduced to date would require bifurcation. Since most parties have not implemented the standard yet, it is difficult to say how the process of identifying which components of a transaction or contract should be included with the derivative and which with the host contract. For example, would one infer a fixed or floating leg to a total return swap embedded into a debt offering? Presumably, there will be a fair amount of discretion involved in making these determinations.

While bifurcated derivatives can be designated as hedging instruments under SFAS 133, securities with embedded credit derivatives that are not bifurcated do not qualify as hedging instruments under the new guidance. Consequently, some transactions will need to be structured to avoid hedge relationships between cash instruments that cause disparate accounting treatments in financial reporting.

DISCLOSURES

Accounting standards around the globe have increasingly required more qualitative and quantitative information about financial instruments, and credit derivative products have not been exempt. Currently, a description of each derivative contract's nature and terms is required, together with the related notional amounts. Depending on whether a contract was entered into for trading or other than trading purposes, additional quantitative disclosures are required.

SFAS 133 has unified the various disclosure requirements for U.S. reporting purposes and when implemented, will reduce somewhat the bulky disclosures that have developed. For credit derivatives that are considered to be derivatives and subject to the requirements of SFAS 133, an entity is required to disclose its objectives for holding or issuing such credit derivatives, the context needed to understand those objectives, and its strategies for achieving those objectives. The description should distinguish between those credit derivatives that are classified as fair value hedges, cash flow hedges, and all other types. Additionally, the description should include a summary of the risk management policy for each of those types of hedges, including a description of the transactions for which risks are hedged. A description of the purpose of the credit derivative activity should be given for those not designated as hedging instruments. Additional quantitative disclosure is required for credit derivatives designated as fair value or cash flow hedging instruments.

For credit derivative products outside the scope of SFAS 133, disclosure requirements will track the requirements for the product to which the credit derivative has been analogized. For instance, just as the nature and amount of a guarantee must be disclosed under Statement of Financial Accounting Standards No. 5, "Accounting for Contingencies," a credit default contract accounted for similarly to a guarantee should disclose the nature and notional value of the contract.

The Securities and Exchange Commission has been proactive in supporting increased disclosures about derivatives and other innovative instruments. New requirements on market risk disclosures have sought to pull information about derivatives and other financial instruments together to give a more comprehensive description of an entity's market risk exposures and how they are managed. Within these requirements, there is a specific requirement to describe the accounting policies used to account for derivative instruments like credit derivatives in greater detail than was historically the case. How each type of derivative is treated for financial reporting purposes, including the criteria used to determine when a derivative will be treated that way, must be disclosed. In addition, where and when the financial effects, that is gains and losses on derivative contracts, can be found in the financial statements is also required, including the implications of terminating a derivative contract or a hedging relationship.

CONCLUSION

It is evident that the many inherent conflicts in accounting come home to roost when addressing credit derivative transactions. The timing of when and manner by which transactions are recognized and reported may differ significantly even though the underlying products are very similar. Careful evaluation of the nature of a contract and of the purpose of a transaction is necessary to ensure a fair presentation of the financial statements. The accounting rules are not uniform, but increasingly, there is definition to the way like transactions should be reported.

Like credit derivatives themselves, the accounting rules employed to report them continue to develop rapidly. Interpretation of the new U.S. guidance, and the effect of international standards in development, will continue to reshape the manner in which these products are reported. While new concepts have been developed for derivatives, there are numerous implementation issues that have yet to be uncovered and resolved. The above framework for accounting for credit derivatives provides fundamental background about how various product types should be treated. Combined with a detailed understanding of a transaction, and professional advice where necessary, even the most complex transaction can be accommodated.

CHAPTER 10

The Federal Income Tax Treatment of Credit Derivative Transactions

Bruce Kayle,* J. D.
Partner, Milbank, Tweed, Hadley & McCloy LLP

INTRODUCTION

The term credit derivative is extremely broad, connoting a wide variety of transactions. The common thread in all credit derivative transactions from a commercial perspective is that one party transfers to another party a specifically identified credit risk (Karol 1995). Despite the common element, as with other forms of derivatives, the tax analysis of credit derivatives must be placed in the context of the particular facts of the particular variety of the species. Whereas, some credit derivative transactions hew closely to traditional products that are used for transferring credit risk and whose tax analysis is entirely settled, others stray into unfamiliar territory. Complicating the process is the fact that the names given to various credit derivative products include words such as "swap" and "option" that are not always reliable indicators of the appropriate tax characterization.

Uncertainty about tax consequences does not appear to have slowed the development of the market for credit derivatives. One might say, somewhat glibly, that a little bit of tax risk is barely on the radar screen of those who take the risks of the derivatives market. As a practical

---

*This chapter has been prepared by Bruce Kayle, a partner at Milbank, Tweed, Hadley & McCloy (LLP) in New York, with the assistance of Thomas F. Brenner. An earlier version of this chapter was published in *50 Tax Lawyer 569* (1997). Unless otherwise specified, all references to "section" or "§" herein are to the Internal Revenue Code of 1986, as amended, and all references to "Regulation" or "Reg." are to the Treasury regulations promulgated thereunder.

matter, however, the tax issues arising from credit derivative transactions probably have received relatively little attention because the main market participants that are U.S. taxpayers have been banks and securities dealers (Baker 1997). Although it is hardly the case that all tax issues are resolved for transactions in this limited domain, there is relatively little for dealers to be concerned with, and banks do not face the most troubling risks that credit derivatives may pose to those who are neither banks nor dealers. There are, however, numerous parties to various credit derivative transactions for whom the tax risks associated with these transactions is a very serious consideration, and undoubtedly many potential parties for whom the tax risks are in fact sufficient reason not to participate.

This chapter outlines certain varieties of credit derivative transactions and begins to explore the federal income tax issues that each one raises. However, not all of the combinations of products and counterparties are covered, and the focus largely is on the treatment of parties that are not dealers. Both the offering of official guidance on at least some of the issues raised and evolution of the products themselves undoubtedly will require further refinements to the analysis and stimulate further writing. As an exhaustive analysis of the tax consequences of every possible type of credit derivative would require an entire book or more, the purpose of this chapter is to identify the issues that must be considered in examining credit derivatives and provide some framework for resolving those issues.

This chapter will briefly outline the essential elements of certain credit derivative transactions that are important to determining their tax treatment, and then analyze the federal income tax treatment of the identified transactions. End results frequently will be compared to those of traditional credit enhancement transactions. A substantial part of that discussion will relate to issues that also are raised by other forms of derivative transactions. Those issues are examined less for the sake of resolving what has not been resolved for other derivatives, than for highlighting what is at stake for market participants in the particular context of credit derivative transactions.

TYPES OF CREDIT DERIVATIVE TRANSACTIONS

Although there are numerous different types of credit derivative transactions, all have a single unifying feature—the transfer from one party to another of credit risk associated with one or more specific debt obligations, each known as a "reference obligation." Beyond this feature, however, the variations in transactions called credit derivatives are sufficient so as to make misleading, particularly from the perspective of tax analysis, the use of a single term to describe all. Even within each of the three broad categories of credit derivatives—credit swaps, credit options, and credit embedded securities—transactions may be of sufficiently different character to prevent meaningful generalization regarding their tax treatment. Thus, clarity requires very careful delineation of the transactions that comprise each category and subcategory. This section describes the various transactions.

Credit Swaps

Of the three broad categories of credit derivatives, the category known as credit swaps includes the most disparate transactions. There are three principal types of credit swaps—the total return swap, the loan portfolio swap, and the credit default swap.

A total return swap is essentially an "equity swap" involving debt obligations. In a typical total return swap, one party ("A") agrees to pay the other party ("B") on a periodic basis amounts equal to interest payments made on a specified principal amount of a reference obligation. B in turn agrees to pay periodically to A either a fixed return on the specified principal amount or a floating return on that principal amount, usually based on an interest index (e.g., LIBOR) (along with A's interest-based payments, the "yield payments"). A also agrees to pay to B the amount of market appreciation with respect to that principal amount and B agrees to pay to A the amount of market depreciation on that principal amount (together, the "value payments"). The value payments, which are combined with the yield payments to result on any particular date in the payment of a single netted amount, can be made periodically or in connection with the maturity or termination of the agreement. If made prior to maturity, the specified principal amount on which the periodic return is paid is adjusted upward or downward to reflect the value payments.[1] Party A in a total return swap relating to a debt obligation often will be a bank that wants to reduce its credit exposure to a particular borrower without selling the borrower's loan or otherwise diminishing its contact (and, hence, customer relationship) with the borrower.[2]

Despite A's presumed primary motive of seeking to shift to B credit risk in the reference obligation, the total return swap does not place A

---

[1]Board of Governors of the Federal Reserve System, *Supervisory Guidance for Credit Derivatives*, SR Letter 96-17 (8/12/96), Appendix.

[2]See *Insurance Finance & Investment*, April 22, 1996, p. 10; *The Economist*, Nov. 2, 1996, p. 73.

in the same position with regard to the borrower's credit risk as traditional credit enhancement devices like a guarantee. Because B is required to make payments to A based merely on a decline in market value of the reference obligation, the total return swap allows A to be compensated for a decline in value of the reference obligation precipitated by the obligor's deteriorating credit in the absence of any actual or imminent default.[3]

In a loan portfolio swap, A and B typically are two banks that simply swap payments received with respect to an identified portion of their respective loan portfolios (Neal 1996).[4] While the swapping of payments in a total return swap may for A have the dominant purpose of shifting credit risk on the reference obligation, the parties to a loan portfolio swap want to shift credit risk in reference obligations *and* take on credit risk on the other party's reference obligations. The loan portfolio swap is considered to be a relatively efficient mechanism for banks to diversify their customer credit exposure without increasing their marketing or administrative activities (Neal 1996). If the basic terms of the loans in each portfolio are similar, the loan portfolio swap functions more like a traditional guarantee than the total return swap. If the borrower on one of the reference obligations held by A defaults, the fact that A is not required to make the corresponding payments to B is for A the functional equivalent of B's providing a guarantee with respect to the particular loan.

A credit default swap, despite its name, is more analogous to a guarantee or letter of credit than to a swap.[5] Upon entering into a credit default swap, A pays either a fixed periodic or a single upfront fee. If the borrower on a specified reference obligation defaults, B pays A an agreed amount (Whittaker and Frost 1997). The amount paid by B upon default normally is the difference between the reference obligation's original principal amount or fair market value at the time the credit default swap is entered into and post-default market value of the reference obligation, but this can be varied by the parties' contract (e.g., B may pay A a fixed

---

[3]Board of Governors of the Federal Reserve System, *supra* note 1, p. 5.

[4]A loan portfolio swap frequently is accomplished through an intermediary that, for a fee, receives the payments from the participating banks and swaps the payments between the two banks.

[5]The tax analysis of a credit default swap also is more closely analogous to that of credit options discussed below. The credit default swap is discussed with other credit swaps here because of the nomenclature used by market participants. This underscores the fact that the commonly used nomenclature can be very misleading in terms of the appropriate direction of tax analysis.

amount). If A owns the reference obligation, the credit default swap functions as a form of insurance against the risk of default.

A credit default swap can be written with respect to a single obligation, but frequently will provide for a payment based on the default of any one or more obligations in an identified portfolio of reference obligations. For example, upon the occurrence of a default with respect to any two obligations in the portfolio, B pays A the agreed amount determined by reference to the particular defaulting obligations and the credit default swap terminates. If A has a relatively high degree of confidence that not more than two of the reference obligations will default, this type of credit default swap can be a more cost effective mechanism for limiting its credit exposure on the portfolio than entering into credit default swaps or procuring other forms of credit enhancement on each obligation. A variation is for the credit default swap to cover not the first, but some subsequent number of defaulting obligations in the portfolio, providing a "layer" of credit protection after the first loss.

Credit Options

The common element in transactions known as credit options is the payment of a single fixed amount or periodic amounts by A to B in exchange for B's obligation to make a payment to A based on an event, not necessarily nonpayment, denoting a deterioration in credit quality of one or more reference obligations. Although typical bond insurance, guarantees, and letters of credit all fit this description, they are not generally considered to be credit options, most likely to distinguish the newer products from these relics. The distinction between a guarantee and certain credit options can be relatively small, however. For example, an "option on credit loss" will provide for A to pay B fixed or periodic payments and B to pay A the amount of loss realized (by a hypothetical holder) if a reference obligation defaults (Neal 1996). Aside from the possible difference in the timing of payments to which A is entitled and the absence of subrogation rights in B, this type of credit option is the functional equivalent of a guarantee if A owns the reference obligation.

More complex (and interesting) credit options call for payments by B to be based not on the failure of the obligor under the reference obligation to make required payments, but on market value changes, or derived amounts approximating market value changes, that are in whole or part occasioned by credit-related events. The credit default swap described above is often referred to as a form of credit option (Neal 1996).[6] There are other variations as well.

One such variation is the "credit risk option" (CRO). In a CRO, A pays a fixed amount to B. Upon exercise, B will pay A an amount based on the extent to which the "spread"[7] on the reference obligation has increased. Specifically, B's payment will equal the excess of a hypothetical market price for the reference obligation over its then actual fair market value (Das 1995). The hypothetical price is determined by discounting the required payments on the obligation at a rate equal to the prevailing risk-free rate plus a fixed number of basis points, known as the "strike default spread."[8] A CRO often, although not always, will be purchased by a holder of the reference obligation. For example, A owns a twenty year fixed rate bond issued by an "emerging market" borrower. The yield on the bond is 400 bp more than the U.S. Treasury obligation with a maturity closely corresponding to the maturity of the bond. A pays B a fixed amount for a CRO with that bond as its reference obligation. The CRO has a strike default spread of 500 bp over the corresponding Treasury obligation. Upon exercise of the CRO, B would pay to A the excess of the present value of required future payments on the bond, discounting at a rate equal to the sum of the yield on the corresponding Treasury obligation and 500 bp, over the actual fair market value of the reference obligation. The CRO may, and usually does, have an expiration date prior to the maturity of the reference obligation. Thus, for example, the reference obligation may have a 20 year maturity, but the CRO can be written for a one year period.

---

[6]The option on credit loss is slightly different from the credit default swap since the latter calls for a payment from B based on a decline in market value as of the time of default, as opposed to the amount of loss as ultimately determined by reference to the amount recovered from the borrower.

[7]"Spread" is the term often used to denote the difference between the yield on a particular debt instrument and the prevailing level of a particular interest rate index, such as LIBOR, or the yield on a reference obligation. Thus, for an instrument that bears interest at a floating rate based on LIBOR, the number of bp (100ths of a percentage point) in excess of LIBOR that the instrument yields is known as the spread over LIBOR. Similarly, the excess of the yield on a fixed rate instrument at any particular time over the yield on the U.S. Treasury obligation with the maturity most comparable to the obligation is known as the "spread to Treasuries."

[8]This form of CRO can be called a "short" CRO. B's payment on a "long" CRO would be based on the extent to which the spread has decreased in which case the payment will equal the excess of the actual fair market value of the reference obligation over its hypothetical fair market value determined by discounting future payments at the strike default spread.

An instrument similar to the CRO is known as an "option on credit spread" (OCS). The OCS functions essentially in the same manner as the CRO, except that the reference obligation is a hypothetical one that has not yet been issued. For example, assume that A plans to issue $100 million of five year bonds in two months and anticipates paying an interest rate 150 bp above the then prevailing five year Treasury note rate. If the appropriate credit risk premium for A (i.e., the "spread" on A's obligations) increases, A's future interest payments would increase by potentially significant amounts, even in the absence of a general rise in interest rates. To hedge against this possibility, A can purchase an OCS from B pursuant to which B will pay A at the time A issues the bonds an amount equal to the present value (discounted at an agreed rate) of future interest payments on the bond in excess of interest at 150 bp over the rate on the five year Treasury obligation. Thus, the OCS is an effective hedge for A against increased borrowing costs caused by a rise in the credit risk premium associated with A's debt.[9] A would pay the additional interest associated with the increased spread, but would receive a payment on the option of an amount that largely compensates it for the increase.[10]

Credit Embedded Securities

We are quite accustomed to having "embedded" in debt or equity securities certain rights or obligations that could be separately created between the issuer and holder of the security. Old fashioned convertible debt can be viewed as a debt obligation with an embedded option to purchase equity in the issuer. Equity-linked debt that calls for payments in part based on the values of certain specified equity securities can be similarly viewed.[11] Finally, debt securities calling for a mandatory conversion of a

---

[9]If A is issuing a fixed rate obligation, the OCS is not a complete hedge for A against an increase in borrowing costs, because it does not protect A against a general increase in the yield on the obligations against which the spread on A's obligation is measured. A can, of course, separately hedge against that risk.

[10]One only can say that A is approximately compensated where A receives a lump sum settlement from B (rather than periodic payments equal to the increased interest payable on the bond issued) because A may or may not be able to invest the lump sum and earn a return equal to the agreed discount rate. Moreover, A is not assured of having the same after-tax consequences from entering into the OCS and receiving a payment thereon than it would from simply having borrowed if its required spread had not changed.

[11]Such instruments were in fact so treated under short-lived proposed regulations. Prop. Reg. § 1.1275–4(g), 56 Fed. Reg. 8308 (Feb. 28, 1991), superseded by 59 Fed. Reg. 64884 (Dec. 16, 1994).

debt obligation at maturity into a specified security (or a payment of like value) can be viewed as a debt obligation with an embedded forward contract.[12]

Thus, the concept of embedding rights and obligations similar to the various instruments discussed above into other securities should not be all that alien. In fact, securities with embedded credit derivatives have long been issued without much notice. A simple example is a floating rate debt obligation that is callable by the issuer. Such an obligation is essentially equivalent to the simultaneous issuance of a debt obligation and purchase of a CRO by the issuer from the investor. If the issuer's credit quality improves so that the spread appropriate for its credit decreases, the issuer can call the obligation and issue a new one at the lower spread. The economic loss suffered by the investor (i.e., forgoing the "excess spread" for the remainder of the term of the obligation) is the equivalent to paying off a CRO. Similarly, floating rate obligations that are puttable by the investor to the issuer are essentially the equivalent of the simultaneous issuance of a debt obligation and purchase of a CRO by the investor from the issuer. Thus, if the issuer's credit quality deteriorates so that the spread appropriate for its credit increases, the investor will accelerate the maturity of the obligation and will realize through the reinvestment of the proceeds at an increased spread (perhaps on an obligation reissued by the issuer) an amount essentially equivalent over time to what it would have received on a CRO relating to the issuer's debt.

The embedding of such credit derivatives has become more obvious as securities of this nature are increasingly issued to transfer credit risk with respect to reference obligations other than the obligation being issued.[13] For example, if A is a credit card issuer holding a portfolio of consumer receivables, it can embed a total return swap relating to that portfolio in a debt obligation. The debt obligation that A would issue would call for A to pay a specified principal amount with interest on the outstanding principal based on the yield from time to time on a portfolio of credit card receivables that A holds. The security effectively transfers

---

[12]See for example, USX Corporation, Debt Exchangeable for Common Stock, Prospectus dated November 18, 1996 and Prospectus Supplement dated November 26, 1996; Salomon Inc., Debt Exchangeable for Common Stock, Prospectus dated April 5, 1996 and Prospectus Supplement dated November 14, 1996; Cooper Industries, Inc., Debt Exchangeable for Common Stock, Prospectus dated December 14, 1995.

[13]In response to the increasing use of credit embedded securities, Moody's Investors Service has recently adopted methodology to evaluate the risk inherent in such securities.

to B at least some of the credit risk with respect to the portfolio (Ainger 1997).[14]

A credit default swap also can be embedded in a debt obligation. Such a security would call for payments based on the value of reference obligations that have defaulted (Firth 1996). For example, A issues a debt security to B that calls for the payment of a specified principal amount plus interest at specified rate. However, if a reference obligation defaults prior to maturity of the security, the amount A is required to pay to B is reduced by the amount of the decline in the market value of the reference obligation from the time the security is issued to the time of its maturity. A less dramatic version of this form of security would involve multiple reference obligations and allow A to reduce the payment at maturity to B only if more than one of the reference obligations defaulted before the maturity of the security. For example, the security may specify ten reference obligations and allow A to reduce the payment at maturity based only on the decline in market value of the third and fourth obligations to default during the term of the security. This type of security also effectively transfers to B a portion of the credit risk relating to the reference obligations. As is true of credit derivatives generally, however, the party who transfers credit risk relating to a reference obligation may or may not own (or otherwise have credit exposure to) the reference obligations.

Other quasi-credit risks can be embedded in a security. For example, the imposition of exchange controls by the country in which a foreign debtor is located could substantially impair the value of a dollar-denominated loan to that debtor. The exchange controls could increase the risk of default by the debtor by making it more difficult for the debtor to obtain dollars or simply diminish the value of the loan if the imposition of controls gives the debtor the right to pay its obligation in units of the restricted foreign currency. The risk inherent in the imposition of exchange controls can be embedded in a security by providing for principal and interest due on the security to be reduced based on the reduction in market value of a reference obligation if exchange controls are imposed or, alternatively, by allowing payments on the security to be made in the restricted currency (Baker 1997).

Credit derivatives can be embedded in obligations other than debt obligations. For example, a party's obligation pursuant to an ordinary interest rate swap transaction may be tied to a credit-related event. The swap

---

[14]In another variation, A enters into a total return swap with a special purpose entity that issues synthetic collateralized notes to investors. In exchange, A receives from the special purpose entity the returns on the proceeds of the notes.

agreement might provide that a party's required payments pursuant to the swap will be reduced if there are defaults[15] or reduced spreads[16] with respect to specified reference obligations. For example, the holder of a fixed rate high yield obligation may hedge its interest rate risk by buying a swap that pays a floating rate that is tied to an interest rate index increased by a spread that varies directly with the spread observed on the debt issuer's obligations. Thus, the combined value of the swap and the high yield obligation will always approximate the obligation's principal amount.

ANALYSIS OF CREDIT DERIVATIVE TRANSACTIONS

Since modern credit derivative transactions will draw inevitable comparisons to their forebears, the guarantee and letter of credit, it is useful to summarize briefly the tax treatment of those ancient, yet living, arrangements. In short, the tax treatment of guarantees and letters of credit is simple, intuitive, and almost entirely settled. The simplicity of their treatment is facilitated by the fact that the guarantee always runs in favor of the holder of the guaranteed obligation. Perhaps more due to this fact than any real analysis of the nature of a guarantee contract, the tax law has settled on a form of "integration" of the guarantee and the guaranteed obligation. Thus, from the perspective of the beneficiary of the guarantee, payments under a guarantee attributable to interest are treated as interest paid by the borrower for purposes of determining the timing of interest inclusion and source (hence, withholding obligations) (Miller 1994). Payments under a guarantee attributable to principal are treated as payments of principal, leaving the beneficiary unconcerned about the character or timing of any deduction for bad debts.

To the extent the credit derivative is a substitute for the simple guarantee, it is natural to look to this simple model as a guide to how the credit derivative should be treated. However, departure from the simple model is inevitable. Two factors contribute to the necessary departure. First, despite the emphasis on credit risk, credit derivatives frequently will in fact involve transfers of risks other than the mere risk of non-payment. And second, the parties to a credit derivative, like the parties to other derivatives, need not own the assets that represent the subject matter of the contract. In the end, the benign results generated by the simple model will in many cases represent little more than a vain aspiration.

---

[15]This is embedding a credit default swap.
[16]This is embedding a CRO.

Credit Swaps

It must be observed at the outset that the term "credit swap" is in part a misnomer. The term implies that the two parties are exchanging credit risk that one or both otherwise would have, essentially guaranteeing the reference obligation or obligations held by the other. In such a simple arrangement, there would be little or no ambiguity about the tax treatment of the parties. However, in those transactions generally referred to as credit swaps, the parties are doing more than providing reciprocal guarantees. To the extent that the credit swap creates more than a reciprocal guarantee, the tax consequences will stray from the simple reciprocal guarantee model.

Total Return Swap

Although A's principal motive in entering into a total return swap may be to shift credit risk on the reference obligation to B, A and B are doing more than shifting credit risk. In addition to credit risk, A has passed on to B the periodic nominal yield on the reference obligation in exchange for a potentially different specified fixed or determinable return, and also has shifted to B the potential for appreciation or depreciation in the reference obligation attributable to factors other than the occurrence of defaults.

Disposition of the Reference Obligation?   If A owns the reference obligation, the initial question that must be asked is whether A's entering into the total return swap constitutes a disposition of the reference obligation for tax purposes. A is in essentially the same economic position as if it had sold the reference obligation to B in exchange for B's installment obligation. Until recently, most commentators in the context of equity swaps[17] concluded that no disposition has occurred based essentially on the absence of an advance of funds by B to A and on A's continued ability to dispose of the property whose returns are swapped away (Kleinbard 1993; Reinhold 1992). Congress apparently agreed with this conclusion as it saw fit to enact legislation changing this result with respect to appreciated equity investments and a limited range of appreciated

---

[17]An equity swap is indistinguishable from the total return swap discussed herein, except that the terms of the equity swap typically relate to a specified equity security or basket of equity securities instead of one or more reference obligations.

debt instruments.[18] Where the total return swap's reference obligation is property, such as private placement securities or a bank's loan portfolio, for which no active and liquid market exists, and the counterparty that owns the reference obligation pledges the reference obligation or otherwise covenants not to dispose of it, the conclusion that there has been no disposition is far murkier, to say the least. Moreover, the stakes are higher than mere gain or loss recognition (which may be trivial)[19] to the counterparty. Concluding that a disposition has occurred can affect the withholding tax consequences of the transaction. In the above example, if B were a bank located in a country that did not have a suitable treaty with the United States, A and B would have to place dubious reliance on the portfolio interest exemption to avoid withholding on payments from A to B.[20] If the total return swap was deemed to effect a disposition of the

---

[18]Code § 1259, enacted as part of the Taxpayer Relief Act of 1997, requires a taxpayer to recognize gain upon entering into a "constructive sale" of an appreciated financial position. A "constructive sale" is generally defined to include total return swaps. Code §§ 1259 (c)(1)(B) and 1259(d)(2). An appreciated financial position includes appreciated stock and debt instruments, but does not include debt instruments satisfying three requirements. A debt instrument is not subject to the constructive sale rules if it unconditionally entitles the holder to receive a specified principal amount, bears interest at a fixed rate or certain qualified variable rates permitted for REMIC regular interests (e.g., a rate based on LIBOR or another index that can reasonably be expected to measure contemporaneous variations in the cost of newly borrowed funds) and is not convertible into stock of the issuer. Code § 1259(b)(2). If constructive sale treatment applies to A in a total return swap transaction, A will be treated as if it sold the reference obligation for its fair market value and immediately reacquired it, receiving a new holding period and a step-up in basis. Code §§ 1259(a). Since most conventional debt instruments will not be subject to the constructive sale provisions of Code § 1259, the remaining analysis assumes that § 1259 does not apply.

[19]If A is a bank and the reference obligations are loans that A originated they usually will have a basis roughly equal to the obligations' principal amount. In such a case, if there is a disposition, A has simply (constructively) received B's obligation with a principal amount equal to the principal amount of the reference obligations bearing interest at a rate that is adequate under § 1274. Because interest on B's obligation is adequate, and neither the reference obligations nor B's obligation are traded on an established securities market (within the meaning of § 1273(b)(3)), A's "amount realized" would be the principal amount of B's obligation. Accordingly, even if a disposition has occurred, A would have little or no gain or loss.

[20]If the reference obligation is not in "registered form" within the meaning of Regulation § 5f.103-1(c), the portfolio interest exemption would not be available. Many bank loans would not be considered to be in registered form. In addition, under § 881(c), the portfolio interest exemption is not applicable to interest "received by a bank on an extension of credit made pursuant to a loan agreement entered into in the ordinary course of its trade or business." Although B may, depending on

reference obligation, it would not be analyzed as a separate instrument and no separate tax consequences would be ascribed to the total return swap. For this reason, and relatively secure in the knowledge that not all total return swaps will trigger a disposition, the remainder of this discussion will focus on the treatment of a total return swap relating to a debt obligation on the assumption that the swap does not represent a conveyance of the obligation.

Integration with the Reference Obligation   If A owns the reference obligation and no disposition has occurred, how then would A and B treat the total return swap? The total return swap almost certainly would be treated as a "notional principal contract."[21] A's consequences then will depend in large part upon whether A is entitled to "integrate" the

---

the circumstances, have some relatively good arguments that it has not made the extension of credit necessary for the exception to apply, these are not arguments that market participants seem anxious to test.

[21] Reg. § 1.446–3 defines a notional principal contract as ". . . a financial instrument that provides for the payment of amounts by one party to another at specified intervals calculated by reference to a specified index upon a notional principal amount in exchange for specified consideration or a promise to pay similar amounts." Reg. § 1.446–3(c)(1)(i). Specified index is defined as ". . . (i) a fixed rate, price or amount; (ii) a fixed rate, price or amount applicable in one or more specified periods followed by one or more different fixed rates, prices or amounts applicable in other periods; (iii) an index that is based on objective financial information . . . ; and (iv) an interest rate index that is regularly used in normal lending transactions between a party to the contract and unrelated persons." Reg. § 1.446–3(c)(2). Notional principal amount is defined as "any specified amount of money or property that, when multiplied by a specified index, measures the parties' rights and obligations under the contract. . . . The notional principal amount may vary over the term of the contract, provided that it is set in advance or varies based on objective financial information. . . ." Reg. § 1.446–3(c)(3). B's payments will be considered to be calculated by reference to a specified index because they are based on "objective financial information." That term is defined as ". . . any current, objectively determinable financial or economic information that is not within the control of any of the parties to the contract and is not unique to one of the parties' circumstances (such as one party's dividends, profits, or the value of its stock)." Reg. § 1.446–3(c)(4)(ii). The value of the reference obligation should be objectively determinable (even if it is not publicly traded), and should not be considered to be "in control of any of the parties . . . [or] unique to one of the parties' circumstances." Reg § 1.446–3(c)(4)(ii). The notional principal amount will be fixed, or if tailored to the amortization schedule of the reference obligation, will be considered to vary based on objective financial information. A's payments either would be considered to be calculated by reference to a specified index for reasons similar to those applicable to B, or may merely be "specified consideration" given in exchange for B's payments.

reference obligation and the total return swap. To qualify for integration treatment the total return swap must be a "§ 1.1275–6 hedge," which is defined as:

> . . . any financial instrument . . . if the combined cash flows of the financial instrument and the qualifying debt instrument permit the calculation of a yield to maturity (under the principles of § 1272), or the right to the combined cash flows would qualify under § 1.1275–5 as a variable rate debt instrument that pays interest at a qualified floating rate or rates (except for the requirement that the interest payments be stated as interest). A financial instrument is not a § 1.1275–6 hedge, however, if the resulting synthetic debt instrument does not have the same term as the remaining term of the qualifying debt instrument.[22]

A "financial instrument" includes for this purpose a notional principal contract, Reg. § 1.1275–6(b)(3).

If B's payments are based on a fixed or interest-like rate (as opposed to, e.g., equity or commodity price changes) and the term of the total return swap coincides with the maturity of the reference obligation, the combined cash flows to A will permit the calculation of a yield to maturity.[23] If, however, the total return swap covers a period shorter than the maturity of the reference obligation, the combined cash flows will not allow calculation of a yield to maturity and integration will not be permitted.[24]

If integration is permitted, A would account for its results as if the reference obligation and the total return swap were a single combined

---

[22]Reg. § 1.1275–6(b)(2)(i). The requirement that the combined cash flows allow calculation of a yield to maturity or otherwise qualify under Regulation § 1.1275–5 hereafter will be referred to interchangeably as allowing calculation of a yield to maturity.

[23]For simplicity, the discussion assumes that the total return swap relates to a single reference obligation. If a single total return swap related to two reference obligations, the conclusion that the combined cash flows of the swap and the two reference obligations allow the computation of a yield to maturity becomes somewhat problematic because the swap will call only for a single payment from B that may reflect the netting of a payment due by B in respect of one reference obligation and a payment due from A in respect of the other. Based on the clear policy of the integration rules, the payments under the total return swap should be treated as being computed and made with respect to each asset separately, even if all such payments are netted. The issue most likely could be avoided by entering into separate total return swap agreements for each reference obligation.

[24]For example, the fact that either A or B will be required to make a payment of indeterminate amount based on a change in value in the obligation would be sufficient to prevent calculation of a yield to maturity.

debt obligation, Reg. § 1.1275–6(f). The effect of doing so, insofar as the character and timing of A's income is concerned, would be to treat A essentially as continuing to own the reference obligation with its yield adjusted to the return promised by B.[25] Thus, for example, A will take into account any built-in gain or loss generally at the same time and with the same character as if it had not entered into the transaction.[26] Most significantly, integration treatment essentially creates parity with a simple arrangement whereby B guarantees the reference obligation in A's hands. In addition, integration prevents application of the straddle rules, Reg. § 1.1275–6(f)(1).

No Integration with the Reference Obligation   If integration is not permitted, A would be required to account for each payment made under the swap separately from any tax consequences of the reference obligation. If A owns the reference obligation, this separate accounting will lead to the first significant difference from the simple guarantee paradigm. If, for example, the nominal interest payments on the reference obligation and B's yield payments are the same, A will recognize periodic appreciation or depreciation in the value of the reference obligation as it makes or receives value payments. Unless A is marking-to-market the reference obligation under § 475, periodic recognition of changes in value obviously is different from how A would be treated had it simply entered into a guarantee arrangement with respect to the reference obligation.

The more difficult issues and the potentially more serious divergence from the simple guarantee paradigm relate to the character of payments under the total return swap. Assuming that A owns the reference obligation, it undoubtedly will want yield payments it makes to be treated as ordinary. It also will want any value payment it makes or receives to match the character of the related gain or loss it may recognize on the obligation. Otherwise A could be in the undesirable situation of realizing

---

[25]Under the "legging rules" of Regulation § 1.1275–6(f)(4), the issue price of the synthetic debt obligation is the adjusted issue price of the reference obligation as of the leg-in date. The effect of this rule is to preserve any market discount, premium, or acquisition premium on the synthetic debt instrument to the same extent as any of these existed on the reference obligation. Because the total return swap may call for periodic adjustments to the notional amount, and, hence, the principal amount of the synthetic debt instrument, there may be certain relatively minor timing differences in the recognition of these items after the leg-in date.

[26]Because the yield on the integrated instrument may be different from that on the reference obligation, there may be some difference in the rate at which original issue discount or market discount is accrued or premium amortized.

a capital loss accompanied by an equal amount of ordinary income. If A had arranged a simple guarantee of the reference obligation, it would have achieved all of these objectives.

However, assuming for the moment that A is not a dealer or a bank, the total return swap is unlikely to allow A to achieve all of its character related objectives. A's most obvious problem is that it is exposed to an adverse mismatching of character of a loss that is eventually realized on the reference obligation and the payment it receives under the total return swap that is attributable to the depreciation in value corresponding to that loss. If the reference obligation is a capital asset in A's hands, a sale of the obligation at a loss upon the maturity of the total return swap would generate a capital loss. Although there are no entirely clear answers regarding the character of payments under the total return swap, none of the possibilities yield results for a nondealer, nonbank A that are entirely satisfactory.

All payments under the total return swap will be treated as ordinary income and deductions unless a "sale or exchange" is deemed to take place. A sale or exchange may be found under § 1234A. That section provides:

> [g]ain or loss attributable to the cancellation, lapse, expiration, or other termination of . . . a right or obligation with respect to property which is (or on acquisition would be) a capital asset in the hands of the taxpayer . . . shall be treated as gain or loss from the sale of a capital asset.[27]

There is as yet no official guidance on how § 1234A might be applied to the total return swap, and the issue has been thoughtfully analyzed elsewhere (Kleinbard 1991). It is sufficient for purposes of our examination to recognize that the answer is uncertain. Unfortunately, however, no plausible interpretation will allow A to avoid a potential adverse character mismatch. To illustrate the possible results, assume that A and B enter into a total return swap with respect to a dollar denominated bond issued by a foreign sovereign with a principal amount of $1 million payable at maturity and a fixed interest rate of 11 percent. The reference obligation

---

[27]§ 1234A. Prior to the Taxpayer Relief Act of 1997, Code § 1234A only applied to rights or obligations with respect to "personal property" as defined in Code § 1092(d)(1). Code § 1092(d)(1) defines personal property as "personal property of a type that is actively traded." This change in law removes one potential problem for A who would, under prior law, suffer a capital loss on sale of the obligation and recognize only ordinary income on the corresponding payment from B if the total return swap related to a reference obligation that was not actively traded property, regardless of the proper interpretation of Code § 1234A.

has a remaining maturity of 10 years. The total return swap has a term of two years, during which A makes annual payments to B equal to the interest payment made on the reference obligation and B pays A an amount equal to LIBOR multiplied by the principal amount of the reference obligation (i.e., the yield payments). The final payment on the swap is adjusted for any appreciation in the reference obligation over the two year period, which A pays to B, or depreciation in the period, which B pays to A (i.e., the value payments). Assume that A has a basis in the reference obligation equal to its principal amount.

The first plausible interpretation of § 1234A is that it applies to *each* payment under the total return swap. Under this interpretation, A can suffer an adverse character mismatch on any payment it makes that is attributable to the excess of the periodic yield on the reference obligation over the stated periodic return on the total return swap. For example, if LIBOR for each of the two years is 6 percent and there is no appreciation or depreciation, A will make two payments to B of $50,000 and have a total capital loss of $100,000. A nonetheless has recognized $220,000 of gross interest income in that two year period. Although A views the payments to B as an adjustment of its yield on the reference obligation, it will not receive any deduction unless it has unrelated capital gains.[28]

The second plausible interpretation of § 1234A is that it applies to *no* payments under the total return swap.[29] Under this interpretation, A can suffer an adverse character mismatch if the reference obligation depreciates. Assume then that the obligor on the reference obligation

---

[28]If A could add the payments to B to its basis in the reference obligation and deduct over time the added amount as amortizable bond premium, it would reduce its problem to one of timing and not character. A might be able to do so if § 263(g) applied to require capitalization of A's payments. Despite the economic similarity of payments on the swap to carrying costs, it does not appear that A's payments to B will fall in the scope of § 263(g), nor does there appear to be any other reasonable theory for A to treat its payments in this case as creating bond premium.

[29]The IRS would appear to support this interpretation as it has ruled that § 1234A does not apply to any payments pursuant to a commodity swap that qualifies as a notional principal contract. According to the ruling, a commodity swap is a "single financial instrument" the periodic payments pursuant to which (including the final payment) are "not gain or loss attributable to the cancellation, lapse, expiration, or other termination of a right or obligation with respect to . . . property. They are simply payments made according to the original terms of a single instrument." This rationale for concluding that § 1234A does not apply to payments pursuant to a commodity swap appears equally applicable to the payments pursuant to a total return swap although the existence of distinguishable yield and capital elements could cause the IRS to reconsider.

defaults immediately after the swap is entered into and makes no interest payments over the term of the swap. LIBOR for the two years is 6 percent and the reference obligation has a market value of $600,000 at the end of the swap. B will pay A $60,000 at the end of the first year and $460,000 at the end of the second year. All of the payments would be ordinary to A. If A sells the reference obligation at the end of two years, it will have a capital loss of $400,000.[30]

A third plausible interpretation of § 1243A offers some hope of saving A from either of these untoward results. Under this third interpretation, yield payments are treated as ordinary and value payments are treated as capital. This interpretation has less promise than may first appear, however, for two reasons. First, although the interpretation has some intuitive appeal, it probably could not be sustained based on existing law. Second, even if it were, its application would be unlikely in practice to achieve the desired outcome.

In the given example, the "desired" interpretation might be reached by claiming that the value payment terminates rights under the swap, while the prior yield payments do not. Even this convenient interpretation will not do justice beyond the specific example, because the total return swap could easily provide for payments based on the value of the reference obligation prior to termination of the swap. In such a case, there would be an absurd distinction in the treatment of the final and each of the earlier payments (Kleinbard 1991), and the character mismatch would persist for all of the earlier payments.

A better argument is that only the value payments represent "rights or obligations with respect to property" since those payments relate to the value of the property and all other payments relate to, in the given example, an interest rate index and other objective financial information. This argument does not depend on the particular value payment being the final one under the swap. Nonetheless, this argument too is problematic. First, although § 1234A was intended essentially to apply to options and forward contracts, settlement of which

---

[30]A would have the same capital loss if it didn't sell the obligation, but simply realized the same loss as a result of the borrower's failure to pay. Under § 166(e), an ordinary deduction for bad debts is not available for any instrument that is a security within the meaning of § 165(g)(2)(C). The latter section defines security as "a bond, debenture, note, or certificate, or other evidence of indebtedness issued by a corporation or by a government or political subdivision thereof with interest coupons or in registered form," obviously including this particular reference obligation.

in practice is based on the value of the subject property and not the income from the property, the statutory language is not confined to rights or obligations derived from the value of property. Moreover, even if one were willing to apply § 1234A only to the value payments, A would need some additional activist statutory construction to avoid the adverse character mismatch. The final payment in the given example illustrates the problem. That payment may reflect a netting of the yield payment and the value payment. Assume in the example that the issuer makes its interest payments when due, that LIBOR is 6 percent for the two year period and at the end of the period the reference obligation has a market value of $950,000. There would be no final payment due in these circumstances because A's yield payment of $50,000 would offset B's value payment of $50,000. To achieve the desired result, the mutual obligations to make value payments would need to be treated as a separate contract from the obligations to make yield payments. A and B would then be treated as making gross payments to each other under the separate contracts and would separately account for the results, treating the yield payments as ordinary and the value payments as capital.

The separate contract treatment is not the inevitable conclusion one would reach in characterizing the economic relationship between A and B. Where value payments are made throughout the life of the swap, the resulting periodic adjustments to the notional principal amount on which the yield payments are based would suggest that the contracts are not separate. In addition, prior to the 1990 amendments to the Bankruptcy Code, parties would go out of their way to disavow the separateness of the offsetting obligations. The reason for doing so was to try to prevent a bankrupt party from avoiding the contract that at the time was unfavorable to it while claiming the right to payment on the other "separate" contract. However, the current Bankruptcy Code would allow parties to net all of their rights and obligations under all of their contracts falling into specified categories, 11 U.S.C. §§ 553, 560. Since deemed separate contracts for the yield payments and the value payments would be in the same category, all of the parties obligations would be netted in a bankruptcy regardless of whether they in fact represented separate contracts. Since there is no substantive difference between a single contract and separate ones in the rights created, the form of the contract being a single one may for tax purposes "break the tie." Clearer support for the separate contract approach can be found, however, in the regulations relating to notional principal contracts. Those regulations would appear to require A and B each to account for the gross amount of their respective periodic payments.[31] Nonetheless, suppose that in this example, LIBOR exceeded the payment that A was required to make based on the current yield of the reference obligation (which does not require a dramatic rise in interest rates, but only a failure of the issuer of the reference obligation to make its payments). B would make a single payment to A that would have two components. The regulations relating to notional principal contracts do not support separating a single party's periodic payment into separate components.

Unfortunately, even if the separate contract interpretation were completely accepted, A would still most likely not achieve its character related objectives. If the swap were separated into two contracts in the desired way, it would only be by rare fortune in any particular case that both separate contracts would be "at the money" (i.e., each contract would be entered into without any upfront payment from either party and without regard to whether the other contract was being entered into simultaneously). It is far more likely that each separate contract would have a value to one party that was equal and offsetting to the value of the other contract. Thus, for example, if without regard to the contract providing for value payments, B would need to make an upfront payment to A of $50,000 to enter into a contract providing for the yield payments, it follows that A would need to make an upfront payment to B of $50,000 to enter into the separate contract providing for the value payments. So long as the contracts were being accounted for as economically separate, it would have to follow that these upfront values should be accounted for with the contracts to which they relate. If so, A's ordinary deductions on its yield payments would be reduced by a total of $50,000 over the period, and A's capital gain upon receipt of a payment from B based on depreciation in value of the reference obligation would be reduced by a like amount.[32] The adverse character mismatch is greatly reduced, but persists to the extent of the imputed initial payment. Even the best of all possible worlds is not a perfect one for A.[33]

---

[31]Reg. § 1.446–3(e)(3), Example 1. Although the value payment in the working example possibly could be considered to be a nonperiodic payment, the example could be modified to provide for value payments every period, which would make those payments periodic.

[32]Alternatively, A would have a capital loss if the value of the reference obligation is unchanged and B does not make any payment to A.

[33]The illustrations have focused on the adverse character mismatch A would suffer if it were to receive value payments. If A is required to make a value payment and received an ordinary deduction, it would have a favorable character mismatch if it simultaneously sold the reference obligation and recognized a capital gain, although only a favorable timing result if it held the reference obligation to

We should revisit our initial assumption that A is not a dealer or a bank. If A is a dealer that enters into a total return swap other than as a hedge of security that it is not marking to market, the total return swap would be marked-to-market annually [§ 475(a); Reg. § 1.475(b)–1(c)] and all gains or losses would be treated as ordinary [§ 475(d)(3); Reg. § 1.475(d)–1(b)]. This result should be satisfactory from the dealer's standpoint, as it is for all other "securities" that the dealer marks-to-market, in the sense that the dealer will not suffer from any adverse character mismatch or distortion of the timing of its income. For any other total return swaps that the dealer enters into, it will expect to be treated like any other taxpayer and have the same timing and character issues.

If A is a bank, with only mild uncertainty, it can ignore all of the potential character problems (and focus only on the timing issues). Section 582(c) provides a bank with ordinary treatment on all sales or exchanges of debt obligations. Although it is possible to argue that § 1234A might nonetheless create capital gains or losses for a bank to the extent that it applied to any transaction, the far better view is that all payments made or received by a bank under the total return swap are ordinary regardless of how section 1234A is applied.[34]

So far, it also has been assumed that A owns the reference obligation. While this assumption may reflect the state of affairs most often found in practice at the current time, it certainly is possible for A to enter into the total return swap without owning the reference obligation. Doing so is a form of synthetic short sale of the reference obligation. In this case, the comparison of the results of the total return swap to those of a guarantee are not especially relevant to A. On the other hand, A would likely

---

maturity. To the extent value payments made by A are capital, A would be forced to sell the reference obligation to recognize a capital gain in order to avoid a different form of adverse character mismatch.

[34]Section 582(c) does not state that debt obligations are not capital assets when held by a bank, but only that their sale or exchange "shall not be considered a sale or exchange of a capital asset." Therefore, if the bank's debt obligations were capital assets, § 1234A could create capital gains and losses where rights or obligations with respect to debt obligations were terminated rather than sold. This possible result should be rejected for two reasons. First, § 1234A is intended to provide the same result upon a termination as if the taxpayer had sold the subject property. For a bank, that sale would have resulted only in ordinary gains or losses. Second, an interpretation of § 1234A that permitted capital gains or losses to be recognized would give banks the unlimited ability to convert ordinary income to capital gains.

have essentially the same character related objectives as if it did own the reference obligation. More specifically, if A had simply entered into a naked short sale of the reference obligation, it would have expected to have had ordinary deductions for the substitute payments it made (analogous to A's periodic payments on the total return swap) and capital gain or loss upon closing the short sale. As the discussion above demonstrates, the total return swap may not replicate these results for A. Similarly, if a nondealer B established a synthetic "long" position by entering into the total return swap, it would under the same analysis have results different from actual ownership of the reference obligation.

Withholding Considerations   If B is a non-U.S. person, A's withholding obligation is not affected by whether the swap and the reference obligation are integrated. Notwithstanding the integration of the total return swap and the reference obligation, the total return swap is treated as a separate instrument for purposes of determining the source of payments and hence the payor's withholding tax obligations, Reg. § 1.1275–6(f)(8). Thus, if B is a non-U.S. person, A will not be required to withhold on its payments to B under the total return swap because they will be treated as having a foreign source whether or not interest on the reference obligation could have been paid to B free of withholding tax, Reg. § 1.863–7. This is a favorable result compared to the treatment of payments to a non-U.S. person under a guarantee, which may be subject to U.S. withholding tax and the 4 percent excise tax under § 4371.

Loan Portfolio Swap
If in a particular loan portfolio swap, all of the loans in the identified portfolios have identical interest rates and identical principal amortization schedules or prepayments, A and B will merely have swapped default risk, effectively creating reciprocal guarantees. Where the portfolios' interest rates and amortization schedules differ, as they inevitably will, A and B will have swapped not just default risk, but other essential economic characteristics of ownership of the underlying loans.

Disposition of the Reference Obligation?   Although many variations on the theme are possible, if A and B are banks and the reference obligations are relatively illiquid commercial loans, upon entering into the loan portfolio swap, A and B would be expected both to own the reference obligations and to covenant not to dispose of the reference obligations. Under these circumstances, it is difficult to conclude that neither A nor B have disposed of their respective loan portfolios and should not recognize gain or loss. Aside from the care that the portfolio swappers in *Cottage Savings Association v. Commissioner* took to document their transaction in a way consistent with a realization event having occurred, there is relatively little to distinguish what A and B have done from what was done in this case. Thus, based on *Cottage Savings,* two principal consequences would appear to result from this loan portfolio swap. First, both A and B would recognize gain or loss based on the difference between their respective tax bases in their portfolios and the fair market value of the other's portfolio. Second, if either A or B is not a U.S. person, the other counterparty will need to consider its withholding obligations as if the non-U.S. person owned the underlying reference obligations.

One possible distinction between the loan portfolio swap and the transaction in *Cottage Savings,* however, is that unlike the portfolio swappers in this case, A and B are taking each other's credit risk. If the principal amounts of the nonbankrupt's original portfolio have been received and paid to the bankrupt more quickly than the principal on the bankrupt's original portfolio, the nonbankrupt party will be just another creditor. This distinction does not lead to a conclusion that A and B have not disposed of their portfolios, but only that A and B each have sold its portfolio to the other in a form of installment sale, taking back the other's obligation to pay principal based on the timing of principal payments on the other loan portfolio with interest based on the weighted average interest rate on the other portfolio. Because neither A nor B's obligation are fixed in amount (because the respective obligations are reduced in the event of defaults on the obligations in the swapped portfolio), the mechanical regulations relating to installment sales calling for contingent payments [Reg. § 15A.453–1(c)] would most likely result in more gain being recognized than would be the case based on the fair market value of the other party's portfolio.

This mutual installment sale construction would appear to be unlikely, however, for two reasons. First, there is longstanding authority treating participation arrangements as interests in the underlying loans, notwithstanding that the participant accepts some bankruptcy risk of the seller of the participation.[35] Second, there is considerable authority for the proposition that a payment obligation that is closely tied to payments on debt obligations is treated as an ownership interest in those debt

---

[35]See, e.g., Rev. Rul. 71–399, 1971–2 C.B. 433; Rev. Rul. 57–509, 1957–2 C.B. 145.

obligations.[36] It is doubtful that the result in *Cottage Savings* would have been different if the portfolio swap had been structured as an exchange of participation interests.

Treatment as a Notional Principal Contact   If A and B are not treated as having disposed of their respective loan portfolios because the facts of their particular swap are sufficiently different from the case described above, the swap would be given tax effect as some form of instrument that does not merely represent ownership in the particular loan portfolio and the consequences of the loan swap to A and B must be considered. The loan portfolio swap would likely be treated as a notional principal contract (Bush and Haspel 1996).[37] As is the case with the total return swap, the next critical issue is whether A or B may integrate the swap and their respective holdings.

To conclude that either A or B can do so requires a little imagination. If both A and B's portfolio involved only a single loan with the same principal amount, it would be possible for both A and B to compute a yield to maturity for the "combined" instrument. If each portfolio had two loans with principal amounts identical to the corresponding loan in the other portfolio, it is only a small stretch to treat the swap as two separate swaps (notwithstanding the netting between payments attributable to the two loans) and to conclude that each loan should be combined with a separate deemed swap relating to that loan.[38] Where loan balances do not so neatly match each other, a further leap must be made to conclude that each loan is a divisible instrument. Each portion of a loan can then be matched to a portion of a loan in the other portfolio to arrive at a yield to maturity. The main obstacle to reaching this conclusion, however, is the absence of any mechanism for specifying which portions of A's loans

---

[36]See, e.g., United Surgical Steel Co. v. Commissioner, 54 T.C. 1215 (1970); Town & Country Food Co. v. Commissioner, 51 T.C. 1049 (1969); Rev. Rul. 65–185, 1965–2 C.B. 153. The fact that each party's "installment obligation" would be based not just on principal and interest payments on the loan portfolio, but in the typical case also on any fees or other amounts received with respect to the loans, would lend additional support to the argument that the installment obligation really represents an interest in the reference obligations.

[37]The analysis of whether a loan portfolio swap satisfies the definition of notional principal contract is essentially the same as for a total return swap, except that the loan portfolio swap may have different notional amounts for A and B's payment obligations. However, nothing in the definition of notional principal contract appears to require the counterparties' obligations to be based on the same notional principal amount.

[38]*See* Note 23, *supra*.

relate to which portions of B's loans.[39] Absent such a mechanism, there is no sensible means of accounting for the accrual and recognition of original issue discount, market discount, and market premium on any particular synthetic loan reflecting the integration.[40] The final and probably conclusive obstacle is that payments by the counterparty on the loan portfolio swap are contingent on the absence of defaults on the reference obligations. While the possibility of a default by the counterparty should not prevent the computation of a yield to maturity, the possible reduction in the counterparty's obligations attributable to defaults by third parties almost assuredly does.

Assuming then that integration will not be allowed, A and B would most likely account for payments under the loan portfolio swap like those under any other notional principal contract. Doing so gives rise to all of the character and timing issues discussed above relating to total return swaps and also to the novel question of how payments attributable to principal are to be treated. It is possible that those payments would be treated as nonperiodic payments within the meaning of Regulation § 1.446–3(f)(1).[41] If so, how those nonperiodic payments are accounted for as a technical matter will depend upon whether the payments are "significant" when made. If the payments are significant, they are treated as loans with no immediate tax consequences. The loan is deemed to be amortized over an appropriate time period, and the deemed amortization will give rise to payments under the swap that are deductible and includible, Reg. § 1.446–3(g)(6), Example (3). If, as appears appropriate, the

---

[39]Informing your clients that such an exercise is necessary is not likely to be a rewarding experience, although probably no less rewarding than telling them there is likely to be a taxable event.

[40]For example, if one loan in A's portfolio had market premium and another loan had market discount, when A received a payment from B attributable to a payment of principal on one of B's loans, A would not be able to determine whether it should recognize additional income in respect of the unamortized discount or a loss in respect of the unamortized premium.

[41]A nonperiodic payment is any payment on a notional principal contract that is not a periodic payment. Reg. § 1.446–3(f)(1). A periodic payment generally is a payment made at least annually pursuant to a notional principal contract that is based on a specific index, and that is based on either a single notional principal amount or a notional principal amount that varies in the same proportion as the notional principal amount that measures the other party's payments. A specified index for this purpose has the same meaning as it does for the definition of notional principal contracts (see Note 21, supra) except that it does not include "a fixed rate, price or amount applicable in one or more specified periods followed by one or more different fixed rates, prices, or amounts applicable in other periods." Reg. § 1.446–3(e).

deemed amortization schedule matches the actual payments of principal on the other portfolio, there effectively will be no tax consequences to payments under the swap attributable to principal because the deemed payments under the deemed loan will offset payments by the other counterparty attributable to principal payments on the reference obligation. If the payments are not significant, they merely are taken into account in the period that they properly relate to, Reg. § 1.446–3(f)(2)(i). Here too, an enlightened application of the rule will conclude that the payments relate to the period in which corresponding payments are made by the other party. Compare to Reg. § 1.446–4(e)(4) gain or loss on hedges of debt instruments spread over term of the hedged instrument as an adjustment to issue price.

Despite this conclusion, there is a possible outcome that is far less lovely. One cannot entirely dismiss the possibility that the payments attributable to principal would be treated as periodic payments since they may be considered to represent depreciation in the value of the reference obligations. In this case, the payments attributable to principal would be deductible by the payor and includible by the recipient as these payments are made or accrue. If the amortization schedules of the loans in the respective portfolios initially were identical, then A or B would suffer accelerations of income or benefit from accelerated deductions depending upon whose loans prepaid first. On the other hand, if one party's loans had a faster amortization schedule that the other's loan, a swap of this sort would be an enormous tax shelter. Given the absurdity of this result and the need to stretch to conclude that the fair market value of particular obligations always will decrease exactly by the amount of principal payments thereon, the better conclusion would appear to be that the payments related to principal should be treated as nonperiodic payments.

Since the analysis so far has lead to comfortably intuitive results, it is almost a shame to introduce as a complicating factor the possibility that one party's payment of amounts attributable to interest could be offset against the other party's payment of principal. Assume, for example, that the portfolios have equal principal amounts, A's portfolio yields interest payments of $100 and no payments of principal, while B's portfolio yields interest payments of $80 and principal payments of $20. No net payments would be made under the swap in this case. As discussed in the context of total return swaps, the more harmonious result can be achieved (in part) only if separate contracts can be imputed relating to interest and principal payments with the result that A would have imputed to it the receipt of a nonperiodic payment of $20 and B would have imputed to it the receipt of a net periodic payment of $20. Doing so would yield the benign results discussed above. Failing to do so will randomize the results to A and B.

Credit Default Swap

The credit default swap is the form of credit swap that involves the most focused transfer of credit risk, as opposed to other elements of ownership. Although one might expect that fact to simplify its tax analysis, the credit default swap is in many respects the most difficult in the genre to analyze.

Treatment as a Notional Principal Contract   Concentrating for the moment on credit default swaps involving a single reference obligation and periodic payments by A (as opposed to a single lump sum), the credit default swap should qualify as a notional principal contract. A is required to make fixed periodic payments and B is required to make a payment that can be calculated based on a notional principal amount and objective financial information (i.e., the diminution in market value of the reference obligation if a default occurs). However, this conclusion is not as clear as in the case of a total return swap for three reasons. First, the occurrence of a default that triggers B's obligation to make a payment to A will terminate A's obligation to continue to make its periodic payments to B. Accordingly, A's payment obligation may be said either not to be payable at specified intervals or not be a fixed amount, in either case because the stated contingency of default will alter the payment obligation.[42] Second, B's making payment will terminate the contract. Even though a contract subject to termination or extension explicitly is included in the definition of notional principal contract, Reg. § 1.446–3(c)(1)(i), it is most likely that the termination contemplated by the definition is not the only event that could give rise to one party's payment obligation.

---

[42]It may be argued that the notional principal amount on which both A's and B's payments are to be based in the undefaulted balance of the reference obligation. Hence, when the obligation defaults, the notional principal amount on which both A and B's future payments are to be made is reduced to zero. Given the absence of any substantive difference between this construction and the mere stating of contingency associated with A's payments, it is hard to conclude with great certainty that notional principal contract treatment is appropriate on this basis. It also may be possible to argue that the occurrence of a default may be considered to be objective financial information based on which subsequent payment obligations are based. It also is hard to rely completely on this argument because the definition of specified index does not allow for combinations of fixed amounts and amounts based on objective financial information. Compare Reg. § 1.860G–1(a)(3)(vi) and Reg. § 1.1275–5(a)(3), both allowing combinations of specified qualifying rates.

Finally, the credit default swap may be sufficiently close in substance to other arrangements, like an option or a guarantee, that it simply should not be allowed to be treated as a notional principal contract to the extent there are substantively different tax results to the parties (and there are). With those caveats, the consequences of treating the credit default swap as a notional principal contract nevertheless should be examined.

1. *Eligibility for Integration.* As with the total return swap, the consequences to A will depend in the first instance on whether A may integrate the credit default swap and the reference obligation. Here the answer appears to be that A cannot integrate. Since B's payment obligation is based on the market value of the reference obligation and not merely the amounts paid on the reference obligation, it will not be possible to calculate a yield to maturity on the combined instruments.[43]

2. *Timing.* Since the credit default swap cannot be integrated with the reference obligation, the more typical timing rules applicable to notional principal contracts would be applied. A's payments are periodic payments that both A and B would take into account in the periods to which they relate. To determine how B's payment is to be treated, it must first be characterized as either a periodic or nonperiodic payment. Although B is required only to make a single payment, that payment probably would be better viewed as a periodic payment, since B is required to make that payment in any period in which the default occurs. In other words, B is required to make a payment based on the same notional principal amount and same specified index in each period. In the absence of a default, of course, B's actual payment obligation will be zero. If B's payment is a periodic payment, it would be taken into account as income by A and a deduction by B in the period in which it is made. Like B's value payment under a total return swap, B's payment here does not benefit

---

[43]Under Regulation § 1.1275–4(a)(3), the possibility of a default on a debt obligation is ignored for purposes of determining whether the debt obligation has contingent payments associated with it. Ignoring default-based contingencies would allow computation of a yield to maturity. However, Regulation § 1.1275–4(a)(3) does not by its terms extend to the integration rules of Regulation § 1.1275–6. Moreover, it would be tortured to say the least to ignore the very contingency that gives rise to a payment obligation.

from the same "shelter" that a guarantor's payment in the nature of principal receives. Accordingly, if A owns the reference obligation, A must sell the reference obligation and recognize the corresponding loss to avoid an acceleration of income.[44]

    A slightly different question arises if A owns the reference obligation and sells it at a loss prior to a default and receipt of payment on the credit default swap. If the reference obligation is actively traded property, the credit default swap would be an "offsetting position" within the meaning of § 1092(c)(2) if it is considered to substantially diminish A's risk of loss with respect to the reference obligation. If so, the reference obligation and the credit default swap would constitute a straddle and A's loss on the disposition of the reference obligation would be deferred until A also disposed of, or received a payment on, the credit default swap. Whether any particular credit default swap would be treated as an offsetting position with respect to the corresponding reference obligation is likely to depend on the characteristics of the particular reference obligation. For a reference obligation that is likely to lose value only because of an impairment in credit and ultimate default by the obligor, the credit default swap could well be treated as an offsetting position. However, for a reference obligation whose value could decrease substantially solely by reason of movements in interest rates, it is less likely that the credit default swap would be treated as an offsetting position.

3. *Character.* A has the same objectives relating to the character of payments under the credit default swap that it did under the total return swap—ordinary deductions for its payments to B and, if it would recognize a capital loss in respect of the reference obligation, capital treatment for the payment that it receives from B.

---

[44]One would probably reach the same conclusion about timing if B's payment obligation were treated as a nonperiodic payment. In that case, the payment must be spread over and taken into account in the periods to which it relates, Reg. § 1.446-3(f)(2). At least in cases where a default on the reference obligation is not imminent or threatened, the effort to try to quantify and allocate B's expected payment would be an arbitrary exercise at best. Recognition of this fact would most likely lead to the conclusion that the period the payment is made in is the period to which it relates.

If A would recognize a capital loss with respect to the reference obligation on account of its default, A would not appear to be in any better position to avoid an adverse character mismatch under a credit default swap than it would be under a total return swap. If § 1234A does not apply at all to the credit default swap, then unless there is an alternative theory for treating B's payment as capital, the payment would be ordinary. On the other hand, even if one concludes that § 1234A applies to B's payment, for A to avoid the adverse character mismatch one must also conclude that § 1234A does not apply to all of A's payments to B. The latter conclusion is particularly difficult to reach since the only consideration A receives for its payments is B's obligation to make a payment based on the value of the reference obligation in the event of a default. In contrast to the case of the total return swap, it is not possible to argue that the periodic payment from A is in respect of some other obligation of B that is not in respect of the value of property. Thus, the natural result of avoiding an adverse character mismatch upon a default on the reference obligation and receipt of payment from B is that all of A's payments would give rise to capital losses and a different adverse character mismatch. A is left to argue (rather uncomfortably) that only B's payment *terminates* a right or obligation with respect to property within the meaning of § 1234A and that A's earlier payments effect no such termination.

Another possible reason for treating B's payments, but not A's, as capital, is that B's payment is properly treated as a "termination payment" under the notional principal contract.[45] A termination payment is defined in relevant part as:

> A payment made or received to extinguish or assign all or a proportionate part of the remaining rights and obligations of any party under a notional principal contract. . . . A termination payment includes a payment made between the original parties to the contract (an extinguishment). . . . [Reg. § 1.446–3(h)(1)]

---

[45]This approach may be somewhat self defeating since it could lead to the conclusion that notional principal contract treatment is inappropriate in the first place.

It is not entirely clear whether B's payment should be treated as a termination payment. The use of the word "remaining" suggests that but for the payment, further payments would be made under the contract. That is the case under the credit default swap, except that the remaining obligations are those of the party receiving the would-be "termination payment." Normally, the termination payment would be made by the same party whose remaining obligations would be terminated. In addition, the words "payment made . . . to extinguish" suggest a motive for making the payment other than compulsion under the contract.

In favor of treating B's payment as a termination payment, it may be said that although B is making its payment because it is required to do so under the terms of the contract, the payment nonetheless has the effect of terminating the contract and, thus, is made to extinguish remaining rights or obligations. This argument would prove too much, however, since any final payment under a notional principal contract would then have to be treated as termination payment, which clearly is not intended. On the other hand, simply to say that a payment that is required to be made pursuant to the terms of the contract cannot be a termination payment is not entirely satisfying, however, since it will exclude certain final payments pursuant to the terms of a contract that are the functional equivalent of the more clearly contemplated *early and voluntary* termination payment. For example, a notional principal contract may call for a final payment based on the present value of expected payments that one party or the other would make under the contract if it continued a specified additional period. Opting to create anomalous results in relatively few cases rather than all cases, one might prefer the interpretation that would not treat B's payment as a termination payment.

The character question then leads to some unsatisfactory answers. Aside from the problem of mere uncertainty, the holder of a reference obligation that would realize a capital loss on its default is facing an adverse character mismatch because there is no entirely satisfactory approach for treating A's payments as ordinary and B's payment as capital. A would need to be a bank or a dealer, then, to avoid this concern.[46]

4. *Withholding*. Notional principal contract treatment has the beneficial consequence of freeing each counterparty from concerns about withholding if the other counterparty is not a U.S. person.

Treatment as an Option   The preceding section examined how payments under a credit default swap would be treated if the credit default swap was a notional principal contract. Nonetheless, the conclusion that the credit default swap should be treated as a notional principal contract does not come easily. Moreover, if the credit default swap calls for A to make only a single payment to B, the absence of multiple payments being required of either counterparty may be an insurmountable obstacle for the credit default swap being treated as a notional principal contract (Bush and Haspel 1996).[47] Accordingly, alternative treatments should be

---

[46]One possibility for self-help exists for A if all payments would be treated as ordinary. A may consider selling its interest in the credit default swap prior to the time that B's payment is made. A cannot be confident that this approach will work, however. Since B's obligation does not become fixed until the reference obligation defaults, it is unlikely that A could sell its right to payment without undue discount prior to that time. By the time B's payment obligation becomes fixed, though, it may be too late for A. If B's payment is a periodic payment, A will take the payment into account when it becomes fixed (if not earlier). Reg. § 1.446–3(e)(2). If B's payment is a non-periodic payment, the timing of its inclusion is somewhat uncertain because the regulations relating to notional principal contracts give no guidance on the manner in which contingent nonperiodic payments are to be treated. However, it is quite possible that A will be required to accrue income in respect of B's payment as of the time that it becomes fixed. Even if A would not be required to recognize income until B actually made its payment, the fact that the payment amount had become fixed may cause the sale proceeds to be treated as ordinary if B's payment otherwise would have been ordinary. *See* Bankers Guarantee Title & Trust Co. v. United States, 418 F.2d 1084 (6th Cir. 1969); Bisbee-Baldwin Corp. v. Tomlinson, 320 F.2d 929 (5th Cir. 1963); Foote v. Commissioner, 81 T.C. 930 (1983).

[47]Even assuming that the absence of multiple payments by at least one party is not fundamentally inconsistent with treating the arrangement as a notional principal contract, the single payment credit default swap resembles an option more than it does a normal notional principal contract. The only difference between a prototypical put option and the credit default swap is the conditions on "exercise" in the case of the latter, the economic significance of which can be relatively trivial. While the economic equivalence of a notional principal contract and a *series* of options are understood and the disparate tax treatment of the two a generally accepted by-product of the desire to provide sensible and intuitive treatment to a wide variety of notional principal contracts, there is no reason why an

examined. One prominent alternative is to treat the credit default swap as an option. There is surprisingly little guidance regarding what essential elements cause an economic arrangement to be treated as an option for federal income tax purposes. An option has been described as involving: "(1) a continuing offer to do an act, or to forbear from doing an act, which does not ripen into a contract until accepted; and (2) an agreement to leave the offer open for a specified or reasonable period of time." *Old Harbor Native Corp. v. Commissioner*, 104 T.C. 191, 201 (1995). The same court noted, "the primary legal effect of an option is that it limits the promisor's power to revoke his or her offer. An option creates an unconditional power of acceptance in the offeree."

A credit default swap arguably meets the above criteria. In a credit default swap, B (1) offers to pay a certain amount upon default of the reference obligation and (2) agrees with the A that the offer will remain open for a specified period of time. Option characterization of a credit default swap also would follow from the fact that B's obligation is to make a single payment based on the diminution in value of the reference obligation, exactly as if it were the writer of a cash settled put option. The main difference between such an obligation and the obligation of the writer of a put option is that B's obligation is conditioned on the occurrence of a default rather than exercise by the option holder after a decline in value below the strike price of the reference obligation. Thus, whereas the writer of a put option takes downside risk in all cases, the B only takes downside risk if a default occurs. This difference is admittedly one of degree. A long term zero coupon obligation issued by a highly creditworthy obligor will have as much if not more downside risk based on interest rate fluctuations than on the risk of default. On the other hand, an obligation with a frequently adjusting floating rate of interest will have the largest part of its downside risk occasioned by default.[48]

---

arrangement that is the economic equivalent of a *single* option calling for a single premium should be susceptible of being afforded treatment that is potentially different from that of an option based simply upon its being called a swap, especially where the significance of the conditions on exercise is not great. Of course, this argument also may be made against treating the credit default swap as a notional principal contract where A is required to make periodic payments, since there is no reason that an option could not call for its premium to be paid in installments.

[48]In the extreme case, if the obligation bore interest at a rate that was to be reset at frequent intervals at a level intended to allow the obligation to be sold at its principal amount, extremely little downside risk exists that is not occasioned by a default.

The question therefore becomes whether a credit default swap "creates an unconditional power of acceptance in the offeree" as contemplated by *Old Harbor*. A's ability to exercise the option is subject to the condition that the reference obligation default. *Old Harbor* and *Saviano v. Commisioner*, 80 T.C. 955 (1983) both held that, in certain circumstances, an arrangement is not an option where the ability to exercise the option is subject to one or more significant contingencies. However, a credit default swap involves a negotiated contingency that objectively defines the parties' rights (i.e., the contingency does not arise from a preexisting impediment to the promisor's ability to perform, as in *Old Harbor*) and that is in neither party's control (i.e., the occurrence of the contingency is not entirely within the control of the promisor, as in *Saviano*). In this sense, the credit default swap is far more analogous to a cash settled put option than the arrangements addressed by the court in *Old Harbor* and *Saviano*. Much rides on the characterization question because treatment of the credit default swap as a form of option would radically alter the timing and character of payments relative to treatment as a notional principal contract.

1. *Eligibility for Integration.* Although an option is a "financial instrument" that may be integrated with a qualifying debt obligation [Reg. § 1.1275–6(b)(3)], the combination of the credit default swap and the reference obligation no more permits the required calculation of a yield to maturity than it did with the credit default swap treated as a notional principal contract. Accordingly, integration would not be permitted.

2. *Timing.* If the credit default swap is an option, A would not be entitled to deduct periodic payments or to amortize a lump sum payment (Rev. Rul. 78–192, 1978–1 C.B. 265; Rev. Rul. 58–234, 1958–1 C.B. 279). A would simply offset the payment or payments it has made against any payment it eventually receives from B [§ 1234(c)(2); Rev. Rul. 88–31, 1988-1 C.B. 302] or would have a loss on expiration of the credit default swap if B is not required to make any payment [§ 1234(a)(2); Rev. Rul. 58-234, 1958–1 C.B. 279]. B would not take either a lump sum or periodic payments into income when made. Rather, B would offset A's payment or payments against any payment it is required to make [§ 1234(c)(2)], or would have income at the expiration of the credit default swap if no payment is required [§ 1234(b)(1)]. These results are obviously fundamentally different from those of treating the credit default swap as a guarantee or notional principal contract.

3. *Character.* If the credit default swap is treated as an option, any lack of clarity as to the treatment of payments associated with

notional principal contract treatment is eliminated. Clarity, however, may be only small consolation for an unsuitable substantive result. Here, § 1234 provides:

> [G]ain or loss attributable to the sale or exchange of, or loss attributable to failure to exercise, an option to buy or sell property shall be considered gain or loss from the sale or exchange of property which has the same character as the property to which the option relates has in the hands of the taxpayer (or would have in the hands of the taxpayer if acquired by him). [§ 1234(a)(1)]

Accordingly, if the credit default swap is treated as an option, and the reference obligation is a capital asset in A's hands, A will have a capital loss equal to the aggregate of its payments to B if the credit default swap expires without any default on the reference obligation.[49] On the other hand, § 1234 does not apply to B's payment to A. B's payment would, however, be capital to A under § 1234A.

A undoubtedly looks at its payments as a reduction in its periodic yield on the reference obligation, much like the payment of guarantee fees. However, unless A receives a payment from B at least equal to A's total payments, A effectively would receive only capital losses for those payments. The capital loss results either upon lapse of the credit default swap or by offset to the capital payment that B makes. Thus, A will still face an adverse character mismatch to the extent of its periodic payments. Although, for A, capital treatment of the periodic payments seems entirely inappropriate, it follows quite clearly from treating the credit default swap as a form of option.[50]

---

[49]As is the case under § 1234A, it will not matter whether the reference obligation is actively traded property.

[50]If A purchased the reference obligation at a market discount, it would not have an adverse character mismatch to the extent of the market discount. This result is achieved more by good fortune than the good workings of the tax system. If A were allowed to treat its payments as additional purchase price of the reference obligation and to amortize that additional purchase price as bond premium, A would then avoid the adverse character mismatch, at least to the extent that enough time had passed prior to the default to allow the "premium" to be amortized. Although this result feels right, it is decidedly integrationist and most certainly would not be allowed so long as the combined reference obligation and credit default swap did not meet the requirements of Regulation § 1.1275–6. This type of imputed premium, as well as integration, becomes problematic as a practical as well as theoretical matter if the credit default swap provides for payment upon the default of one of several reference obligations.

4. *Withholding.* If the credit default swap is treated as an option, neither A nor B would be required to withhold with respect to its payments if the other were not a U.S. person.

Treatment as a Guarantee To the extent that it can be argued that the credit default swap should be treated as an option because it so closely resembles the economic arrangements embodied in an option, the same argument can be made, and perhaps with greater force, for treating it as a form of guarantee. Just as there is little guidance about what are the fundamental elements of an option for tax purposes, there is no real guidance about what are the fundamental elements of a guarantee. Surely one fundamental element is that a payment must be required only if there is nonperformance by the primary obligor. Another fundamental element must be that the payment by the "guarantor" bear some relationship to the nonperformance by the primary obligor.

The first element clearly is present in the credit default swap. The second element is not so clearly present, however, for four reasons. First, the default that triggers a payment obligation may be a default, such as breach of a net worth covenant, that does not involve nonpayment. Second, the decline in market value upon the default does not measure the amount of the borrower's nonperformance, but only the market's expectation about the amount of nonperformance. Third, the credit default swap does not confer on the guarantor any right of subrogation. Fourth, and maybe most important, the beneficiary of the guarantee does not necessarily own the reference obligation and, thus, is not the party who is seeking the performance that is guaranteed. This fourth reason, if not fatal for a party that owns the reference obligation, certainly is fatal for a party that does not own the reference obligation. Assuming, however, that the intended beneficiary of the credit default swap owns the reference obligation, the possibility that the credit default swap would be treated as a guarantee cannot be that readily dismissed.[51] In light of the previous discussion and the likely treatment of a guarantee in most respects, the party that owns the reference obligation will not want the possibility dismissed.

---

[51] If the credit default swap is treated as a guarantee so long as the reference obligation is owned, it would have to be treated as a form of "springing" notional principal contract or option when the reference obligation is transferred (unless it were transferred with the reference obligation). The necessity of doing so suggests that the credit default swap should never be treated as a guarantee. On the other hand, to the extent that treatment as a guarantee would be unfavorable, merely providing for the possibility of separation should not allow a different result to be achieved.

1. *Timing and Character.* The credit default swap, if treated as a guarantee, could not be integrated with the reference obligation under Regulation § 1.1275–6 unless it were a "financial instrument." The definition of financial instrument for this purpose does not include a guarantee [Reg. § 1.1275–6(b)(3)]. However, if the credit default swap is treated as a guarantee, integration under Regulation § 1.1275–6 is not necessary to avoid the undesirable timing and character results that may follow from notional principal contract treatment. Rather, the common law treatment of guarantees would achieve a satisfactory measure of integration.

Treating the credit default swap as a guarantee then would at least begin to achieve the harmony in both character and timing that is lacking if the credit default swap is treated as a notional principal contract or option. A's payments are relatively easy to deal with. A will receive ordinary deductions for its payments to B in the periods to which the payments relate. B's payments to A are a little more difficult to analyze, however. Although largely analogous to a guarantor's payment of principal on a guarantee, no principal payment may yet be due at the time B makes its payment. Moreover, if the obligor later makes its payment in full, A would be entitled to keep B's payment as the credit default swap does not provide any right of subrogation that a typical guarantee would. The fact that A is entitled to retain any later principal payments that the obligor makes may well undermine its ability to treat the payment from B as a nontaxable payment of principal under the obligation.[52] Assuming, however, that A can so treat B's payment, if A subsequently sells the reference obligation and recognizes a capital loss, A should be required to reduce the amount of the capital loss by the previously nontaxed payment from B and would not suffer an adverse character mismatch. If A is fortunate enough to realize a gain with respect to the reference obligation, either because it sells the obligation at a price higher than its fair market value at the

---

[52]In contrast to the conclusion reached in G.C.M. 38646, that a guarantee payment merely shifts the debtor's obligation, in a credit default swap the debtor remains obligated to A and has no obligation to B. It is, therefore, more difficult to conclude that payments made by B are a substitute for the principal and interest obligations of the debtor. This may simply confirm that the credit default swap should not be treated as a guarantee.

time B makes its payment on the credit default swap or
because the obligor ultimately pays all principal due, the
character of A's gain may be called into question, but A is not
in jeopardy of an adverse character mismatch.

2. *Withholding.* As satisfied as A might be to treat the credit
default swap as a guarantee from the perspective of the timing
and character of its income tax consequences, if B is not a U.S.
person, A would need to consider carefully whether it is
required to withhold any amounts from the payments it makes
to B. In general, under §§ 1441 and 1442, the payor of fixed or
determinable annual or periodical amounts ("FDAP") that
have a U.S. source is required to withhold at a rate of 30
percent. If A makes periodic payments under the credit default
swap, those payments certainly would meet the FDAP
requirement. Even if A is required to make only a single
payment, that single payment nonetheless also may meet the
FDAP requirement [Reg. § 1.1441–2(a)(1)]. Accordingly, if the
credit default swap is characterized as a guarantee, the source
of A's payments must be identified to determine A's
withholding obligations.

No statutory sourcing rule indicates the appropriate
manner for sourcing guarantee fees. See §§ 861–865. In *Bank of
America v. United States,* the court addressed the question of
how to determine the source of acceptance commissions, which
are essentially equivalent to guarantee fees. The court
concluded that acceptance commissions compensate the
acceptor for assuming credit risk, and, hence, should be
sourced by analogy to the interest payments that are being
guaranteed. Since interest generally is sourced according to the
residence of the obligor, A would be required to withhold on
payments to B respecting reference obligations with a U.S.
obligor unless a favorable treaty applied.[53]

The 30 percent withholding tax may not be the only issue
A confronts with respect to payments made to B if B is not a

---

[53]The *Bank of America* decision has been criticized on the grounds that guarantee fees,
unlike interest, are not payments for the use or forbearance of money. The Service
has held, for purposes of allocation under § 482, that guarantees are services.
However, the characterization of guarantee fees as payments for services might
not affect A's withholding obligations. Payments for services are sourced
according to where the services are performed. Even if B is not a U.S. person, its
guarantee services may be considered to be performed within the United States
where it accepts the credit exposure of a U.S. obligor.

U.S. person. Section 4371 imposes a 4 percent excise tax on insurance premiums paid to a foreign insurer with respect to an insurance policy covering risks located in the United States. The regulations define an insurance policy as an instrument, "by whatever name called, whereby a contract of insurance or an obligation in the nature of an indemnity, fidelity, or surety bond is made" [Reg. § 46.4371–2(a)]. A foreign insurer is "an insurer or reinsurer who is a nonresident alien individual, or a foreign partnership, or a foreign corporation" [§ 4372(a)]. The person who pays the insurance premium is responsible for remitting the tax [Reg. § 46.4374–1(a)]. Since a credit default swap may be said to indemnify A for losses associated with the default of a reference obligation, it appears that A would be responsible for paying a 4 percent excise tax when it makes its payments to B where B is a foreign insurer. Whether B is a foreign insurer for purposes of § 4371 may not always be obvious. It is unclear whether the term "insurer" refers to entities actually engaged in the business of insurance or whether it also encompasses any person who enters into an insurance-type relationship. Thus, for example, in the absence of a favorable treaty provision (e.g., Income and Capital Gains Convention, Dec. 31, 1975, U.S.-U.K. Protocol, art. II, which provides an exemption from the § 4371 excise tax for payments to U.K. insurers), premiums paid to a foreign company engaged in the business of providing casualty insurance would clearly be subject to the excise tax if the risk insured against is located in the United States. However, if a foreign company that is not otherwise engaged in the business of insurance enters into a credit default swap, a question exists as to whether such company is an insurer for purposes of § 4371. In most situations where § 4371 has been applied by the Service and by the courts, the foreign entity issuing the insurance policy has been a traditional insurance company.[54]

---

[54]For examples see Neptune Mutual Ass'n v. United States, 862 F.2d 1546 (1988); Rev. Rul. 78-277, 1978-2 C.B. 268; P.L.R. 8816019 (Jan. 13, 1988); P.L.R. 8507003 (Nov. 6, 1984). However, Private Letter Ruling 9349007 (Sep. 8, 1993) considered the application of § 4371 to premiums paid by U.S. persons to a public international organization that guaranteed against specified losses on certain investments. In that ruling, the Service concluded that the premiums were not taxable under § 4371 because all of the risks guaranteed against were foreign risks, but did not address the question as to whether the international organization was an insurer for purposes of § 4371.

Credit Options

Like the term "credit swap," "credit option" connotes a sufficiently wide variety of transactions so that there is no single approach to the tax analysis of this genre. Rather different considerations apply to the individual transactions.

Option on Credit Loss

An option on credit loss (OCL) is the credit derivative most similar to an ordinary form of guarantee or credit insurance arrangement. If an OCL requires B to pay A the exact amount of any credit related losses suffered on a particular reference obligation that A owns, A is in exactly the same economic position as if it had purchased traditional bond insurance. A would certainly expect to be able to deduct the periodic fees paid to B[55] and to ignore any credit loss or related payment from B, essentially treating the receipt of payments from B as payments on the reference obligation (Rev. Rul. 76–78, 1976–1 C.B. 25; Rev. Rul. 72–134, 1972–1 C.B. 29). B would expect to include the periodic fees in income and, assuming B was in the business of supplying such credit protection, to take ordinary deductions for any payments it made to A.

However, the OCL is not a traditional guarantee or bond insurance. A may or may not own the reference obligation. A may own the reference obligation, but transfer either the reference obligation or the credit option without transferring the other. B may not be given the rights of subrogation that a guarantor normally would have. Moreover, B may enter into OCLs with respect to an aggregate principal amount that exceeds the outstanding principal amount of the reference obligation. What then is the OCL?

The theme is now a familiar one. Aside from a guarantee, two possible ways to characterize the OCL are as a notional principal contract or as a traditional option. Both characterizations are somewhat flawed. Assuming that A is required to make multiple payments or that the single payment objection to notional principal contract treatment is overcome, the OCL may qualify as a notional principal contract based on B's payment to A being considered to be "based on objective financial information." So long as the reference obligation was issued by a third party, B's payment to A would appear to meet this standard. However, as was the case with the credit default swap, the contingent nature of B's payment (i.e., the fact that B does not make the payment based only on the objective financial information, but based also on the existence of a specified contingency

---

[55]The deduction would be subject to the limitation of § 67(a) if A is an individual.

(the obligor's default)) may be enough to cause the OCL not to be a notional principal contract.[56] The alternative, treatment of the OCL as an option is tenable, but has the same potential flaw as would treating the credit default swap as an option (i.e., the deemed option would only be exercisable upon occurrence of a specified contingency—nonpayment).[57]

Although the issue of how to characterize the OCL is very much the same as how to characterize the credit default swap, the stakes may be considerably different. So long as A owns the reference obligation and the OCL calls for the payment of amounts that match the nonpayment of the obligor, A would be entitled to integrate the reference obligation with the OCL under Regulation § 1.1275–6 if the OCL is treated either as a notional principal contract or as an option. Since the payment on the OCL by definition only replaces the amounts that were required to be paid on the reference obligation, the combined OCL and reference obligation would have a yield to maturity equal to that of the reference obligation adjusted for the amounts paid by A on the OCL.[58] If, on the other hand, the OCL is treated as a guarantee, effectively the same result as integration would be achieved.

Unfortunately, the inquiry cannot stop at this point. Two important issues remain, and resolution of these issues requires reaching a conclusion about the proper way to characterize the OCL. The first issue is whether A must withhold on payments to B if B is not a U.S. person. No withholding would be required if the OCL is either a notional principal contract or an option. If, however, the OCL is treated as a guarantee, withholding is likely to be required absent a favorable treaty, and the 4 percent excise tax under § 4371 may apply as well. The characterization of the OCL then becomes a matter of great significance where B is not a U.S. person. The second issue is how to treat the OCL if A does not own the reference obligation. Here all of the timing and character issues discussed in connection with credit default swaps return.

If A owns the reference obligation, the link between the amount of the obligor's nonpayment and the amount of the payment required of B

---

[56]See Note 42, *supra*, and accompanying text.

[57]See text accompanying Note 48, *supra*.

[58]This assumes, of course, that the reference obligation bears interest at a fixed rate or a rate specified in Regulation section 1.1275–5(a)(3) and the amount of the obligor's nonpayment is finally determined (this may occur only with a delayed payment on the OCL that bears interest). In addition, if the OCL is of a variety that calls for a fixed payment regardless of the amount of the obligor's nonpayment, then it will not be possible to calculate a yield to maturity on the combined OCL and reference obligation and integration will not be permitted.

makes the guarantee shoe fit so closely that it probably should be worn. The fact that A may transfer the reference obligation without simultaneously transferring or terminating the OCL should then be ignored until the transfer occurs. As of that time, the OCL should be treated as either a notional principal contract or as an option. As between the two, option treatment would appear more appealing.

Credit Risk Option

In an economic sense, the credit risk option is the most novel of all of the instruments discussed in this chapter. For different reasons, the three different characterizations, guarantee, option, and notional principal contract, that have provided the guideposts for analyzing how the other instruments should be treated, do not beckon quite so loudly.

Guarantee characterization is quite easy to dismiss. The payoff on an CRO is not contingent on a default by or measured by the nonperformance of the obligor on the reference obligation. This fact makes it all but impossible to treat the CRO as a form of guarantee.

Notional principal contract characterization is similarly problematic. A typical CRO calls for only a single payment from each party. Although this fact alone should eliminate notional principal contract from contention, there is a somewhat subtle but potentially important distinction from a credit default swap or even an OCL. Unlike the credit default swap or the OCL, the payment made in exchange for the upfront or periodic payments is not made automatically by reason of external events, but upon the act of the other party in exercising the option. Thus, even if A and B were to enter into an CRO that required A to make periodic payments to keep the option open, it would not be at all clear that the CRO could be treated as a notional principal contract.[59]

Does this all mean that the CRO should then just be treated as an option (which is what it is called after all)? Unfortunately, even that conclusion is not entirely obvious. While we operate without a definitive statement of what constitutes an option for tax purposes, we can at least observe that the parties to an option agreement usually have allocated between themselves the upside rewards and downside risks in an item of property and that the results of that allocation can be measured by reference to changes in fair market value of the property. In other words, the holder of a call option on specific property should benefit from

---

[59]The distinction is a much finer one, however, in the case of a cash settled European style option, which simply requires a payment based on external criteria on the expiration date. See text accompanying Note 47, *supra*.

increases in value of the property, or the holder of a put option from decreases in value, and the grantor of the option should suffer by a corresponding amount. This simple phenomenon does not occur in the case of an CRO.

The simplest case to observe is a CRO relating to a reference obligation that is an outstanding publicly traded bond. At the time the option is written, the bond trades at a spread of 100 bp to the comparable U.S. Treasury obligation and has a fair market value of exactly 100 percent of its principal amount. For an upfront lump sum, A purchases a CRO from B under which B pays A any excess of a hypothetical fair market value of the bond, determined by discounting future payments on the bond at 100 bp more than the then current yield on the comparable Treasury obligation, over the actual fair market value of the bond at the time of exercise. Between the time the option is entered into and the time of exercise, two variables change. The issuer's credit deteriorates and the yield on the comparable Treasury obligation goes down. These two factors offset, and the fair market value of the bond at the time of exercise is still exactly 100 percent of its principal amount. Notwithstanding the absence of a change in value of the obligation, A is entitled to a payment from B because the value of the future payments, discounted at the Treasury rate plus 100 bp, is more than the actual fair market value of the bond. Further confounding efforts to consider the CRO to be an option, other examples can demonstrate that if the issuer's credit spread remains constant, all changes in the value of the reference obligation upward or downward (which would be attributable only to changes in interest rates) will not affect the payoff on the option.[60] A correlation between the payoff and the value of the reference obligation exists in the limited case where the interest rate on the comparable Treasury obligation stays exactly the same

---

[60]If the yield on Treasury obligations decreases and the issuer's credit spread remains the same, the market value of the reference obligation will in theory increase by the same amount as the hypothetical market value of the reference obligation (i.e., the strike price of the CRO), because the actual fair market value in theory can be derived in this case by discounting future payments at the Treasury yield plus the strike default spread of 100 bp, which is exactly how the hypothetical fair market value is derived. Accordingly, to the extent that the actual fair market value increases to the degree that it in theory should, there is no payoff on the CRO in this situation. Conversely, if the yield on the Treasury obligations increases and the issuer's credit spread remains constant, both the actual and hypothetical market values should decline by equal amounts, and the holder of the CRO similarly would not receive a payoff. Thus, the CRO does not behave like either an ordinary put or call option because the holder cannot expect a payoff correlated either to a decrease or increase in value of the reference obligation.

and the issuer's credit deteriorates in the case of a "short" CRO, or improves in the case of a "long" CRO. Accordingly, it is fair to conclude that the payoff on the CRO is not necessarily measured by changes in fair market value of the reference obligation. Thus, to conclude that the CRO can be treated as an option, one must accept the proposition that an instrument could be treated as an option on an item of property even if payment to the holder of the obligation is determined by something other than changes in the fair market value of the property.

One may nonetheless be able to harmonize the economic behavior of a CRO with the behavior of an ordinary option by viewing the CRO as a traditional option with a strike price that happens to change (a lot). We would think nothing of treating as an option an arrangement where, for a fixed payment, B grants A the right to buy Blackacre for $1000 any time within one year and for $1100 any time within two years. In a CRO, the parties do not fix the multiple strike prices, but allow the strike price at any particular time to be derived from then prevailing interest rates. To the extent that the value of the reference obligation varies from that derived strike price, the required payment on the CRO tracks our traditional expectation of the performance of an option.[61]

Treating the CRO as an option generally will result in the more or less expected consequences, nondeductibility of the premium and capital treatment of the payoff or lapse (except for dealers and banks). Assuming the purchaser of the option owns the reference obligation, a capital loss on lapse cannot be amortized as bond premium, but the same result would occur upon the lapse of an entirely traditional option on a debt obligation.

One other possible characterization of the CRO that should be considered if one party owns the reference obligation is that it creates a partnership since the CRO may be said to represent an agreement on dividing the value derived from the reference obligation. Whether an arrangement is a partnership for tax purposes depends upon an analysis of a number of factors, the most significant of which is an intention to share profits and losses.[62] In the end, it is unlikely that a partnership could be found. If A owns the reference obligation and purchases a CRO from

---

[61]Before getting too comfortable with this conclusion one should consider an option on an equity security that isolates one or more of many factors that affect the value of a security. Suppose A bought an option from B with respect to a publicly traded Mexican company with a strike price derived by determining a hypothetical value that assumes a constant dollar to peso exchange rate. Can there really be such a thing as a "synthetic letter stock option"?

[62]For example, Luna v. Commissioner, 42 T.C. 1067, 1077-1078 (1964): "[T]he following factors, none of which is conclusive, bear on the issue. . . . The agreement of the parties and their conduct in executing its terms; the contributions, if any, which

B under which B will pay A if the spread on the obligation widens, B has made no initial investment in the "venture." B's opportunity for profit is limited to the option premium it has been paid and B's "profit" above is not necessarily related to whether there is income or gain derived from the reference obligation. For example, if the value of the reference obligation decreases by an amount equal to current income on the reference obligation, but its credit spread remains constant, the "venture" has derived no economic income, yet B will enjoy its maximum return as the option lapses (i.e., B's income would exceed the economic income of a holder of the reference obligation that did not enter into a CRO).[63] In these circumstances, it would be a wild stretch to treat the CRO as creating a partnership for tax purposes.

A slightly harder case is where A owns the reference obligation and sells B a CRO under which A will pay B if the spread on the reference obligation tightens. Here, B may be said to have made an initial investment in the venture equal to the option premium paid to A. If the spread on the reference obligation tightens and interest rates stay relatively level, the value of the reference obligation will increase and B will receive a payment from A, in effect participating in the income of the venture. However, B will receive the same payoff even if interest rates were to rise sufficiently to cause the obligation to fall in value, perhaps by more than current interest payments. In the end, the fact that B can profit to a degree greater than the gross income of the venture should preclude finding that the CRO creates a partnership.

Option on Credit Spread

Although the option on credit spread is very similar in its terms and analysis to the CRO, its likely user will have a considerably different outlook on the desired tax consequences. Since the OCS is the form of

---

each party has made to the venture; the parties' control over income and capital and the right of each to make withdrawals; whether each party was a principal and coproprietor, sharing a mutual proprietary interest in the net profits and having an obligation to share losses, or whether one party was the agent or employee of the other, receiving for his services contingent compensation in the form of a percentage of income; whether business was conducted in the joint names of the parties; whether the parties filed Federal partnership returns or otherwise represented to [the Service] or persons with whom they dealt that they were joint ventures; whether separate books of account were maintained for the venture; and whether the parties exercised mutual control over and assumed mutual responsibilities for the enterprises."

[63]Another factor tending to negate the existence of a partnership is that B has no control over the enterprise. B has simply agreed to compensate A for losses associated with an increase in credit spread on a reference obligation owned by A.

CRO acquired by a future borrower to lock in or at least hedge the expected spread on its future borrowing, capital treatment for lapse would be decidedly unwelcome, and immediate income recognition upon settlement of the OCS only slightly less unwelcome. Two possible avenues exist for the future borrower to avoid the unwelcome results. First, it may be appropriate to revisit the characterization of the OCS as an option since the context in which it is created is different from that surrounding a CRO. Although options are written on property on a "when issued" basis, the fact that the property in this case is a debt obligation of the holder of the option may make the OCS appear to be more like a commitment fee than a true option. If treated as a commitment fee, the holder of the option would be entitled to an ordinary deduction on its lapse (Rev. Rul. 81–160, 1981–1 C.B. 312). The problem with treating the OCS as a commitment fee is that if it is exercised, the exercise does not result in a borrowing from the writer of the option, but a payment from that party. Nothing that has been settled in regard to the tax treatment of commitment fees prepares us to determine the character or timing of that payment.

A second and more promising avenue is for the future borrower to accept treating the OCS as an option, but to treat the OCS as a hedge under Regulation § 1.1221–2. There are a few potholes on this street too. That regulation excludes property that is part of a "hedging transaction" from the definition of capital asset, causing gain or loss realized with respect to that property to be ordinary, Regulation § 1.1221–2(a). A hedging transaction is defined as one that is entered "into in the ordinary course of the taxpayer's trade or business primarily . . . [t]o reduce the risk of interest rate . . . changes . . . with respect to borrowings made or to be made . . . by the taxpayer" [Regulation § 1.1221–2(b)]. The key to application of the definition is the meaning of "interest rate . . . changes." If this means overall interest rate changes, the OCS will not qualify because the future borrower remains exposed to general rises in interest rates. "Interest rate . . . changes" alternatively could mean changes in the interest rate that the particular borrower will pay (Bush and Haspel 1996). If this meaning is accepted, it requires only the small further leap to accept that the relevant "benchmark" interest rate is a changing one that depends on the yield on the comparable Treasury obligation at the relevant time. This further leap is very much the same one that had to be made to treat the CRO as an option. If one makes it all the way to the end of this street, Regulation § 1.446–4 is waiting to allow the borrower to spread any payment it receives on the OCS over the life of the issued debt obligation, avoiding the unwelcome acceleration of income.

Credit Embedded Securities

This section will focus on two variations mentioned in the Types of Credit Derivative Transactions section in which credit derivatives are embedded in debt obligations. Although these two variations are hardly exhaustive, they will as a practical matter illustrate the principal issues that arise. The first variation is embedding a total return swap in a debt obligation. The second is embedding a credit default swap in a debt obligation.

In general, when a credit derivative is embedded in a debt obligation, three principal issues arise. First, whether the instrument with the credit derivative embedded can properly be characterized as debt for tax purposes (and what are the consequences if it cannot)? Second, what is the timing of interest income and deductions if the instrument is treated as debt? Third, whether, and to what extent, withholding is required if the instrument is not held by a U.S. person?

Total Return Swap Embedded in a Debt Obligation

In this variation, A issues to B a debt obligation that requires repayment of its stated principal amount and periodic payments of interest that vary based on the level of credit related losses on an identified portfolio of reference obligations. In practice, A will either hold the reference obligations or bear credit risk on them, perhaps as guarantor. For example, if the reference obligations are a portfolio of consumer credit card receivables, the debt obligation may call for interest at a specified fixed or floating rate reduced, but not below zero, by one percentage point for each percentage point by which the amounts charged off with respect to the portfolio exceed 5 percent.[64]

The analysis of this instrument is not that complex. Since the instrument provides for the unconditional payment of principal, the variability of the interest payments based on the performance of the reference assets should not prevent the instrument from being treated as debt of A (Plumb

---

[64]This is not an entirely "pure" form of embedding a total return swap, since no attempt is made to value the reference obligations. Thus, the issuer is not paying to the investor any appreciation in the reference obligations and will not receive any payment if the value of the reference obligations in the aggregate fall below their aggregate principal amount by reason of experiencing significant losses. Nonetheless, as a practical matter, the example is reasonably close to the "pure" case because the potential for appreciation is relatively small (since the receivables are short term) and the likelihood of losses that would require a reduction in principal payable to the investor is considered to be extremely unlikely.

1971).[65] Interest on the obligation will be contingent interest. Accordingly, the rules of Regulation § 1.1275–4 will apply, and A will be entitled to deduct interest and B will be required to include interest based on the yield of comparable obligations of A that do not bear contingent interest and the particular projected payment schedule prepared by A based on that yield, with adjustments made as the actual payments differ from the projected payments, Regulation § 1.1275–4(b)(2). A will not be entitled to integrate the credit card receivables and the obligation it has issued under Regulation § 1.1275–6(b)(2)(ii)(A).[66]

Because the interest payments on the obligation are based on the performance of assets held by A, the portfolio interest exemption will not be available if B is not a U.S. person. Accordingly, withholding will be required at a rate of 30 percent unless a lower treaty rate applies. A more difficult question that arises where B is not a U.S. person is whether the interest payments on the obligation should be treated as something other than interest. In particular, the question is whether the instrument should be treated as a unit consisting of a debt obligation bearing interest at a fixed or floating rate and a guarantee by B of the reference obligations for which it receives a separate fee (i.e., a portion of each nominal interest payment represents a guarantee fee). Payments by B, the "guarantor," are made by way of offset of the interest payments. If the instrument were so treated, there could be a different withholding rate under an applicable treaty for the portion of each payment by A that is treated as interest and the portion that is treated as a guarantee fee. In addition, the 4 percent excise tax of § 4371 could also apply to the guarantee portion.[67]

Although there is no authority that would bifurcate interest payments on a debt obligation into interest and something other than interest in circumstances such as these,[68] it is not hard to imagine the IRS or a court adopting the view that it is possible to do so. Suppose that B is in the business of supplying financial guarantees and A wanted to have B

---

[65]If the instrument takes the form, as many credit card receivable backed securities do, of certificates of beneficial interest in a trust, the conclusion that the instrument can be treated as debt if it explicitly shares the credit risk of the reference obligations is problematic.

[66]Debt instrument held by the taxpayer cannot be integrated with a debt instrument issued by the taxpayer.

[67]If B is a U.S. person, the consequences of this alternative characterization would likely be relatively trivial.

[68]*But see* Farley Realty v. Commissioner, 279 F.2d 701 (2d Cir. 1960); Richmond, Fredericksburg & Potomac R.R. v. Commissioner, 33 B.T.A. 895 (1936), both of which are factually distinguishable.

provide some form of guarantee of the portfolio of reference obligations. If the guarantee would have attracted more withholding tax than interest and also have attracted the 4 percent excise tax, could A and B have so easily avoided those consequences if B were willing to make a loan to A at the same time? In any particular case, the determination is likely to be made based on the particular facts of the transaction. If B is not given any of the rights normally given to a guarantor, such as the right of subrogation or other rights to control foreclosure or other form of workout with a defaulting borrower, it seems unlikely that the bifurcated interest and guarantee could be sustained. On the other hand, to the extent that B is given any of those rights, A's withholding obligations become more ambiguous.

Credit Default Swap Embedded in a Debt Obligation

A security with an embedded credit default swap may be more difficult to analyze than one with an embedded total return swap of the type just discussed. The typical case is described in the Types of Credit Derivative Transactions section, and the main difficulty arises because the embedded credit default swap may result in the investor receiving considerably less than the amount paid for the security.

Whether a security that does not promise the return of (at least most of) the amount advanced can be treated as debt of the issuer is a question that is now most frequently debated in the context of DECS (Pratt 1993).[69] In fact, the security with an embedded credit default swap bears more of a resemblance to DECS than would appear at first. That the security has most of the downside risk attributable to default in the reference obligation is obvious, but depending on the terms of the security, it also can have much of the upside and downside attributable to interest rate changes and changes in the creditworthiness of the issuer of the reference obligation. For example, if the issuer of the security is highly creditworthy and the issued security has the same maturity and bears interest on the same basis as the reference obligation (i.e., both are fixed rate or both are floating rate and based on the same interest index) then the issued security should tend to increase and decrease in value based on interest rate changes and on the perceived creditworthiness of the issuer of the reference obligation with a relatively close correlation.

---

[69]"DECS" is an acronym for "debt exchangeable for common stock" or "dividend enhanced convertible stock." DECS is mandatorily convertible into the issuer's common stock.

Having established that the analogy to DECS is apt, rather than rehash the entire DECS debate, the remainder of this section will simply identify what is at stake where the embedded instrument is a credit default swap instead of a forward contract. First is the question of whether the issuance of the security results in the issuer being deemed to have disposed of the reference obligation (if it owns the reference obligation). This can be a more difficult question than is the case in a typical DECS transaction. In the extreme case, the purchaser of the security will experience economic performance that more closely tracks the performance of the reference asset than does the purchaser of a DECS with respect to the security into which the DECS is convertible.[70] Although the absence of a pledge of the reference obligation or the ability of purchaser of the security to obtain the reference obligation along with the issuer's continued ability to dispose of the reference obligation, create a respectable position that no disposition has occurred by reason of the issuance of the security,[71] as a practical matter, enough variance in the economic performance of the reference obligation and the issued security can be created to be confident of this result.[72]

If no disposition has occurred, the basic characterization of the security must be determined. Conventional although not universal conclusions

---

[70]The seller of a typical DECS will reserve through the conversion formula the benefit of all appreciation in the property into which the instrument is convertible, up to a specified amount (e.g., 10 percent) and a percentage of appreciation in excess of that amount.

[71]The constructive sale provisions of Code § 1259 should not apply to most transactions of this type inasmuch as the reference obligations are typically debt instruments described in Code § 1259(b)(1) (i.e., conventional debt). See Note 18, *supra*, and accompanying text. Even if the reference obligations are not conventional debt, Code § 1259 would not by its terms apply to this transaction. That section treats an appreciated financial position as constructively sold when the holder of such position enters into a short sale, an "offsetting notional principal contract" or a futures or "forward contract" with respect to the same or substantially identical property. Code § 1259(c)(1). However, Code § 1259 provides the Treasury with the authority to issue regulations prescribing constructive sale treatment for transactions having substantially the same effect as a transaction listed in Code § 1259. Although the Treasury has not yet exercised the discretion accorded it by Code § 1259, a security with an embedded credit default swap has much the same effect as the transactions listed in Code § 1259 if its terms (and the terms of the reference obligation) are such that it substantially reduces or eliminates the A's exposure to risk of depreciation in value of the reference obligation.

[72]For example, the issued security can be given a shorter maturity and a different interest rate basis than the reference obligation.

would be that the security either is a combined noncontingent debt obligation of the issuer and credit default swap or a debt obligation of the issuer that provides for contingent principal. In neither case would integration of the reference obligation and the issued security be permitted under Regulation § 1.1275–6(b)(ii)(A). Thus, the issuer would account for the reference obligation separately from the issued security, and in the case of the former construction, the noncontingent debt obligation separately from the credit default swap.

Treating the security as a combined noncontingent debt obligation and credit default swap requires the issuer and investor to come to grips with all of the same timing, character, and withholding issues raised by credit default swaps generally. This treatment also requires the issuer and investor to address which payments on the security should be treated as being made in respect of the debt security and which payments in respect of the credit default swap. The first and most obvious question is how much of the nominal return (i.e., without regard to a reduction in principal repayment) on the security represents interest and how much is attributable to the credit default swap? The answer most likely can be found by comparing the yield that the issuer otherwise might be required to pay with the nominal yield on the security. The difference essentially reflects the amount being paid that is attributable to the credit default swap.

Having identified the economic cost of the credit default swap, it also must be determined whether the swap should be deemed to have been paid in a lump sum (i.e., the security is deemed to have been issued at a premium, reflecting its higher than market nominal yield, with the issuer paying over to the investor the amount of the premium as a payment on the credit default swap) or through periodic payments (i.e., a portion of each interest payment is treated as a payment on the credit default swap). Whether the premium is deemed paid in a lump sum or periodically will affect whether the debt instrument has original issue discount and otherwise will have an effect, although a relatively minor one, on the timing of interest income and deduction on the security. In addition, if the investor is not a U.S. person and withholding is required, the determination would significantly affect the issuer's withholding tax obligation. In choosing between the periodic and lump sum characterization, the two are economically equivalent if the security issued has a fixed maturity, and neither choice appears to be a superior characterization. However, the two are not entirely equivalent if the security, as often will be the case, has its maturity accelerated if the reference obligation defaults. In this situation, neither choice would appear to be superior in theory, but periodic payment treatment has the benefit of relative simplicity.[73]

If instead of being treated as a combined debt obligation and credit default swap, the issued security is treated solely as a debt instrument subject to the rules of Regulation § 1.1275–4(b), the issuer and investor would accrue interest deductions and interest income based on the issuer's projections of actual payments, which projections must be consistent with an overall yield to maturity equivalent to the yield on comparable noncontingent debt obligations of the issuer. Doing so would most likely result in a portion of the nominal interest payments on the issued security being treated as a return of principal for both the issuer and the investor. This result is similar to the timing result achieved if payments by the issuer on the credit default swap would have been nondeductible, but has the effect of deferring recovery of payments on the credit default swap if they would have in fact been deductible.

A more significant effect of treating the security as a single debt obligation is on character. Curiously, the effects are different for the issuer and the investor. Even more curiously, for the investor, the result is different and less favorable than any of the possibilities for a separately accounted for credit default swap. For the issuer treating the security as a single debt instrument has the effect of causing all payments on the credit default swap to be ordinary in character. If there is no default on the reference obligation, the issuer will deduct as interest all payments made on the security in excess of its principal amount; thus, receiving ordinary deductions for payments attributable to the credit default swap. If the security defaults, the issuer will recognize ordinary income (from the cancellation of indebtedness) with respect to the amount that it effectively is paid by the investor under the credit default swap (i.e., the portion of the principal amount that the issuer does not have to repay). For the investor, however, all payments from the issuer will be treated as ordinary because they represent interest, Regulation § 1.275–4(b)(6)(ii), yet a loss on the credit default swap represented by a foregone principal payment

---

[73]Since the pricing of the credit default swap will imply some likelihood of a default at or before maturity of the issued security, it stands to reason that the premium is priced to reflect some expectation of recovery prior to maturity. Thus, recovery over a longer period, like the stated maturity of the issued security would be too slow as an economic matter. The result of simply reducing the stated interest payments is not superior because the reduction also would be computed on the assumption that the security is repaid at maturity, producing an almost equivalent deferral of premium recovery.

in excess of previously included interest income will be treated as capital, Regulation § 1.1275–4(b)(6)(iii)(C).

To illustrate, assume A issues a security with a principal amount of $1000, a maturity of three years and an annual interest payment of $100. The principal amount of the security is reduced by the diminution in value of a reference obligation between the time the security is issued and the time of a default in the reference obligation if a default occurs before the maturity of the security. B purchases the security at original issuance at its stated principal amount. Assume the comparable yield for A is 8 percent. The projected payment supplied by A provides for a payment of $935 of principal at maturity, which with the annual interest payments results in a yield of 8 percent. Immediately prior to the maturity of the security, it will have an adjusted issue price of $1035 and B will have included only $235 of the $300 of accrued interest. If the reference obligation defaults immediately before the maturity of the issued security and B receives a payment of $600 at maturity, reflecting the final $100 payment of interest and $500 of principal, B would have an ordinary loss of $235, equal to the total interest it had included over the life of the security and a capital loss of $200.

Given this unattractive scenario, it is not surprising that investors in securities of this nature in practice have been non-U.S. persons, bringing to the fore the withholding issues. Even if all of A's payments in excess of principal on the security are treated as interest, the portfolio interest exemption will be unavailable because of § 871(h)(4)(A)(i)(II), which denies the exemption to interest that is based on the value of any property of the debtor. Thus, to avoid withholding, either the issuer must be a bank [§ 871(i)] or the investor must be entitled to the benefits of a favorable treaty.

CONCLUSION

Credit derivatives have proven themselves in the marketplace to be powerful and versatile tools for market participants to manage credit risk. Like other powerful tools, they have their dangers too. In no small part, those dangers relate to their tax consequences. The pages above emphasize the dangers for potential users of credit derivatives, but there are dangers for the Treasury as well, as taxpayers may resolve doubts in their own favor using the benefit of hindsight. Thus, uncertainty surrounding the tax treatment of credit derivative transactions is in the interest neither of the Treasury nor the commercial public. The stakes are highest for nonbank, nondealer holders of reference obligations that enter into credit derivative transactions, and this is the area that needs the greatest attention. Given the growth that the credit derivatives market has already experienced and can be expected to experience in the future, the Treasury Department cannot wait long to wade into the area.

BIBLIOGRAPHY

Ainger, Will: "SBC Plans the Largest Credit Derivative Deal to Date." *Derivatives Week*, August 18, 1997, p. 1.

Baker, Marci: "Exploring the Risk Frontier: Commercial Banks Joust with Wall Street Firms for Control of the Burgeoning Credit Derivatives Market." *Investment Dealers' Digest*, August 18, 1997.

Board of Governors of the Federal Reserve System: *Supervisory Guidance for Credit Derivatives*, SR Letter 96-17, August 12, 1996, p. 5, Appendix.

Bush, John N., and Ahron H. Haspel: "Deciphering the Taxation of Credit Derivatives." *Journal of Taxation of Investments*, Autumn 1996, pp. 35, 38, 41.

Conlon, Steven: "U.S. Tax Issues Relating to Credit Derivatives," *Derivatives*, May/June 1998, p. 203.

"Credit Derivatives." *Insurance Finance & Investment*, April 22, 1996, p. 10.

Das, Sanjiv Ranjan: "Credit Risk Derivatives." *Journal of Derivatives*, Spring 1995, pp. 7, 9.

Firth, Simon: "The Credit Derivatives Market Expands, but Many Issues Remain Unexplored." *Credit Derivatives*, November/December 1996, pp. 77, 78.

Joint Committee on Taxation: *General Explanation of the Economic Recovery Tax Act of 1981*. JCS-71-81, December 29, 1981.

Karol, Bernard J.: "Symposium: Regulation of Financial Derivatives: An Overview of Derivatives as Risk Management Tools." *1 Stan. J. L. Business & Finance*, 1995, pp. 195, 203.

Kleinbard, Edward D.: "Risky and Riskless Positions in Securities." *Taxes*, 71, 1993, pp. 783, 794–796.

Kleinbard, Edward D.: "Equity Derivative Products: Financial Innovations' Newest Challenge to the Tax System." *69 Tex. L. Rev.*, 1991, pp. 1319, 1341–1346.

Miller, David: "Tax Consequences of Guarantees: A Comprehensive Framework for Analysis." *Tax Lawyer*, 48, 1994, pp. 103, 115–116, 130–131.

Miller, David: "An Overview of the Taxation of Credit Derivatives." *Tax Strategies for Corporate Acquisitions, Dispositions, Spin-Offs, Joint Ventures, Financings, Reorganizations & Restructurings*. Practising Law Institute, 1998.

"Moody's Expands to Include Credit Derivatives." *Derivatives Week*, July 7, 1997, p. 3.

Neal, Robert S.: "Credit Derivatives: New Financial Instruments for Controlling Credit Risk." *Economic Review*, Federal Reserve Bank of Kansas City, 1996, pp. 19, 21, 22, 23.

"Passing on the Risks." *The Economist*, November 2, 1996, p. 73.

Plumb, William T.: "The Federal Income Tax Significance of Corporate Debt: A Critical Analysis and a Proposal." *26 Tax Law Review*, 1971, pp. 369, 431–432.

Pratt, Tom: "Salomon and Amed Unveil New Exchangeable Debt." *Investment Dealers' Digest*, December 20, 1993.

Reinhold, Richard L.: "Tax Issues in Equity Swap Transactions." *Tax Notes*, 57, 1992, pp. 1185, 1201–1203.

Whittaker, Gregg, and Joyce Frost: An Introduction to Credit Derivatives, *The Journal of Lending and Credit Risk Management*, May 1997, p. 15.

CHAPTER 11

Credit Derivatives: Legal and Regulatory Issues

David Felsenthal, J. D.
Partner, Clifford Chance

M. Sharmini Mahendran, J. D.
Associate, Clifford Chance

INTRODUCTION

A credit derivative may, depending upon the terms of and the parties to the credit derivative, be subject to different laws and regulatory regimes within one jurisdiction and may also be subject to the laws of many different jurisdictions. In this chapter, we briefly describe certain legal and regulatory issues that should be considered by parties to a credit derivative. These issues relate to bank regulation, insurance regulation, gaming laws, confidentiality laws, netting laws, and securities laws. The principal types of credit derivatives that we refer to in this chapter are total rate of return swaps (TRORS) and credit default derivatives, such as credit default swaps and credit-linked notes. We primarily describe New York and U.S. law but, because credit derivatives often involve more than one jurisdiction, we also provide brief comparative analyses of the analogous laws of three important European jurisdictions: the United Kingdom, France, and Germany. We do not provide an exhaustive analysis in this chapter of all of the relevant issues. In the Bank Regulation section, we address issues that are specifically relevant to bank users of credit derivatives. In the balance of the chapter we address issues that are generally relevant to all users of credit derivatives.

BANK REGULATION

Banking regulations will be applicable to banks that are a party to a credit derivative transaction. Banks have been active in the credit derivative markets both as protection purchasers and as protection sellers. Basic issues that arise for a bank counterparty to a credit derivative include the following: (1) Do banking regulations permit banks to enter into credit derivatives? (2) What are the risk-based capital requirements applicable to the bank when entering into credit derivatives? (3) What are the supervisory requirements for risk management procedures for credit derivatives? (4) How are credit derivatives affected by requirements applicable to ordinary bank credits, such as limits on loans to one borrower? We do not address risk-based capital requirements for credit derivatives in this chapter.[1] With respect to the other issues listed above, we briefly discuss such issues first in the context of U.S. federal banking laws and regulations and, where applicable, the banking law of the State of New York (NYBL), and then provide a comparative perspective by considering the relevant laws of the United Kingdom, France, and Germany.

The United States

Guidelines relating to credit derivatives have been issued by all three federal bank regulators: the Office of the Comptroller of the Currency (OCC), which regulates national banks, issued its *Guidelines for National Banks* on August 12, 1996 (the *OCC Guidelines*); the Board of Governors of the Federal Reserve System (Federal Reserve), which regulates state member banks and bank holding companies, issued its *Supervisory Guidance for Credit Derivatives* on August 12, 1996 (*Federal Reserve Guidelines*); and the Federal Deposit Insurance Corporation (FDIC), which provides deposit insurance to U.S. banks, issued its *Supervisory Guidance for Credit Derivatives* on August 19, 1996 (*FDIC Guidelines*). The Federal Reserve also issued, on June 13, 1997, guidelines on the application of market risk capital requirements to credit derivatives. The Banking Department of the State of New York (NYSBD) issued a memorandum on credit derivatives to its examiners on December 23, 1996 (*NYSBD Memo*).

Permissibility
The releases issued by each of the three federal regulators and the NYSBD recognize that banks within the jurisdiction of such regulator enter into credit derivatives.

Internal Risk Management
The *OCC Guidelines* state that banks interested in using credit derivatives should use proper care and due diligence, and banks acting as protection

---

[1]See Chapter 12, The Supervision of Credit Derivative Activities of Banking Organizations.

sellers should thoroughly evaluate their credit portfolios to identify credit concentrations and risk interconnections. The OCC believes that national banks should subject credit derivatives to a uniform product assessment process to ensure that all significant risks have been addressed in the context of changing markets, and the bank's organizational structure, systems support, operational capacity, policies, and procedures. The *OCC Guidelines* also state that the OCC's Banking Circular 277, which provides guidance for financial derivatives activities, is applicable to users of credit derivatives.

The Federal Reserve Guidelines state that a bank should not enter into credit derivative transactions unless its management has the ability to understand and manage the credit and other risks associated with these instruments in a safe and sound manner. Management expertise in evaluating credit derivative products, the adequacy of relevant policies, including position limits, and the quality of the bank's relevant information systems and internal controls will all be reviewed by the bank's examiner as part of the bank's supervision by the Federal Reserve.

The *FDIC Guidelines*, which apply generally to U.S. banks with FDIC-insured deposits, state that a bank's examiner should review the bank's exposure to the credit protection seller, if applicable, under the credit derivative, as well as to the reference asset if the asset is owned by the credit protection buyer under the credit derivative.

The *NYSBD Memo*, which applies to New York State-chartered banks, states that the NYSBD examiner should thoroughly review the management of credit derivatives to determine if the bank's operating management is knowledgeable of the risks involved, the appropriateness of internal control safeguards, and the ability of the board of directors of the bank to exercise its oversight responsibilities with respect to credit derivatives.

Bank Credit Requirements

Existing banking laws in the United States and other jurisdictions impose requirements on banks' credit exposures, such as a limit on the total amount of loans to a single borrower. Banks must consider how credit derivatives fit into such existing laws. Specific bank credit requirements are discussed below.

Concentration Limits   The *Federal Reserve Guidelines* state that, for supervisory purposes, a concentration of credit generally exists when a bank's loan and other exposures, such as federal funds sold, securities and letters of credit, to a single obligor, geographic area, or industry exceed a stated percentage of the bank's capital and reserves for losses. The *Federal Reserve Guidelines* state that the Federal Reserve's bank examiners will not consider a bank's asset concentration to a particular borrower reduced because of the existence of a nongovernment guarantee on one of the borrower's loans, because the underlying concentration to the borrower will still exist. However, bank examiners are advised under the *Federal Reserve Guidelines* to consider how the bank manages the concentration, which could include the use of nongovernment guarantees. Examiners will also look at a bank's asset concentrations because the ultimate risk to the bank stems from asset concentrations, although the associated credit risk may be mitigated by the existence of nongovernmental guarantees or other credit protection products.

Lending Limits   The OCC, for national banks, and the New York State Banking Department, for New York State-chartered banks, impose lending limits on the amounts that a bank can lend to any single borrower, calculated as a percentage of capital. As of the time of writing, the OCC had not issued any specific guidance with respect to the impact of credit derivatives on lending limits.

The *NYSBD Memo* states that the regulatory approach accorded credit derivatives follows that which is applied to guarantees. A memo from NYSBD counsel attached to the *NYSBD Memo* states that, for purposes of the lending limits, a bank selling protection should be treated as having extended credit to the obligor on the reference asset. However, the *NYSBD Memo* also states that actual treatment by the NYSBD of credit derivatives may vary widely, depending for example, on how completely credit risk is transferred from one party to the other.

Asset Classification   Regulators require troubled loans and other assets, if they meet certain criteria, to be classified as "substandard," "doubtful," or "loss." The *Federal Reserve Guidelines* state the following about the effect of credit derivatives on classification. Credit derivatives may be used by a bank to preclude the classification of a reference asset or to reduce the severity of the classification of such asset. To accomplish this, the credit derivative must have the following characteristics: (1) the credit risk must be transferred to the protection seller; (2) the protection seller must have the financial capacity and willingness to pay; (3) the credit derivative must be legally enforceable; and (4) the credit derivative must provide protection during the remaining term of the reference asset. Where the term of the credit derivative is shorter than the maturity of the reference asset, the effect of the credit derivative would generally not be recognized for purposes of classifying the reference asset.

Non-U.S. Law: The United Kingdom, France, and Germany

The United Kingdom

Banks licensed to do business in the United Kingdom may generally use credit derivatives. The Financial Services Authority (FSA) has maintained the policy of its predecessor regulator, the Bank of England, in maintaining that the same rigorous standards of risk management and control should be applied to credit derivatives as to other similar products. The FSA has expressed concern regarding the extent to which credit protection sellers and total return swap buyers have access to information regarding a reference borrower where there is no publicly traded security of such borrower. The FSA has noted, in this context, that information is generally passed from protection seller to protection buyer as part of the initial transaction process in a credit derivative, but that this information is not updated during the life of a swap. The FSA has also stated that banks should consider the extent to which controls are needed to prevent credit protection being purchased from a counterparty whose default is significantly correlated to that of the reference credit (e.g., credit protection from sovereign default that is provided by a bank situated in the same country).

The FSA has also stated that there is room for doubt as to whether dealer polls and/or auctions will prove effective in practice as a means of establishing recovery values. The FSA believes that bank management should carefully review the fall-back provisions in credit default contracts if a dealer poll were to fail to establish a recovery value for the reference credit. The FSA has also expressed concerns regarding maturity mismatches of a credit default derivative and its reference asset and set down criteria which must be satisfied before such mismatches are allowed.

France

Banks that are licensed to do business in France may use credit derivatives. Banks that use credit derivatives will be subject to similar risk management and exposure limits as those that are applicable to the use of other financial derivatives. The Commission Bancaire (CB) has published guidelines regarding the prudential treatment of credit derivatives for the purposes of the solvency and capital adequacy ratios (Bulletin n° 18, April 1998). These guidelines only deal with risk calculation issues, but in a working paper released in June 1997, the CB stated that the banking profession should pay particular attention to "the fundamental qualitative aspects" of the organization, management, and control of risks induced by credit derivatives, including legal risks.

Germany

Banks licensed under German law may enter into credit derivatives. The German Bundesaufsichtsamt fur das Kreditwesen (BAKred) has issued draft guidance relating to the capital and risk weighting of credit derivatives. It is currently assimilating comments on the draft circular with a view to publishing a final edition later this year. The legal and regulatory requirements regarding credit derivatives applicable to banks will be clearer once the BAKred has issued its final guidance.

INSURANCE REGULATION

The use of credit default products, such as credit default swaps and credit-linked notes, raises the issue of whether they may be considered to be insurance against nonpayment or insolvency of the reference borrower and, therefore, subject to insurance regulatory requirements. TRORS do not appear to raise such issues because payment to the protection purchaser under the TRORS does not generally depend upon the occurrence of a specified event, such as an insolvency. In determining whether a credit default product may be deemed to be insurance, a user of such a product may need to consider the laws of the jurisdictions where the protection purchaser and the protection seller are located, as well as the contractual choice of law governing the credit default derivative. We describe below certain important concepts of New York's insurance laws, as well as a comparative analysis of the laws of the United Kingdom, France, and Germany.

The United States: New York

The New York Insurance Law (NYIL) provides that any person engaging in financial guaranty insurance or other insurance business in New York must be licensed as an insurer by the New York Superintendent of Insurance. "Financial guaranty insurance" is defined to include the issuing of any indemnity contract by a person doing insurance business under which loss is payable to an insured claimant upon proof of occurrence of financial loss. The NYIL does not define "proof of occurrence of financial loss," but the use of the term implies that the insured must demonstrate that it has incurred loss. Typically, credit default products do not require the protection purchaser to have to demonstrate any loss to the protection seller to obtain payment under the credit derivative. Upon notification by either the purchaser or the seller that a credit event has occurred, the swap contract would terminate. Any payment made by the protection seller is typically not linked to the protection purchaser's loss (if any) relating to the credit event.

However, even if the credit default product does not qualify as financial guaranty insurance, it may still constitute "doing an insurance business" in New York. A person may do an insurance business in New York by either (a) making or proposing to make an insurance contract to a person resident in or an entity authorized to do business in New York or (b) making or proposing to make any contract of warranty, guaranty, or surety, the making of which is a vocation rather than an incidental line of business of such person.

Making an Insurance Contract

The NYIL defines "insurance contract" to mean "any agreement or other transaction whereby one party, the insurer, is obligated to confer benefit of pecuniary value upon another party, the insured or beneficiary, dependent upon the happening of a fortuitous event in which the insured or beneficiary has, or is expected to have at the time of such happening, a material interest which will be adversely affected by the happening of such event."

New York case law suggests that the credit event may not be a fortuitous event if it is an event with respect to which the protection purchaser performed reasonable diligence. In such a case, the credit derivative would not be an insurance contract under the NYIL. New York courts have also held that where an indemnity was part of a contract and was incidental to the subject matter of the contract, the indemnity did not involve a fortuitous event and would not be deemed to be an insurance contract under the NYIL. It is also possible that a protection purchaser under a credit default product may not have, and may not be expected to have, a material interest that may be adversely affected by the occurrence of the fortuitous event underlying the protection being purchased, which would prevent the credit default product from being viewed as an insurance contract. In general, credit derivatives do not require the protection purchaser to have any interest in the reference asset.

If the protection purchaser is not resident in, or organized to do business in, New York, it is also possible that the protection seller will not be deemed to be doing an insurance business in New York.

Making a Contract of Warranty

As discussed above, a protection seller would also be engaged in an insurance business if it was viewed as making or proposing to make contracts of warranty, guaranty, or surety as a vocation rather than an incidental line of business. New York case law suggest that, even if the credit derivative was viewed as a contract of warranty, guaranty, or surety, the seller would not be engaged in making such contracts as a vocation unless a majority of its business revenues were derived from issuing such contracts.

Finally, we note that the NYIL provides that contracts that violate the provisions of the NYIL will, despite such violation, generally be enforceable by the protection purchaser against the protection seller.

Non-U.S. Law: The United Kingdom, France, and Germany

The United Kingdom

Any person that carries on insurance business under the Insurance Companies Act of 1982 (ICA) must be authorized to do so pursuant to the ICA. If such person is not so authorized, then § 132 of the Financial Services Act of 1986 (FSA) provides that the contract may not be enforceable by the insurer and the other party may be able to recover money and property paid to the insurer (including premiums), together with compensation. The legal analysis of whether a credit derivative is a contract of insurance is relatively complicated under English law because such analysis is based on the judgments in several court cases. Generally, however, an insurance contract under English law requires that the credit protection buyer suffers, or has a risk of, loss or that the credit protection buyer has an insurable interest which is protected by the contract, and the payor's obligations are conditional upon the risk of loss, or loss being incurred by the credit protection buyer.

If the payor's obligations under the contract are not conditional on the credit protection buyer having an insurable interest or on any loss or risk of loss being incurred by the credit protection buyer, such a contract should not be considered to be a contract of insurance under English law. In determining whether a contract is an insurance contract, an English court will generally look beyond the terminology of the contract to the substance of the transaction.

France

Credit derivatives that quality as transactions on financial instruments under the law of July 2, 1996 (Investment Services Law) do not constitute insurance contracts. As for other derivatives, there are reasons to believe that they should not be considered to constitute insurance under French law. However, the issue is not definitively settled, and a fact-specific analysis of French insurance laws should generally be undertaken by a party to a credit derivative that may be subject to French law.

Germany

Similar to the English legal analysis of insurance contracts, the German legal analysis of whether a contract may be deemed to be an insurance contract generally looks to whether the payment to a credit protection buyer is dependent on the credit protection buyer's loss. If the credit derivative contract or a related confirmation is drafted to cover actual losses of the credit protection buyer with respect to a reference asset or reference obligor, such a contract may be deemed by Germany's Federal Insurance Supervisory Authority to be an insurance contract.

GAMBLING LAWS

Many jurisdictions have laws against gambling. If a credit derivative were viewed as a bet on the occurrence of bankruptcy or other credit event, it might be subject to such gambling laws. Credit derivatives that violate gambling laws may be deemed to be unenforceable. Potential gambling law issues may arise under the laws of the jurisdiction of the protection seller, the protection buyer, and the governing law of the contract.

The United States: New York

The New York gaming laws prohibit and render unenforceable contracts pursuant to which persons may stake something of value upon contingent outcomes. If a credit derivative were viewed as an illegal gambling transaction, the New York gaming laws could allow a party to avoid its obligations under that credit derivative. New York courts, however, have carved out two relevant exceptions to the New York gaming laws. First, if a protection purchaser has a bona fide business interest in the outcome of the future event being insured against, the contract providing this protection will generally not be subject to the New York gaming laws. Second, if the parties intended at the time of entering into the credit derivative transaction to settle the transaction through physical delivery of the reference asset, such a credit derivative should generally not be subject to the New York gaming laws.

The New York bucket shop laws prohibit transactions involving the sale of a security or a commodity in which the parties do not intend the actual bona fide delivery of such securities or commodities, but intend instead to settle such transactions based upon the market prices of such securities or commodities. It can be argued that the bucket shop laws should not apply to credit default derivatives because the payment to the protection purchaser on a credit default derivative depends on the occurrence of a credit event, and not on the market prices of securities or commodities. In addition, the bucket shop laws should not be applicable to physically settled credit derivatives.

Non-U.S. Law: The United Kingdom, France, and Germany

The United Kingdom

Section 63 of the FSA provides a statutory exception from the United Kingdom gaming and wagering laws with respect to contracts where one of the parties enters into the contract for commercial reasons and the making or performance of the contract constitutes a "dealing" in an "investment," as defined under the FSA. Generally, entering into, or performing under, a credit derivative should fall within § 63's exception. However, certain products, such as bilateral or syndicated loans, may not constitute "investments" under § 63, and credit derivatives relating to such products may not benefit from § 63's exception to the gaming and wagering laws. English caselaw indicates that one of the parties must intend a contract to be a gaming and wagering contract for such a contract to be unenforceable, and like New York courts, English courts have generally viewed financial transactions entered into in good faith for a commercial purpose as not gaming or wagering contracts.

France

Credit derivatives that are considered to be forward financial contracts under the Investment Services Law would not be subject to French gaming laws. With respect to credit derivatives that would not be considered to be forward financial contracts, it is unclear whether, in practice, French gaming laws will be applied to render such credit derivatives unenforceable.

Germany

Similar to New York and English law, credit derivatives that are entered into for a commercial purpose should generally not be subject to the prohibitions against gaming and wagering contracts under German law.

CONFIDENTIALITY

Concerns relating to confidentiality are relevant to financial institutions which may deal with the same client in different capacities. For example, if a bank is party to a credit derivative involving a reference obligor that is a borrower of the bank, the bank may be subject to confidentiality laws that may restrict the bank from divulging nonpublic information to the bank's counterparty in the credit derivative that was obtained as part of its lending relationship with the reference obligor. Such restrictions may pose difficulties where the information needs to be provided in order to trigger the credit event provisions under the credit derivative. Some credit derivatives address this concern regarding confidentiality by requiring that publicly available information (PAI) be available before a credit event may occur under the credit derivative. However, PAI may not be a suitable trigger for payment defaults under bilateral loan or derivative contracts if PAI is defined to exclude either of the parties to the credit derivative being the source of the PAI.

The United States: New York

Privacy legislation at the federal level restricts federal governmental access to financial data but does not relate to private third-party access to such data. New York case law suggests that a cause of action exists based upon a breach of confidence theory in the context of bank/depositor relationships. However, as to the relationship between a bank and a borrower, New York courts have held that, in the absence of contractually agreed upon confidentiality provisions, the relationship is solely that of creditor and debtor and thus there is no basis for imposing a duty of confidentiality on the bank. If a bank is subject to confidentiality agreements with its customers or is otherwise concerned about disclosing information regarding its customers, credit derivatives involving such customers as the reference obligor may raise concerns for the bank. A bank that is a party to a credit derivative involving a reference obligor with a preexisting relationship with the bank should evaluate the type of relationship that the bank has with the reference obligor to determine if any confidentiality concerns may be involved in divulging information regarding the reference obligor to the bank's counterparty in the credit derivative.

Non-U.S. Law: The United Kingdom, France, and Germany

The United Kingdom

Confidentiality duties are applicable to fiduciaries, including banks, under English law, and provide that a fiduciary must only use information obtained in confidence from its customer for the benefit of its customer and not for its or any third party's advantage. Banks or investment compa-

nies that have a preexisting relationship with a reference obligor will need
to consider carefully the type of information relating to such a reference
obligor and the manner in which it was obtained before they provide
such information to a counterparty under a credit derivative.

France

French bank secrecy laws impose confidentiality duties upon French credit
institutions, and should be carefully considered by such institutions when
providing information to a counterparty in connection with a credit derivative. The violation of such banking secrecy laws is a criminal offense
and will also be a basis for civil liability.

Germany

German bank secrecy laws may apply to the release of confidential information by a bank to counterparty under a credit derivative, where the
confidential information relates to a client of the bank.

NETTING

Users of credit derivatives who enter into multiple derivative transactions
with the same counterparty may wish to net the amounts owed under
the credit derivative transactions and other transactions so that each party
owes the other a single amount. Such netting is often accomplished
through the use of a master agreement, such as the Master Agreement
(ISDA Master Agreement) published by the International Swaps and Derivatives Association, Inc. (ISDA). The ISDA Master Agreement may be
used for credit derivatives as well as other types of credit derivatives.
Netting may be done both outside of and in the context of insolvency
proceedings. The enforceability of contractual agreements relating to netting, termination and closeout in insolvency will depend upon whether
the relevant netting law is drafted broadly to cover generic types of
financial instruments or agreements, or is drafted to cover specific financial products.

The United States

U.S. federal law provides, pursuant to the Federal Deposit Insurance
Corporation Improvement Act of 1991 (FDICIA), broad general protections for netting contracts that are governed by the laws of the United
States, or any state thereof, and that are between certain types of financial
institutions. In addition, the Financial Institutions Reform, Recovery, and

Enforcement Act of 1989 (FIRREA) protects, subject to certain requirements and limitations, the netting of certain types of financial contracts
entered into by U.S. banks if such banks are involved in FDIC-supervised
insolvency proceedings. Also, the U.S. Bankruptcy Code, as amended
(Bankruptcy Code), provides product-specific netting protections for nonbank entities that are subject to proceedings under the Bankruptcy Code.

Whereas the netting protections of FDICIA would generally apply
to any qualifying netting agreement regardless of the type of product
covered by such netting agreement, FIRREA and the Bankruptcy Code
apply only to certain types of financial agreements, including swap agreements. The term "swap agreement" under FIRREA and the Bankruptcy
Code does not explicitly include credit derivatives, but credit derivatives
using the standard ISDA form appear to be sufficiently similar to other
derivatives that they should be included within the definition of "swap
agreement."

Non-U.S. Law: The United Kingdom, France, and Germany

The United Kingdom
Credit derivatives will generally be treated similarly to other off-exchange
derivatives and will enjoy similar netting protection.

France
Netting protection under French law apply to transactions on financial
instruments that are off-exchange and are documented using a market-
recognized master agreement, such as the ISDA Master Agreement. Credit
derivatives that are deemed to be transactions in financial instruments
under the Investment Services Law, involve at least one party that qualifies
as an investment services provider under the Investment Services Law,
and that are documented under a qualifying master agreement, will be
subject to netting protection under French law.

Germany
German civil code provisions relating to netting may apply to credit
derivatives. However, it is unclear at present whether German regulators
will accept the application of the civil code netting provisions to credit
derivatives.

SECURITIES LAWS AND INSIDER DEALING

Credit derivatives that involve securities as reference assets may be considered to be options on a security and, thus, be subject to securities laws and regulations. Related insider dealing rules may also apply in cases where users of credit derivatives have the opportunity to use information obtained by them while acting in another capacity with respect to a reference obligor. For example, a financial institution may be subject to certain restrictions when entering into a credit derivative transaction which involves as reference assets securities that have been underwritten by the financial institution. Additionally, material nonpublic information may be obtained by parties to a credit derivative about the reference obligor and issues may arise regarding the use of such information.

The United States

A credit derivative involving securities as reference assets might be deemed to be an option on a security and, thus, be considered to be a security subject to the U.S. securities laws. Many credit derivatives are individually negotiated bilateral contracts and should qualify for the private placement exemption from the registration requirements of the U.S. securities laws. However, the antifraud, insider trading, and other restrictions of U.S. federal and state securities will apply to credit derivatives that qualify as securities. Credit derivative transactions that involve the transfer to U.S. persons of reference assets that are securities should be structured so that the transfer of such securities are effected in accordance with applicable U.S. securities laws and regulations. Securities transactions in the United States must generally be effected through a U.S. bank or a U.S.-registered broker-dealer.

Non-U.S. Laws: The United Kingdom

The United Kingdom

Credit derivatives, like other financial derivative instruments, should generally be considered to be investments subject to the FSA. Like other investments subject to the provisions of the FSA, credit derivatives may only be dealt in by persons authorized under, or exempt from, the provisions of the FSA. With respect to insider dealing, the United Kingdom's insider dealing legislation generally applies to instruments that are listed or dealt on, or are admitted to or quoted on, or under the rules of an authorized exchange, or that are based on such instruments. It is important to note that criminal or civil consequences may flow from activities not covered by the United Kingdom's insider dealing legislation where dealings in credit derivatives involve using information that is not widely disseminated or shared equally between both parties.

France

Credit derivatives should generally not be covered by French securities laws. With respect to insider dealing, a person acquiring unpublished information during the course of such person's professional activities would be regarded as a "primary" insider under applicable French law and would be strictly liable for insider dealing under French law. A person acquiring information outside the scope of such person's professional activity must generally be shown to have known that the information was confidential to be held liable under French insider dealing laws.

Germany

Credit derivatives should generally not be covered by German securities laws. However, insider dealing prohibitions under German law may be applicable to credit derivatives involving the release of information relating to an exchange-listed security that is a reference asset, where such information is not publicly available and may have an impact on the price of such security.

CHAPTER 12

The Supervision of Credit Derivative Activities of Banking Organizations

Daniel C. Staehle*

Capital Markets Examiner, Office of the Comptroller of the Currency

With contributions from Christina M. Cumming

Although small when compared with other derivatives markets, the credit derivatives market has grown to the point where financial institution supervisors have developed considerable interest in these transactions. As discussed earlier in this volume, credit derivatives reflect the efforts of financial engineers to apply derivative structures and technology to the transfer of credit exposures in traditional credit instruments, such as bank loans and bonds. Ultimately, credit derivatives may well represent an important new means of managing credit risk, and the analytical techniques developed to manage credit derivatives may provide new insights into the nature of credit risk and how it is best measured. As often occurs with innovative financial instruments, credit derivatives raise fairly difficult questions about how existing supervisory rules and prudential guidance should be interpreted with respect to these products. As hybrids of traditional credit products and derivative instruments, credit derivatives do not always fit well into existing regulatory and supervisory frameworks.

---

*The authors are Capital Markets Examiner at the Office of the Comptroller of the Currency and Senior Vice President at the Federal Reserve Bank of New York, respectively. The views expressed in this chapter are those of the authors and do not necessarily correspond to the views of the Federal Reserve Bank of New York, the Federal Reserve System, or the Office of the Comptroller of the Currency. We would like to acknowledge helpful comments on this chapter from Brian Peters and the benefit of collaboration on this subject area with colleagues at the Federal Reserve Bank of New York and the Federal Reserve Board. We alone are responsible for the content of this chapter.

At the outset, it is important to note that credit derivatives are just one of several recent innovations in the management of credit risk. The development of credit risk measurement models, along with considerable advances in credit scoring models and securitization, are changing the way credit is managed at banks and other financial institutions. The combined effect of credit derivatives and these new or enhanced tools is to create considerable potential to enhance the credit risk management process. This potential includes such elements as the initial credit underwriting and pricing decision, the analysis of credit portfolios, and the ability to adjust the portfolio's credit risk profile over time by shedding and assuming credit exposure to individual obligors.

The changes under way in credit risk management provide financial supervisors with new opportunities. Financial institutions employing credit models and credit derivatives in their risk management process can provide the supervisor with new analysis to understand the risk profile, asset quality, and risk management decisions of financial institutions. Such longer run developments as effective stress testing and more liquid markets for credit derivatives and other credit instruments offer new potential to identify and manage concentrations, long the most difficult and damaging credit risk problem.

These same developments also provide financial supervisors with new challenges. The analytic framework used by bank supervisors is rooted in the credit risk approaches banks have employed through the last few decades. Thus, as banks move to a new approach to credit risk measurement, monitoring, and management, supervisors will need to update their approaches. The simplicity of the regulatory credit risk capital framework in particular is challenged by the new developments as the market continues to refine both the pricing of credit and the mechanisms for transferring credit exposures within and outside of the banking system. The combination of credit derivatives, credit risk modeling, and securitization, in particular, create new potential for wholesale, and not just retail, credit risk exposures to be originated by banks and transferred to the general market.

Thus, many of the opportunities and challenges for supervisors associated with credit derivatives cannot be viewed as uniquely the result of credit derivatives. The sweep of innovation in credit risk analysis and management techniques creates a basic question for supervisors. How much should supervisors direct their scarce resources to enhancement of the existing framework to accommodate innovations such as credit derivatives and how much to a more thorough reassessment and updating of the framework?

This chapter will review several of the more common credit derivative structures and the issues which these products pose for financial institution supervisors. Significant supervisory issues with respect to credit derivatives relate to sound risk management practices, appropriate capital treatment, effects on concentrations and legal lending limits, and assessment of a bank's asset quality. Accounting treatment and legal issues are also important supervisory considerations and are addressed in Chapters 9 and 11, respectively. Finally, the bibliography contains a list of recent supervisory guidance or discussion papers on credit derivatives issued by banking regulators globally.

WHAT ARE CREDIT DERIVATIVES?

Credit derivatives do not yet have a commonly agreed upon definition in the marketplace and are not a sharply defined class of financial instrument. From a supervisory perspective, credit derivatives are perhaps best described as off-balance sheet financial instruments used to assume or transfer away credit risk. Sometimes the risk assumption or transfer occurs only to a limited extent, under very specific circumstances or for a limited period of time. In general, the presence of three features sets a credit derivative apart from both market risk derivatives and traditional credit instruments. They are:

1. The transfer of credit risk associated with a third-party "reference" asset through contingent payments based on either the performance of the reference asset over time or the price behavior of the reference asset at, or shortly after, a predefined credit event, such as a credit rating downgrade or a default;

2. The structuring of cash flows such that the transactions resemble traditional derivatives such as swaps or options, that is, periodic exchanges of payments or the payment of a premium; and

3. Use of an International Swaps and Derivatives Association master agreement and the legal format of a derivative contract.

The most widely used types of credit derivatives to date are total rate of return swaps (TRORS) and credit default swaps. While the timing and structure of the cash flows associated with TRORS and credit default swaps differ, the economic substance of both transactions is that they seek to transfer the credit risk on the asset(s) referenced in the transaction. The counterparty seeking to transfer the credit risk (the beneficiary) often owns the reference asset or a similar instrument issued by the reference obligor. The counterparty receiving the credit risk of the reference asset (the guarantor) is able to do so without purchasing the reference asset directly. For example, the beneficiary may pay the total return on a reference asset, including any price appreciation, to a guarantor in exchange for a spread over funding costs (a TRORS structure). Alternatively, a beneficiary may pay a periodic premium to the guarantor in exchange for a guaranty against any loss that may occur if the reference asset defaults (a credit default swap). The following sections describe the basic structure of these transactions and set out the terminology used through the balance of this chapter.

Total Rate of Return Swaps

The TRORS appears to be the most popular form of credit derivative transaction as of this writing. In a TRORS, one counterparty (Bank A in Figure 12–1) agrees to pay the total return on a specific reference asset to its counterparty in exchange for a LIBOR-based return. Reference assets may be bank loans, although swaps based on corporate and sovereign debt securities are also popular.

F I G U R E   12–1

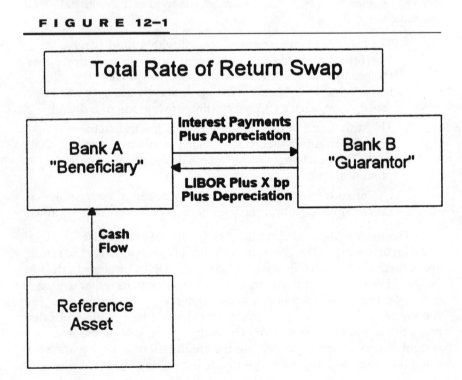

Total Rate of Return Swap

In the example in Figure 12–1, the total return payments due to Bank B include not only contractual cash flows (e.g., coupon payments) of the reference asset, but also any appreciation on the reference asset. The payments due to Bank A include a LIBOR-based return and any depreciation on the reference asset. Consequently, for the term of the swap, it is as if Bank B actually owns the reference asset. Bank A, in turn, often holds the reference asset on its balance sheet, receiving from Bank B some spread above its own funding costs for doing so (assuming Bank A funds itself at LIBOR). Because Bank B is required to make up any depreciation on the reference asset over the life of the swap, Bank B is termed the guarantor and Bank A the beneficiary.

At each payment date, the reference asset is priced for purposes of determining swap obligations. The price of the reference asset is determined either by a poll of dealers or by reference to a direct market quotation. In the event of a default by the reference obligor, the swap may either terminate, in which case a final dealer poll is conducted to facilitate settlement, or the swap may continue to maturity with each counterparty paying subsequent appreciation or depreciation, as the circumstances warrant. This approach assumes that there will be a market for the defaulted reference asset. If instead the swap is terminated, the counterparties will owe each other accrued interest plus any appreciation or depreciation evident from the final dealer poll. Usually, Bank B (the guarantor) has the option of purchasing the reference asset from Bank A and pursuing a workout with the reference obligor directly. Bank B will exercise this option if not satisfied with the dealer poll (i.e., Bank B believes the valuation is too low). Alternatively, in rare circumstances, Bank A may have the option to put the reference asset to Bank B in lieu of cash settlement.

Credit Default Swaps

In a credit default swap, one counterparty (Bank A) agrees to make periodic payments to its counterparty in exchange for a payment in the event of the default of the reference asset (Figure 12–2). Since the payoff of a credit default swap is contingent upon a default event occurring, which may include bankruptcy, insolvency, delinquency, or even a credit rating downgrade, calling the structure a swap may be somewhat of a misnomer: the transaction more closely resembles an option with a strike event rather than a strike price. In fact, similar transactions which require delivery of the reference asset upon default are called default puts.

The occurrence of default is contractually well-defined and often must be publicly verifiable. These default definitions must be sufficiently specific to exclude events whose inclusion would be undesirable, such as

F I G U R E   12–2

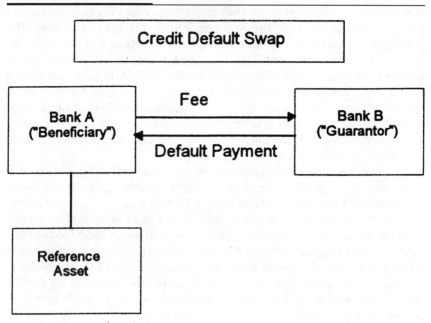

when an reference obligor is delinquent due to the intentional withholding of a payment in a legal dispute that does not effect the credit worthiness of the organization. Further, a materiality threshold is usually involved, that is, a default event must have occurred and the loss on the reference asset must exceed a certain percentage of its predefault value. Materiality thresholds may also be expressed in terms of a minimum required widening of the reference asset's spread. The materiality threshold increases the likelihood that only significant changes in credit quality of the reference asset will trigger the default payment (rather than smaller fluctuations in value that may occur over time).[1]

Upon default, the swap is terminated and a default payment is calculated. As with a TRORS, the default payment is often calculated by sampling dealer quotes or observable market prices of the reference asset and may involve averaging results over some prespecified period. Averaging dealer prices over time is used to reduce post-default price volatility. As was true with TRORS, the guarantor often has the option of purchasing

---

[1]Note that the materiality threshold is not a deductible: it is used to determine when a payment is to be made, not how much the payment will be.

the reference asset directly rather than cash settling the swap. Alternatively, the default payment may be specified in advance as a set percentage of the swap notional amount (e.g., 15, 25, or 50 percent—called binary default swaps). Binary default swaps may be used for reference assets that aren't traded but which belong to an asset class whose recoveries in default may be somewhat predictable. For example, if senior secured bank loans typically recover 85 percent of their value after default, a binary default swap paying 15 percent in the event of default may be attractive to senior, unsecured bank lenders.

Finally, when there is more than one reference asset included in the swap, which is often found in basket structures, the guarantor is usually exposed to only the first reference asset to default. Basket default options can also be embedded in cash instruments, such as notes, in order to increase the yield to an investor.

HOW ARE BANKS USING CREDIT DERIVATIVES?

Banks may utilize credit derivatives in several ways. Banks may choose to receive credit exposure (provide protection) for a fee or in exchange for credit exposure which they already own in an effort to better diversify their credit portfolio. Banks may also elect to receive credit exposure through credit derivatives rather than through some other transaction due to a relative yield advantage.

Alternatively, banks may use credit derivatives to reduce either individual credit exposures or credit concentrations in their portfolios by purchasing credit protection from another institution. Banks may use credit derivatives to synthetically take a short position in an asset which they do not wish to sell outright, perhaps for relationship or tax reasons. From the bank customer's perspective, credit derivatives may be written by banks to allow a nonbank customer to obtain access to bank loan exposures and related returns either as a new asset class (for credit diversification) or without up-front funding (perhaps to increase return on equity). Here, the bank is essentially performing credit intermediation using a new off-balance sheet vehicle.

Finally, banks may seek to establish themselves as dealers in credit derivatives. Rather than pursuing credit portfolio efficiency or seeking enhanced yields, dealer banks seek to profit from buying and selling credit derivatives quite apart from their portfolio management goals. Dealer banks may or may not hold the assets referenced in their credit derivative transactions, depending on their risk tolerance and (ultimately) their ability to offset contracts in the marketplace.

WHAT IS NEW AND UNIQUE ABOUT CREDIT DERIVATIVES FROM A SUPERVISOR'S VIEWPOINT?

Credit derivatives pose significant challenges to the way bank supervisors normally view credit risk. Perhaps the most fundamental challenge of credit derivatives is that they unbundle credit risk in new ways, often creating a focus on asset price behavior given a credit event, such as a default. The potential for gains and losses as a result of changes in the value of assets around an event of default, while a traditional banking risk, has until now not been used as a basis for payments in a cash-settled, traded financial contract. Credit derivatives are often designed to price and trade this risk separately from the ownership of a financial asset.

Bank supervisors have traditionally viewed credit risk as a cradle-to-grave phenomenon where the focus is upon principal repayment. Banks historically held credit exposures until maturity and could be expected to work out any problem exposures. Returns on equity in lending depended not only on the probability of default, but also on the management of the post-default recovery process. As illustrated in Figure 12–3, a good

F I G U R E   12–3

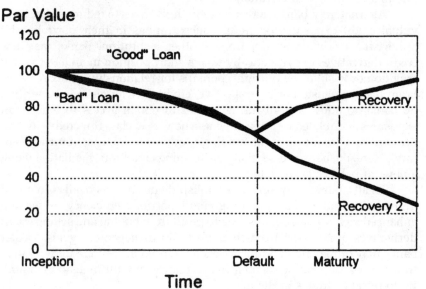

Traditional Supervisory View of Credit

Par Value

- "Good" Loan
- "Bad" Loan
- Recovery
- Recovery 2

Axis labels: 120, 100, 80, 60, 40, 20, 0

Time axis: Inception — Default — Maturity

Time

loan is one that is fully performing through maturity. Bad loans deteriorate in value prior to maturity, perhaps defaulting before maturity. Thereafter, the recovery experience on the bad loan has a meaningful impact on the loss suffered by the bank. In this traditional view of the credit process, portfolio management is achieved largely through underwriting standards and monitoring of individual credits over their life. The bank's risk profile is evolutionary, rather than actively managed.

Reflecting the loan-by-loan nature of traditional credit risk management, bank supervisors have used a weighted summation approach to measure aggregate asset quality or capital adequacy. Bank supervisors use such measures as the ratio of nonperforming loans to total loans and the weighted classified assets ratio, where the weights reflect the historical average rate of value repaid given a loan's regulatory classification (special mention, substandard, doubtful, or loss). A risk measure based on weighted summation cannot distinguish between concentrated and diversified portfolios, and, thus, the potential for future problems, except belatedly, when a concentration of credits has deteriorated in credit standing. Supervisors have, therefore, supplemented their measures of asset quality and capital adequacy with an assessment of concentrations.

Finally, traditional measures of asset quality and capital adequacy stress the importance of the bank as principal to a transaction. For example, a bank providing a letter of credit on a commercial credit exposure is seen to substitute its credit risk for that of the original borrower by the bank beneficiary of the letter of credit. In this case, the bank beneficiary of the letter of credit experiences a reduction in its regulatory capital requirement, since the obligations of banks receive a lower risk weight than commercial obligors. This process of risk substitution, however, does not always result in a reduction of capital charges, since even high-quality nonbank, nongovernment guarantee providers receive the same risk weight as commercial borrowers.

Credit derivatives challenge the traditional credit perspective on all three counts—buy and hold, weighted sum aggregation, and credit substitution. These three features lie at the heart of the challenge in integrating credit derivatives into the supervisory framework.

Credit derivatives allow for the application of active—or dynamic—risk management strategies, rather than buy and hold strategies, to portfolios of traditional credit instruments such as bank loans. While larger banks have been active originators and sellers of credit for over a decade, the usefulness of loan sales as a portfolio management tool is limited to a short period after origination. Credit derivatives, by contrast, make it possible for banks to take on both long and short positions, to actively manage credit exposures by entering into additional or offsetting credit derivative transactions over time, and to employ option strategies to limit downside risk. In short, the bank can alter its credit risk profile over time.

In addition, credit derivatives arguably serve to differentiate the pre- and post-default markets for loans, reinforcing an existing trend toward segmentation arising from the growth of the distressed credit market. Credit derivatives generally stipulate that the contract will end if there is an event of default. The termination feature generally leaves the management of the risk beyond default in the hands of the protection buyer. By contrast, with a letter of credit, the beneficiary bank is taken out of the bad loan completely, which then becomes a funded asset of the guarantor. Despite the termination feature, it can be argued that credit derivatives transfer substantially all of the expected value of a credit over its life since the value around default will reflect prospects for future recoveries.[2]

Credit derivatives also create the potential for new approaches to credit pricing based on marginal contribution to portfolio credit risk, thus taking into account portfolio concentrations. For example, the marginal required return of taking on additional credit exposure to ABC Corporation depends not only on the inherent risk in the exposure, but also the nature of and amount of ABC credit exposure already in the bank's portfolio and on the degree to which ABC Corporation credit risk is correlated with other credit risks in the portfolio. Consider a bank with a large exposure to the petroleum industry that will suffer credit losses as the price of petroleum products declines. Such a bank might reasonably be willing to pay a higher price than the market to obtain credit exposure to airline or other transportation firms whose credit profile would improve with a decline in the price of petroleum products. Contrast this bank with one that already has significant transportation-related credit exposure and no petroleum exposure. That second bank will be much less willing to take on additional transportation exposure, and is likely to demand a lower price (higher yield) for the credit exposure because of its concentration.

While analytical measures of the marginal contribution of individual credit exposures to overall portfolio risk are still developing, the advent of portfolio pricing raises the possibility that banks could move much closer to efficient credit portfolios. If traditional credit management can be viewed as maximization of revenue or volume given the combined constraints of current underwriting standards and capital, marginal

---

[2]An interesting question is whether credit derivatives will alter the loan workout process and whether changes in the likelihood of recoveries through workout will be sufficiently great to alter the overall rate of return in lending.

pricing of credit risk based on contribution to overall portfolio risk points to an approach based on maximization of return per unit of credit risk. That different banks will require different returns (hence, prices) for the same credit instrument, depending on their current credit portfolio composition, implies that credit exposures may be traded profitably and that market-making services may have economic value-added.

Finally, both the dynamic management of credit risk and pricing based on marginal portfolio risk rest on a view that reference credit exposures can be fully or partially offsetting. The derivative structure suggests a recharacterization of the benefits from buying credit protection from simple risk substitution for the reference asset, like a letter of credit, to the substitution of counterparty credit risk for reference asset (commercial loan) risk. Thus, the principal-to-principal nature of back-to-back, fully offsetting credit exposures is not lost, but recharacterized. As discussed later, this recharacterization—and the adequacy of the measurement approaches to capture it—is among the most difficult issues in addressing credit derivatives in the current framework.

CAPITAL TREATMENT OF CREDIT DERIVATIVES FOR BANKS

Among supervisory issues, the regulatory capital treatment of credit derivatives has drawn the most attention from financial market participants since the early days of the market. The 1988 Basle Accord and the 1996 Market Risk Amendment to the Accord, as well as the national rules that implement the Accord, do not directly address the capital treatment of credit derivatives for banks, given the innovative nature of the instrument. Thus, bank supervisors have needed to interpret their national rules, and a number of have done so, including the U.S. banking regulatory agencies in the form of interim guidance.[3]

The capital requirements for banks contemplate two principal types of credit risk: banking book exposures arising from traditional lending activities and counterparty credit risk arising from over-the-counter (OTC) derivatives activities. Credit derivatives have elements of both exposure

---

[3]See Federal Reserve SR Letter 96–17, *Supervisory Guidance for Credit Derivatives*, August 12, 1996, SR Letter 97–18, *Application of Market Risk Capital Requirements to Credit Derivatives*, June 13, 1997, OCC Bulletin 96–43, *Credit Derivatives: Guidelines for National Banks*, Office of the Comptroller of the Currency, Washington, D.C., August 12, 1996; FIL 62–96, *Supervisory Guidance for Credit Derivatives*, Federal Deposit Insurance Corporation, Washington, D.C., August 19, 1996.

to a reference asset, which resembles a traditional lending exposure, and exposure to the counterparty to an OTC derivative transaction. As discussed earlier, several features of credit derivatives and their use by banks, as well as a broader set of concurrent advances in the management of credit risk, represent departures from the traditional supervisory framework for lending activities. These features all create challenges in interpreting the existing capital rules to cover credit derivatives, but the primary focus of this discussion will be on the dual nature of credit exposure in a credit derivative.

An uppermost concern for banking supervisors is that the capital level at individual banks and in the banking system is adequate for the nature and amount of risk borne by banks. If risks are not adequately supported by the capital of market participants, the market's vulnerability to credit shocks increases. Therefore, in reviewing the potential capital treatment for credit derivatives, the key considerations are:

1. The nature of the credit risk assumed or transferred,
2. The duration and extent of the transfer or assumption of credit risk, and
3. The size and appropriate measurement of that credit risk.

Since credit derivatives can embody credit exposures to a counterparty and to a reference asset, a useful starting point for analysis is the possible capital treatment of each exposure under the current rules. Figure 12–4 outlines these two possible capital treatment approaches for credit derivatives using a TRORS as an example. The first approach, which we will call the derivatives approach, treats credit derivative swaps in the same manner as the capital guidelines treat interest rate swaps and other derivatives. Since TRORS involve two-way payments of interest as well as payments reflecting appreciation of the reference asset by Bank A and depreciation of the asset by Bank B, both banks have counterparty credit risk. A key question of interpretation is the capital treatment of the asset held by Bank A which presumably was seeking credit protection by entering into the TRORS. In Figure 12–4, we assume conservatively that Bank A holds capital against the reference asset, without recognition of the transfer to Bank B of the credit risk of the reference asset. We also assume that the reference asset is a loan to a commercial firm, causing the loan to be risk weighted at 100 percent. A variant of this treatment would consider Bank A's counterparty exposure to Bank B as substituting fully for the exposure to the reference asset, reducing Bank A's capital charge on the asset to 20 percent or eliminating it altogether.

A second approach treats the TRORS as a transaction closely resembling traditional credit instruments like letters of credit and guarantees.

Two Capital Treatment Possibilities

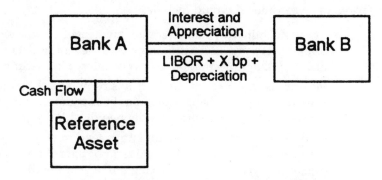

	Bank A	Bank B
Derivatives Approach	Asset at 100% RW Swap MV at 20% RW	Swap MV at 20% RW
Direct Credit Substitues Approach	Guaranteed Asset at 20% RW	Guaranty at 100% RW

The approach therefore recognizes the transfer to Bank B of the credit risk of the reference asset and patterns the capital treatment after that of a letter of credit. We will call this the direct credit substitutes approach. A key feature of this approach is that Bank B holds capital against the reference asset, reflecting the transfer of the credit risk of the reference asset from Bank A to Bank B. Meanwhile, the existence of the credit derivative transaction would allow Bank A to treat the reference asset as being guaranteed by Bank B. Therefore, Bank A would be allowed to reduce the risk weight of the reference asset to 20 percent, the appropriate risk weight for an asset guaranteed by a bank from an OECD country. As is the case with guarantees and letters of credit, Bank B would be responsible for the full risk-weighted capital charge associated with the reference asset.

Clearly, the degree to which credit risk transfer is recognized has a significant impact on the distribution of capital charges between the counterparty banks. Further, these two approaches may be viewed as representing, in effect, two endpoints on a continuum with respect to the credit risk of the reference asset (i.e., all of it either stays with Bank A or is fully transferred to Bank B). Given the heterogeneous nature of the credit derivative market, however, neither of these approaches may accurately portray the true extent of reference asset credit risk transfer. Additional factors to be considered would include:

- Credit default swaps only require payments from the swap counterparty providing protection in the event of default, so that only the protection buyer has counterparty credit risk.

- Measuring counterparty credit risk is complicated by the fact that adverse price changes may not be associated with an increase in the probability of a defined default event.

- Both TRORS and credit default swaps tend to be written for terms which are shorter than the term of the reference asset (e.g., a two year swap referencing a five year bond). Consequently, the full credit risk of the reference asset does not appear to be transferred for a bank hedging a reference asset with a credit derivative.[4]

- Some assets which banks wish to hedge, such as loans, may not be traded instruments. If the loan obligor has issued a traded instrument such as a bond, a bank may hedge its cash loan exposure with a credit derivative referencing a bond of the same obligor. In such a case, the degree of risk transfer depends on the relationship between the two instruments.

- Some credit derivative products use an averaging of post-default market prices to determine default payments, while others may specify a fixed default payment in advance (e.g., 15 percent of notional value if a default occurs). Consequently, banks may still have exposure to the reference asset even after default payments have been made and perhaps after credit risk has been deemed transferred.

For example, Figure 12–5 provides an example of a TRORS where a $100 reference asset has defaulted and the final swap payment is the

---

[4]If the reference asset owner, a bank, sells the reference asset at the maturity of the swap, and the sales price is certain to be the same as the price which is used to settle the swap, then the bank will have no gain or loss on the position, and the credit risk can be viewed as fully transferred. In the more likely event that the prices are not the same, perhaps due to timing problems or market disruptions, or the asset owner decides not to sell the reference asset, the bank will face some basis risk or forward credit risk, respectively.

F I G U R E   12–5

Default Pricing Scenario

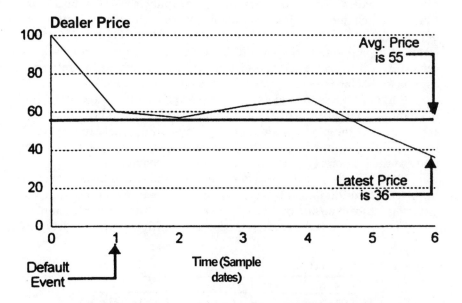

average of six weekly, post-default samples of dealer prices. An averaging of post-default prices might be used to smooth out price volatility immediately following the default event, the idea being that a price at a particular point in time after default might be a uniquely good or bad price. Note that the average of the six weekly dealer polls is $55. Note further that the value of the reference asset at the conclusion of the default pricing process is $36. Therefore, the beneficiary would own an asset worth $36 in the marketplace and would receive a default payment from the guarantor bank of $45. In this case, the beneficiary receives a total value of $81 after default, representing a $19 loss on the original exposure. Both the guarantor and the beneficiary are exposed to significant loss. Rather than risk transference, this appears to more closely resemble risk sharing.[5]

---

[5]Alternatively, the beneficiary bank could sell one-sixth of the exposure on the six consecutive dealer poll dates, receiving from the guarantor six partial default payments. In this case the beneficiary would be fully protected against loss.

CAPITAL CHARGES UNDER THE DERIVATIVES APPROACH AND THE DIRECT CREDIT SUBSTITUTES APPROACH

Because credit instruments and derivatives instruments are treated quite differently under risk-based capital rules, the capital impacts of the derivatives approach and the direct credit substitutes approach on bank users of credit derivatives are widely divergent. To illustrate, Figure 12–6 calculates the capital charge that would be assigned to a guarantor (risk receiver) in a five-year total rate of return (TRORS) where the reference asset is a $10,000, five-year traded commercial loan.

If the TRORS is treated as a direct credit substitute, such as a letter of credit or guaranty, the guarantor would be required to hold 8 percent capital against the nominal amount of the guaranty under current credit risk capital rules. In our case, the guarantor would hold $800 of capital (the required 8 percent of the reference asset exposure).

If the TRORS is treated as a derivative, capital would be held against the market value of the swap as well as against an add-on representing the potential future exposure of the swap, risk-weighted according to counterparty. In this case, it is the credit risk associated with the counterparty that

F I G U R E   12–6

Capital Treatment Illustration

Scenario:
Five year TROR swap
Five year reference asset
$10,000 notional amount
Reference asset appreciates 3%

Bank B
("Guarantor")
Capital Charge:

Credit Analogy:
$10,000 x 8% = $800.00

Derivatives Analogy:
MTM: $300 x 20% x 8% = $4.80
Add-On: ($10,000 x 15%) x 20% x 8% = $24.00
                                                                                             $28.80

T A B L E   12–1

Capital Treatment Illustration

Before TRORS:			After TRORS:		
Beneficiary Bank Capital	–	$800	Beneficiary Bank Capital	–	$160
Guarantor Bank Capital	–	N/A	Guarantor Bank Capital	–	$28.80
Total Capital Required	–	$800	Combined Capital	–	$188.80
Result: Less capital in the banking system.					

is assessed a capital charge, not the credit risk associated with the reference asset. For the sake of computational simplicity, in Figure 12–6 we assume that the referenced loan appreciates by 3 percent, that the proper add-on matrix factor is the one used for commodities, and that the counterparty (beneficiary) is a bank (a 20 percent risk-weighted counterparty). The resultant capital charge at 8 percent is only $28.80.

As Figure 12–6 illustrates, capital charges can be dramatically different depending on whether the reference asset risk or the counterparty credit risk is viewed as the dominant risk in a credit derivative. In determining which approach should be applied to credit derivatives, a supervisory concern is maintaining the adequacy of the levels of capital as well as preventing the creation of opportunities for regulatory arbitrage under the current credit risk capital rules.

The potential for regulatory arbitrage can be illustrated by the example from Figure 12–6. Assume that the guarantor treats the TRORS as a derivative, while the beneficiary treats the transaction as a guaranty. As Table 12–1 shows, the guarantor would hold $28.80 of capital against the TRORS counterparty exposure, while the beneficiary would reduce the risk weight of its traded commercial loan to $160 (i.e., a 20 percent risk weight being that it is now guaranteed by another bank). The result is that both banks combined do not hold the level of capital required for the underlying loan exposure. In this fashion, capital could drain out of the banking system. Moreover, a bank investing solely in credit derivatives rather than loans could take on almost 30 times more credit exposure through TRORS than it could through funding a commercial loan outright on the same capital base.

These calculations, as well as the historical importance of credit risk in producing large-scale losses at individual banks, explain why bank supervisors have been inclined to view credit derivatives use in association with traditional credit extending activities as more appropriately treated as direct credit substitutes than as interest rate or other market risk derivatives in their interim guidance.

CAPITAL TREATMENT FOR BANKS DEALING CREDIT DERIVATIVES

Banks that are dealers in credit derivatives usually seek to earn profits from intermediating credit derivatives, as depicted in Figure 12–7, but not from taking outright positions in credit exposures. Thus, a dealer bank frequently runs some combination of derivatives positions hedged with cash positions and a matched book of offsetting swaps. Risk in such a portfolio arises from counterparty exposure as well as basis risk and forward credit risk, depending on the degree of offsetting or hedging achieved by the dealer, rather than outright credit positions in credit derivatives.

Given this risk profile, dealer banks are likely to find capital charges under the direct credit substitutes approach onerous. For example, assuming that the reference asset in Figure 12–7 is a corporate loan or bond, the dealer (guarantor) would be responsible for maintaining 8 percent capital against a 100 percent risk-weighted asset. The capital charge may be partially mitigated if the dealer's other counterparty (the investor in Figure 12–7) is also a bank. In that case, the dealer can treat its guaranty to Bank A as being guaranteed by the investor bank and the dealer

F I G U R E   12–7

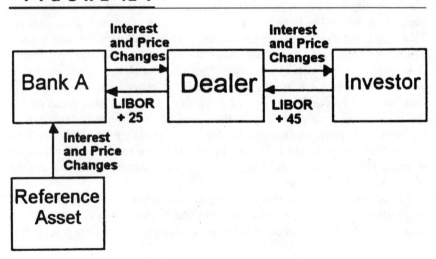

may reduce the risk-weight of its guaranty to Bank A to 20 percent (the appropriate risk-weight for a guaranty from a bank).

If the dealer bank's exposure to the reference asset is largely hedged, the bank's dominant credit risk is counterparty risk. Whether the reference asset appreciates, depreciates, or defaults, the dealer bank's concern about the performance of the reference asset is secondary, as long as the counterparty is creditworthy. This last qualification is important, because the bank is still exposed to reference asset risk in that the counterparty can encounter unexpected difficulty leading to default. Default creates an open position in the dealer's book. Yet this risk would appear to be far less than the risk associated with owning the reference asset outright.

The Market Risk Amendment (Amendment) to the Basle Accord provides another avenue to handle the capital treatment of credit derivatives held in the trading books of dealer banks, where credit derivatives dealing is generally booked at U.S. banks.[6] In general, the Amendment requires counterparty and market risk capital charges for OTC derivative transactions, while requiring market and specific risk capital charges for debt and equity securities in the trading account, as defined in Figure 12–8. Specific risk, in contrast to general market risk, is the risk of adverse price movements as a result of idiosyncratic factors related to the issuer. Conceptually, specific risk would include the effects of a change in credit quality of the instrument's issuer. The Amendment became generally effective January 1, 1998, although in the United States, it generally applies only to large banks with sizable trading activities. While the Amendment provides for both a standardized and an internal models approach, our discussion will focus on the model-based approach.

U.S. banks subject to the Amendment are required to measure the general market risk of their trading account positions using internal models, and have the option of using either the standardized or internal models approach for measuring specific risk. Therefore, banks will have the option to calculate the specific risk of net risk exposures, including any credit derivatives, in their trading portfolios for market risk capital purposes and to reflect the benefits of any diversification within the debt

---

[6]12 CFR Parts 208 and 225, Federal Register, Vol. 61, No. 174 dated September 6, 1996, page 47358 ff. and Vol. 62, No. 249 dated December 30, 1997, pp. 68064 ff. The Amendment generally applies only to the trading account, but some foreign exchange and commodities transactions in the banking book are to be included in the market risk capital charges. A further interim rule was issued for comment in December 1997 to implement more detailed Basle requirements on recognition of specific risk models and eliminating an interim approach to calculating specific risk capital in the Amendment.

FIGURE 12-8

Definitions

- **Counterparty Risk: The credit exposure arising from amounts owed by the counterparty to the credit derivative transaction.**

- **Market Risk: The risk arising from changes in the reference asset's value due to changes in market interest rates.**

- **Specific Risk: The risk of changes in the reference asset's value apart from changes in market interest rates, primarily due to changes in credit risk.**

and equity instrument portfolios. Consequently, where the benefits of matching and offsetting of positions can be estimated, this alternate capital treatment could allow for capital charges that are better aligned with the risks borne by dealers and much lower than the direct credit substitutes approach.

A credit derivative in the trading account can have three types of risk: general market risk, specific risk, and counterparty credit risk. In assessing the market and specific risks in credit derivatives, positions can be described in three ways: matched, offsetting, and open. Matched positions are those where the dealer has identical long and short positions, as depicted in Figure 12–7. Offsetting positions are nearly matched positions, for example, long and short positions in the reference assets of the same issuer that are not exactly matched in maturity, coupon, priority in bankruptcy, etc. Open positions include all others. Figure 12–9 indicates which risks are present in each type of position.

As Figure 12–9 indicates, all credit derivative positions have counterparty risk. The method used by regulators to assign capital charges for counterparty risk involves adding the market value of the position, if positive, with an estimate of potential future credit exposure (PCE). PCE, in turn, is derived by multiplying the notional value of the derivative by

F I G U R E   12–9

Risk / Position	Counterparty	Market	Specific
Open	Y	Y	Y
Matched	Y	N	N
Offsetting	Y	Residual	Residual

an appropriate add-on factor. Currently, add-on factors exist for such products as interest rate, foreign exchange, equity, and commodity derivatives, but not for derivatives based on specific debt instruments. Therefore, regulators need to determine an appropriate add-on factor in providing interim supervisory guidance.

Open positions have general market and specific risks, in addition to counterparty credit risk, and the Market Risk Amendment calls for capital charges for those risks. (For perfectly matched positions, the market and specific risk elements cancel each other out.) In implementing the Amendment for credit derivatives, it seems natural to associate the reference asset risk as a form of specific risk which can be captured using either the standardized or the internal models approach.[7]

The treatment of offsetting positions, that is, dynamically, partially, or imperfectly hedged positions, diverges significantly between the standardized and the models approaches. The standardized approach recognizes only two categories of positions: matched and open. By matched,

---

[7]It should be noted that no clear dividing line exists between general market and specific risks, since a general market risk model can be very disaggregated, modeling risks down to the individual instrument level. The December 1997 interim rule focuses on specific risk and provides some general guidance on principles for estimating the general market and the specific risk of portfolios in the trading account in order to facilitate consistent implementation of the rules.

the standardized approach means perfectly matched positions, identical in every significant feature. The models approach by construction is not explicit about the degree of matching, but sets out an expectation that all significant risks will be modeled. Hence, if a bank has significant residual or forward risks in offsetting positions, the component risks should be modeled, but the correlation between the various constituent elements in the positions will be recognized and reflected in the capital charges. Where the residual and forward risks are *de minimus*, they do not have to be modeled.

Because credit derivatives are relatively new and complex instruments, their treatment under the Amendment is likely to evolve along with market practices, advances in modeling the several market and credit risks of credit derivatives, and the broader evolution of credit risk measurement and management techniques. U.S. and foreign bank regulators are working on frameworks to incorporate credit derivatives into the market risk capital framework, and the Federal Reserve has published interim guidance to assist dealer banks.[8]

THE IMPACT OF CREDIT DERIVATIVES ON ASSESSMENTS OF BANK'S ASSET QUALITY

In addition to capital standards, another key component of the supervision of banking organizations is an assessment of the bank's asset quality, especially in the banking book. During on-site examinations, bank examiners review loan files and other pertinent documentation in order to rate individual credits. Examiners will assign pass ratings to those credits whose prospects for repayment remain sound, note credits showing special vulnerability, but no credit weakness, and classify credits which are developing (or already demonstrate) various credit weaknesses. Classifications are weighted according to severity and compared with the level of the bank's loan loss reserves and regulatory capital. A consequence of a high level of classified assets may therefore be unsatisfactory regulatory ratings for both capital and asset quality. Table 12–2 provides a short synopsis of the ratings used by examiners to classify weakening credits.

As a risk management tool, credit derivatives allow banking organizations to transfer credit risk to counterparties or assume risk from them. From a regulatory viewpoint, the issue is how to treat an asset which would normally be classified when that asset is credit enhanced by a

---

[8]Federal Reserve System, SR Letter 97–18, *Application of Market Risk Capital Requirements to Credit Derivatives*, June 13, 1997.

T A B L E 12-2

Asset Classification Definitions

Special Mention: Assets specially mentioned have potential weaknesses which may, if not corrected, weaken the asset or inadequately protect the bank's credit position at some future time.

Substandard: A substandard asset is inadequately protected by the current sound worth and paying capacity of the obligor or the collateral pledged, if any.

Doubtful: A doubtful asset has all the weaknesses inherent in a substandard asset with the added characteristic that the weaknesses make collection or liquidation in full, on the basis of currently existing facts, conditions, and values, highly questionable and improbable.

Loss: Asset classified loss are considered uncollectible and of such little value that their continuance as bankable assets is not warranted.

credit derivative. For example, consider a bank with a five year commercial loan that would be rated substandard on a stand-alone basis. If the bank also has entered into a credit derivative swap transferring the credit risk to its counterparty, how should the loan be rated?

The example points to several factors to be considered. First, the continuing creditworthiness of the credit derivatives counterparty is a necessary precondition to any easing of the loan's classification. Second, consideration needs to be given to the particular terms of the credit derivative relative to the exposure on the bank's books. For example, is the maturity of the credit derivative also five years or something less? Is the credit derivative a credit default swap, which only pays off in the event of default, or a TRORS, which requires the guarantor to pay the bank for any depreciation in value? Finally, what if the reference asset in the credit derivative is another obligation of the loan obligor and not the loan itself? Bonds, for example, are often a preferred reference asset as they are more liquid and easier to value than loans.

The source of existing supervisory guidance that perhaps comes closest to addressing this situation is the *Commercial Bank Examination Manual* discussion of the classification of assets which are backed up by a guaranty. In general, the existence of a guaranty may preclude the classification of an asset or lessen its severity if the guarantee has been provided by a financially responsible guarantor. The following characteristics define a financially responsible guarantor:

- The guarantor must have both the financial capacity and willingness to provide support for the credit;

- The nature of the guarantee is such that it can provide support for repayment of the indebtedness, in whole or in part, during the remaining loan term; and
- The guarantee should be legally enforceable.[9]

In general, U.S. bank supervisors have tended to apply these guidelines loosely to credit derivatives, relying more heavily on the professional judgment of bank examiners and case-by-case evaluations.

Closely related to the issue of asset classification is the effect of credit derivatives on the loan loss reserve process and the categorization of assets as nonperforming for accounting purposes. That is, should an asset still be reported as nonperforming if it is protected by a credit derivative? Should the value of the credit derivative be included in the valuation of the nonperforming asset? In a similar fashion, when a credit derivative payment is triggered by a decline in market price or a default, how should the beneficiary treat receipt of this payment (income/basis adjustment to the nonperforming asset/addition to the loan loss reserve, etc.)? Since Generally Accepted Accounting Principles (GAAP) are relied upon by bank supervisors to address these issues, readers should refer to Chapter 9 of this text relating to accounting issues.

IMPACT OF CREDIT DERIVATIVES ON CREDIT CONCENTRATIONS

One of the most important, but analytically difficult, issues for financial institutions and their supervisors is the identification and management of credit concentrations. In banking especially, but in other financial activities as well, the presence of credit concentrations has been a major factor in episodes of financial distress at both the individual institution and industry levels. Credit concentrations can take an easily recognized form, such as large exposures to a single obligor, to a set of related obligors, or to an industry. Credit concentrations can also develop when several large exposures are linked by macroeconomic forces, market dynamics, or other factors. The linkages may be difficult to detect in relatively benign market conditions and only emerge under stress.

Advances in credit risk measurement techniques offer the potential to facilitate the identification of emerging credit concentrations or reductions in diversification. In particular, the high-quality, integrated

---

[9]"Classification of Credits: Treatment of Guarantees," *Commercial Bank Examination Manual* (March 1994), Section 2060.1.

management information system necessary for a comprehensive credit risk management process can enhance the overall quality and availability of information. A strong information and risk analysis infrastructure also facilitates stress testing, which can assist management in identifying and sizing up more subtle linkages among credit exposures. While much work remains to be done in the development of credit risk measurement techniques and analysis of concentrations, the readily apparent possibilities in the new approaches hold out promise for a breakthrough in an area known for its analytical difficulty by both financial institutions and supervisors.

Credit derivatives create new opportunities to manage credit concentrations and increase risk diversification in credit portfolios by providing a new avenue for shedding risk, or taking on diversifying or offsetting exposures, and, potentially, by drawing new market participants into the market for credit risk. The enhanced ability to transfer risk becomes all the more powerful when combined with better and more penetrating identification and analysis of concentrations.

To date, supervisors have had two principal approaches to dealing with concentrations. The first is reliance on legal lending limits in order to limit the credit exposure of banking institutions to specific borrowers or a group of closely-related borrowers. These limits also function to promote equitable access to banking services by requiring banks to extend credit to a variety of customers. In the United States, legal lending limits are promulgated by the Office of the Comptroller of the Currency for nationally-chartered banks (12 USC 84) and State Banking Departments for state-chartered banks.[10] In addition, the Federal Reserve has established legal lending limits for Edge Act Corporations in Regulation K. Typically, legal lending limits prescribe a maximum amount of credit exposure that a banking institution may take on with respect to one obligor, usually calculated as a percentage of capital. The second approach used by supervisors is a qualitative analysis in which supervisors review bank methodologies for identifying, monitoring, and managing concentrations, as well as the examination of large exposures selected by the examiners.

As with capital and asset quality issues, credit derivatives raise some interesting questions in the area of legal lending limits. Given that credit derivatives are used by banking organizations to reduce credit exposures to individual borrowers, should these transactions be recognized in calculating legal lending limits? At the present time, legal lending limits do

---

[10]For example, New York State Banking Law 103 establishes legal lending limits for banks chartered by the State of New York.

not address the treatment to be accorded to credit derivatives. Legal lending limits do require banks which have provided guarantees to include the exposure that is guaranteed in their calculations. However, it is not clear that a bank benefitting from a guarantee will always be able to deduct its exposure to the guaranteed asset.

RISK MANAGEMENT AND INTERNAL CONTROLS

As banking activities become increasingly complex and varied, bank supervisors have been working to reformulate examination practices into approaches that adapt well to new banking products, practices, lines of business, and business strategies. The traditional paradigm of reviewing historical financial data and reviewing credit files in a standard manner for all banks is no longer seen as always the most efficient and effective way to evaluate the current condition and future prospects of a banking company, given the panoply of new risks and opportunities banks face today. While this observation seems especially apt for large, complex banking companies, the observation has general applicability. In the United States, bank supervisors have been moving towards a risk-focused approach to examinations of financial institutions since the early 1990s. For example, the Federal Reserve initiated an *Rx21* project to develop a risk-focused approach to examining financial institutions.

A principal objective of the new risk-focused approach is to obtain an understanding of the risk profile of a banking institution in some detail and assess whether risk management practices and internal controls are adequate as designed, given the nature and volumes of the bank's activities, and whether those processes are functioning properly. Therefore, the new approach has been aptly characterized as a more process-oriented approach to examinations, as opposed to a transaction—or proving the balances—approach. Risk-focused examinations, much like the movement towards internal models for regulatory capital requirements, is meant to accommodate the rapid advances in risk measurement and internal control approaches, as well as the diversity in risk profiles of banking institutions.

Bank supervisors, at both the international and national levels, have set out a basic framework for describing sound risk management practices. For example, the Federal Reserve's description of basic risk management principles for banks' trading and derivatives activities was set out in 1993[11] and includes:

---

[11]SR Letter 93–69, *Examining Risk Management and Internal Controls for Trading Activities of Banking Organizations*, December 20, 1993.

- Active board and senior management oversight;
- Adequate risk management policies and limits;
- Appropriate risk measurement and reporting systems; and
- Comprehensive internal controls.

These principles are grounded in the elements of sound corporate governance, namely, that the Board of Directors is ultimately responsible for the safe and sound operation of the bank, and that they may delegate, with proper oversight, day-to-day decision-making to members of management.

Banking organizations conducting credit derivatives activities will be evaluated in a risk-focused context on how well they implement these basic principles. In 1995, the Federal Reserve formalized the process of evaluating risk management and internal controls in all activities using these principles and required examiners to provide a rating of risk management as part of the rating of management assigned during the examination process.[12] (Appendix to this chapter describes each numerical rating in the new rating system.) The following discussion will describe how bank supervisors evaluate the risk management and internal control practices of banks conducting credit derivative activities in the new risk-focused examination environment.

Active Board and Senior Management Oversight

Boards of directors and senior management take ultimate responsibility for the safe and sound conduct of business activities. The board should approve all significant business strategies associated with credit derivatives and should clearly communicate the risk tolerance of the organization in these businesses. Given that credit derivatives are new products with unique, customized characteristics and risks, senior management should ensure that the bank has followed a new product approval process in developing its business strategy. For example, Federal Reserve supervisory guidance states that an institution not obtain significant positions in any new financial instrument "until senior management and all relevant personnel (including those in internal control, legal, accounting, and auditing functions) understand the product and can integrate it into the

---

[12]SR Letter 95–51, *Rating the Adequacy of Risk Management Processes and Internal Controls at State Member Banks and Bank Holding Companies*, November 14, 1995.

institution's risk measurement and control systems."[13] This guidance
seems especially relevant to credit derivatives given their importance as
innovative instruments in managing a risk as major as credit risk, as well
as the uncertainties associated with their appropriate legal, regulatory
and accounting treatment.

Another key focus of the board and senior management is to ensure
proper staffing and expertise in the business line and support areas. Not
only must senior management ensure competent staffing, but depth of
staffing should also be a focus in new product areas. Where expertise is
highly concentrated, control weaknesses may exist, as well as the potential
for key staff to be hired away with no suitable internal candidates for replacement.

Adequate Policies, Procedures, and Limits

An important element of any risk management system is a set of policies,
procedures, and limits to govern risk-taking in its activities. The extent
to which the bank will require detailed day-to-day policies is a function of
the size, sophistication, and complexity of the activities being conducted.
Nevertheless, the creation and updating of written policies and procedures, especially in a dynamic area such as credit derivatives, provides
both a process for establishing the rules of the road in a business, and a
means to communicate the rules to all bank staff involved.

With respect to credit derivatives, management should assure that
there are adequate limits or other controls in place to guard against an
imprudent level of risk-taking. Limits may be established by counterparty,
reference obligor, business unit, portfolio, or instrument. For large, complex banking organizations which are (or intend to be) particularly active
in credit derivatives, a combination of limits may be necessary to constrain
risk-taking within the board's approved tolerance level.

One key function which the bank's policies and procedures should
serve is to clearly identify the bank's objectives behind using credit derivatives. If, for example, the bank plans on using credit derivatives only as
an end-user to hedge existing credit positions, policies should clearly
convey this. Further, management should describe how credit derivatives
are to be used to manage credit exposures, when transactions are appropriate and what approvals are required to execute a trade. Of course,
hedging is not the only use of credit derivatives. Credit derivatives may

---

[13]SR Letter 95–17, *Evaluating the Risk Management and Internal Controls of Securities and
Derivative Contracts Used in Non-trading Activities*, March 28, 1995, p. 7.

be used to generate trading income, to enhance yields on investments, to allow otherwise problematic or costly access to certain markets, to obtain leverage, to manage funding, or to take advantage of arbitrage opportunities. However the bank intends to participate in the market, policies, and procedures should describe the objectives of these activities and the limitations to be observed in their conduct.

Appropriate Risk Measurement and Reporting Systems

In order to monitor and control credit derivative activities and assess their effectiveness, management must receive timely and accurate reports depicting the operational performance and risk exposure of these activities. Reporting should be sufficiently detailed so that management can determine whether its stated objectives are being met and its risk limits observed.

Risk measurement for credit derivatives at this relatively nascent stage of market development can present some difficult problems. For example, a dealer may find it difficult to revalue or mark-to-market its positions with a high degree of precision. Credit derivative prices established at the inception of a trade may be based upon circumstances that are unique to the buyer, the seller or the reference obligor (or all three) at the time of the trade. For this reason, dealers need to document, monitor, and revisit key assumptions used in pricing and revaluation on a regular basis. Financial controllers at a dealer bank may consider making valuation adjustments against pricing uncertainties resulting from market illiquidity.

End-users of credit derivatives may face greater risk measurement obstacles in credit derivative transactions than dealers. As a general rule of prudent risk management, end-users should not rely on a single counterparty such as the dealer when revaluing trades or assessing the effectiveness of hedging activity. Wherever possible, end-users should attempt to gain independent, third-party pricing sources.

Across the spectrum of risks which banks must manage when engaging in credit derivative transactions, one particular subjective risk that needs to be addressed is reputational risk. Reputational risk occurs when negative publicity about the bank's activities, litigation or regulatory sanctions or strained relationships with its customers adversely affect its business reputation and, thus, its earnings prospects. Reputational risk can arise in several ways with an innovative product such as credit derivatives. Dealers in credit derivatives should ensure that they know their customers and that the customers understand the product and its risks. End-users of credit derivatives need to ensure that they evaluate the dealer they are transacting with, understand the instruments they enter into, and have the risk management and internal control infrastructure in place to manage them. Where an end-user is relying on the dealer for advice, it is prudent for the dealer and end-user to enter into a written understanding of their relationship. Both dealers and end-users need to be careful that they are not exploiting gaps in the accounting, legal, and regulatory framework created by the newness of credit derivatives in a manner that could later raise questions about the quality of financial statements or compliance with applicable law and regulation.

For example, some investors may be restricted by law, regulation, or specific governing documents from purchasing the obligations of certain issuers, or may be limited to purchasing only highly-rated credits. Credit derivatives may allow investors to indirectly create exposure to prohibited or lower-rated counterparties and thereby skirt the intentions of these limitations. Managements should be aware of the legal and reputational risks associated with transactions of this kind.

Comprehensive Internal Controls

The final requirement for an effective risk management process is a comprehensive system of internal controls. Internal controls should be designed to promote efficient operations, to safeguard assets and to foster reliable internal and external reporting. Further, internal controls play a major role in ensuring compliance with laws, regulations, and internal management policies.

A strong and independent internal audit function plays a vital role in any system of internal controls. Management should ensure that the scope and frequency of internal audit coverage is sufficient and that audit staff has the appropriate level of expertise to evaluate credit derivative activities and risks.

CONCLUSION

Credit derivatives are products that have the potential to revolutionize the way credit risk is conceptualized, measured, managed, and priced, along with advances in credit risk modeling and refinements of credit scoring and securitization techniques. Credit derivatives may prove to be convenient, cost-effective means of reducing credit concentrations, diversifying credit risk, and enhancing yield at any given level of credit risk. Over time, the underlying economic benefits will eventually determine the size and appeal of these products. Bank supervisors' understanding and treatment of credit risk must necessarily continue to evolve with market innovation and the increasing use of these products. Banking supervisors in the G-10 countries have begun to grapple with the supervisory issues posed by credit derivatives, as have many other financial supervisory bodies, including the National Association of Insurance Commissioners in the United States. Credit derivatives, taken together with advances in credit risk modeling and securitization, herald a wave of change in the management of credit risk that will engage financial institutions and their supervisors for some time to come.

B I B L I O G R A P H Y

Bank of England, Supervision and Surveillance Discussion Paper, *Developing a Supervisory Approach to Credit Derivatives*, London, England, November 1996.

Board of Governors of the Federal Reserve System: *Risk-Based Capital Standards; Market Risk*, 12 CFR Parts 208 and 225, Federal Register, Vol. 61, No. 174 dated September 6, 1996, p. 47358 ff. and Vol. 62, No. 249 dated December 30, 1997, pp. 68064 ff.

Board of Governors of the Federal Reserve System: SR Letter 97–18, *Application of Market Risk Capital Requirements to Credit Derivatives*, Washington, DC, June 13, 1997.

Board of Governors of the Federal Reserve System: SR Letter 96–17, *Supervisory Guidance for Credit Derivatives*, Washington, DC, August 12, 1996.

Board of Governors of the Federal Reserve System: SR Letter 95–17, *Evaluating the Risk Management and Internal Controls of Securities and Derivative Contracts Used in Non-trading Activities*, Washington, DC, December 20, 1995.

Board of Governors of the Federal Reserve System: SR Letter 95–51, *Rating the Adequacy of Risk Management Processes and Internal Controls at State Member Banks and Bank Holding Companies*, Washington, DC, November 14, 1995.

Board of Governors of the Federal Reserve System: SR Letter 93–69, *Examining Risk Management and Internal Controls for Trading Activities of Banking Organizations*, Washington, DC, December 20, 1993.

Commission Bancaire, Discussion and Research Paper: *Credit Derivatives: Initial Policy Directions for Prudential Treatment*, Paris, France, June 4, 1997.

Federal Deposit Insurance Corporation: FIL 62–96, *Supervisory Guidance for Credit Derivatives*, Washington, DC, August 19, 1996.

Office of the Comptroller of the Currency: OCC Bulletin 96–43, *Credit Derivatives: Guidelines for National Banks*, Washington, DC, August 12, 1996.

Securities and Futures Authority: Board Notice 414, *Guidance on Credit Derivatives*, London, England, April 17, 1997.

Risk Management Ratings

The rating for risk management is based on a scale of one through five in ascending order of supervisory concern. The rating should be consistent with the following criteria:

RATING 1 (STRONG)

A rating of 1 indicates that management effectively identifies and controls all major types of risk posed by the institution's activities, including those from new products and changing market conditions. The board and management are active participants in managing risk and ensure that appropriate policies and limits exist, and the board understands, reviews, and approves them. Policies and limits are supported by risk monitoring procedures, reports and management information systems that provide management and the board with the necessary information and analysis to make timely and appropriate responses to changing conditions.

Internal controls and audit procedures are sufficiently comprehensive and appropriate to the size and activities of the institution. There are few noted exceptions to the institution's established policies and procedures, and none is material. Management effectively and accurately monitors the condition of the institution consistent with standards of safety and soundness and in accordance with internal and supervisory policies and practices. Risk management is considered fully effective to identify, monitor, and control the risks to the institution.

RATING 2 (SATISFACTORY)

A rating of 2 indicates that the institution's management of risk is largely effective, but lacking to some modest degree. It reflects a responsiveness and ability to cope successfully with existing and foreseeable exposures that may arise in carrying out the institution's business plan. While the institution may have some minor risk management weaknesses, these problems have been recognized and are being addressed. Overall, board and senior management oversight, policies and limits, risk monitoring procedures, reports, and management information systems are considered satisfactory and effective in maintaining a safe and sound institution. Generally, risks are being controlled in a manner that does not require additional, or more than normal, supervisory attention.

Internal controls may display modest weaknesses or deficiencies, but they are correctable in the normal course of business. The examiner may have recommendations for improvement, but the weaknesses noted should not have a significant effect on the safety and soundness of the institution.

RATING 3 (FAIR)

A rating of 3 signifies risk management practices that are lacking in some important ways and, therefore, are a cause for more than normal supervisory attention. One or more of the four elements of sound risk management are considered fair, and have precluded the institution from fully addressing significant risk to its operations. Certain risk management practices are in need of improvement to ensure that management and the board are able to identify, monitor, and control adequately all significant risks to the institution. Weaknesses may include continued control exceptions or failures to adhere to written policies and procedures that could have adverse effects on the institution.

The internal control system may be lacking in some important respects, particularly as indicated by continued control exceptions or by the failure to adhere to written policies and procedures. The risks associated with the internal control system could have adverse effects on the safety and soundness of the institution if corrective actions are not taken by management.

RATING 4 (MARGINAL)

A rating of 4 represents marginal risk management practices that generally fail to identify, monitor, and control significant risk exposures in many material respects. Generally, such a situation reflects lack of adequate guidance and supervision by management and the board. One or more of the four elements of sound risk management are considered marginal and require immediate and concerted corrective action by the board and management. A number of significant risks to the institution have not been adequately addressed, and the risk management deficiencies warrant a high degree of supervisory attention.

The institution may have serious identified weaknesses, such as an inadequate separation of duties, that require substantial improvement in its internal control or accounting procedures or in its ability to adhere to supervisory standards or requirements. Unless properly addressed, these conditions may result in unreliable financial records, or reports, or operating losses that could seriously affect the safety and soundness of the institution.

RATING 5 (UNSATISFACTORY)

A rating of 5 indicates a critical absence of effective risk management practices to identify, monitor, or control significant risk exposures. One or more of the four elements of sound risk management are considered wholly deficient and management and the board have not demonstrated the capability to address deficiencies.

Internal controls may be sufficiently weak as to jeopardize seriously the continued viability of the institution. If not already evident, there is an immediate concern as to the reliability of accounting records and regulatory reports and about potential losses that could result if corrective measures are not taken immediately. Deficiencies in the institution's risk management procedures and internal controls require immediate and close supervisory attention.

CHAPTER 13

The Use of Credit Derivatives in Credit-Enhanced & Credit-Linked Structured Notes: A Former Rating Analyst's Perspective*

David K.A. Mordecai
Vice President, AIG Risk Finance

With contributions from Robert J. Grossman

THE ROLE OF CREDIT DERIVATIVES IN OFF-BALANCE SHEET AND NONRECOURSE FINANCING

Credit risk is one of the fundamental risks of finance. Credit derivatives have traditionally existed, for at least twenty years, in the form of bond insurance, and in other forms of credit protection constructed from more conventional credit facilities (e.g., special-purpose or standby letters of credit). However, current credit derivative instruments are specifically designed to strip out and trade credit risk, to have a well-defined payoff and, hence, to be priced efficiently, based on the perceived risk of a specific credit event, such as a default.

---

*This chapter is based on Mr. Mordecai's presentation at the 1998 IFR Credit Symposium in London and cites other published references by Mr. Mordecai on the subject. Mr. Mordecai was a Director and the lead analyst for catastrophic risk, structured notes and other exotic pooled credit instruments within the Commercial Asset-Backed Group at Fitch IBCA, Inc. Mr. Mordecai wishes to acknowledge Robert Grossman's contribution in reviewing the contents of this chapter for its consistency with Fitch IBCA's rating approach. Mr. Grossman is a Group Managing Director and a member of the credit policy committee at Fitch IBCA, Inc., where he directs the activities of the Loan Products Group.

Credit derivatives, in one form or another, have enjoyed a long history in off-balance sheet and nonrecourse structured financing as traditional contingent products. For example:

1. Back-to-back loans have facilitated cross-border corporate borrowing.
2. Backup lines of credit have contributed to securitization of corporate credit by supporting commercial paper issuance.
3. Other contingent credit issuances have served to guarantee project, equipment, and trade financing:
   - Standby LOCs forward contracts
   - Limited guarantees or third-party financial insurance
   - Defeasance, escrow, reserve, and collateral accounts
   - Backup and liquidity facilities

Increasingly, these traditional credit facilities are being replaced in special-purpose credit-enhanced structures, by over-the-counter, market-traded credit derivatives.

In their simplest form, credit derivatives involve an exchange of cash flows between two counterparties, based on some underlying notional amount, typically related to a traditional credit facility. Just like other derivative products, simple credit derivatives can be broadly classified as swaps, options, or forwards. More complex structures combine simpler credit derivatives to incorporate the correlation of state-dependent payoffs. Closely related to credit derivatives are insurance derivatives, which are tied to discrete events within an insurance portfolio, an index of losses or damage, or some event-intensity parameter.

Credit-linked notes (CLNs) are debt securities issued by an entity with conventional coupon, maturity, and redemption features, similar to traditional notes or bonds. A credit-linked note differs from a more conventional debt instrument in that, by design, the performance of the credit-linked note is dependent on the performance of a prespecified reference asset. In this way, credit risk can be unbundled and traded separately from interest rate and price volatility. Credit-linked notes achieve this redistribution of credit risk by incorporating a credit derivative into the structure of the note. Unlike traditional credit issuance, where credit risk remains irrevocably linked with the asset of original issuance, credit derivatives permit the segregation and restructuring of the credit risk of an underlying financial instrument.

Credit-linked notes, as a special class of synthetic securities or structured notes, typically utilize the set of bankruptcy-remote mechanisms that are common to the asset-backed securities market. These structures were developed in secondary-market for mortgages and trade claims (inventory and receivables), and in the nonrecourse financing of stand-alone projects, sale-leasebacks, leveraged leases and recapitalizations, and LBOs. As an asset class, credit-linked investment vehicles provide access, at lower transaction costs, to both investment and risk management opportunities, for investors and hedgers seeking to achieve specific risk-reward profiles. The result is a redefined relationship between supply and demand for credit.

Since credit-linked note structures enable entities to synthesize their own AAA-rated swap counterparties, issuers may capitalize on comparative borrowing advantages. The off-balance sheet treatment of credit derivatives enables participants restricted to investment-grade investments to gain access to higher returns, while buyers of noninvestment-grade assets exchange a fraction of their higher spreads for a lower cost of funds. Credit-linked notes and CBO/CLO structures effectively arbitrage the default-risk, maturity, liquidity, tax, and regulatory premiums existing in the market. One could view the growing trend toward securitization of credit-risk and event-risk as "intermediation to the nth-degree."

In 1996, the notional volume of the corporate and sovereign credit derivatives market grew tenfold, from $5 billion to more than $50 billion, approximately two-thirds the size of the new issuance of other structured notes during the same period. With the potential to become the least expensive means to finance the assumption or off-loading of credit risk, credit derivative-based structures provide the basis for a more complete market for risk. Although closely related to the interest rate and asset swap markets, the market for credit derivatives is less likely to be commoditized. Even in their simplest forms, credit derivatives are highly structured and tailored to specific end-user needs. Since the causes of credit-risk are diverse, credit derivatives shall likely remain highly credit- or "name-" specific (despite the adherence of credit swap documentation to ISDA conventions). This heterogeneity of credit-risk limits the scope for a standardized, generic credit derivative. This may be limiting market liquidity in the short-run however, it also assures robust spreads for these structured credit instruments.

Similar development can be observed in the parallel histories of insurance risk management and commodity price-risk management, and the extension in to financial market-risk management, over the past 25 years. Alternative risk financing techniques, such as self-insurance, self-funding, financial reinsurance, and "captives," now common to the insurance industry, bear close resemblance to the structures now emerging in the synthetics and credit derivatives markets.

Structured or synthetic notes refer to a broad category of instruments (including CLNs) that utilize swaps, options, and other derivative structures to reengineer or "repackage" cash flows and reallocate risks from a financial claim or portfolio of such claims. Synthetic securities and related credit-linked and insurance-linked structured notes, promise to be among the fastest growing segments of the debt capital markets for years to come. In order to distinguish the credit-linked or insurance-linked structured note from other synthetic notes, this chapter refers to all synthetic notes other than CLNs and insurance-linked notes as *repackaged notes*. These securitized asset swaps reengineer the cash flows of existing securities to meet custom-tailored investor demands (i.e., asset/liability and risk management motivations). These instruments, issued by bankruptcy-remote trusts, meet the typical structured finance standards: legal forms, payment conventions, and credit considerations. As a risk-allocation mechanism, synthetics also resolve the investment market's dual problem of constrained optimization: return maximization subject to variance minimization.

The repackaged or synthetic note bridges the debt market and the structured securities market, while maximizing collateral efficiency, in order to capitalize on price inefficiencies. For this reason, an alternative name for these instruments might be *price-indexed synthetic notes*. In mediating between these markets, repackaged notes arbitrage relative-value mispricings between bonds, asset-backed securities, equity and commodity prices, and fixed versus floating rate obligations. Alternatively, as a risk allocation mechanism, synthetics can reallocate diverse risks from other securities. These risks include: interest rate and currency exchange-rate risk, reinvestment risk, call optionality, liquidity, as well as credit-risk and event-risk. By redistributing or segregating these risks, these synthetic structures create a customized combination of risk for a particular investor clientele, thus maximizing the value of the security. They also can result in more efficient pricing for the asset.

Credit-linked structured notes, as investment vehicles, can be classified into two general categories: *synthetic* instruments (e.g., CLNs) that share or transfer risk and *pooled* instruments (e.g., CBOs, CLOs, CP conduits). Synthetic structures include both swap-dependent and swap-independent instruments. "DPCs" or "swapcos," are special-purpose subsidiaries of securities dealers that originate these instruments, warehouse the "books" (i.e., the portfolios of swaps and derivative trades), and serve as stand-alone counterparties for these transactions.

All structured synthetic notes fall into four generic structural categories: *swap-dependent, asset-dependent, swap-independent,* and *custodial receipt.* The legal form of the trust is classified as either a continuation or termination structure. In *swap-dependent structures,* the rating relies on both the

F I G U R E 13–1

Synthetic Note Examples

Swap-Dependent Structure (Wrapped)

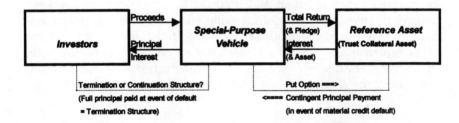

Swap-Dependent Structure

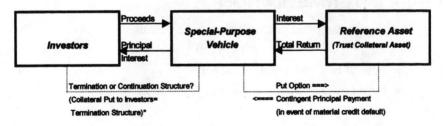

Asset Dependent/Swap-Independent Structure

collateral and the credit of the swap counterparty. The rating will be linked to the weaker of the two credits. Swap-dependent structures are often "credit-wrapped," with third-party credit enhancement.

In contrast, *swap-independent structures* have collateral distribution features, in which a termination event like default or an unwind results in each party receiving a pro rata share of the collateral. These structures typically take the form of grantor trusts or partnerships, and any credit analysis focuses exclusively on the underlying collateral. In the swap-independent structure, an investor can be made no worse off than outright ownership of the underlying assets. These structures bear many similarities to default swap structures, in which one party pays a spread to put an asset to another. Institutional investors with excess "off-the-run" credit analysis capacity will conceivably enter the credit enhanced note market to compete with and potentially displace the traditional monoline insurers. As the credit swaps market becomes broader, deeper, and more liquid, credit enhancement may become even more commonplace in the synthetics market place, especially for below investment grade issuers and counterparties.

In as much as synthetic securities maximize collateral efficiency for purposes of investment and market-risk allocation, market-based credit derivatives can potentially maximize collateral efficiency for credit enhancement purposes, relative to these traditional forms. For example, a total return swap provides off-balance sheet economic exposure to the credit-risk of the underlying asset for a synthetic financing cost typically lower than the market rate, especially for a lower-rated buyer of the swap.

CREDIT ARBITRAGE AND DEFAULT RISK INTERMEDIATION[1]

In short, credit-wrapped synthetic structures permit arbitrage of all of the following risk-adjusted price relationships:

■ default risk and credit sensitivity
■ term structure risk (i.e., volatility, duration, and convexity)

[1]Credit arbitrage, pricing, and default-risk intermediation concepts borrowed from chapters by Mordecai on credit-linked and insurance-linked structured notes, have been published in the following books: *Credit Derivatives: Applications for Risk Management*, by RISK (1998), *Credit Derivatives: Applications for Risk Management*, and *Alternative Investment Strategies* by Euromoney Books (1998).

- term structure of credit risk (i.e., the correlation and integration of credit risk and market risk)

Credit derivative arbitrage applies the principle of arbitrage between separate or separable markets. Analogous to the interest rate swap market, in which different markets price fixed-rate assets and liabilities differently from floating rate assets and liabilities, some credit markets price a given level of expected default risk (or event-risk) differently.

First, institutional, tax, regulatory, or market frictions often result in distinct and separate clienteles with divergent prices for a given level of risk. Second, demand and supply shifts in submarkets for certain risky assets (e.g., issuers, covenants, etc.), or for capital, result in disparities or anomalies in pricing similar credit risks. Third, divergent default or event expectations in closed or restricted submarkets can result in pricing disparities.

Ideally, a liquid credit derivatives market could bridge the discrepancies in these markets to ultimately achieve a market equilibrium. When supply and demand for risk in these submarkets become equal, these markets will clear, and the markets for credit risk will become "complete," or "efficiently priced." In such an instance, the expectations for default and the prices for a given level of credit risk in different submarkets should converge much as the interest rate and currency swap markets have done.

Driving much of the demand for credit derivative strategies, is their ready packaging as structured notes for consumption by institutional investors. With a CLN, as with any structured financing that employs a special purpose vehicle or entity (SPV or SPE), the rating agencies' primary concern is bankruptcy remoteness of that entity. The rating affects not just the pricing of a CLN, but the breadth and depth of the market for the instrument and thus, to some extent, its liquidity. The growing institutionalization of investment capital and competition among managed funds increases the role of reverse inquiry. Reverse inquiry represents an opportunity for investors and trading desks, rather than issuers and bankers, to drive the supply of transactions in the capital market. Consistent with the tenets of Miller-Modigliani, investors can demand, and issuers can supply, securities with payoffs prespecified to fit investors' particular risk-return preferences, in this case their credit views.

DEFAULT ESTIMATION AND CREDIT DERIVATIVE PRICING

In principle, a credit swap, currently the most common and simplest credit derivative to execute, resembles the financed purchase of a bond.

It requires no initial outlay of cash, yet generates a regular stream of income, in the form of the premium or compensation for the assumption of credit exposure. Credit swaps are priced to trade at the same approximate level of return as an asset swap on a similar credit. Because a credit derivative is considered to be equivalent to a financed position based off of LIBOR, dealers compare the relative value of credit swaps against comparable credits in the asset swap market, rather than to the spread over treasuries for a comparable bond. From a practical position, the credit swaps dealer begins with the theoretical price for the trade (based on the zero coupon spread curve for the credit), then checks for liquidity in the underlying asset (this will affect the secondary market price of covering the swap). The premium is determined by the pricing of the underlying credit. The base rate approximates the cost of funds plus the spread. If the dealer cannot find liquidity for the underlying at a particular price, then the spread widens until the market clears for the swap or it becomes uneconomical for the swap to be transacted.

One reason that the benchmark for a credit swap is the asset swap market, is because a credit swap is an unfunded transaction which requires no initial cash outlay. Most derivatives dealers price according to the credit rating of the counterparty in a trade. However, a credit swaps dealer, unlike an asset swap or interest rate swap dealer, must also consider the following issues in the market for the underlying: the default probability, the expected recovery (loss), and the liquidity of the market for the underlying asset. Dynamic hedging in the credit derivatives market is not yet feasible. In this sense, credit swaps are treated like a hybrid between an asset swap and a conventional credit instrument like a bond or a loan (to be addressed further in the next section).

The downside risk to a buyer of a credit swap is a function of the occurrence of default, the use of leverage, and the expected recovery rate, as evidenced by the price of comparable bonds or loans in the market at the time of the event. One proxy for potential losses are published historical default and recovery rates compiled by the rating agencies and other sources.

Rating agencies, and buyers of corporate, mortgage-backed and asset-backed securities, typically model and measure default risk in terms of the frequency and the probability of default, and expected loss. The probability of loss measure can be interpreted as the marginal probability of losing even a single dollar. This measure of risk represents the risk aversion profile for an investor who is sensitive to losing any amount. Alternatively, it can be viewed as a risk measure that treats any default as a total loss. (In the simplest cases, the frequency of default is similar to the probability of default.) Expected loss is conditioned upon a given level of defaults:

Expected (Net) Loss = Gross Defaults*(1–Expected Percent Recovered)

or alternatively, expected losses can be described as the net difference between expected defaults minus expected recoveries.

Predominantly, derivatives dealers, swapcos, and DPCs,[2] portfolio managers of CBOs/CLOs, buyers of MBS or ABS residuals, and risk managers currently use different variants of value-at-risk. Value-at-risk (VaR) approaches employ methods like Monte Carlo simulation, in order to forecast and summarize with a single statistic the expected maximum loss, over a target horizon, and a given confidence interval. A correctly implemented Monte Carlo approach to VaR can capture both market risk and credit risk of a portfolio, and can compute both probability of default and expected loss as by-products. In addition, VaR directly calculates portfolio value losses from an asset's migration in credit quality to default by inferring a transition matrix from historical data.

The difference between systematic market risk and idiosyncratic (i.e., asset-specific) price risk can be illustrated in simpler context using metaphors from cross-sectional regression analysis of risk factors and event studies of pricing residuals. In market model event studies, abnormal idiosyncratic returns in pricing residuals signal changes in market expectations regarding future cash flows to an asset as a function of new information:

$$r_i = \alpha + \beta(R_m) + \varepsilon_i$$
where, r_i = return on asset "i"
α = *abnormal return*
β = *the coefficient of variation*
R_m = *the return on the market*
ε_i = *error term ($E[\varepsilon_i] = 0$)*

In the CAPM and other equilibrium asset-pricing models, excess

---

[2]Swapcos and Derivative Product Companies (DPCs) are stand-alone or special-purpose entities sponsored and capitalized specifically to trade and warehouse derivative exposures by serving as highly-rated counterparties for these transactions. The balance sheets of these entities are limited exclusively to liquid and highly-rated investments that are segregated from the other activities of their parent companies.

returns (returns in excess of the risk-free rate) represent idiosyncratic returns not priced by the market:

$$r_j - r_f = \alpha_0 + \beta(R_m - r_f) + \varepsilon_j, \text{ where } \alpha_0 = 0$$
$$\text{where, } r_j = \text{return on asset "}j\text{"}$$
$$r_f = \text{risk-free rate of interest}$$
$$\alpha_0 = \text{excess returns}$$

The discount factor for the idiosyncratic price risk of an asset (as a present value of expected future cash flows) includes the market expectation of credit risk. Credit risk is the product of probability of default times the market's sensitivity to losses from defaults. Since all defaults are not directly observable, the historical data for bonds and loan prices are incomplete. There is missing data for the trading prices in both of these debt markets. Also, debt prices suffer from problems with discontinuous trading, illiquidity, and distorted bid-ask spreads. Although noisier, equity prices tend to provide smoother, more observable measures of asset volatility. To determine when a default will be "costly" (i.e., when expected net losses are expected to be significant), credit swap traders employ tests of the *materiality of default* using prices, or the market value of debt. The market value of debt can be derived from option value of default, based on asset volatility inferred from equity prices. *KMV's model* is particularly well-known for applying contingent claims analysis to imply default probabilities from firm equity prices and correlations. The KMV approach employs an estimate of the value of corporate liabilities and a long-run average of the standard deviation of equity returns to compute the *distance to default* for a particular credit or portfolio of credits.

Both market value and credit quality correlations for corporate debt can be inferred from equity prices. However, this requires a model that links the asset value of the firm to changes in firm credit quality. If we assume that firm value is randomly distributed according to some distribution, and that liabilities are constant, then the face value of the firm's liabilities act as the critical threshhold level for triggering default when firm value approaches this level, much like the exercise price of an option. In this way, the option of default can be modeled as a barrier option. If we treat default risk as a barrier option, then both defaults and recoveries are a function of the variability of equity prices (i.e., asset volatility or the variability of expected future cash flow).

THE ROLE OF ASSET VOLATILITY IN VALUING THE OPTION OF DEFAULT

Credit risk can be described as the sensitivity of the market value of an asset or a portfolio to expected losses on future payments. Default risk can be defined as the realization of those losses on future payments. The credit-risk premium prices the risk of migration to a state of default for a loan or bond (and the related deterioration in market value).

A risky bond can be analyzed as the combination of a risk-free bond (e.g., U.S. Treasury bond) and a long call (short put) option on some asset (i.e., the underlying assets of a firm in the case of a corporate bond). In pricing the call (put) option embedded in the bond, one can derive the probability of default for that bond. The value of the call (put) option and the implied credit-risk premium is a function of the volatility of the underlying asset values. Assuming constant interest rates, these underlying asset values vary with changes in the future cash flows expected to accrue to those assets.

If we model default risk as a barrier option, then the volatility of asset values directly predict the probability of default. The relationship between market risk and credit risk is based on the valuation of the option of default. Black-Scholes-Merton provide an option-theoretic approach for using equity prices to value a risky debt claim on corporate assets.

According to Merton, the option value of debt is a function of the face amount (K) and maturity of the debt (T), the risk-free rate of interest (r), and the volatility of the equity price (σ), where σ is a measure of the operating risk of the firm.

$$Bond = V\,N(-z) + Kr^{-T} * N(z - \sigma\sqrt{T}),$$

$$where\ z = \frac{\log(V/Kr^{-T})}{\sigma\sqrt{T}} + \tfrac{1}{2}(\sigma\sqrt{T})$$

In the *Black-Scholes-Merton* model, the default premium depends solely on firm leverage, operating risk, and debt maturity. Hence, the volatility of equity serves as an informative signal on cash flow variability in relation to business risk, and financial and operating leverage.

For a portfolio, much of the covariance dominates the variance of any single credit. Covariance is the product of the variances of the assets and the correlation between those assets. The sign and magnitude of the correlation determines the extent to which individual credit variances can offset one another.

THE ECONOMICS OF CREDIT DERIVATIVES AS CREDIT ENHANCEMENT

As illustrated throughout this chapter, the economics of credit derivatives facilitate their use as substitutes or complements for more traditional credit enhancement approaches. For example, three key differences distinguish a credit swap from an outright purchase (assignment or participation) of a loan:

■ ease of off-balance sheet treatment
■ flexibility of structure and terms
■ optional use of (implicit) leverage

For credit-enhanced synthetic or structured notes, appropriately structured, a credit derivative can sometimes serve as a cost-effective alternative (substitute *or* complement) to a third-party financial guarantee. In this role, the credit derivative exchanges counterparty credit risk for the credit risk of the underlying asset. As the market for active counterparties becomes broader and deeper with entry, it will augment the greater liquidity and rational pricing of the current market for credit insurance.

Market risk and credit risk are distinct, but interrelated. Market risk represents the variation in market expectations about future expected returns, supply and demand for investment capital and investment opportunities, and the term structure of interest rates (i.e., future expectations of the risk-free rate). In the debt markets, the primary focus of market risk is on duration and convexity. However, market risk and credit risk are related, because credit events are often triggered by extreme downward market movements. In other words, credit events are by their very nature extremal events (rare probabilistic events). Credit risk represents the losses in the market value of an asset (i.e., a financial claim or portfolio of financial claims) that are correlated with changes in default expectations related to that asset or portfolio. The market value of an asset or portfolio is credit sensitive (to expected losses in credit quality or the asset's migration toward default), inasmuch as duration loosely represents the yield sensitivity of a debt instrument to risk-free interest-rate volatility. Hence, credit risk could be loosely interpreted as the market sensitivity of an asset or bundle of assets to default expectations. Extreme downward market movements often correlate with trading gaps and illiquidity related to defaults. As markets become more volatile, they also become more correlated. *This is especially evident when markets are volatile downward.*

Credit risk is idiosyncratic and heterogeneous and, hence, not readily diversified away because of its heterogeneity and the contagion of extreme (downward) volatility. Equity or price risk is more easily diversified, because it is homogeneous in its relationship to discount factors and expectations about the residual claims on future cash flows. In addition, credit risk has its own term structure.

In keeping with the modern portfolio theory of Markowitz, two loans or bonds that are held to maturity will have a default correlation much lower than the equity price correlation of their respective firms, given the lower likelihood that two extremely low-probability events will occur simultaneously. Hence, the consequence of low default correlation is that the systematic risk in a portfolio of credit instruments is small relative to the risk contributed by each individual credit. Assuming a low (or zero) correlation with the rest of the portfolio, the lower the relative weight of an individual credit within a portfolio, the smaller its contribution to the risk of that portfolio. Higher correlation results in higher volatility (i.e., risk) of the portfolio.

Risk-pooling obtains benefits from diversification by optimally combining financial instruments with statistically independent or uncorrelated risks in a portfolio. The objective of pooling these instruments (loans, bonds, etc.) is to reduce the relative weighting of any single risk exposure with respect to the average return of the portfolio. Examples of risk-pooling include Collateralized Bond Obligations (CBOs), Collateralized Loan Obligations (CLOs), and commercial paper (CP) conduits. *Risk-sharing* attempts to achieve benefits of diversification by contractually swapping risk exposures with uncorrelated risks in portfolios or instruments held by other parties. Examples of risk-sharing include derivative product companies (DPCs or swapcos) and certain types of reinsurance (coinsurance). *Risk-transfer* attempts to immunize the returns of a portfolio or instrument from certain risks by paying a third-party to contractually assume exposure to those risks. Examples of risk-transfer are primary insurance policies, excess-of-loss reinsurance, financial guarantees, bond insurance, portfolio insurance, and hedging with swaps, options, forwards, and futures. An extension of both the risk-sharing and risk-transfer concepts is *risk-spreading,* or the transfer of risk over among many parties, the fundamental principle of the financial markets.

Traditional credit-risk management methods such as covenants, collateralization, and portfolio diversification provide only partial protection. Cash market diversification is often not feasible, because of a constrained supply of "primitives" (nonderivative instruments). Credit risk tends to be "lumpy," in that notes and bonds are not sufficiently divisible, or there may not exist a supply of comparable instruments with the covenants, features, terms, or principal amount necessary to provide adequate diversification. With credit swaps, asset managers have been able to rebalance portfolios and diversify away excess concentration risk with the ability to synthetically sell (short) credit exposures to loans, bonds, and insurance portfolios. Credit-linked notes permit investors and hedgers to cost-effectively monetize their credit views. These vehicles provide access for new investors to otherwise closed markets. They also enable portfolio managers to more effectively implement strategies in the credit markets based on modern portfolio theory. Risk managers can now construct more efficient portfolios by reducing high portfolio concentrations while retaining the underlying cash market assets and possibly some of the returns.

Credit and insurance derivatives could effectively delink pricing from supply and demand. In previously thinly-traded or restricted markets, these instruments provide solutions to the following optimization problem: What is the maximum return (i.e., cheapest cost of funds), given a particular level of credit risk (or in the case of insurance derivatives catastrophic event-risk)?

The flexibility of credit derivative terms and leverage enable investors to run a "matched" credit book by specifying the terms, seniority, and maturity of credit exposures which are not readily available in the cash market. The ability to pay an actuarially-fair premium to immunize a portfolio on a contingent basis from a particular credit event, eliminates the need to prematurely sell an illiquid asset in a distressed market, provided there is a liquid market for the credit derivative. A premature sale might lead to a lower recovery value than holding the asset until full recovery value is achieved.

There are numerous regulatory and market-structure motivations for these innovations in banking, insurance, and money management. A more liquid market for credit-linked notes and other credit derivatives can reduce capital requirements by allowing more favorable risk-based capital treatment for banks and insurance companies. By year-end 1997, somewhere between \$10 to \$25 billion of synthetic loan securitizations were issued as either portfolio CLOs or hybrid CLNs by banking institutions, seeking more efficient capital treatment while retaining loans on their books. These issues provided the capital market with access to "virtual banks," highly-rated investment vehicles with access to short-duration, floating rate, senior priority financial assets.

By referencing an index of default events and credit spreads, credit-linked notes and credit swaps can relieve the administrative burden and duplication of capacity in the analysis and processing of underlying credit instruments. Credit-linked notes that utilize credit swaps share similarities with other synthetics linked to asset swaps or equity swaps that allow for tax-advantaged structuring to minimize withholding tax, estate tax, and other tax liabilities.

Among pooled instruments, CP conduits, like the Alpha and Beta Funds, that are simply commercial paper-funded, hedged portfolios of investment-grade fixed income instruments, are often called "credit arb vehicles." The asset distinction between CBOs and CLOs, of holding bonds versus loans has been blurred. The distinction between *static* or *cash-flow* pools and actively-traded *market-value* pools remain. Various CBO/CLO structures are also distinguished based on structuring motivations (e.g., credit arbitrage versus bank balance sheet management). A recurring challenge is to design a capital structure with optimal leverage for a credit-linked note, leverage that will maximize return and minimize risks, in particular, credit risk.

The pursuit of lower funding costs and more sophisticated arbitrage strategies require more active trading and greater trading flexibility. This is leading to a convergence between CP conduits, CBO, CLO, and CLN submarkets. Increasingly, the preferred structure is a tranched capital structure for CBO, CLO, and CLN vehicles that includes the following elements: commercial paper, repo and securities lending, senior bank revolving and term debt, multiple mezzanine tranches and equity sponsorship, and often credit swaps, as well.

These hybrid vehicles match the credit risk, and the cash flow volatility of assets and liabilities, as well as their interest rate duration and convexity. These vehicles also attempt to maximize the benefits of diversification by investing in mixed asset classes. The global financial community is witnessing the emergence of stand-alone portfolio structures that synthetically replicate finance and insurance companies, as well as "virtual banks." The secular trend toward the intermediation of corporate credit risk increasingly dominates the latter 1990s and potentially the next decade. This is analogous to the dominance of securitized mortgages, the intermediation of interest rate and liability management in the 1970s, and the dominance in the 1980s of the LBO funds which employed leverage and nonrecourse financings to intermediate control of corporate assets and restructure corporate balance sheets.

CREDIT-WRAPPING STRUCTURED NOTES: CREDIT DERIVATIVES FROM THE SIMPLE TO THE COMPLEX

Embedded default puts and credit swaps are becoming common fixtures in structured note programs, much like total return swaps. Rating language will often specify the ability to exchange one counterparty for another suitable counterparty. The extent to which these contingent features can be priced and traded separately in a secondary market will rely upon the availability of economically-attractive spreads quoted by suitable counterparties.

What's motivating these trades? The ability to build complex credit-linked structures from simpler credit derivatives, by balancing cost, credit, and pricing considerations:

- role of "implicit leverage" and "all-in-cost" concepts in pricing and structuring a credit wrap

- credit spread intermediation (i.e., the certainty-equivalent or "break-even" spread)
- default substitution
- Capital Structure Arbitrage

The breakeven spread on a risky debt instrument is the calculated yield-spread to Treasuries at which an investor is indifferent between investing in an instrument with a given level of credit- or event-risk versus investing in a risk-free (e.g., Treasury) instrument. Market spreads tend to exceed break-even spreads for reasons related to regulation, risk aversion, liquidity, or taxes.

As with other derivative instruments, constructing and valuing credit derivatives and CLN structures involves the use of default estimation applications like the Stein estimator and volatility estimation and simulation methodologies, like Markov Chain Monte Carlo algorithms and stratified sampling techniques. As a rating agency, Fitch IBCA has conducted research to incorporate elements of JP Morgan's *CreditMetrics* and CSFP's *Creditrisk+* models into its rating analytics. *CreditMetrics* employs a value-at-risk approach to default and recovery estimation. In contrast, *Creditrisk+* is a sensitivity analysis tool that employs an actuarial approach to correlation and volatility similar to the methodology employed for insurance portfolios. McKinsey & Co. subsequently introduced its *Creditview* model to the marketplace. *Creditview* employs cross-section and time-series regressions to empirically estimate the incidence of default for various credit instruments relative to changing economic variables (e.g., GDP, interest rates, etc.) on a regional and an industry basis. The Creditview model is not a factor model in the sense that it does not analytically incorporate term structure into its parameter specification as do the Asset Value Models or the Spread Models.

Exhibit:

Black-Scholes-Merton (Contingent Claims Analysis)

1st Generation: Asset Value Models

    Merton (1974)

    Black-Cox (1976)

2nd Generation: Asset Value Models

    Hull-White (1995)

    Longstaff-Schwartz (1995)

3rd Generation: Term Structure Models
> Jarrow-Turnbull (1995)
>
> Jarrow-Lando-Turnbull (1995)
>
> Das-Tufano (1996)

Contingent Claims-Based Risk Management Models

KMV, CreditMetrics

Creditrisk+

Creditview

RATING CREDIT-LINKED STRUCTURED NOTES

Credit (and equity) derivative structures supply securities to the marketplace that more efficiently capture the payoff distribution of a specific pool of assets, particular industry structures, or the unique investment opportunity set of an individual firm. The potential for merchant banking and corporate finance to use fundamental option and portfolio theory applications of credit derivative products is leading to further development of the contingent claims analysis of firm value and default risk for reducing the cost of capital via structured note issuance.

With the rise of tailored investment products, the distinction between investment management and investment banking continues to blur, as buy-side and sell-side firms both participate in principal investment and proprietary trading and market making of credit. Credit spread technology and trades quoted off the term structure of credit risk (i.e., zero-coupon forward spreads) continue to proliferate. Products in development include:

- Basket Options
- Credit Spread Options
- Correlation Products

As mentioned in a previous section, the key consideration in assigning a rating to a synthetic asset, such as a structured or credit-linked note, is that the investor should be no worse off than with a comparable direct investment in the reference asset. Typically, in the case of credit-linked notes, the direct investment alternative is an asset swap or a financed purchase of a bond.

Only 2 to 3 percent of over-the-counter structured notes that are issued are rated. So, why rate CLNs? One motivation for rating CLNs, and for rating structured notes in general, is distribution to a broader, deeper, more liquid market, those institutions that require investments to be rated. Another related motivation is to provide exposure to enhanced yields for these institutions that are restricted to investing in rated instruments.

Since the guiding principle for rating derivative-dependent structured notes is *credit equivalence*,[3] the credit derivative should be structured to minimize tracking error between the credit performance of notes issued and the reference asset(s), subject to the stated objective of the transaction. The underlying asset generally tends to be either a financed purchase of the reference credit instrument (note, bond, or loan) or an asset swap involving the reference credit.

In principle, assigning a rating to the structure involves the inference of a default probability or probability of downgrade for the reference credit. Based on this inference, the secondary consideration is estimating the expected loss. From a credit rating perspective, the underlying default probability and expected loss of the reference asset is the benchmark for designing the default and recovery performance of a CLN. In accounting for sources of tracking error in a CLN or credit derivative structure, issues of basis risk or moral hazard must be addressed. The latter two notions refer to circumstances or transaction terms that result in significantly greater credit risk accruing to the structure than to the reference asset(s).

Key issues in assessing the appropriate default probability and expected loss for a CLN include:

- the definition of the credit event(s)
- the *materiality* of a credit event, and the relationship between credit risk and market risk
- the recovery value (i.e., market value of the reference asset conditioned on the occurrence of a credit event, this determines the redemption value if a credit event were to occur, and, hence, the expected loss of the notes being rated)
- the correlation of credit (default) exposures (events) between reference credits and counterparties
- the form of settlement (physical, cash, digital) and settlement risk

---

[3] The notion that an investor should be no worse off from a credit perspective than investing directly in the underlying asset.

■ the discretion of the counterparty in declaring a credit event (especially when the counterparty is also acting as the calculation agent), basis risk, and moral hazard

Volatility and correlation (uncorrelated credit/default events) structured notes, like CLNs and other swap- or derivative-linked securities usually exhibit ratings that are referred to as *structural ratings*. Ratings generally address the likelihood that a transaction will comply with promised objectives (i.e., the timely payment of interest and the ultimate return of principal at the stated maturity of the issue). Structural ratings typically reference the rating of the weakest link in the structure, either that of the reference party/asset or of the counterparty. In many cases, Fitch IBCA's long-term structural ratings can often substitute the higher short-term rating of the counterparty for its lower long-term rating, subject to provisions for the posting of collateral and replacement of counterparty, should the counterparty short-term rating fall below some critical trigger level. This approach relies on the liquid market for suitable counterparties, and somewhat addresses the compounded probability of downgrade (or ultimate) related to correlated exposures of the counterparty to the reference credit. At the same time, this feature does not unduly constrain counterparties from economically constructing higher rated transactions.

As with other structured notes, rated (and most unrated) CLNs rely on ISDA master agreements and confirmations for establishing triggers and covenants. Specifying the credit implications of these triggers and covenants for a particular structure involves addressing three fundamental issues related to the payoff distribution of the credit derivative. The first consideration involves identifying credit events that are events related to the payment or rating performance of the reference party or reference asset. Secondary considerations are related matters of notification and materiality (i.e., what economically constitutes a credit event and why). Third is the likely impact to the credit losses for the notes by including a particular trigger in the definitions of credit events.

Alternative credit event triggers that are listed in the ISDA documentation include nonpayment, downgrade, moratorium, merger, exchange, acceleration, bankruptcy, distressed restructuring or reorganization, rescheduling, or renegotiation. The appropriateness of a defined event trigger is a function of the *basis risk* between the defined event and the stated risk-reward profile of the transaction. In other words, the suitability of an event trigger should be determined by the extent to which that particular trigger matches the potential set of economic events that could materially impact credit losses to the structure.

In assessing credit equivalence, an understanding of the motivation for a CLN is even more critical for rating a CLN than for rating other repackaged notes. For example, a CLN that creates credit exposure to a reference credit in a currency other than the currency of issue, is a substitute for an asset swap on the reference asset, rather than a substitute for a direct purchase of the asset itself in its currency of issue. This nuance is especially pertinent when addressing risks related to the recovery value of the asset (i.e., the expected loss assessment of the CLN, basis risk, and moral hazard [extent of discretion on the part of the counterparty, especially when the counterparty is also acting as calculation agent]).

Examples of Simple Credit Derivatives, Complex Strategies, and Their Rating Implications

Simple credit option strategies include: selling a covered call, selling a naked put, and hedging with credit puts. A structured note with an embedded covered call can be structured as an SPV collateralized with the reference bond and/or zero-coupon Treasury strips, and the relevant swap agreement.

Selling a covered call is a yield enhancement strategy, where the market risk to the seller is the foregone opportunity cost if the credit spread tightens more than the amount of the yield enhancement (i.e., the premium received from the sale of the call). The credit risk to the seller of a covered call is that the underlying/reference asset defaults or is downgraded, and that the additional yield (call premium) received is not adequate to compensate for the lower recovery value of the asset in the defaulted or downgraded state. In this case the asset is the net value between the long asset and the short call position.

A CLN that incorporates a total return swap, and assumes the first-loss risk (e.g., the Chase SLT note), is equivalent to a structured note with a levered short exposure to an embedded call. Generally, the rating analysis will decompose the expected interest coupon into a contingent component and a nominal, stated interest component. The default and recovery scenarios stress the sensitivity of transaction cash flows to expected losses against principal and the *promised* (versus contingent) components of the interest payment. Based on the sensitivity of the various components to the stress scenarios, a structural rating can be assigned to the transaction. That rating addresses the likelihood of credit losses that may accrue to principal and the nominal stated (promised) interest coupon.

F I G U R E   13–2

Covered Call

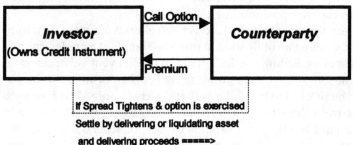

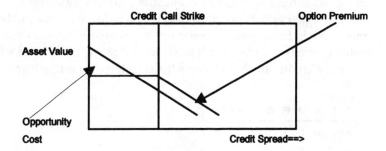

A substitute to credit enhancement by purchasing a letter of credit or a credit guarantee (a *credit-wrap*) on a long bond position is to hedge the credit position with credit puts. Hedging with credit puts provides credit protection by purchasing options payable in future periods. Traditionally, similar features have been implicit in many, if not most, repackaged or synthetic notes, especially those note structures where the originator of the structure also serves as the counterparty that guarantees the minimum return to the trust that issues the notes. Whether traditional implicit guarantees are priced as efficiently (i.e., competitively) as an explicit market-priced credit option by either the investor or the originator of the structure is an empirical question.

The economic objective for a credit put or protection buyer (aside from absolute downside protection) is obtaining an premium per unit of expected loss that on average is fairly priced. In contrast, the economic objective for a seller of the credit put or protection provider is to obtain surplus premium on average, relative to expected and unexpected losses. A money manager with a credit line for exposure to a specific credit (for which no issuance is available in the cash market) might sell default protection and earn a premium on the underutilized line, much like a bank receiving a commitment fee for a standby facility. That money manager has synthetically created a position in an asset.

In essence, the counterparty (protection seller) is acting as a guarantee-provider by selling an obligation to purchase bonds at a predetermined spread-to-treasuries. Selling a naked put on a credit event enhances yield and lowers the long-run average funding cost of the portfolio for the put seller. Here, the risk to the put seller is that the credit spread widens such that the loss from the exercised purchase obligation exceeds the yield enhancement (and funding cost savings to the put seller). Although the probability of a credit event (downgrade or default) remains the same, in the occurrence of a credit event, the recovery value on the reference asset is higher and, hence, expected loss is reduced for the put buyer. The put seller is being paid a premium to provide a floor on the recovery value of the reference asset. The structural rating analysis of a CLN that is long, a credit put should stress the counterparty rating (the put seller's

F I G U R E 13–3

Naked Put

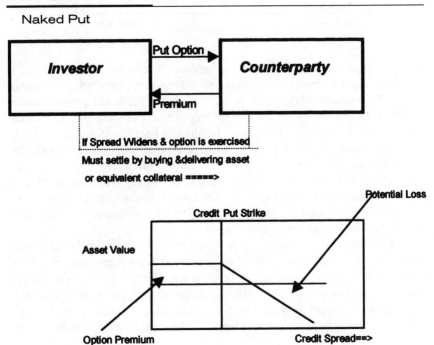

FIGURE 13-4

Credit Exchange Bond

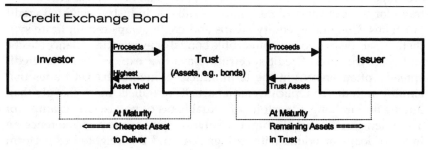

rating) as the weakest link in the transaction, since this is the factor that would drive the recovery value of the issued notes.

A credit exchange bond is an example of a CLN linked to a complex credit derivative that allows an investor to earn excess returns relative to a traditional bond with comparable default risk. With this structure, the investor in a credit exchange bond may achieve an enhanced return without necessarily assuming additional interest rate or call risk. An example of a likely issuer of a credit exchange bond is an asset manager holding the residual tranche of a CBO. By issuing the bond, the CBO manager is buying first-to-default credit protection by paying a premium to the investor in the credit exchange bond.

A credit exchange bond is a basket trade (i.e., an obligation issued by a financial intermediary, in which the reference asset is the credit performance of a basket of underlying corporate bonds). In addition to an incremental spread paid to the investor during the option period, and a lower additional spread paid after the option period to the maturity of the bond, the investor will be delivered the cheapest of the underlying corporate bonds at option maturity. If all of the bonds in the basket have the same rating *and* the counterparty is rated higher than the bonds in the reference basket, the structural rating of this transaction should conceptually bear the average rating on the basket of bonds. If the ratings of the reference bonds in the basket differed, then a rating would be assigned the transaction somewhere between the weighted average rating of the basket and the lowest rated instrument in the basket.

CREDIT ARBITRAGE STRATEGIES

Examples of credit arbitrage strategies that allow investors and issuers to express credit views include: balance sheet restructuring, credit-spread arbitrage (intertemporal credit spread plays similar to yield-curve arbitrage for interest rate volatility), and synthetic industry-weighted credit portfolios. Combining equity swaps and credit swaps can replicate synthetic assets (leases, loans, convertible bonds) or even entire balance sheets, and cost structures. Credit spectrum plays that exploit nonlinear credit spreads, often present in the term structure, involve basket trades that employ an index to replicate credit barbells or bullets, more cheaply than buying and holding a portfolio of actual loans or bonds. One example of a synthetic credit barbell might involve writing a swap to reference an index of loans or bonds with ratings AA- and B-, weighted to perform to meet an undersupply of BBB- with a given maturity. Credit and equity derivatives can be combined to construct options on synthetic convertibles as a play on both future credit and equity volatility. Credit wrapping other synthetic notes can often provide a cost-effective substitute for financial guarantees or fixed income portfolio insurance from a traditional bond insurer.

CREDIT-ENHANCING SYNTHETIC NOTE STRUCTURES

As suggested by Merton, the evolution of the legal forms, financial structures, and computing technology drives the capital market toward financial intermediation and the production of state-dependent financial products to meet demand driven by diverse investor preferences. A revolution in merchant banking and principal investing is reemerging with developing corporate finance applications of contingent claims analysis that blend both equity and credit derivative-based products.

CLNs are often structured to arbitrage cross-border anomalies. These arbitrage strategies express views regarding disparities in spreads due to the illiquidity or undersupply of securities in a particular maturity or currency. A classic example of just such an opportunity would be a mismatch in Mexican bond spreads between U.S. dollars and either Deutschemark or Yen. Supply-demand dynamics or market technicals often result in wider spreads in DM/Yen than in USD-denominated instruments with the same underlying credit risk. An asset swap equivalent to buying the DM-denominated bond and a DM/USD currency swap. The final leg of the trade would involve buying default protection on a liquid USD reference security of the same underlying credit. In the past, the spread pickup on the trade typically has varied between 40 to 100 basis points with the level of swaps rates and spread differentials.

A ratable CLN with a payoff distribution similar to this asset swap might be structured using simple credit derivatives to synthetically replicate the credit exposure. In addition, the level of credit exposure can be tailored by creating a floor for the recovery value with credit protection (by purchasing default swaps or options). In a similar manner, long asset positions can be monetized to synthetically replicate and issue credit-enhanced, leveraged lease instruments, by bundling total return swaps with default options and treasury strips.

Asset managers are increasingly focused on the spread between their Weighted Average Cost of Capital (WACC) (i.e., the Weight Average Coupon [WAC] of their fixed obligations), and the Weighted Average Price (WAP) and Weighted Average Maturity (WAM) of assets in their portfolio. This has further stimulated the other side of yield management, the modeling and managing of expected losses using credit derivatives. Bankers and portfolio managers are adopting more sophisticated credit models based on VaR or actuarial approaches. Similar market pressures are driving credit and bond underwriters to adopt financial and derivative market vehicles to expand capacity and lower cost. Financial guarantee insurers, in underwriting credit risks, are subject to more stringent regulatory and rating agency treatment than other sectors in the insurance industry.

Rating agencies and regulators mandate rigorous underwriting standards and capital requirements for financial guarantee insurers, based on perceived levels of underwriting risk. The result is that credit insurance tends to be a very capital-intensive sector of the insurance industry. Although analysts continue to utilize liability models, based on capital resources relative to underwriting exposures, a growing population of analysts are beginning to adopt models with an emphasis on assets in a credit insurer's portfolio, including the value of the assets that comprise unearned premiums. With the ongoing evolution of the credit-, insurance-, and asset-swap markets, even rating agencies are being required to price assets in order to derive credit-risk estimates and the probabilities of default. This trend towards convergence between credit-risk and event-risk is expected to persist, as the market risk approach and the statistical risk approaches of the financial and insurance markets continue to converge.

B I B L I O G R A P H Y

Credit Derivatives and Credit-Linked Notes

Allen, W. Robert: "Integrating Credit and Risk Management," *Journal of Lending and Credit-Risk Management*, Robert Morris Associates, February 1996.

Das, Satyajit: *Credit Derivatives: Products, Applications and Pricing*, Wiley, New York, 1997.

Hart, David: "Managing Credit Risk and Market Risk as a Buyer of Credit Derivatives," *Journal of Commercial Lending*, Robert Morris Associates, November 1995.

Irving, Richard: "Credit Derivatives Come Good," *RISK*, December 1995.

Smithson, Charles: "Credit Derivatives," *RISK*, June 1996.

Mordecai, David, et al: "Emerging Market CBO Concentration Limits: Volatility, Business Cycle Correlation and the Diversification of Industry," (unpublished study) *Fitch IBCA*, January 1998.

Mordecai, David: "Credit Arbitrage Investment Opportunities in Credit-linked Synthetic & Structured Notes: Introduction and Overview." In *Alternative Investment Strategies*, Euromoney Books/AIMA, London, 1998.

Mordecai, David: "Employing Credit Derivatives to Credit Enhance Structured Notes." In *Credit Derivatives: Applications for Risk Management*, Euromoney Books/AIMA, London, 1998.

Mordecai, David: "Emerging Market Credit Derivatives and Default Estimation: Volatility, Business Cycle Correlation and the Diversification of Industry, Region & Country Risk in a Global Credit Portfolio." In *Credit Derivatives: Applications for Risk Management*, RISK, 1998.

Models and Model Risk

Credit Suisse Financial Products: *Creditrisk+ Technical & Marketing Documents*, CSFP, 1997.

Derman, Emanuel: "Model Risk," *RISK*, May 1996.

J.P. Morgan: *Creditmetrics Technical & Marketing Documents*, JPM, 1997.

Jorion, Philippe: *Value-at-Risk: The New Benchmark for Controlling Derivative Risk*, Irwin, Homewood, IL, 1997.

McKinsey & Company: *Creditview Technical & Marketing Documents*, McKinsey, 1997.

Synthetic and Repackaged Securities

Das, Satyajit: *Swap & Derivative Financing*, Irwin, Homewood, IL, 1994.

Konishi, A., and R. Dattatreya: *Handbook of Derivative Instruments*, Irwin, Homewood, IL, 1996.

Peng, Scott, and Ravi Dattatreya: *The Structured Note Market: The Definitive Guide for Investors, Traders & Issuers*, Probus, Chicago, 1997.

Smithson, Charles: "Hybrid Securities," *RISK*, April 1996.

Financial Engineering, Intermediation, Option Pricing, and Portfolio Theory

Markowitz, Harry: *Mean-Variance Analysis with Portfolio Choice and Capital Markets*, Blackwell, Malden, MA, 1994.

Markowitz, Harry: *Portfolio Selection*, Blackwell, Malden, MA, 1990.

Marshall, J.F., and V.K. Bansall: *Financial Engineering*, NYIF, 1992.

Merton, Robert: *Continuous-Time Finance*, Blackwell, Malden, MA, 1990.

Nelken, Israel: *Exotic Options*, Irwin, Homewood, IL, 1995.

Shimko, David: *Finance in Continuous Time: A Primer*, Kolb, 1992.

Insurance and Financial Market Convergence

Embrechts, Paul, C. Kuppelberg, and T. Mikosch: *Modeling Extremal Events*, Springer-Verlag, New York, 1997.

International Risk Management: *The Convergence of Financial and Insurance Markets*, EMAP, 1996.

International Risk Management: *The Practical Application of Financial Market Tools to Corporate Risk Management*, EMAP, 1997.

Shimko, David: *The Valuation of Multiple-Claim Insurance Contracts*, USC, 1991.

Lamm, R. McFall: *The Catastrophe Reinsurance Market: Gyrations and Innovations Amid Major Structural Transformation*, Bankers Trust, January 1997.

Lane, Morton: *The Year of Structuring Furiously*, Sedgewick-Lane Financial, January 1997.

Litzenberger, Robert, David Beaglehole, and Craig Reynolds: *Assessing Catastrophe-Reinsurance-Linked Securities as a New Asset-Class*, Goldman Sachs, July 1996.

PART FIVE

The Future of Credit Derivatives

CHAPTER 14

The Future of Credit Derivatives

Alden L. Toevs*, Ph.D.
Executive Vice President, First Manhattan Consulting Group

The basic concept behind credit derivatives is not that new. In fact, it has been around for years in the form of letters of credit, loan commitments, and bond insurance contracts. As a formal product idea in its own right, credit derivatives have been on the radar screen only since the early 1990s. In the most recently available regulatory-mandated reporting period (1997), U.S. commercial banks reported period-over-period growth of more than 40 percent in their use of credit derivatives. Credit derivatives usage stands at about $50 billion in notional value; this total could be doubled if usage by all financial institutions were included.

Despite the presence of familiar precursor products and a simple, yet powerful, product design, credit derivative outstandings are dwarfed by the more than $8 trillion notional value of over-the-counter interest rate and currency swaps and by exchange-traded derivative contracts on many financial and physical products. After more than five years in the marketplace, it is clear that credit derivatives have not yet emerged as a blockbuster product.

What follows is FMCG's point of view on the question, "Will the credit derivative product take off and become highly successful in the long run?" To us, it seems that:

- Credit derivatives pass the tests necessary for successful financial products;

*The author wishes to thank Kenneth Zaslow, Emil Matsakh, and Kalliopi Lekas for their research support.

- Other factors currently affect the pace, but not the ultimate success, of credit derivatives; and
- Forces are now at work to address these limiting factors; thus, credit derivative use will grow, likely to levels that will make this product an important financial innovation.

CREDIT DERIVATIVES PASS THE TESTS NECESSARY FOR SUCCESSFUL FINANCIAL PRODUCTS

The fundamental condition for a financial product's success is the presence of a significant issue that can be addressed using the product. The product must then effectively enable end users to do one or more of the following:

- Segment and adjust risk levels
- Increase transactional efficiency by improving:
  1. pricing transparency, segmentation, and convergence
  2. market liquidity, leverage costs, etc.
- Lower ancillary costs such as margin, back office, regulatory, accounting, and tax costs
- Reduce excuses that otherwise lead to inertia.

If a new financial product can pass many of these tests, thereby increasing end users' overall risk/return efficiency, the product will likely succeed. If, on the other hand, a new product can only pass one or two of these tests, the product might still succeed if the market situation(s) to which it is applied is sizable.

Credit derivatives have been designed to focus on a huge market in which participants face a number of significant risk issues, any one of which can create "killer" losses. That is, credit risks are innately big in terms of outstandings and potential volatility. For example, there is $6 trillion of credit-exposed debt outstanding in the United States alone.

As shown in Figure 14–1, the big U.S.-dollar investors in credit-risk-exposed debt are commercial banks ($1.5 trillion), insurance companies ($1.4 trillion), mutual funds ($0.7 trillion), and pension funds ($0.3 trillion). Add to these figures the $13 trillion U.S. equity markets, which clearly have credit risk exposure, and you have a sizable and growing market (24 percent growth year-end 1996 to year-end 1997).

Pundits predict that credit derivatives will fail because they address only one side of the market are unfounded. All cash markets with credit risks are fundamentally two-sided; that is, sellers of credit risk all find

F I G U R E   14–1

U.S. Commercial Debt Size and Ownership

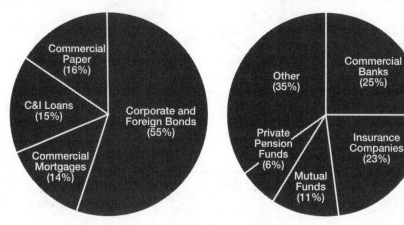

Credit-Intensive Debt Outstanding

- Commercial Paper (16%)
- C&I Loans (15%)
- Commercial Mortgages (14%)
- Corporate and Foreign Bonds (55%)

Credit-Intensive Debt Owned by Sector

- Other (35%)
- Commercial Banks (25%)
- Private Pension Funds (6%)
- Insurance Companies (23%)
- Mutual Funds (11%)

1997 Total = $6.1 Trillion

Source: Federal Reserve Flow of Funds data for December 31, 1997.

buyers. Why, then, would we expect derivatives of these cash markets to be one-sided? More directly to the point, credit derivative dealers and end users both note that end users frequently ask for two-way pricing and transact upon them. For example, a number of mid- to large-sized commercial banks have both bought and sold credit risk exposures as end users.[1]

* * *

Let's now look at how well credit derivatives pass the functional tests of new financial products.

Test One: Credit Derivatives Help End Users Segment and Adjust Risk Levels

Risk segmentation alternatives created through credit derivatives can be quite broad. Any market participant can synthetically issue (originate) or

---

[1]See *Winning The Credit Cycle Game: A Road Map for Adding Shareholder Value through Credit Portfolio Management*, Ronald Reading, Alden Toevs, and Robert Zizka, January 1998 (a monograph published by Robert Morris Associates), p. 63.

F I G U R E   14–2

Total Return Distributions with, and without, Credit Puts

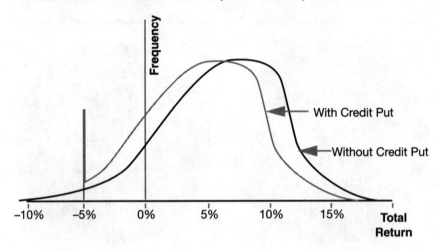

purchase his/her own or someone else's credit. There are no restrictions in size, although there are some round lot conventions. The start date of the exposure can be agreed upon in an adaptable manner; a contract can have any maturity and can begin on any date in the future.

For example, without AT&T's knowledge or consent, a credit derivatives user can issue or purchase AT&T credit risk for any amount, term, and start date. Accordingly, end user XYZ could buy, say, $100 million of notional credit risk on AT&T from a swap counterparty for five years starting today, one year in the future, or whenever. Theoretically, with the use of credit derivatives, the total AT&T credit risk issued could one day exceed AT&T's total bond and loan outstandings.[2]

Risk/return characteristics can be altered or segmented via credit derivatives. Using credit options, for example, the credit risk held by an end-user can be attenuated so that the "fat-tail" risk outcome distribution can be reshaped in any number of ways. The simplest example, illustrated in Figure 14–2, is to purchase a loan, bond, or a credit swap, and a default

---

[2]If this strikes the reader as odd, remember that the total amount of S&P 500 equity exposures is well in excess of the aggregate amount directly issued by the firms in the index. Equity index derivatives make up the difference, many of these derivatives are held by mutual funds that issue "cash" market mutual fund shares. This mechanism of converting derivatives into cash market instruments is one of many forms of risk securitization.

put option that limits the total return downside outcome to a loss of, say, 5 percent of notional value.[3]

Credit derivatives provide risk-magnitude-sharing alternatives, not unlike those in insurance markets where risk takers elect to take first, second, third, etc. loss positions.

- First-loss positions can be created simply (e.g., by purchasing a default or total return swap and a credit put option) as just illustrated. In general, first-loss positioning can be created a number of ways and has multiple uses, including:
  1. Hedging credit-exposed portfolio positions against unacceptably large worst-case losses;
  2. Constructing catastrophic loss protection for a bank that is in the process of syndicating loans, issuing a collateralized loan obligation (CLO), etc.; and
  3. Hedging one's own *future* debt issuance costs to be no worse than a prespecified amount.[4]

- Second-loss positions can be created in several ways, most straightforwardly through buying a credit put option for the maximum loss level desired and selling another credit put option that obligates the seller to pay at a lower loss level.

Tenor strategies can be usefully exotic. Suppose that investors generally like company ABC's prospects, but some worry about ABC over the intermediate period. ABC's yield curve could then look "humped," as shown in Figure 14–3.

A viable risk-taking strategy for the proponents of ABC would be to buy an intermediate-term, total return swap and simultaneously sell short- and longer-dated total return swaps. This combination, properly weighted to have a neutral stance vis-à-vis changes in interest rate levels and an overall tightening or widening of credit spreads, would benefit from a reversion to a normal credit spread (*à la* a typical peer company in terms of industry and credit rating). Executing this "butterfly" trade with credit derivatives may be superior to doing so in the cash markets:

- The trade can be structured to be simultaneously put into place at the outset; this is more difficult to do in cash markets where

---

[3]The typical "fat-tail" return distribution of a bond or a loan can be made nearly normal (bell-shaped) through a series of credit options at various strike prices.

[4]One popular parallel strategy in equity markets has companies that engage in stock buybacks use equity puts and calls to manage their repurchase program returns, including those on the "downside."

F I G U R E 14–3

Example of a Maturity Sector Credit Opportunity

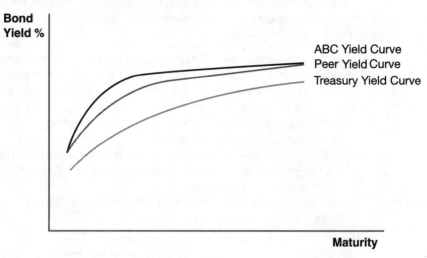

the purchases of intermediate maturity ABC bonds and the short sale of short and long maturity ABC bonds often has to be "legged-into"

■ Availability of bonds to end the trade when the equivalent of the short sale needs to be covered need not be as great a concern as it would be in the cash market butterfly trade—the derivatives trade could be closed out by properly structuring offsetting swaps.

Risk segmentation can also be undertaken by specifying the payout "trigger event" in credit derivatives. For example, the triggering event in a derivative contract on the reference company in the swap contract can begin (or end) with a rating decline to a specified level, a particular type of default (e.g., payment or covenant), its filing for bankruptcy protection, or a later event in the downward credit spiral. [Note: this flexibility is a strength of credit derivatives; yet, as we are finding out from the Russia defaults of 1998, careful documentation of the trigger event has not yet become a standard practice in the credit derivative marketplace.]

Credit losses come from the intersection of default likelihood and loss-in-event-of-default (LIED) outcomes. Figure 14–4 is an illustrative example of the distribution characteristics of default likelihood and LIED for loans of double-B rated obligors. These separate drivers of ultimate

F I G U R E   14–4

Default and LIED Distributions

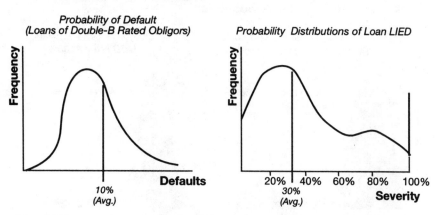

Source: FMCG's analysis of a portfolio of loans of Double-B rated obligors.

loss can be thought of as two separable transactable risks in credit derivative markets.

The resulting difference in loss distributions that comes from a range of possible LIEDs versus a fixed, average LIED of 30 percent is shown in Figure 14–5. Many bankers incorrectly assign risk-adjusted capital allocations to cover the difference between expected losses and those at a given confidence level (e.g., 99 percent, using a fixed LIED estimate). The reality is LIEDs vary and because of this required capital levels rise considerably.

Default and severity risk segmentation can already be found in credit derivative instruments. For example, one end user may choose to receive a fixed payment for a default and, therefore, take the risk that the loss severity upon a default differs from the amount specified in the swap contract. Another end user may structure a different payout (e.g., by selecting a derivative that pays all severity losses above, say 30 percent, in exchange for making payments when recoveries exceed 70 percent).

Test Two: Credit Derivatives Increase Transactional Efficiency

Credit derivatives can add pricing transparency through more precise valuation of credit costs and facilitation of price convergence, leverage, and other means. In their simplest forms, credit swaps create purer credit

F I G U R E 14–5

Impact of LIED Variance on Loss Distributions and, hence,
Risk-Adjusted Capital Allocations

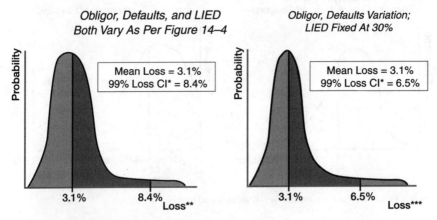

*Statistical confidence interval
**Loss = loss derived by paired random draws from the two distributions in Figure 14–4
***Loss = loss derived by random draws from the default distribution in Figure 14–4 with a 30 percent severity

products than loans or bonds. These swaps are priced based on the cost of the underlying's credit risk and the credit risk of the swap counterparty.

Pricing fixed-income cash products, on the other hand, combines credit and financing costs.[5] When credit and financing costs are linked, as they always are in a cash investment, investors with lower credit ratings face heavy costs of carrying (financing) investments in higher-rated companies. By allowing investors to avoid these financing costs, credit swaps expand the investor universe, thus creating a broader-based investor group and, likely, better credit spread assessments.

Credit options also provide pure, tradable information on credit insurance prices. These are useful in many ways (e.g., as an alternative to bond insurance or as an input when letters of credit, financial performance guarantees, etc. are priced/hedged).

Although elements of credit risk can be found in bond, loan, equity, and other market prices, the convergence of views among these markets has been hampered because available information is imprecise and be-

---

[5]Liquidity factors must be considered for both cash and off-balance sheet transactions.

cause there are barriers that limit actions of otherwise willing market participants. For example, corporate loan markets have long been the sole domain of local banks; through CLOs and other derivatives, this is changing rapidly.

Pricing efficiency has been further impeded by a persistent dearth of quality data on expected and worst-case default rates, default correlations, and loss-in-event-of-default estimates. This surprises many casual observers who justifiably note that there has been plentiful opportunities to record and analyze this type of information, which in turn has high potential value to creditors. Credit derivatives can help reduce these data gaps. Swaps, CLOs, and credit-linked notes can, for example, be created on baskets of credits. Prices for these instruments can now be done with explicit recognition of the diversification "index" among the credits in the basket. (Some end users are increasing their knowledge of diversification benefits by having dealers price different baskets of credit exposures.)

Some investors appear to want to increase exposures in areas not easily accessible to them. As previously mentioned, credit derivatives help nonbank investors participate in the bank loan market. Insurers, pension funds, mutual, and hedge funds have already increased their credit-based income by purchasing commercial and industrial (C&I) and commercial real estate (CRE) loan exposures via CLOs and credit swaps.

Another topical credit market is emerging-market government and corporate debt. Some already feel overexposed; others wish for more exposure to diversify their portfolios and/or enhance portfolio earnings. Credit derivatives are now commonly used to change emerging market credit exposures, without requiring the sale of the underlying instrument.

Arbitrage opportunities (some of them major) exist in credit markets that cannot now be easily traded upon. Investors can use total return swaps, however, to arbitrage a perceived mispricing between bank loans and subordinated debt of the same issuer. For example, suppose that both assets are priced at par, but the loan yields LIBOR plus 325 basis points while the debt yields LIBOR plus 300 basis points. Clearly, in the absence of some overriding technical or other nonmarket factors, a mispricing exists since the loan has seniority in a default yet it yields more than subordinated debt. To efficiently exploit this opportunity, total return swaps could be executed to create a long position in the bank loan and a short position in the subordinated debt.

Undertaking these or more complex transactions will reduce inappropriate credit spread differentials. It is, of course, not quite this simple. Full convergence is unlikely because:

- Loans and bonds of the same company differ in their LIED

- Accounting and tax treatments of the transactions needed to effect this arbitrage may prove to be onerous, particularly for non-dealers
- Regulatory capital requirements may limit the trade's viability
- Transaction costs limit full price parity.

Liquidity and leverage are enhanced through the use of credit derivatives; consider these two quick examples:

- Potential investors in bank loans can achieve about the same yield as available in loans by purchasing credit derivatives; often liquidity can also be superior. For example, money managers can invest in Treasuries and purchase total return swaps. If short-term cash requirements spike quickly, Treasuries can be sold or repaid for "emergency" cash faster and more cheaply than bank loans can be sold[6]
- Leverage is facilitated through a variety of credit-linked notes;[7] credit options also offer more plentiful credit risk leverage than unleveraged purchases of loans, bonds, etc.

Thus, credit derivatives increase transactional efficiency by opening up markets to nontraditional investors and traders; help establish purer credit risk markets; and enable end users to take actions that lead to better pricing parity by overcoming entry barriers in cash markets and other inefficiencies.

Test Three: Credit Derivatives Help Lower Ancillary Costs

"Back office" costs of running a servicing group to collect commercial loan payments are not required if credit risk is obtained via credit derivatives with payouts linked to loan performance. The cost of posting collateral (if required) is also reduced when using credit derivatives—margin is needed only for changes in value arising from credit spread movements,

---

[6] In addition, the tax implications of selling and then repurchasing Treasuries may be less onerous than doing the same with loans.

[7] FMCG cautions end users to use credit-linked notes carefully. Some forms can be quite useful; others are complex, difficult to value, and prone to high amounts of risk leverage. Some end users currently buy these notes for their apparent yield and investment-grade-rating "cosmetics"; they may be surprised at how low their risk-adjusted returns might become under a wide variety of circumstances.

not this amount plus the changes in value arising from general changes in interest rates, as would be the case with bonds. Regulatory constraints can sometimes be avoided or reduced using credit derivatives; this is a factor in the decision-making process pay for many credit-linked note purchases. (Obviously, those who do so should pay careful attention to the concerns regulators had when promulgating their regulations before attempting to avoid the application of these regulations through the use of credit derivatives.)[8]

Test Four: Credit Derivatives Help Reduce Internal Management Inertia

Because credit derivatives offer fundamental building blocks of credit risk, it is easy for end users to find ways to change their credit risk profiles. Many bankers, for example, are asked by their clients to lend them money in ways that create sizable risk concentrations. Conventional efforts to mitigate these concentrations only partially succeed. Figure 14–6 demonstrates the loan concentration problem at a typical regional bank.

Most bankers deem the following conventional techniques/tools for credit risk management as being too blunt:

- Lower credit risk concentrations by turning away some loan requests made by large borrowers—a useful risk management approach, but with the downside of increasing competition as borrowers develop additional banking relationships to ensure they have access to funds;

- Sell risk via loan syndications/participations and CLOs—again useful, but competitors are introduced to larger borrowing clients via loan document disclosures. In addition, clients may have agreements with the bank that prevent the inclusion of their loan in a CLO;[9] and

- Expanding the geographic footprint to increase the number of client relationships.

---

[8]There have been many memorable losses/embarrassments associated with many types of derivatives that have arisen from their use to avoid or limit application of regulatory requirements.

[9]Recently, CLOs have been issued disclosing the ratings but not the names of the underlying borrowers. This shows how the CLO market is becoming a market based on ratings, rather than fundamental analyses of underlying credits. Some investors balk at such "blind pool" purchases.

F I G U R E 14–6

Typical Loan Concentration in U.S. Commercial Banks

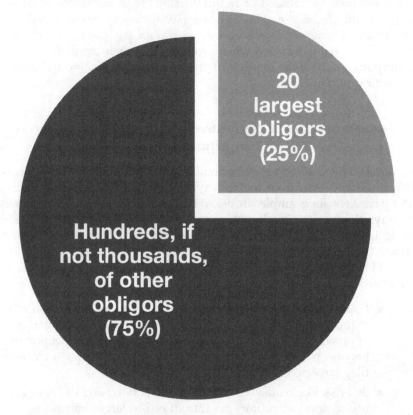

% of total C&I loan portfolio outstandings

Source: Typical findings from FMCG's client work on credit risk concentrations in C&I loan portfolios.

Credit derivatives help overcome potential new "investor" inertia. For example, insurers can use simple-to-understand credit derivatives to expand their lists of available credit-risk prone investments.[10] As a result, end-users need not develop loan origination capabilities or find traders and supporting analysts capable of judging credit quality of market offer-

---

[10]Insurance regulations now often require insurers to do this in the form of CLOs, reinsurance contracts, or credit-linked notes.

ings with the quickness often demanded during loan package sales. (Because credit derivatives have no formal issuance date, campaigns need not be as marketing can be less pressured.)

* * *

In summary, credit derivatives create the means for lenders, investors, issuers, underwriters, and others to adjust their collectively large credit risk exposures. They address, therefore, a fundamental need of the marketplace.

In addition, credit derivatives pass all of the functional tests for success. Innovations in this derivative marketplace will continue at a fast pace, but current product offerings already help market participants:

- Segment/reposition credit risk in terms of amount, tenor, start date, loss position, and trigger event
- Improve transactional efficiencies
- Lower ancillary costs of the back office, margins, etc.
- Overcome several important inertias in credit risk management.

OTHER FACTORS AFFECT THE PACE, BUT NOT THE ULTIMATE SUCCESS, OF CREDIT DERIVATIVES

Despite their many powerful applications, the worldwide total notional value of credit derivatives slightly exceeds 1 percent of U.S. cash market commercial credit exposure.[11] Notional placements and mark-to-market values of credit derivatives also slightly exceed 1 percent of that values outstanding in the interest rate and currency swap markets.

What primary forces hold back the use of derivatives to transform credit risk, an old and potentially fatal risk? The best view may come from commercial banks. Recently FMCG, under the aegis of the Robert Morris Associates, undertook a comprehensive assessment of the credit

---

[11]This estimate uses a conservative, year-end 1997 estimate of $100 billion in total notional credit derivatives outstandings, of which $50 billion is held by U.S. commercial bank end users versus $6 trillion in U.S. corporate debt and commercial loans.

T A B L E   14–1

Use of Credit Derivatives by U.S. Commercial Banks

North American Commercial Bank Use of Credit Derivatives*	Advanced Credit Risk Management Banks (15 out of 64 banks)	Traditional Credit Risk Management Banks (49 out of 64 banks)
Have done at least one trade	47% ⎫	22% ⎫
Plan to begin using them soon	13 ⎬ 93%	8 ⎬ 55%
Actively researching the market	33 ⎭	25 ⎭
No activity underway	7	29
Decided not to pursue	0	16

*Based on a survey of 64 banks with large commercial lending exposures.

risk measurement and management practices of the largest North American commercial banks.[12]

Among many topics, the survey covered credit derivative usage, and found that a total of 19 banks (30 percent of those sampled) have entered into at least one credit derivative trade. Table 14–1 provides more detail on the current state of play. By the way, in answering another survey question, 20 banks said that they would expect to count credit derivatives among one of their most often used management tools by 1999.

In answering the question, "Used for what purpose?" The surveyed banks gave the answers in Table 14–2.

Most banks gave the same reasons why credit derivatives will mature more slowly than financial logic may suggest: Transactional efficiency in the product has been hampered by unclear regulatory, accounting, tax, and legal treatment. Using the bankers in our study as bellwether indicators, issues on end users' minds include:

- How much benefit, if any, will regulators and rating agencies attribute to institutions that hedge large credit exposures? Will these benefits depend on the type of swaps used (e.g., total return swaps versus default puts)? Do risk exposures have to be micro-hedged or will macro hedges (say, hedges placed on

---

[12]For more on the survey findings see *Winning the Credit Cycle Game: Adding Shareholder Value through Credit Portfolio Management*, op. cit. (A summary of this monograph has also been published in the Summer 1998 issue of *Journal of Lending and Credit Risk Management*; this article can also be found on FMCG's website, www.fmcg.com.)

T A B L E   14–2

Purposes for Which Commercial Banks
Use Credit Derivatives

	Advanced Credit Risk Management Banks (15 out of 64 banks)	Traditional Credit Risk Management Banks (49 out of 64 banks)
Hedge an obligor or specific group of exposures	80%	37%
Create a macro hedge	60	33
Add credit risk if the price is right*	47	14

*The frequency of using credit derivatives to add risk provides an interesting, secondary indicator that the credit derivative market is developing good two-way flows.

the credit risk performance of an industry) also provide regulatory benefit? What will the capital treatment be on credit risk purchased in a credit derivative? What hidden regulatory issues lie ahead; e.g., will selling credit put options create the risk of oversight by insurance regulators? (See Chapter 12 of this book for added perspective.)

■ What accounting treatment will auditors give credit derivatives? Does hedging a loan exposure with a credit derivative create the possibility of having to mark the derivative to market while the loan is subject to accrual accounting? How will credit option premiums be treated on the income statement? (See Chapter 9 of this book for a full discussion.)

■ What tax treatment will be settled upon? Under what circumstances will the credit derivative be allowed to be integrated with the underlying cash instruments to create appropriate ordinary income and capital gain offsets? How will withholding tax issues for nondomestic end users be resolved? (See Chapter 10 of this book for the troubling taxation details; there you will see that the tax issues for even the simplest derivatives are complex, particularly for nondealers/banks.)

■ What legal issues might be encountered? Will ISDA documents hold up in court on netting and other issues? Are there unknown "ultra vires" type risks? (See Chapter 11 of this book for a full discussion.)

There are more subtle and, ultimately, insidious issues that also hamper the maturation of credit derivative products. Credit risk portfolio management has become an extremely hot topic at banks, insurers, money managers, and other credit-risk-product end users. That is the good news for the viability of credit derivative products. The bad news, derived from FMCG's consulting work, clearly suggests that many executive managers, who must ultimately approve risk altering profiles by actions such as purchasing and selling credit derivatives, are reluctant to act.

All too often, buyers of credit risk do so for its apparent yield rather than risk-adjusted yields or risk-adjusted return on capital. Therefore, they are reluctant to pay the price needed to reduce their risks. Risk concentrations, as previously illustrated in Figure 14–6, are more the rule than not. Credit risk is actually even more concentrated than this example indicates—firms using accrual accounting (e.g., banks) often have heavy concentrations in geographic regions and in limited spectrums of the credit risk continuum.

The heavy concentration of bank credits in similar risk grades is particularly worrisome. Many bankers have 70 percent+ concentrations of their C&I portfolios in credits that have (or would warrant) double- or triple-B ratings. These credits often share quite common macroeconomic risk exposures. That is, as a group these loans can be highly interdependent in their credit risk outcomes, regardless of their industry group associations. (Figure 14–7 depicts the high degree of loan concentrations in the most heavily assigned risk grades in commercial banks.)

These same buy-and-hold commercial bankers underappreciate the stock market's differentiated reaction to credit loss performances. While many remember the substantial credit losses incurred in the early 1990s, most have forgotten the differential impact these losses induced in bank stock total returns. Let us "relive" the stock market results achieved by high-loss versus low-loss banks in the credit downturn of 1990–1992/3. To let the lenders with poor credit underwriting have a chance, let us look at the period October 1989 to October 1997. The average annual total equity return of the best credit-performance banks from 1989 to 1997 was 56 percent higher than that of banks with poor credit performance (25 percent versus 16 percent). Yet, the best banks had only half the price volatility as these extra returns were earned. This results in a Sharpe ratio for equity holders of low loan loss bank stocks that is 4 times better than that for high loan loss banks (see Table 14–3).

Clearly, limiting large risk concentrations and otherwise diversifying credit risks can have large paybacks to shareholders of financial institutions. Attaining a more balanced risk exposure proves to be difficult. Even committed executives face conflicts/constraints such as these:

F I G U R E   14–7

Concentration of Credit Exposures in Similar Credit Ratings/ Grades

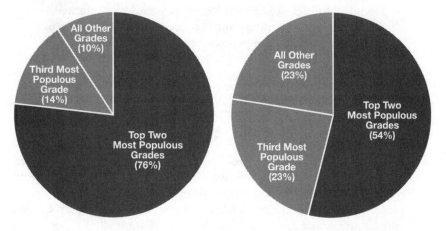

Median for All Banks   *Median of Best Practice Banks*

- Quarrels on whether or not credit should be extended when relationship managers wish to do so, but loan portfolio managers urge caution

- Data and risk measurement quality that limits the accuracy of correlation-adjusted returns needed to get full benefits from

T A B L E   14–3

Stock Market Reactions to Portfolio Credit Losses

Bank Stock Market Performance: 1989–1997	Low Loan Loss Banks*	High Loan Loss Banks**
Average annual total return to shareholders	25%	16%
Risk (annual standard deviation of stock price changes)	22%	44%
Sharpe ratio (a return/risk measure)	0.8	0.2

*There were 8 banks among the 50 largest banks that had materially lower than average loan losses in 1990–1992/3.

**There were 7 banks among the 50 largest banks that had high, but survivable, loan losses in 1990–1992/3. (Note that another 11 high loss banks did not survive as independent entities, largely because of their high credit losses.)

credit hedges, plus sorting out differences of opinion when opposing sides present highly complex, mathematical arguments still daunts many executives

■ Hedging to limit additional losses, which can substantially reduce reported earnings and may accelerate the timing of what would be for the moment opportunity losses.

FORCES ARE NOW AT WORK TO ADDRESS THESE LIMITED FACTORS; THUS, CREDIT DERIVATIVE USE WILL GROW

As is the case in derivative markets that have already matured, a compelling product can grow to significant volumes prior to having a well-defined regulatory, accounting, tax, and legal environment. Solutions to the issues faced by credit derivative end users will continue apace and will not be the major hold-up. The volume of transactions per credit derivative end user will be more impeded by softer issues.

What is most needed to quicken the acceptance by a broad base of end users is education and product design that fosters:

1. A growing realization by the executives in end-user companies that credit risk portfolio management is being practiced at a level of proficiency by some peers in ways that create competitive advantage via:
   - more efficient risk/return profiles in their portfolios exposed to credit risk
   - arbitrage-based earnings, that is, taking advantage of mispriced credits in the market
   - for lenders, flexible accommodation of borrower requests in ways that create better risk-adjusted returns
2. The emergence of specific cases where risk-adjusted earnings levels (and growth rates) become the envy of executives at more traditional institutions
3. Differentiated stock price performance for those institutions that weather the next credit downturn noticeably better than their peers
4. Guidance that others are able to manage credit exposure in a portfolio context; that is, manage them similarly to a value-based bond mutual fund

5. Executives who educate their peers on the practical power of risk diversification using business contextual examples rather than blackboards full of mathematics and statistics.

Market makers, consultants, regulators, rating agency analysts, and equity analysts all are working on these issues with varying degrees of success. Software and databases provided by some vendors are helping internal risk managers create real life, risk-adjusted cases for executives to review. What is missing most is a cathartic triggering event for the recalcitrant executives—which, unfortunately may only come during or after the next credit downturn.

Resolution of the above issues is, however, inevitable because:

- Compelling risk arbitrage profits are being earned by leading insurers, investment banks, and commercial banks.

- Capital market securities, such as CLOs, are being packaged in ways that create portfolios envied by many geography-bound credit originators. These transactions are being examined by an increasing number of risk managers who in turn are learning a great deal about the cost of being under-diversified.[13]

- Risk-based measurements that have been embraced by some investment and commercial banks are becoming more commonplace and are now being sought out by insurers, banks, and other financial firms that historically have focused on accrual-based accounting results.

- Role models have been created—some firms have worked out better ways to organize how credit portfolio investments are selected and managed than are found in firms that have not had risk-based performance reporting. And, importantly, in the last four years, the increased cross-hiring of bank and insurance executives has spread knowledge of better credit practices across many insurers and banks.

- Databases with more credible information than those developed from any single institution's past credit events can be purchased (from rating agencies and vendors) and used to support decision making in portfolio-wide contexts.

- Firms that sell credit risk management products are reorganizing themselves in ways that further promote research

---

[13]Much can be learned on what the market charges for underdiversified credit risk in the structuring process of CLOs and basket credit swaps.

and education on these topics. For example, J.P. Morgan and
Credit Suisse offer credit risk management models at nominal
cost; and, several investment banks are combining all credit-
risk-exposed debt sales and trading operations into one
management hierarchy. One outgrowth of this type of sell-side
organizational change is an increase in research reports and
seminars on the power of managing credit in a day-to-day
portfolio context.

* * *

With these forces at work, credit derivatives will grow in popularity.
Looking forward, the credit derivative market will soon become a large
one; it is easy to imagine over $1 trillion in notional outstandings within
three years or so. Fortunately for end users, this market is not likely to
be as lucrative for dealers as were the first $1 trillion in interest rate and
currency swaps: (1) end users are likely already experienced users of other
types of derivative products, and (2) the bulk of the first trillion dollars
sold will be plain vanilla credit derivatives, which end users should be
able to value with decent, if not high, levels of competency. From an end-
user perspective, credit derivatives may become one of the best-value-
for-money innovations of the Street.

Credit Derivatives Glossary

Judah Kaplan, Associate
Credit Derivatives, Chase Securities, Inc.

Douglas S. Rolph, Ph.D., Candidate
Finance Department of the Graduate School of Business,
    University of Washington

asset swap   A simultaneous bond purchase and an interest rate or currency swap in which an investor swaps the fixed coupon on the bond for a floating interest rate. Premiums, discounts, and accrued interest are made as an upfront payment by (to) the investor to (from) the swap counterparty so as to make the notional amount on the swap equal to the par value of the asset. Asset swaps are the first pricing tool for many credit derivatives.

available-for-sale securities   Investments which are not classified for accounting purposes as either trading securities or held-to-maturity securities. Although the investor must use the mark-to-market method, unrealized price changes are reflected on the balance sheet instead of through the income statement.

Bank of International Settlements (BIS)   International central bank that has produced guidelines for capital adequacy requirements. These guidelines are then adapted by member countries.

banking book   The ledger on which banks have historically recorded most bank assets such as loans, revolving credits, and letters of credit. Items in the banking book are generally held-to-maturity securities that are accounted for using the cost method.

basis risk   The risk that the gains or losses on a hedging instrument will not completely offset the losses or gains on the underlying exposure.

basket default swap   See *first to default swap*.

BISTRO   The Broad Index Secured Trust Offering, a proprietary product introduced by J.P. Morgan in December 1997, in which a bank sells its exposure in a high grade credit portfolio through a default swap to a special purpose vehicle (SPV). The SPV issues notes to investors which allow the investors exposure to the portfolio with limited recourse.

call option   The right to purchase a fixed quantity of an asset or index at a given date in the future for a price agreed upon when the option is purchased.

capital adequacy requirements   Rules which define the amount of capital that banks are required to set aside for protection against business losses.

cash settlement   One means of settling a total return or default swap in which the risk buyer (protection seller) pays the counterparty a cash amount. The amount of the cash payment may either equal the decline in market value of the reference asset times the notional amount or may be a binary payment which is a fixed amount determined at the inception of the contract. If the contract calls for a binary payment, then upon a credit event, the protection seller (risk buyer) pays the counterparty the fixed amount irrespective of where the reference asset trades in the market.

Chase Secured Loan Trust (CSLT) Note^{SM}   A proprietary investment structure developed by Chase Securities Inc. utilizing credit derivatives technology. The trust issues investment grade rated notes to investors reflecting the economics of an underlying portfolio of leveraged bank loans or other high yield assets. The CSLT has been described as a second generation CLO.

collateralized bond obligation (CBO)   A note issued by a trust as a claim against an underlying portfolio of bonds. Often these notes are issued in multiple tranches, based on different credit risk characteristics, varying from AAA to unrated equity, to investors with different investment objectives.

collateralized loan obligation (CLO)   A note issued by a trust as a claim against an underlying portfolio of bank loans. Often these notes are issued in multiple tranches, based on different credit risk characteristics, varying from AAA to un-rated equity to investors with different investment objectives.

concentration risk   The risk that an investor has too great a concentration of his portfolio in a particular asset class, geographic location, obligor or industry, etc. and is therefore exposed to potential losses more than an investor with a more diversified portfolio.

convexity   A measure of the price volatility of a bond with respect to its yield. Convexity measures the percentage price change not explained by duration due to the non-linearity of the price-yield relationship.

cost accounting (method)   The practice of accounting for an investment at its historical cost rather than at its current market value. It is most often used for held-to-maturity securities and assets held in the banking book.

counterparty credit charge (CCC)   The adjustment made to the price of a swap contract to account for the credit quality of the swap counterparty.

counterparty risk   Risk that the counterparty to a financial transaction will default.

credit derivative   Financial instrument which derives its value from the credit quality of a bond, loan, or other financial obligation.

credit event   Event which triggers an early termination of a total return or default swap resulting in either cash or physical settlement. Examples include payment default, bankruptcy, default or obligation acceleration, repudiation/moratorium and restructuring.

credit intermediation swap   See *dynamic credit swap*.

credit-linked note (CLN)   A note in which cash flows are based off of a bond, loan, or other financial obligations and in which the ability to make those cash flows is linked to an underlying asset or group of assets. See also *repackaged notes*.

credit option   An option which derives its value from the credit quality of a loan, bond, or bond index.

credit rating   Measure of a firm's credit risk. Firms that produce such ratings include Moody's Standard and Poors, Dun and Bradstreet, and Fitch IBCA.

credit risk   Risk that a borrower will default on a commitment to repay debt or bank loans.

credit risk premium (spread)   The difference between the yield earned on a credit-risky asset and the yield earned on a risk-free asset such as a U.S. Treasury Obligation.

credit swap   A credit derivative contract that protects a protection buyer (risk seller) against a credit event. The swap is settled by either cash settlement or physical settlement. In return for providing this protection, the protection seller (risk buyer) receives a fixed series of cash flows.

credit wrap   Credit protection of a debt instrument issued by an insurer, bank, or other entity to increase the credit quality of an underlying debt instrument.

CreditMetrics®   A portfolio model developed by J.P. Morgan for evaluating credit value-at-risk across an array of different instruments in a mark-to-market framework.

Creditrisk+   A portfolio model developed by Credit Suisse Financial Products for evaluating credit risk using an actuarial approach.

default risk   Risk that an obligor will not make interest, principal, or other contractual payments on a financial obligation.

default swap   See *credit swap*.

documentation   Legal agreement that defines the structure of a financial contract.

duration   A measure of the price volatility of a fixed income instrument with respect to changes in interest rates, credit spread, or both. Duration measures the present value weighted average term to maturity of the security's cash flows.

dynamic credit swap   A default swap in which the notional amount is linked to an underlying swap or portfolio of swaps so that the contingent payment is linked to the performance of both a counterparty's credit and to the mark-to-market value, if positive, on the reference swap.

"fallen angel"   A company which was formerly of an investment-grade quality but which has since become a below-investment-grade (high yield) credit.

Federal Reserve System (FRS)   Regulator for state-chartered banks. One of two main banking regulators in the United States. See also *Office of the Comptroller of the Currency.*

financial guaranty insurance   A contract in which an insurance company receives a fee to provide credit protection on a debt instrument.

first loss risk   A position in a portfolio or repackaged note which will be in the first position to lose value if there are realized credit losses suffered on the underlying portfolio. Alternatively, this will be the last tranche of the issue to receive cash flows from the portfolio. First loss risk is often referred to as an equity interest in the portfolio.

first to default swap   A credit swap which references a portfolio of credits in which the risk buyer (protection seller) makes a contingent payment to the counterparty only for the first (if any) obligor in the portfolio to incur a credit event.

fractional exposure (FE)   An estimate of the expected percentage of loss if a counterparty defaults on a derivative contract without any recovery. This is sometimes referred to as the "worst case" exposure to a counterparty.

guarantee   A contractual agreement by one party to pay the debts of an obligor if the obligor is unable to make the required payments itself. The market views the guarantor as the ultimate credit risk on the debt.

held-to-maturity securities   Investments in debt securities which an investor has the ability and intent to hold to maturity. These may be accounted for using the cost method.

idiosyncratic risk   Risk that is specific to each entity and that can be mitigated via diversification or hedged by a credit derivative.

index swap   A type of total return swap in which the value is derived from a specific bond index, such as a high grade or high yield bond index.

insurance contract   A contract in which one party pays another (the "Insurer") a fixed fee in return for a contingent payment from the Insurer if specified losses occur.

ISDA   International Swaps and Derivatives Association. Industry association for the global derivatives community.

ISDA Master Agreement   Standard legal documentation for financial transactions developed by ISDA. Along with various annexes also developed by ISDA, serves as basic legal documentation for derivative transactions, including credit derivatives.

legal risk   The risk that a derivative contract may be deemed illegal, unsuitable, or non-binding.

letter of credit (LOC)   A contract between a bank and an obligor whereby the bank agrees to pay a third party (the "Beneficiary") in the event that the obligor does not fulfill its contractual obligations. If the letter of credit is drawn upon, the bank may seek full recourse from the obligor.

leveraged loans   Bank loans extended to below investment grade companies (rated less than Baa3/BBB-) which have a credit spread of greater than 125 basis points.

liquidity risk   The risk that an investor will not be able to close out an open position in a security or a derivative contract at a given time due to the fact that there is not another party who wishes to assume the investor's position.

loan participation   An arrangement in which an investor agrees to purchase the risk of an underlying loan while allowing the holder of the loan to maintain ownership, collect payments from the obligor and pass them on to the investor. The investor ultimately holds the credit risk of the obligor and the performance risk of the loan holder.

London Interbank Offered Rate (LIBOR)   Rate which banks lend funds to each other on the international interbank market. Key rate which is often used as a variable rate in swaps.

Loss-In-Event-of-Default (LIED)   The amount of the face value of an investment an investor is unable to recover if the obligor suffers a credit event.

marginal risk   The difference between a portfolio's risk before and after an additional marginal transaction.

mark-to-market (MTM) accounting (method)   The practice of recording an asset's current market value in the financial statements with unrealized changes from its previous value also being reflected in the financial statements.

market risk   Risk associated with movements in market prices, most often risk-free interest rates.

matched position   Long and short positions in identical credit derivative structures over identical maturities referencing identical assets. Defined by the Federal Reserve.

materiality   The requirement in some credit derivatives contracts that a reference asset must fall in value by more than a minimum amount in order for a credit event to trigger swap termination and settlement. Originally this was required so as to prevent technical defaults from terminating the swap. Less commonly used these days.

mean reversion   The tendency of a variable (interest rates, default rates, recovery rates, etc.) to drift toward its historical average.

National Association of Insurance Commissioners (NAIC)   Association of insurance regulators that develops model laws and rules that are adapted by state insurance commissioners.

Notice of Intended Settlement (NIS)   An irrevocable notice from the protection buyer to the protection seller that confirms the buyer will settle the credit swap and, in the case of a physically settled credit swap, contains the details of the assets that the buyer will deliver to the seller.

notional amount   Amount on which the cash flows for a derivatives contract are calculated.

obligation acceleration   The occurrence of a default, event of default, or other similar condition or event (however described), other than a failure to make any required payment, in respect of the reference entity under one or more obligations in an aggregate notional amount of not less than a threshold amount which has resulted in such obligations becoming due and payable before they would otherwise have been due and payable. This is one type of credit event.

obligation default   The occurrence of a default, event of default, or other similar condition or event (however described), other than a failure to make any required payment, in respect of the reference entity under one or more obligations in an aggregate notional amount of not less than a threshold amount which has resulted in such obligations becoming capable at such time of being declared due and payable before they would otherwise have been due and payable. This is one type of credit event.

Office of the Comptroller of the Currency (OCC)   Regulator of nationally chartered banks. One of two main regulatory agencies in the United States. See also *Federal Reserve System*.

offsetting position   Long and short credit derivative positions in reference assets of the same obligor with the same level of seniority in bankruptcy. These positions may otherwise be considered matched positions except for different maturities or different structures (i.e., one position is a default swap and the other position is a total return swap). Defined by the Federal Reserve.

physical settlement   One means of settling a total return or default swap in which the risk buyer (protection seller) pays the counterparty the notional amount times initial price and receives the reference asset through physical delivery.

publicly available information   Information which has been published or electronically displayed in any two or more internationally recognized financial news sources and which reasonably confirms any of the facts relevant to the determination that a credit event has occurred. However, if either of the parties or any of their respective affiliates is cited as the sole source for such information, then such information shall be deemed not to be Publicly Available Information. Written information from either the Reference Entity, any Guarantor, Paying Agent, Fiscal Agent, Administrative Agent, Arranger, or Clearinghouse shall form Publicly Available Information whether or not published or displayed. This is often used to prove the existence of a credit event.

put option   The right to sell a fixed quantity of an asset or index at a given point in the future for a price agreed upon when the option is purchased.

rating migration   The movement of an obligor from one credit rating to another.

recovery rate   The percentage of face value of an asset that a creditor will be able to recover (typically in bankruptcy court) in the event of a default.

recovery risk   The risk that an investor will not be able to recover the full face value of the investment from the obligor if the obligor defaults on the obligation.

reference asset   Loan, bond, or other financial obligation on which the cash flows and/or credit event for a credit derivative are based.

reinvestment risk   The risk that an investor, upon receiving cash, will not be able to reinvest its money at the same yield as earlier investments.

repackaged notes   Structured notes that use swaps and other derivatives to repackage cash flows and reallocate risks from a financial claim or portfolio of claims. Examples include CLNs, CLOs, CBOs, BISTRO, and CSLTs.

repudiation/moratorium   The reference entity disaffirms, disclaims, repudiates, or rejects, in whole or in part, or challenges the validity of, any obligation in any material respect. Also, the reference entity declares or imposes a moratorium, standstill, waiver, or deferrral, whether de facto or de jure, with respect to any obligation in any material respect. This is one type of credit event.

restructuring   With respect to one or more obligations of reference entity, one of the following occurs in a material respect: (i) a reduction in the rate or amount of interest payable, or the amount of scheduled interest accruals; (ii) a reduction in the amount of principal or premium payable at maturity; (iii) a postponement or other deferral of a date or dates for either (A) the payment or accrual of interest or (B) the payment of principal; or (iv) a change in the ranking in priority of payment of any obligation, causing the subordination of such obligation. This is one type of credit event.

reverse inquiry   A request from investors and traders to banks and debt issuers for new credit-related investment products and opportunities to fit the investor's particular preferences.

risk based capital standards   The amount of capital required to be allocated by banks against losses caused by credit risk.

risk pooling   The combining of many financial instruments with uncorrelated risks into a single portfolio to reduce the relative risk-weighting of each instrument in the portfolio. This procedure allows an investor to benefit from the portfolio's diversification.

risk sharing   The exchanging of uncorrelated risk exposures with other parties in order to benefit from portfolio diversification.

risk spreading   The transfer of risk over many parties such as is often the case in the financial markets.

risk transfer   The attempt to hedge one portfolio by paying another investor to contractually assume exposure to the risks in the first portfolio.

spread option   An option which derives its value from the level of credit spreads.

systemic market risk   Risk borne by all investors in a market that cannot be mitigated by diversification. One example is the interest rate risk borne by investors in fixed-income investments.

term structure of credit risk   Forward credit spreads, also known as the "credit curve."

threshold amount   A dollar or percentage amount which must be exceeded in order to trigger a credit event. A threshold amount may be used to determine if materiality has been met or if a payment default is large enough to warrant a credit event.

total rate of return swap (TRORS)   See *total return swap*.

total return swap (TRS)   Credit derivative in which one party pays the total positive return of a bond, loan, or other financial obligation, while the other party pays a fixed or variable rate payment plus any negative total returns on the reference asset.

trading book   The ledger on which banks record trading securities such as securities, options, interest rate swaps, bonds, and credit derivatives. Items in the trading book are generally accounted for using the mark-to-market method.

trading securities   Investments a company intends to sell in the short term as part of a strategy to buy and sell, thereby generating profits based on short-term price movements. These must be accounted for using the mark-to-market method.

Value-at-Risk (VaR)   A methodology often utilizing Monte Carlo simulation to forecast and summarize the maximum expected loss of a portfolio over a given horizon and with a given confidence interval.

INDEX